THE PRINCIPLES OF POLITICS

Oxford University Press, Ely House, London W.1

GLASGOW NEW YORK TORONTO MELBOURNE WELLINGTON
CAPE TOWN SALISBURY IBADAN NAIROBI LUSAKA ADDIS ABABA
BOMBAY CALCUTTA MADRAS KARACHI LAHORE DACCA
KUALA LUMPUR HONG KONG TOKYO

Politics 8'14' 15. 19². ∧ 27 ⁴/₀ ∧ 50'12' 32³ 34². 35²·

37'1.2' 41'23f £5 49' 57² 52' 55' 66³

68" 70·2·3'f 72² 75² 76' 77'¹₂ 79· 80' ₒ₄ 83²·

85' 874² 89' 41'23' 96²·34 f' 98'¹·² 101'·

102²·ff 108.7 109³ 114³f 115²· 116²³ 118.4'56 119'· 133³·

138²· 140' 142² 145²· 149²· 150²· 157²· 158²· 159'·161·

162³ f 165 168²⁴ 169 170²³ 174²· 175² 177³· 178² f

180/ ½ 184³ 185²· 186³ 190²·3' 195' 197''f 20·1²

202' 203'f' 205' 206²· f 208²· 209/ 211·²·3 213·

214' 216 217'/ 218³ 219/ 221'⁎/ 222³ 224' 227³ 228·

228³45² 230· 232'· 239²· PAd ₒ₉ 249 252'¹³ 262²·³ 263²·

265²·34' 266³ 267/ 268/ 275' 264/ 287'³ 289²· 24 2²f

30AA 310₂/₂ 316 327²f 532².

TOPₐ Lucas .

THE PRINCIPLES
OF POLITICS

BY
J. R. LUCAS
Fellow of Merton College, Oxford

CLARENDON PRESS
OXFORD
1966

Made and printed in Great Britain by
William Clowes and Sons, Limited, London and Beccles

To H. M. L.

APOLOGY

THREE apologies are required for writing a book on political philosophy: to the politicians for professing to know more about politics than they do: to the historians for not treating the subject in a reputable, that is historical, manner: to the philosophers for maintaining that philosophy has anything to say about politics at all.

English public life appears to have no place for books on politics. In Europe and in America political theorising is an amateur's activity, and the enlightened educated man is felt to be competent to discuss and determine all public questions. Books on politics can be addressed to him, and can seek to demonstrate to him what arrangements ought to be made, or what policies undertaken, by appeals to general and generally accepted profundities. In England, however, the educated man fights shy of political speculation in the abstract. He thinks that politics requires practical know-how much more than a set of theoretical principles. He defers to the man with particular, local knowledge and special experience, who is thereby enabled to reach a sound judgement. The fruits of acquired and transmitted experience are what we most value, and for this reason public life is run on the *college system*, through a series of corporations—the Cabinet, Parliament, the Civil Service, benches of magistrates, chambers and Inns of Court, the City, the world of letters, the bench of Bishops, Colleges, Chapters, and Headmaster's Conferences—all composed of, and producing, groups of mutually interacting colleagues, engaged in, and expert in, the same line of country. An Englishman faced with a problem does not ask "What is the book which contains the answer?" but "Who are the people who know how to deal with this sort of thing?", and if he wishes to master some branch of practical affairs himself, he starts as a junior member of the relevant group, and learns the way to do things from his seniors, as he goes along, by constant contact with them and observation of what they do. He therefore has little use for books on the principles of politics, for England seems to have no one philosophy of politics, but only a diversity of political practices. If an Englishman determines, as many do, to devote his life to the public service, he is not primarily concerned to reach abstract conclusions about the nature of the State, the bindingness of political obligation, or the legitimate aspirations of nationality; nor even to decide *in abstracto* whether nationalisation, Imperial Preference or social services are a good thing. Books which argue about these things have no appeal to him. Rather, he is concerned to imbibe and acquire a traditional method, formed by the collective experience of the group concerned, which will enable him to deal with particular problems of a certain type. Such books as he does consult are not tracts for the general reader, but handbooks for the expert. Stone's *Justices' Manual* and Erskine May are for the English what *De l'Esprit des Lois* and *Du Contrat Social* are for the French. Therefore it might seem that there was no place for a book on the principles of politics in England: abroad the political theorist can address himself to the encyclopaedist; at home only to the expert, who needs no instruction in the principles of his practice.

The English distrust of abstract theorising in politics is well founded. Nevertheless it does not preclude all political philosophy. A theorist may be *doctrinaire* in his politics, but he does not have to be; and if it is possible to formulate political principles which are not doctrinaire, it is important to do so. For, however great our belief in an unarticulated political know-how, we need on occasion to articulate our principles as best we can, in order to discuss and assess them. For one thing, the possession of practical know-how does not prevent practitioners from sometimes disagreeing; quite apart from the conflicts of political parties, there are serious disputes among, say, lawyers, or civil servants, or "educationalists". Furthermore, although it is true that public life in England is organised through a series of groups or corporations, they are none of them completely independent or insulated from the rest of the national life. The principle of "lay control" is as important in politics and the law as it is in the affairs of the Church. The layman does not possess the expertise of the expert, and should not meddle incautiously: but that is no reason for attempting to exclude the layman from the mysteries of any practical art; on the contrary, he should be instructed and informed as fully as possible, so that his criticisms shall be based on understanding rather than ignorance.

The historians will allow that the principles underlying our political life ought to be revealed and expounded, but they will claim that the only useful exposition of political thought is a historical one: the only way to understand the ideas that move us now is to trace the course of their development, and show how we have come to hold them. I do not wish to deny the importance of the historical approach for understanding human institutions and human affairs; and in order to understand one's own society and its political ideals, it is necessary to know the history of that society and its thought. But this is not enough. We study Locke's *Treatises on Government*, or Mill's *Utilitarianism*, but much seems out of date, or irrelevant, or simply wrong, and we have to extract what is of value in their work from much that is not, and to reformulate it for ourselves and transpose it into the idiom of our own age. In doing this, we are, in effect, having to think out afresh the principles of our own political thinking, and are therefore being not simply historians reporting on the past but also critics reflecting on the present. Moreover, while the historian can help us to understand how our society and our thinking came to be as it now is, he cannot claim to be able, *qua* historian, to give us guidance on which of various possible courses open to us in the future we should choose. But politics is concerned with making choices. And therefore we need, besides a historical exposition of political principles, a critical under-standing and assessment of them as well.

Philosophers no longer regard political philosophy as a possible subject for rational discussion. The philosophy of science, of mathe-matics, of ordinary language, even of history, may be profitably pursued: but about politics there is nothing the philosopher can say. It is partly a matter of fashion. The Idealists were strong on political philosophy; and therefore the Logical Positivists and their successors turned their attention to other topics. More important has been the Logical Positivists' doctrine that the only rational arguments are those that are either deductive or inductive. Since the arguments used in political philosophy are for the most part neither deductive nor inductive, it seemed that they were not rational, and not susceptible of philosophical assessment at all. In particular, the Logical Positivists were convinced that value-judgements were irrational, and outside the scope of philosophical consideration. Political philosophy has, traditionally, involved many value-judgements, and therefore could not be a reputable intellectual discipline. Modern philosophers, while repudiating the doctrines of the Logical Positivists, have often retained their prejudices. They hanker for arguments whose validity can be definitively assessed and for disciplines which are demonstrably value-free. And although many philosophers now will allow that moral judgements are possible, and are neither meaningless nor merely emotive utterances, they can give only a somewhat existentialist account of personal morality, in which the private individual faced with a predicament makes a decision and commits himself to one course of action rather than another. No account is given, or is on their terms possible, of public morality, or of the complex evaluations a political thinker must make, when he weighs one good against another, and balances different, and entirely sound, considerations against one another. And therefore political philosophy has remained under a cloud longer than almost any other branch of philosophical enquiry.

For my own part, I do not share in the fashionable unconcern with politics. I have a less restricted notion of reason than Hume, and arguments which fail to conform to the canons of deductive or inductive inference can still, I believe, be reasonable and sound. And I do not hold that a discipline, in order to be rational, must be value-free; indeed, I do not know what subject could be more worthy of the ratiocination of a rational agent than to consider what things are valuable, and to deliberate how we can achieve them in our common life together.

CONTENTS

SECTION 1

HUMAN NATURE

HUMAN beings, as we know them, are often selfish, but sometimes unselfish; their judgement is fallible, but sometimes in the course of argument different people come to hold the same view, which is, as far as we can see, reasonable and right; they are infinite in their complexity and aspirations, but finite in their capacities and achievements; they occupy the same public external world, but are each the centre of a private perspective, not necessarily shareable with others; they have values, which are neither necessarily the same for all, nor actually different for each; they can help one another, and need to, but can hurt one another, and often do.

These propositions about human nature are not self-evident, though I believe them to be true. They have been, and still are, often denied, at least implicitly, but I shall not in this book attempt to show that they are true. I shall assume their truth and show what then will follow if human beings are living together in communities, and what different things would follow if human nature were different. Many of the varying political ideals that have been put forward from time to time have drawn their strength from some other idea of human nature, perhaps partial, perhaps wrong, but such as to warrant the different form of society that is being argued for.

We can see how political institutions depend upon the nature of the men constituting political communities by considering one by one the propositions I have put forward about human nature, and how things would differ if each in turn were false, while the others remained true. There would be no conflict, no law, no State, if men did not live in the same public external world in which they could interact with one another: nor if they had no values in common, and could neither hurt one another nor be in need of another's help. No coercive machinery would be needed, either, if no men were ever "bloody-minded"—that is, if men, though having different desires and interests and different ideas of what was right, were all prepared to abide by decisions duly made by the proper authorities in the proper way. Again, if men's judgement were not fallible, and we all knew what in general ought to be done even though we were often not willing to do it, we should not

need the present apparatus of legislatures and law courts to establish
laws and determine their application. Or again, if human affairs were
not so complicated, or if we were all omniscient, it would be feasible,
as Locke believed, to draw up a precise constitutional determination
of areas of potential conflict where governmental adjudication was
needed, and areas which should be guaranteed free from governmental
interference.

These primitive polities, ἀναγκαιόταται πολιτεῖαι, reveal the
rationale of different facets of our own more complicated political
institutions. We shall think them out further in the next section as
foils to illustrate, by contrast, the social organisation required by
human beings as they actually are, capable of interacting in the same
world, having some values the same; sometimes selfish, fallible in their
judgements, and imperfectly informed.

These five characteristics of human nature fall into two groups.
First the two general conditions, which are necessary if there is to be
any possibility of communal co-existence at all:

A(i)   Some Interaction.
A(ii)   Some Shared Values.

Second, three conditions of *imperfection*, or, to use a more neutral
word, limitation:

B(i)   Incomplete Unselfishness.
B(ii)   Fallible Judgement.
B(iii)   Imperfect Information.[1]

The first two conditions are prerequisites of there being any
community at all. If we were disembodied spirits not inhabiting any

---

[1] Compare the characterisation of human nature given by H. L. A. Hart in
The Concept of Law, Oxford, 1961, Ch. IX, § 2, pp. 189–95, which can be sum-
marised again under five heads, namely:
    (i)   Human Vulnerability.
    (ii)   Approximate Equality.
    (iii) Limited Altruism.
    (iv) Limited Resources.
    (v)   Limited Understanding.
Hart's condition (iii) corresponds to B(i) above; his condition (v) to B(ii) and
B(iii) together. His condition (i) states the most important part of what is covered
by A(i) and A(ii) together. His condition (iv) is important for a lawyer or an
economist developing the concept of property, but does not hold in his sense of
all communities—for example, intellectual or religious ones. His condition (ii)
is better expressed by saying that human powers are *comparable*. See further
below p. 64.

common world and incapable of impinging on one another—incapable even of communicating with one another—, then we could not co-exist in any common life. Equally, if we co-existed, but had no values in common, then, although we might impinge, we could not communicate or co-operate at all. But although it is necessary that we should be able sometimes to interact and have some values in common, it is not necessary that we should always be interacting, and have all values the same. Indeed, it is barely possible that we should, if we are to remain separate individuals. Each man, if he is to be different from other men, must have some sphere of consciousness and thought, of experience and aspiration, that is his own, and is not shared with everybody else: and each man, if he is to be a man, and conscious of himself as an agent, and not merely a puppet, must have some angle on life that is peculiarly his, some realm of choices that is under his own control, and therefore likely to be different from those that others might have chosen. I would not be a man at all, if, besides my publicly observable behaviour, I could not think to myself, feel feelings, contemplate ideas, and make plans for my future actions before carrying them out. To have a mind of my own is to be able to wish, privately, as well as to act, publicly. Nor could I call even my soul my own unless I could choose for myself, and not be bound always to endorse some common set of values. Although it is a good and joyful thing to dwell together in unity, we cannot—logically cannot, if we are to be *we*, in the first person plural—be entirely of one mind or share all our experiences or live all our lives together. We are individuals, different, unique. And therefore we can have no absolute community with other people, but must always remain to some extent strangers and aliens, as all the others are.

Human beings are able to interact and do have some shared values. It is a contingent but highly important fact that all, or nearly all, men can feel physical pain, and that physical pain can be caused to one man by another, and will be felt by that one man alone, and not by the other who is causing it, nor by anybody else. Pain is not only regarded as bad: it is an irruption into one's private personal experience which demands one's attention, and in extreme cases absorbs it so much that one cannot attend to or think about anything else. It is also a contingent and highly important fact about men that one man can kill another, and that death is generally regarded as something bad and to be avoided. Also that men need food, drink, and many other material goods, which other men may hinder them from obtaining, but which they can no less help them to secure. Also that human beings at some stages in their life need, and often enjoy, the companionship of other human beings.

These contingent facts about human beings mean that there are a number of shared values, of evils to be avoided and goods to be pursued, common to all, or almost all, mankind; and therefore that there can be a set of pains and penalties and of rewards and inducements that will be effective in conforming human behaviour to required patterns. But although these contingent conditions are highly important in shaping human life as it actually is, it is possible to erect a system of coercion and enforcement on a much more slender and less contingent basis than these. Whenever we have autonomous agents interacting with one another or acting in a common world, each with some set of values, not all of them concerned exclusively with his private experience, then each agent will be liable to be caused distress through the actions of another agent. To have a set of values— that is, to care for something—is, for any being not totally omnipotent, to be *vulnerable*.[1] And therefore anyone who ever wants to *do* anything in a public external world, as well as anyone who ever wants the co-operation of anybody else, or who even values the good opinion of anybody else, is vulnerable. Even tortoises[2] are vulnerable in this way, and could be subject to a form of coercion. Although a recalcitrant tortoise could not be killed or made to suffer pain by other tortoises, it could be prevented from doing anything. Anything it did, a group of other tortoises could undo: or they might stand in a circle round it, and in effect imprison it. This is not a contingent fact about tortoise life, but a necessary consequence of there being a common, public, external world in which individuals can do things. If one individual can do something, another may be able either to prevent him doing it or to undo it: and unless one is incomparably stronger than all the others, a sufficient number of them will be able to prevent or frustrate all his actions: for an action that cannot be prevented or frustrated by no matter how many other individuals is *eo ipso* not an action in a public world at all, but must, by definition, be confined to some private sphere of activity. Nobody can stop a tortoise from speculating: but if that is all that a tortoise wants to do, so that he will not regard it as an evil to be prevented from doing anything else except speculate, then he will not want to do anything to which any other tortoise

---

[1] But see below, § 15, p. 57.
[2] Compare H. L. A. Hart, *The Concept of Law*, p. 190.

might object, so that there will be no need of any penalty or punishment to prevent or deter him from doing anything that other tortoises might not want him to do.

Imprisonment is the paradigm punishment. A man who is imprisoned is thereby debarred from doing anything, whatever it is, that he may want to do in the public, external world. So that if there is anything that he wants to do in the public, external world, imprisonment will be regarded by him as an evil and something to be avoided, and if there is nothing in the public external world that he wants to do, if he has achieved an attitude of utter ἀταραξία, complete indifference, towards external things, then he is harmless, and it does not matter that he cannot be influenced or deterred. For all other men, the loss of liberty is an evil on a different logical level from the infliction of pain: it is an evil we are vulnerable to simply because we are rational agents. It is for this reason we are peculiarly sensitive on the score of the liberty of the subject,[1] and it is for this reason that while we have been able to dispense with the rack and the thumbscrew, and perhaps the gallows, gaols will continue to be necessary, and adequate, as means of coercion, so long as there are men recalcitrant enough to need to be coerced.[2]

SECTION 2

OTHER NATURES AND IDEAL COMMUNITIES[3]

IF HUMAN nature were different, human society would be different also. The first two conditions—A(i), that human beings inhabit the same public, external world, in which they can interact with one another, and A(ii), that they have values which are neither necessarily the same for all, nor actually different for each—cannot be other than they are if communal life is to be possible at all. The three principles of imperfection, however, could be different, and if they were, communal life would be very different also. Many political ideals have drawn their strength from some variant view of human nature.

The three principles of imperfection have the same logical form. Each says that human beings are *sometimes, but not always,* unselfish,

---

[1] See further below, § 20, pp. 86–87.
[2] See further below, § 15, pp. 59–60.
[3] See also table on p. 371.

right, well informed. They deny that we are never unselfish in our decisions, right in our judgements, well informed in our opinions, as well as that we always are. In the terminology of the schoolmen, they are of the form I as well as O, and rule out the corresponding E propositions as well as the A ones.

The principles can thus be denied in two ways. They can be denied pessimistically, by denying to man even the limited excellences they ascribe to him. Or they can be denied optimistically, by denying that man's excellences are limited at all or are in any way less than perfect.

Of the pessimistic alternatives, one need not detain us. Nobody denies B(iii), Imperfect Information, in a pessimistic vein, and maintains that men never know anything. It is a pessimistic denial of B(i), denying that men are ever the least bit unselfish, that underlies the political philosophy of Hobbes. Hobbes misconceived human nature as being entirely selfish, and therefore altogether precluded the possibility of moral government freely supported by reasonable men, and made government out to be necessarily a tyranny, only tolerable in that the selfishness of tyrants was likely to be less obnoxious than the law of the jungle. More recently, thinkers have despaired more of man's reason than of his unselfishness, and have denied B(ii), that men have any judgement, albeit only fallible, rather than B(i), that men are ever the least bit unselfish: people may be willing to compromise, and not pursue their own interests without regard to other people's interests, but, they say, we cannot conceive of a discussion or an argument leading to a solution which can be held to be fundamentally reasonable and right. On such a view, all principles of Natural Law or Natural Justice are mistaken; there is no room for the Reasonable Man of the English common law; political philosophy can discuss forms and procedures, but not questions of substance and principle.

Most political thinkers have erred, however, in thinking too much rather than too little of human capacities, and have denied the O part, rather than the I part, of some of the principles of imperfection, assuming that men were perfectly unselfish, perfectly rational, or perfectly informed.

Let us first consider the assumption of perfect information—the denial of B(iii): it is often felt that obedience, far from being a virtue, is a vice. To act in obedience to another's wishes is to act heteronomously, and only autonomous actions are really moral, are the authentic actions of a self-respecting man. And so we yearn for a society in which nobody is ever told to do anything, but each person knows for himself what he ought to do. The Stoics had such an ideal. If each man were to recognise his station and its duties and perform the task that fell to him, then indeed all men could live together in a universal commonwealth. The kingdom of autonomous agents continues to fascinate us to this day. We feel that to each of us there is a job assigned and waiting to be done, and that we should all be allowed to get on with our respective tasks without interference from outside.

Only when we reflect on our being but imperfectly informed, do we accept the need for some outside organisation of our activities, and are reconciled to some degree of heteronomy. I am not able to will many maxims to be universal laws because I do not know enough about the rest of mankind, where they are, what they need, or what they are doing, to be able to legislate for them. Even in deciding my own course of action I am often ignorant of how other people are situated and what they expect of me. Often therefore I must obey orders, carry out instructions, or take things on trust, because I have not the time or the opportunity to make an independent assessment of my own. More than this, often it is a condition of the success of an enterprise that independent assessments shall not be acted upon: in an army or a business it is more important that bad orders shall be carried out than that subordinates should remedy the mistakes of their superiors. In less extreme cases the Stoic and Kantian ideal of the independent individual's determining for himself by exercise of pure practical reason his station in the universe and the path along which duty calls him is still misleading, because the universe is not so determinate as to fix either my particular moral position in it, or the particular actions I ought to undertake. Rather, the universe affords many indifferent positions and paths of duty, and it is only in virtue of my own or other people's, often arbitrary, decisions that a particular moral situation arises, or a particular course of action is marked out as obligatory. Arbitrary decisions are rationally opaque, and other men's reasons, even where they exist, are often unknown to me. Therefore, knowing that I do not know everything, and believing that morality is largely other-regarding, I must be prepared, if I wish to be moral, to let my actions be determined by other men's wills, and to some extent and in this sense to act heteronomously, and to allow that obedience must, on occasion, be a virtue.

If we assume not perfect information, but complete unselfishness, we have the conditions for what I might call an "Areopagite" community, of the type envisaged by Milton and Mill. They assume the conditions of Some Interaction and Some Shared Values A(i) and A(ii), Fallible Judgement B(ii), and Imperfect Information B(iii). Areopagites are fallible and not perfectly informed, but they are possessed by a deep love of truth, and are anxious only to discover the truth, and not to establish the rightness of their own views because they are their own. An absence of intellectual *amour propre* character- ises the Areopagite frame of mind, and it is only in the absence of this species of selfishness that Milton's and Mill's argument for freedom of discussion holds good. Provided everyone puts forward opinions only because he thinks them to be true and not because they are the ones he happens to hold, and provided he will abandon them if they are shown to be false, and would prefer to be cured of his own errors rather than have to point out those of other people, unfettered debate and dis- cussion is possible. And if each Areopagite is liable to some errors of judgement or information, then the more debate and discussion there is, the more errors will be exposed, and the more the truth will be established.[1]

If we allow that men are sometimes selfish and sometimes misin- formed, but deny that their judgement may ever be at fault, our view of society will be that which lies behind the thought of Mr. Frank Buchman. People are selfish, but if only people could get over their selfishness, then, granted they were correctly apprised of the facts, they could live lives of Absolute Honesty, Absolute Integrity, Abso- lute Justice, and the like. There is no allowance for the fact that men can in good faith still disagree, or that men with the best intentions can still be utterly wrong; and, correspondingly, there follows the con- clusion that where people disagree, it must be due to bad faith. There is a suggestion of this view of human nature, characterised by Some Interaction and Some Shared Values A(i) and A(ii), Incomplete Unselfishness B(i) and Imperfect Information B(iii), but not Fallible Judgement B(ii), in President Eisenhower's belief that if only all men of Good Will could get together, a satisfactory solution of all problems must emerge.

If we drop two of the conditions B(i), B(ii), B(iii) at the same time, we develop even more idealised visions of communal existence. Thus if we assume Some Interaction and Some Shared Values A(i) and A(ii) and Fallible Judgement B(ii), but not Incomplete Unselfishness B(i) nor Imperfect Information B(iii), we have the form of life assumed in

[1] See further below § 22, pp. 91–94, and § 70, pp. 308–311.

the higher ranks of the Civil Service. Civil Servants are unselfish and devoted to the public interest: they are well informed, and believe themselves to be perfectly informed—they believe that everything that can be said can be said on paper, and that all papers are to be found in the files of their own department. But they recognise that their judgements may be wrong, and that therefore an exchange of views between departments or mutual discussion and criticism within a department is the proper way to conduct the administration of State.

If to the Stoic assumption of perfect information we add that of perfect rationality, while still allowing that men are often selfish, we approximate towards the position of Kant or, in our own time, Professor R. M. Hare.[1] Both writers acknowledge that men are often guided by self-love or self-interest, but both play down the significance of ignorance and fallibility: they believe not only in Autonomy but in Universalisability, and believe that on this basis a complete system of morality can be erected. Kant assumes without question that there is always only *one* maxim which the man possessed of Good Will can at the same time will to be a universal law of nature: and although Mr. Hare allows that "Fanatics", as he terms those who disinterestedly differ from normal moral standards, do exist, it is, he believes, an important and fortunate fact that they are few in number.[2]

The nearest we can get to a community of individuals characterized by Imperfect Information B(iii), but not Incomplete Unselfishness B(i) nor Fallible Judgement B(ii), is the Visible Church as sometimes idealised. The body of Christian people are, ideally, completely unselfish. Unlike the Areopagites, they have little feeling for their own fallibility—partly perhaps because they avoid contentious topics of debate,[3] partly because they often construe Our Lord's promise that the Holy Spirit will guide them into all truth[4] as meaning also that the Holy Spirit will guide them into nothing but the truth. Christians differ from Stoics in their strong sense of non-self-sufficiency, their sense of being only children who do not know enough to be completely independent autonomous agents, and in their consequently heteronomous ethics. And we may represent this, with some considerable strain, as the acceptance of B(iii), the principle of Imperfect Information.

[1] R. M. Hare, *Language of Morals*, Oxford, 1952; *Freedom and Reason*, Oxford, 1963.
[2] R. M. Hare, *Freedom and Reason*, Oxford, 1963, p. 172.
[3] Romans xiv. 1.   [4] John xvi. 13.

We end with the completely ideal society, characterised by Some Interaction and Some Shared Values A(i) and A(ii) only, without any principles of imperfection. We may reach it in three ways. It is clear that if the Visible Church on earth is what is characterised by Some Interaction and Some Shared Values A(i) and A(ii), together with Imperfect Information B(iii), then what is characterised by Some Interaction and Some Shared Values alone, without Imperfect Information, will be the Church above, in which we have perfect information, and know even as we are known.[1] If Kantian man is perfected from his self-love, his Good Will becomes a Holy Will, and the Kingdom of Holy Ends-in-themselves clearly constitutes a heavenly city for that philosopher. The passage from the higher Civil Service to Heaven is more difficult, but we can follow it out if we look back to the origins of the Civil Service beyond Jowett to Plato's *Republic*, where διαλεκτική, the method of discussion in which the Guardians engage in their pursuit of truth and the common good, is transmuted, in the metaphysical books of the Republic, from a tentative method of winnowing out truth from error by the give-and-take of argument, to a mystical and infallible intuition of the Forms as they really are; and as the philosopher comes to apprehend the Form of the Good, he is, as it were, transported into the world of the Forms, the Platonist's Heaven.

SECTION 3

COMMUNITIES AND DISPUTES

A COMMUNITY is a body of individuals who have a common method of deciding questions that may arise among or between them. It is by virtue of their having in common a way of deciding questions, a way of achieving a common mind about important matters, that a number of individuals who necessarily are not *necessarily* going to agree about everything, are united into a single body. Two may walk together so long as they happen to agree; but for them to be more than casual companions who happen to have fallen into each other's company, they must acknowledge some principle for determining where they are to go and what they are to do, other than the contingent concomitance of their separate wills. Even a married couple counts as a community in this sense because they must have some way of settling disputes—

[1] I Corinthians xiii. 12.

e.g. that in the last resort the husband shall decide, as laid down in the 1662 Prayer Book, or that in the last resort the wife shall decide, as in America—so that they may stick together and not drift apart or break up like couples engaged in some passing love affair.

For human beings disagree. They inhabit the same world and have different points of view. There will be disagreements not only about ideas, but about actions; in particular, members of a community will disagree about what shall be done by, or in the name of, their community. These disagreements we shall call disputes. A dispute is about how a community shall act—though often the "action" in question is that the community shall let one, or the other, party get his own way.[1] Often disputes can be resolved by rational discussion and argument, but since men are less than perfectly rational and their judgement is fallible, their disputes will not always be resolved by argument alone, but will be unresolved disputes; if human beings are also both bloody-minded and able to hurt one another, they will be tempted to settle their unresolved disputes by force, each party trying to bring about the state of affairs that he desires by every means within his power, hurting anyone who attempts to stop him, and avoiding being hurt himself, so far as he can.[2] It is a characteristic of civilised life that unresolved disputes do not become conflicts of force, but are settled some other way.[3] Philosophers have often imagined what life would be like if unresolved disputes were settled by force, and have given vivid descriptions of how unpleasant it would be.[4] I go further, and make it part of the *definition* of a community that disputes between its members are never settled by force, but by some method common to all its members. It is in virtue of this that we can talk of a community's being a single entity. The members of a community are not always of one mind, necessarily not always of one mind. What is common to them is not their views on all questions, but a way, a *method*, of settling, or at least of *deciding*, those *disputes* that cannot be resolved by argument alone. A community, therefore, is defined as a body of individuals who have a common method of deciding disputes.[5] There are, of course, other, more amorphous groups[6] which lack a common

---

[1] See further below, § 36.
[2] For definition of force see below; § 15, p. 57; see also § 16, p. 63.
[3] For an apparent exception, see below p. 65.
[4] See below, § 16, pp. 62–63.
[5] For convenience, the definitions are listed together at the end, pp. 366–70.
[6] See below, § 64, pp. 275–276.

method for settling disputes, but they are for that reason less definite entities than communities.

Hobbes' contention that every Commonwealth must have a Sovereign can be understood, and seen to be by and large true, if we take it as meaning that every community must have a supreme method of settling disputes. For if, as with the married couples, there is only one rule, it is supreme; and if there is more than one rule, there must be some further rule, a "meta-rule" to adjudicate between the two rules in cases of conflict and to decide which one is applicable; for example, the Anglo–American couple who agreed that the husband should decide all important, the wife all unimportant, issues, and that the wife should decide which issues were important and which not.

In a sense, therefore, and subject to certain qualifications,[1] there must be only one method of settling disputes within a given community, if it is to be an alternative to recourse to force. This is not to say that all disputes must be settled in exactly the same way, but that all the methods must form a single coherent system. In Great Britain we have in one sense many methods of settling disputes—the Queen's Bench, the Courts of Equity, the Appeal Court, the High Court of Parliament; but in another sense we have only one, namely that in no dispute that is likely to arise are there two methods available, likely to give different results, both equally applicable, neither superior to the other, and with no method of deciding which method is to be preferred. Usually it is obvious from the nature of a dispute which method is the correct one to apply; the Queen's Bench Division does not prove wills or grant divorces. Sometimes, when more than one method is available, some definite person, say the plaintiff, has the right to choose which one shall apply in his case. On other occasions, where two jurisdictions appear to compete, one jurisdiction is authorised to decide whether itself or the other is the appropriate one for the case; or one court is superior to the other, and can always overrule its decision, as in this country the High Court of Parliament can override any judicial decision. In this sense, then, a society can have only one method of settling its disputes. For suppose there were more than one. Then there would be a possibility of their giving different results. It would be in the interests of the one party that one method should be the method adopted and of the other that the other should. There would thus be a dispute about methods of settling the original dispute. And with *this* dispute there would be no *method* for deciding it. So that if there

<hr/>

[1] See below, § 8, pp. 31–32.

really are two distinct methods, which are not woven together, by a method for deciding between them, into a single system, then there will be no method of always obtaining settlement of disputes; and if a dispute that was irresoluble by other means arose, the community would fall apart.

SECTION 4

DECISION PROCEDURES

IT IS because human nature is as we have described it, and, in particular, because of the fallibility of human judgement, that we need to have, and can have, the methods of settling disputes that we actually do have. If men were all much more reasonable than they are, there might be differences of opinion among them, but these would be easily resolved by discussion and argument, and they would all agree in the end on how a question ought to be decided. There might still be difficulty in carrying out the decision, but there would be none in knowing that it was the right decision. In fact, however, even when fully informed of the relevant features of a case, we often disagree about the right solution, and this disagreement often remains unresolved by argument. It is of crucial importance, however, that although we often do have irresoluble disagreements it is not the case that we always disagree. Even on moral questions we sometimes reach agreement, and there are other types of question on which agreement is almost invariable. We nearly always agree about the number of people in a given room at a given time, about the date, about questions of personal identity. And this fact, that we can recognise procedures more easily than right results, enables us to agree on methods of settling disputes even if we cannot agree on a solution directly. As in other branches of philosophy, we can set up a "decision procedure" on whose validity we agree and about whose application there can be little doubt; and by means of such a decision procedure we can settle indirectly issues on which we could not reach agreement direct.[1] Two friends, each of whom thinks it is the other's turn to buy the drinks, may agree to toss for it. This is an effective method for settling the dispute, because they both know without any serious doubt what

[1] The term 'decision procedure' is used in mathematical logic in a technical sense, different from that in this book.

constitutes tossing for it, the way in which one sets about doing it, and how the fall of the coin is to be interpreted. In a similar vein they may agree on a more serious matter to refer the dispute to a third friend to arbitrate: and again this is an effective method, because they can have no serious doubt whether the person they address is that third friend or not, nor how the words he utters are to be taken. Thus it is often possible to have almost complete agreement about a method, a procedure, or a form, for settling disputes, when we are unable to reach any sort of agreement about the rights and wrongs of the dispute itself, the content of the dispute, the substantial issue at stake. Therefore, if we attach, as we do, paramount importance to being able to settle disputes, we shall need to establish *methods* of settling disputes, about which methods themselves there can be very little dispute.

In order that there should be no dispute about methods, it is necessary that the established method shall have or shall be given some identifying marks so that every party to a dispute shall be able to recognise it as *the* method to which he should have recourse. The mediaeval monarchs wore their crowns and modern states put their policemen into uniform. An American story illustrates the logical importance of uniform.[1] A leading bandit in New York State was arrested; "Will you go quietly?" asked the officer who arrested him, "or must I handcuff you?" "What's the charge?" "Income-tax." "I'll come along", and he entered the waiting police-car without resistance, and was driven to the police station, which was full of policemen. Only as his executioner drew his gun, did the bandit realise that these were no policemen at all, but members of the rival gang, dressed for the occasion. The policeman's uniform, like the crown of the mediaeval monarch, or the *fasces* of the Roman magistrate, commands immediate respect, so that people obey without actually having to be coerced. It is obviously better that physical violence should not have to be employed, if only for reasons of economy, to save wear and tear on the police force: on reflection, we can go further than this and see that it is logically necessary for people to be able to recognise "Authority" and give way before it, if they are to be members of a community at all, and not outlaws. If a man involved in a dispute with his neighbour was unable to call a policeman, unable to find a magistrate to summon his neighbour to appear,

---

[1] Also actual incidents in Britain: see *The Times*, 11 December 1965, p. 8, col. 5, and 11 May 1966 p. 12, col. 2. For the citizen's views of the problem, see letter in *The Times*, 2 February 1966, p. 13, col. 5.

unable to invoke the protection of a king, because there was no means of telling policemen, magistrates or kings apart from other folk, then there would be no way of settling the dispute. If there was a State in which bandits regularly dressed up as policemen, people would not obey putative policemen for fear they might be bandits, unless compelled to at pistol point. A policeman could not stop a car by holding up his hand, but must always shoot its tyres. People would obey only when coerced, and might then be obeying the police or bandits for all they knew: one lot of people dressed as policemen meeting another lot of people dressed as policemen would shoot it out: and every encounter and dispute would end in a resort to violence.

For these reasons, the officers of the law need to be clearly recognisable as such, and legal systems characteristically secure this by making it an offence for any persons or procedures to appear to be authorised when they are not.[1] Hobbes makes the same point, that there is "requisite, not only a declaration of the law, but also sufficient signs of the author and authority. The author, or legislator is supposed in every commonwealth to be evident because he is the sovereign, who having been constituted by the *consent*[2] of everyone, is supposed by everyone to be sufficiently known."[3] The 'consent' here mentioned is that when, at the institution of a commonwealth "a multitude of men do agree, and covenant, every one, with every one, that" whatever body the majority of them shall choose, "every one, he that voted against as well as he that voted for, shall *authorise*[4] all the actions and judgements of that body."[5] Hobbes' account here has often been criticised, as being broken-backed—because on his view agreements are not binding unless and until there is somebody in a position to enforce them—and as being redundant—because once a sovereign is established, any contract there might be would be between individual subject and sovereign, and not between subject and subjects. These criticisms are cogent. Nevertheless it is at this point that Hobbes comes nearest to realising that sovereignty is a matter of agreement as well as of coercion, and that for a sovereign to be a sovereign he must be able not only to coerce the recalcitrant, but to be recognised as

---

[1] See below, § 42, pp. 175–177; § 69, p. 303.
[2] My italics.
[3] *Leviathan*, Part 2, Ch. 26, ed. Michael Oakeshott, Basil Blackwell, Oxford, 1946, p. 178.
[4] Hobbes' italics.
[5] *Leviathan*, Part 2, Ch. 18, *init*. Oakeshott, p. 113.

sovereign, that is, for it to be agreed by his subjects, however un-willingly, that he is their sovereign. This is true not only of a Hobbesian sovereign, but of any method of settling disputes. The method must be one about which there is agreement, at least to the extent of its being agreed that it is the relevant method, that is, of its being recog-nised as *the* method. Various methods of settling disputes have been adopted in their time. The ancient world looked for omens and auspices, the Middle Ages had trial by ordeal and trial by combat,[1] often recourse has been had to some random process, but the pre-eminent method has always been the decision either of one person or of more than one person after the arguments on each side of the case have been put. Such a body is said to have *authority* to decide the question in dispute. The sense of the word 'authority' in ordinary usage shades over into the senses of the words 'power' and 'influence', but we need to distinguish them sharply for the sake of clarity. Let us define authority with respect to a given decision procedure by saying:

A man, or body of men, *has authority* if it follows from his saying, 'Let X happen', that X ought to happen.

In contrast, let us define power by saying :

A man, or body of men, *has power* if it results from his saying 'Let X happen' that X does happen.

And again:

A man, or body of men, *has influence* if the result of his saying, 'Let X happen', is that other people will say (perhaps only to them-selves), 'Let X happen'.

Similarly, I use the phrases 'an authority', 'the authority', 'the authorities', 'a power', 'the power', 'the powers', 'the powers-that-be', etc., to refer to a person, or persons, or a body, or bodies, which have authority or have power. The content of these definitions varies with the context. Normally we shall speak of a man having authority with respect to a given decision procedure, in virtue of which it follows from his saying, 'Let X happen', that X ought, according to that decision procedure, to happen. Similarly we speak of a man having power against the background of a particular set of circumstances. Furthermore, it depends very much on what X is, whether a man has authority to say that X shall happen, or any power or influence in the matter. If father, at the driving wheel, says, 'Let us go to the sea', he

---

[1] See further below, § 17, p. 65.

has authority and power: the same words in the mouth of the children can at most have influence, and such power as results from that: and the same father saying, 'Let Parliament be dissolved,' is in that matter without authority, power, or influence.

The definitions here given are not the only senses in current use. We often use the words 'authority' in a sense resembling that of 'influence' as I have defined it—as in 'He is a great authority on Chinese history': and lawyers use the word 'power' in exactly the sense here given to 'authority'—as when a court "exceeds its powers" or when a man is "empowered to act".[1] It is natural that the words should be used often interchangeably. For power (in my sense) often creates authority, and *vice versa*, and authority influence, and influence power. Nevertheless, even though authority, power, and influence go together, often necessarily so, it is useful to distinguish them. And therefore I adopt these definitions, with the *caveat* that they do not cover all the ordinary senses of the words.

SECTION 5

THE ARBITRATION OF ARBITRATORS

WE CONFER authority on men because we want to settle disputes by recourse to human judgement. The use of human judgement as a method of settling disputes is possible because human judgement although fallible is not hopelessly fallible. Men may err: but they are not bound to err, and we find in practice that they do better, far better, than a random process. The fact that we have judges and find their judgements more or less satisfactory, and do not feel inclined to replace the judges of the High Court by tossers of coins is powerful evidence that human beings are reasonable, that is to say, that they can be reasonable, and have a better chance of reaching the right solution than they would if their judgements were, as some writers allege,[2] purely a reflection of their emotional state, and entirely unguided by rational considerations.

Indeed, if we could not trust human judgement at all, we should be

---

[1] See also, for example, § 10, p. 40.
[2] e.g. Jerome Frank, *Law and the Modern Mind*, New York, 1930, pp. 104–6, 115, or Theodore Schroeder, 'The Psychological Study of Judicial Opinions', 6 *Calif. L. Rev.* (1918), 89, 93.

unable to have any method for settling disputes. Suppose it were true that the judgements of even the best judges were entirely unguided by rational considerations, were entirely random so far as the merits of the case were concerned; so that we could replace the judge's decision by a simple toss of the coin. What then would be the consequences? The consequences would be twofold. First, that it would always be worth picking a quarrel, no matter how weak one's case, because one would always have a fifty-fifty chance of winning. I would always lay claim to everyone else's property, because the more I claimed, the more I should be likely to get. I would always maintain that it was the other man's turn to pay for the drinks, no matter how clearly I remembered that he had paid last time, because the toss of the coin is not only no respecter of persons but also no respecter of truth. Secondly, no sooner had the coin given a verdict against me than I should query it and try to put it in question, because again there would be a fifty-fifty chance of its not upholding its previous verdict. If the coin decided that it was my turn to pay, I should immediately maintain that I had paid, and ultimately suggest recourse to the coin to settle that dispute. A settlement is no settlement unless it is usually, and in general, more or less lasting. A dispute is not settled if it is always possible for the loser to reopen it, or raise another dispute very similar to it, with as good a chance of getting a settlement in his favour as if the first decision had never gone against him. It does not do to appear before a court a second time with exactly the same pleas and arguments as the court rejected the first time one appeared before it: this is not due to the impatience of judges or the frailty of human institutions: it is a logical necessity deriving from the concept of what a settlement of a dispute must be. So, too, the rule of precedents is not just a quirk of Anglo-Saxon common law but again a logical necessity.[1] Thus if our decision procedure really gave random results we should lose the two features of external predictability and internal stability that are essential to any effective method of settling disputes. If people can know in advance what the judge's decision is going to be, they will settle out of court, and the court will not be swamped with an endless flood of litigation: and a procedure that produces internally inconsistent decisions will be totally ineffective in settling disputes between parties, at least one of whom, *ex hypothesi*, is recalcitrant to reason and likely to be contumacious. Something much

---

[1] See further below, § 29, p. 133.

more goal-directed than the toss of a coin is required in order to master human self-will.

To put it another way, we can only settle disputes in unclear cases against a background of agreement about clear cases. Unless we sometimes agree, no method is possible of settling disputes in which we cannot reach agreement: and unless we agree on matters of substance pretty often, it will neither be practicable to adjudicate all our disputes nor tolerable to enter into such doubtful relations with other people. Therefore besides the unclear cases which are in dispute there must be many clear cases which are not disputed. But there is no clear distinction between clear and unclear cases, any more than there is between cases that are clearly to be decided in favour of one party and cases that are clearly to be decided in favour of the other party; so that even if we agreed to toss a coin in unclear cases, we should still need judges to decide the second-order dispute whether a particular case was a clear one or an unclear one. Thus we cannot dispense with judges: and if we use judges from the outset to adjudicate unclear cases we shall have the advantage of generally diminishing the range of uncertainty, whereas if we use random methods the tendency will be to increase the range of uncertainty.

SECTION 6

POLITICAL REASONING

WE HAVE argued that judges are necessary because of the fallibility of human judgement, and possible because of the possibility of human judgement—if we all could judge perfectly, we should not need judges, and if nobody had any capacity to judge at all, nobody would be capable of being a judge, or rather, there would be no point in having a judge rather than a random process. In contrasting judges with random processes, we are making a point of the greatest importance not only for political but for all philosophy, namely the essential non-arbitrariness of arbitrators. Judges, and all other arbitrators of disputes, would be of no use at all if they were no better than really arbitrary, that is, random, processes. Judges in fact are required not to be arbitrary in their judgements but to be reasonable, and to base their decisions on rational consideration.

Many philosophers have despaired of the power of reason to give guidance on political[1] issues. To do so is absurd. Political decisions must be guided by reason, because they are concerned with collective action, and men do not all always happen to act together in the required way,[2] so that some people have to be told what to do, and not usually merely coerced into doing it, and some rationale of action is implicit in asking people to do anything. Separate, different, individuals cannot act together without some agreement on concerting their individual actions. To reach agreement they need to use words. And words, λόγοι, are instinct with reason.

Crude scepticism about the rôle of reason in politics is absurd. Usually, however, the apparent sceptic is prey to other doubts. He may be doubtful about human nature. Men often are unreasonable. Often, though they reason, they fail to reach the right conclusions: and often they will not reason, or will not act on what, in their heart of hearts, they know to be right. This is true. Men often are unreasonable, both in the sense of having fallible judgement,[3] and in the sense of being selfishly wilful and perverse.[4] But men are not always unreasonable in either sense. Not only is the cynic's view contrary to common observation, but, if it were always and unreservedly true, communal existence would be impossible. Except there be ten or twenty righteous and reasonable men found in it, not even God can save Sodom from destruction.

More sophisticatedly, the sceptic may entertain too exalted notions about reason for it to be applicable to the humdrum affairs of ordinary life. Geometry and mathematics generally have been taken to be the paradigm forms of reasoning, and by these standards political arguments appear sloppy and not at all compelling; perhaps psychologically persuasive, but not rationally cogent; a form of propaganda, not reasoning of any real sort. The only valid arguments, on this view, are those where it would be unintelligible, because self-contradictory, to controvert them.

Some philosophers have thought that the lack of stringency in our moral and political arguments was remediable, and that if only we would set ourselves to do it, we should be able to "place *morality amongst the sciences capable of demonstration*" in which "from self-evident propositions, by necessary consequences, as incontestable as those in

---

[1] Taking this word, as always in this book, in its wide, original, sense, in which it applies not only to politics in the modern, narrow, sense, but to social and legal affairs, and all that pertains to men's public life.
[2] See below § 65, p. 279–80.   [3] B(ii) on p. 2.   [4] B(i) on p. 2.

mathematics, the measures of right and wrong might be made out".[1] In recent years philosophers have offered "rational reconstructions" of moral arguments in purely mathematical terms,[2] and have attempted to reduce moral argument to a nearly pure deductive form.[3] These attempts have not been convincing. Arguments on moral and political questions are unlike many other arguments, in that they are interminable; that is, they lack a rigid decision procedure, whereby we can demonstrate the cogency of valid arguments, and point out the invalidity of others.

There are two reasons why moral and political arguments should lack the clear-cut criteria of validity that are characteristic of, say, geometry; or, perhaps better, why geometry and allied disciplines should possess a definiteness that moral and political thinking lacks. The first is that there are many questions that the geometer can refuse to answer, as being irrelevant to his discipline, whereas a man making a moral or political decision cannot antecedently lay down rules that will guarantee the irrelevance of some question. The geometer knows, as soon as it is asked, that the question, 'Is an equilateral triangle blue or green?' is not a question he has to answer. But irrelevant though such a question may also seem to a politician, he cannot be sure of its irrelevance—and indeed, if he had been living in Byzantium in the time of Justinian, the distinction between blue and green would have been of crucial political significance.[4]

More generally we may say that political and moral thinking differs from more academic disciplines in that in the former we often have to reach a decision and give an answer, and cannot, as academics can, "suspend judgement". The principle 'Tertium non datur' cuts much more deep in moral and political life than it does elsewhere, and when we have to make up our minds and cannot postpone decision, then weak arguments are better than no arguments; weak arguments are not fallacious arguments, but only ones that are not as conclusive as we could wish. Where we have time or opportunity to think more deeply or find out more fully about a situation, we should. But often in life, time and opportunity are not given us, and yet we must decide;

---

[1] John Locke, *Essay Concerning Human Understanding*, Bk. IV, Ch. 3, § 18.
[2] R. B. Braithwaite, *The Theory of Games as a tool for the Moral Philosopher*, Cambridge, 1955.
[3] R. M. Hare, *Freedom and Reason*, Oxford, 1963.
[4] Procopius, *Wars*, I.xxiv.2–3; *Secret History*, vii.15–16.

and therefore must decide in the light of the best available, rather than the best possible, arguments.

In geometry there are no weak arguments which are not fallacious. Arguments are either valid or invalid, and those that are not completely conclusive and compelling carry no weight at all. On this score, moral and political argument are not alone in being different. Apart from the purely deductive arguments of mathematics and logic, arguments are characteristically *dialectical* in form, because argument characteristically goes on between *two* persons, the one putting forward a thesis, the other making objections to it, which the first one in turn tries to counter. The logic of moral and political argument—and also of argumentation in history, philosophy, and most disciplines other than the mathematical ones—is a logic of one side of an argument and another, of *prima facie* cases which may be countered, and presumptions which may be rebutted. The parallel is with the law courts, not with a text-book of geometry, and the typical connective of argument is not 'therefore' but 'but'.[1]

The appropriate style of argument is thus radically different from those of geometry. Except in those urgent questions mentioned earlier where there is not time to defer decision, the proponent of an argument should "wait for an answer". He should give his opponent, real or imaginary, time either to agree that he is convinced, or to point out weaknesses in the proponent's own argument. An argument is not conclusive unless, although there are opportunities for countering it, no reasonable man feels himself able to do so.[2] A geometrical, or any deductive, argument leaves the hearer or reader no room to make objections, no option but to agree. Americans, perhaps under the influence of Locke, make the same point when they end a verbal argument with the word 'period'. But in truth, dialectical arguments, unlike deductive ones, do not end with a period or a full stop, but with a pause, in which further objections could be made, further qualifications called for. They do not finish with a flourish, Q.E.D.,

---

[1] See W. D. Ross, *The Right and the Good*, pp. 19–20; *The Foundations of Ethics*, pp. 83–86. H. L. A. Hart, 'The Ascription of Rights and Responsibilities', *Proceedings of the Aristotelian Society* 1948, pp. 171–94; reprinted in A. G. N. Flew, *Logic and Language*, Vol. I, pp. 145–65; and J. R. Lucas, 'The Philosophy of the Reasonable Man', *Philosophical Quarterly*, 1963, pp. 97–106. See also below § 7, p. 25, and § 27, p. 127.

[2] Compare J. S. Mill, *On Liberty*, Ch. II (Everyman ed.), p. 81: "There is the greatest difference between presuming an opinion to be true, because, with every opportunity of contesting it, it has not been refuted, and assuming its truth for the purpose of not permitting its refutation."

but tail off tentatively with a '*ceteris paribus*' clause. And therefore we cannot give an adequate account of reason, or say in advance what reason is, or what a man must do to be sure of reaching the right conclusion.

The view of Descartes, that complete and precise rules could be given for directing the reason aright, is a dream. Even in mathematics, the paradigm, deep and difficult researches have demonstrated beyond doubt that there is not—cannot be—any one method for the solution of all problems.[1] Much more so in politics. We may be able to work out solutions for those problems that arise, but we cannot have all the answers in advance. We can reason about political questions, but cannot specify in advance exactly what constitute good or sound reasons. Sometimes we can go some of the way, and say roughly what political reasoning is *like*; in particular, some of the things that it is *not*.[2] But we can never formulate completely in advance what it is to be reasonable in politics, or how exactly right solutions are to be found. The one thing we can know is that we do not know all the answers.

SECTION 7

LAWS AND MEN

THE two facts, that decisions should characteristically be reasonable, and that we have no antecedently specified method, no algorithm, for reaching rational decisions in politics, are, together, of the greatest importance. For, as we have seen,[3] we must have a decision procedure available, if a community is to go on being a community. Some decision must be reached; if not always the right one, then sometimes the wrong one; but at least some decision. Any decision, we are tempted to say, is better than no decision. But that will not do either, as we have seen: completely arbitrary decisions are insupportable.

Thus we are torn. We need definiteness: we need reasonableness. As soon as we have achieved one, we feel bound to qualify it, in order not to lose the other. We establish highly definite decision procedures, which all may observe and all may abide by; but immediately begin to blur the sharp outlines to leave room for the pressure of reason to be

---

[1] See, for example, W. & M. Kneale, *The Development of Logic*, Oxford, 1962, Ch. XII, § 4, esp. pp. 735–6.
[2] See below, §§ 26, 27, pp. 123–7.   [3] § 3, pp. 10–13.

effective; and then having made rational discussion possible, find that it is interminable, and have to cut short the debate to secure crisp and sharp decisions we can actually accept.

Because we have no algorithm, we rely on the reasoning of reasonable men. If we identify the reasonable men individually, by name,[1] we secure definiteness for our decision procedure, but leave open the possibility that the *soi-disant* reasonable men may turn out not to be reasonable after all, and give unreasonable decisions. We want to ensure that arbitrators are not arbitrary, and therefore we do in fact require judges not simply to give decisions, but to observe principles, and be guided by them in reaching their decisions.[2]

If we can say that a judge is observing principles, it would seem that we should be able to say what those principles were. But it is not so. Often we can formulate principles of justice, but we can never specify them with complete precision. The tags of the jurists—*suum cuique, pacta sunt servanda, audi alteram partem*—these and many others are true and worth saying; but they do not tell us how to determine, what is often the most difficult question, whose the property is, or what exactly was promised. Many attempts have been made, for reasons which will appear later,[3] to lay down the law exactly and unambiguously, so that everyone shall know what the law is, and the judge's function shall not ever be to decide a case, but only to make the appropriate court order which each case automatically calls for. But no attempt has ever been successful. Even the Code Napoléon has required judicial interpretation. However many types of case the legislator distinguishes and deals with, further cases crop up which he had not envisaged, and for which the application of the law is not automatic. Ideally, we are tempted to think, the law should be stated in universal terms, and any particular case should clearly either be subsumed or not be subsumed under a given law. But this ideal of deductive adjudication fails on two counts: first, we do not have available a standard complete description of each particular case, but rather a number of rival incomplete descriptions; and many legal disputes are about which description is to be taken as the right one: secondly, laws are never stated so as to detail all possible combinations of features which could turn up in particular cases; so that always there will be the unexpected case, characterised by two features, in virtue

---

[1] Compare the story of Deioces in Herodotus, I.96–101.
[2] See further below, § 30, pp. 135–6.
[3] §§ 10, 27, 30 and 31.

of one of which the case should be dealt with one way, and in virtue of the other of which the case should be dealt with the other way.

How far it is a contingent matter that human beings have not been able yet to enunciate a set of laws that are perfectly precise, or how far it stems from something deeper, is not clear. It is sufficient for my purpose here that it is only a contingent truth about mankind, but my own opinion is that it is something more. I believe that it is due to the infinite complexity of human beings, which makes it impossible for us ever to specify human affairs completely and with perfect precision. The ideal of deductive adjudication seems therefore inapplicable to any controversy concerning human affairs, and especially to those involving evaluations or moral matters. Such controversies must be two-sided: there naturally are rival descriptions, neither of which can be ruled out of court on formal grounds or by any mechanical procedure; some features tell one way, and some another; and so, only by the exercise of reason, and not by the automatic application of any rigid, precisely formulated, rule, can we weigh the two sides of the argument, and come down on one side or the other. The principles of right reasoning are not fully formulable. It is a know-how, which cannot be reduced to any finite number of know-thats.[1] And therefore, if we regard as "information" only what can be considered as a know-that, our information about human affairs is always and necessarily imperfect. Although we can know many things that are true and important, we can never master a list of things that are all the things there are to know: and although we can give many useful, but incomplete, formulations of the principles of reasoning, and can often give in words our reasons for deciding particular cases, we cannot reduce right reasoning to a formula, nor can we formulate in advance how every possible type of case is to be treated.

Whether the metaphysical doctrine of the last paragraph is accepted or not, the practical conclusion remains the same, that no set of laws that are complete and perfectly precise has ever yet been formulated, nor is likely to be. We are able to make any point clear, but we cannot make every point clear. Any particular set of circumstances may be considered and a decision for those circumstances given, but no formula can be constructed that will unambiguously cover all sets of circumstances. And therefore we need judges, to decide difficult cases which cannot always be straightforwardly subsumed under general

[1] See Gilbert Ryle, 'On Knowing How and Knowing That', *Proc. Arist. Soc.*, 1945–6, and *The Concept of Mind*, London, 1950, Ch. 2.

principles, but call for some measure of judgement. The common saying that government should be a government of laws not men, cannot be completely realised. We always need some men, judges, to say what the law is, and although we may demand that they be not arbitrary in their judgements but observe principles, we cannot tie them down completely, and completely specify the principles, except as being what the judges say they are.

The fact that we cannot make government be completely one of laws not men has had great consequences for political thinking. It has led philosophers to conclude that it is men not measures that matter, not simply as something to be desired, but as something inevitable, inherent in the very nature of the community. To argue thus might seem to be rushing unnecessarily from one extreme to the other: after all, although we cannot lay down laws that are perfect, we can make them tolerably clear for most cases, and the *rôle* of the judges is limited in scope; to ask for more, and complain that the laws were not absolutely precise, might seem to be a case, as Aristotle would say, of demanding greater precision than the subject-matter can admit.[1] To counter the objection thus, however, would be to miss the point. For decision procedures do need to be formally specified and precise, because they must be agreed and recognisable in advance, and because they have to be able to deal with an indefinite range of possible cases. There must be no doubt about what the procedure is: and if we cannot completely formulate the procedure in words, but must rely on human beings to adjudicate cases, we must specify those human beings in advance: and, secondly, we cannot lay down definite limits to the jurisdiction of judges, because if the jurisdiction is limited, we have to have, as with the Anglo-American couple,[2] a second-order jurisdiction to decide which cases do, and which do not, fall within these limits, and this jurisdiction too must involve the judgement of human beings. In the sense, therefore, in which a community has only one decision procedure, that decision procedure must be able to adjudicate on its own competence, so that no firm boundaries can be set to its competence.

From this it is a short step to the first thesis of Unlimited Sovereignty, that in each community it will always be possible to point to supreme judges or law-givers, whose *dicta* have supreme authority,[3]

---

[1] *Nicomachean Ethics*, 1094 b 23, 1098 a 27.
[2] See above, § 3, p. 12.
[3] See § 4, pp. 16; or p. 366.

which we cannot formulate laws or principles to shackle. The body with supreme authority we call the sovereign. Every community must have a sovereign, whose authority is necessarily unlimited.[1]

The first thesis of Unlimited Sovereignty is generated by the antithesis between the requirement of the decision procedure for precision and antecedent agreement, and the complexity, uncertainty and imprecision of human affairs. It is only by stressing in turn formal precision and material imprecision that the argument can be made plausible; but if so, the argument must be internally inconsistent. The inconsistency can perhaps most clearly be seen if we recall that the whole point of having persons to decide difficult cases was that they were not completely arbitrary, and were for that reason preferable to, for example, roulette wheels. Having introduced persons to be judges and law-givers, on the grounds that they were not arbitrary, it would be absurd to conclude that they were sovereigns, who necessarily were arbitrary after all.

Hobbes had other reasons for formulating his doctrine of sovereignty in terms of persons rather than procedures. One can point to persons with one's finger, whereas one cannot point to procedures with one's finger, and Hobbes was sceptical of the existence of anything he could not touch and see. He could accept persons, who had bodies, but not procedures or methods, which can only be apprehended by the mind, and whose ontological status must always be suspect to the materialist. Moreover Hobbes, taking a lower view of human nature than we do, regarded men as less amenable to authority and more in need of coercion, if the decisions of the decision procedure were to be enforced. By identifying the coercer with the decider in the person of the sovereign he secures the maximum enforcement of, and needs minimum agreement with, the settlement of each dispute.

Against these and other arguments, we may point out that a government of men not laws, is open to much the same objections as a government of laws not men. Just as we need men to interpret the laws, so we need laws to identify the men. This is clearest if we consider the case when the sovereign is not a single person but a body of persons. For with a body of persons we have to have *rules*—rules of membership, rules of procedure, rules of voting—to determine who are the members of the sovereign body, what constitutes a meeting of that

---

[1] The special sense given to the word 'authority' in § 4, pp. 16–17, should be remembered. We distinguish the thesis of unlimited authority, stated here, from that of unlimited power, stated in § 18.

body, what is to count as a decision of the sovereign.[1] These rules are of the same logical and ontological status as laws; often, indeed, they are laws, as for example those that determine membership of Parliament.

Even the most personal sovereignty is not entirely free of some element of law or principle. The absolute monarchs of the sixteenth, seventeenth and eighteenth centuries were hereditary monarchs: they were sovereign because of a law of succession which said that they should be. It could be argued even against Louis XIV that he was not sovereign enough to alter the law of succession, to which he owed his own occupancy of the throne. Although a king, unlike a law, can be pointed at, it is not by virtue of his being pointed at that he bears rule, but by virtue of his satisfying a certain description—being the heir of the preceding monarch—in a law which designates the person entitled to bear rule: and the being designated by a law of succession is again of the same ontological status as laws generally; as it was put in 1441: "The law is the highest inheritance which the king has; for by the law he and all his subjects are ruled, and *if there was no law there would be no king and no inheritance*";[2] and we can no more point with a finger to what it is that makes this man rather than any of his fellows king than we can point to any other law. Hereditary monarchs, therefore, are not completely Hobbes-type sovereigns.[3]

Nor, for different reasons, are dictators. Dictators depend for their authority not upon a law of succession but upon their embodying an aspiration or an ideology.[4] They may be able to shape the development of their ideology, but they are themselves also subject to it, and their room for manoeuvre limited by it. Hitler did not speak only of Hitler, but of the German *Volk* of which he was the *Führer*. Napoleon was supported for many different reasons; but not for that of simply

[1] Most notably, when we say that the Queen-in-Parliament is sovereign of the United Kingdon, we are referring to a complicated *procedure*, of first, second and third readings of both Houses, or under certain, very complicated, provisions of the Parliament Acts of 1911 and 1950, of the House of Commons only, together with the Royal Assent, constituted either by the Queen in person, or by a body of commissioners on her behalf, reciting the words, '*La Reine le veult*'. The Queen-in-Parliament is neither a person, nor a body of persons, but a highly complicated procedure.

[2] Year Book 19 Henry VI Pasch. pl. 1, my italics; compare Bracton, *De Leg. et Consuet. Ang.*, 1.8.5.

[3] See also H. L. A. Hart's analysis of the sovereignty of Rex I and Rex II in *The Concept of Law*, pp. 52–53.

[4] I use ideology in a wide sense, to include negative ideologies, e.g. anti-Communism.

being Napoleon—not even by his Marshals. The dictators with wide mass-appeal which makes them appear to be Hobbes-type sovereigns, obtain that mass-appeal by virtue of some universal principle which is widely accepted and which they are thought to embody.

We are thus unable to resolve the tension between laws and men, so as to be able to give a theory of decision procedure solely in terms of either of them. A decision procedure cannot be solely in terms of laws, rules, principles, or conventions, because these cannot be formulated precisely enough to cover all cases, and we need a man to exercise judgement in interpreting them. But equally there is no virtue in obtaining decisions from a ruler, who does not observe any rules or principles, nor is it possible to designate a man as ruler without some law or convention of designation. We therefore cannot give a completely adequate formal account of a legal system. Such account as we can give will be formal, because it is upon forms and procedures for settling disputes that we have to rely when we cannot reach agreement without recourse to law: but an entirely formal account will be misleading, because it is only against a background of substantial agreement that any form for settling disagreements can be workable. We would like to lay down in advance principles which would define clear limits to the legitimate authority of judges, rulers, and law-givers, but cannot because of the complexity of human affairs, and the ineliminable margin of ambiguity in human language. We are left therefore with an essentially *untidy* account of the basis of law: we cannot ignore the content of law and speak only of its form; but neither can we say anything very clear-cut or definite about its content. Political philosophy is neither a formal nor a very precise discipline, being formed by a constant interplay between laws and men, between the need for arbitrators and the need for them to be non-arbitrary in their arbitration.

SECTION 8

SOVEREIGNTY

THE thesis of Unlimited Sovereignty was open to attack, in its classical form, because it was expressed in terms of sovereign persons; and no account of authority in terms of persons alone can be adequate. We have phrased our discussion in terms of methods, rules of procedure, or laws, rather than of persons, sovereigns, or subjects. The analogue to the doctrine that there can only be one sovereign in a State is, therefore, that there can only be only one—in the sense specified in Section 3—method of settling disputes, binding on all members of a given community.

This proposition is substantially true; and is not open to the objections that can be made to the doctrine of sovereign persons. But it needs careful qualification if it is not to be open to other objections. We must, in the first place, make sure that we are not unwittingly involved in an illegitimate reversal of quantifiers, from the true proposition that for every question arising in a community there must be some method (which, we saw in Section 7, requires that there should be some body) authorised to decide it, to the false conclusion that in every community there must be some method, and therefore some body, authorised to decide every question.[1]

It may indeed be true that there is no legal limitation on a court of ultimate appeal, because there cannot be: but it does not follow that the court must therefore be *legibus solutus*, like the absolute autocrats of the Roman Empire. Although it is possible to have a sovereign procedure which has supreme authority and which is subject to no formal limitations on its competence—for example, the Queen-in-Parliament in Great Britain—it is also possible to have a set of procedures which enable enough questions to be decided for the community to continue as a community, but in which it is implausible and unhelpful to single out a sovereign procedure—for example, in the United States of America, where different questions are settled by different procedures, involving different bodies, but none of them can be unqualifiedly maintained to be supreme.[2]

The example of the United States, important though it is as a counter-example to some theories of sovereignty, does not blunt the

[1] This can be conveniently represented in symbolic logic by saying that from $(x)(\exists y)F(x,y)$ there does not follow $(\exists y)(x)F(x,y)$. In this case x ranges over questions to be decided, y ranges over bodies authorised to decide questions, $F(x,y)$ is to be interpreted as y *is authorised to decide* x. The fallacy in the attempted derivation can be easily seen if we consider the interpretation in which x and y both range over the natural numbers, and $F(x, y)$ is interpreted to mean y *is greater than* x. Then, while it is true that for every number x there is some number y, which is greater than x, it is false that there is some number y, which is greater than every number x.

[2] Not the Supreme Court, because its decisions can be overridden by Constitutional Amendment; nor Constitutional Amendment, because no State may be deprived without its own consent of its equal representation in the Senate even by Constitutional Amendment (Art. V, last sentence). See further below § 10, pp. 40–41.

rigour of the argument which claims, not that every community does, but that every community must, have a decision procedure, or hierarchy of decision procedures, which is authorised to decide all questions whatsoever. This is the modern version of the first thesis of Unlimited Sovereignty, and seems to be inescapable, if anything more inescapable than the classical doctrine of sovereign bodies, because procedures and laws, along with principles, methods and theories, are peculiarly liable to appear more clear and distinct in the mind of man than they ever are exemplified in practice. The administrators' vice of producing schemes which are very well on paper, but would never in fact work, is paralleled by the academic vice of giving an account that is beautifully clear and tidy, but not quite faithful to the facts, and disastrous in its implications. Thus it was argued in Section 3, that a community must have one method of settling disputes, and it is easy to construe this as requiring that there must be one and only one rigidly formulated constitutional law establishing a hierarchy of courts and legislatures competent to pronounce on every question whatsoever.[1] But our argument has not proved this. The arguments of Sections 3 and 4 established the need for there being a standard procedure for deciding those disagreements which actually arose and which were otherwise irresoluble. But many disagreements that might arise do not, and many that do are resolved amicably. Furthermore, not all disputes need to be settled at once, at least not in the terms in which they were posed, nor is it insupportable to have more than one decision procedure, so long as the decisions they yield are not at variance with one another. We thus need to make four qualifications on the competence and uniqueness of a community's decision procedure.

(1)   A community needs to be able to settle only those questions which actually do arise. There may be hypothetical questions which a community would have no way of answering, and which would, if they did arise, split the community and destroy it. But so long as such divisive questions are not raised, the community can survive its inability to cope with them.

(2)   A community needs to have a *procedure* for settling only those disputes which cannot be resolved amicably. We always have to envisage the possibility of our not being able to find a resolution of our disagreements, but it is importantly the case that very often we can agree without resort to any formal decision procedure.

[1] See e.g. Hans Kelsen, *General Theory of Law and State*, tr. A. Wedberg New York, 1945, pp. 407–8.

(3) A community's decision procedure needs to be capable of settling only those disputes and questions that have to be settled. Supreme though the Queen, or the Queen-in-Parliament, may be, she does not have to say whether the Monadic Predicate Calculus is, or is not, complete, nor whether there are, or are not, any synthetic *a priori* propositions. The Royal Society can continue to exist although some of its Fellows are advocates of the duodecimal system and others of the binary system. Some questions can be left unanswered without the community falling apart; and these the decision procedure does not have to be able to cope with.[1]

(4) Where there is more than one procedure, a superior procedure to adjudicate between them is required only if the different procedures do in fact give incompatible decisions, not if merely they formally could. In the constitution of the Roman Republic the *Comitia Tributa* and the *Concilium Plebis* were both sovereign assemblies, and if they had fallen out with each other there would have been no way of deciding the dispute. But since their membership was almost identical, the problem was not a real one. So too in the Universities of Oxford and Cambridge the formal possibilities of conflict between the University and the Colleges are great, and without there being any means of settling their disputes: but since the same persons run the Colleges as run the University, the possibility of irresoluble conflict is more formal than real.

A community, therefore is not bound to have one rigidly formulated procedure for deciding all questions, nor, more importantly for our present argument, is a decision procedure the only way of reaching agreement. Disagreements are often resolved by argument, and, when not by argument, sometimes by compromise. Provided the machinery of the law can prevent disputes breaking out into violence, it does not have to furnish a decision procedure for every disagreement. It is enough if the machinery of the law can, as it were, hold the ring while agreement is reached in other, informal ways. Men are reasonable, though not completely so, and often in the fulness of time come round to a more reasonable view. Some issues drag on for generations, before being either resolved or buried. Some—the most momentous—may engage everybody's attention for a time, at the end of which a very large measure of agreement—"the General Will"—may emerge. These agreements are as important to the life of a community as the settlement of disputes between members, and we must not allow the

---

[1] But see § 7, p. 26, and § 17, pp. 68–71.

possibility of unresolved disagreement to obscure the community of sentiment and purpose that exists between the various different members. If we consider only the disagreements and disputes between people, we shall inevitably be led to think about forms and procedures; because, as we have seen, it is easier to agree about procedures than about the decisions themselves, about methods than about results. But in fact forms and procedures are not the only things we can agree upon, and are merely the things we need agree upon for the settlement of some disagreements—those we cannot otherwise resolve—and not for all disagreements.

Since only by virtue of our being able to agree, can we have a decision procedure at all, it must be possible for us to agree, on occasion, that it is not working, and no longer worthy of respect. More generally we may point out that although we need to have decision procedures because of our disagreements, we are able to have decision procedures only because of a much greater measure of agreement amongst us. Not only must we agree about forms and procedures, but a community cannot exist at all, unless condition A(ii) holds of its members, that they agree about at least some of their values. It is only against this background of agreement that disagreements can arise. Although it is necessary, if it is to continue, that a community should have a procedure for deciding questions that are otherwise irresoluble, the possession of a decision procedure is not, or at least is not necessarily, the *raison d'être* of a community. And therefore it is a mistake to generalise from those relatively few issues on which there is serious disagreement to those relatively many on which there is none, and to suppose that a decision procedure represents the whole being of a community, and to say on behalf of any person or procedure, *L'état, c'est moi.*

The argument for Unlimited Sovereignty fails, first because it argues from the fact that there cannot be a *definite* limit set to the competence of a certain authority to the conclusion that *everything whatsoever* lies within its competence; and secondly because it over-stresses the importance of the formal decision procedures of a community, and neglects the various qualifications in practice on the sort of question the decision procedures must be able to decide. The thesis itself is false because it is only against a background of agreement, including some agreement on values, that a decision procedure can exist: and therefore there must be some decisions the decision procedure may not give, namely those that run counter to the shared values of the members of the community. What these decisions are that the decision procedure has no authority to give we shall not attempt to determine; indeed, we cannot determine them exactly. All we can say for certain, is that there are *some* decisions the decision procedure may not give. And we therefore deny the first thesis of Unlimited Sovereignty and say instead: "Not all things are lawful to the supreme authority in a community."

SECTION 9

CONSTITUTIONALISM

THE denial of Unlimited Sovereignty may be taken in two ways. We may go on from saying that not all things are lawful to the supreme authority, and lay down *some* of the things that are not lawful. We cannot, as we have seen, specify exactly the limits of lawful authority, but we might hope to lay down not exact, but outside, limits to the supreme authority. This was suggested by Locke,[1] and has been put into practice by the Americans. Or, alternatively, we may not commit ourselves in advance to limits, which since they must be outside limits must allow too much, but rather reserve the right to criticise at any time the decisions of the supreme authority as being "unconstitutional" or "not in accordance with the spirit of the constitution". This has been the British practice. We may call the former the principle of *Constitutional Limitation*, the latter the principle of *Constitutional Criticism*. Each has its advantages and disadvantages. Neither need exclude the other.

There is not much we can say here about the latter principle, of Constitutional Criticism, because it consists in not making general pronouncements but in criticising particular decisions. Whether a particular decision is open to criticism or not, will depend upon circumstances. Thus, if in October 1964 a Bill extending the life of the Parliament then assembled, notwithstanding the provisions of Section 7 of the Parliament Act 1911, had been passed by both Houses of Parliament, and given the Royal Assent, there is no doubt that this would have been a valid law, and would have been accepted as such by all courts. Nevertheless it would be proper to call such an Act unconstitutional, meaning not that it was *ultra vires*, legally outside the competence of the Queen-in-Parliament, but that it was against the "spirit of the constitution". But nobody claimed that a similar measure

---

[1] *True End of Civil Government*, Ch. IX, §§ 135–42; see also §§ 95, 132, 149.

actually enacted in 1940 was unconstitutional; for then there was clear and compelling reason why it was in the Public Interest that Parliament should not be dissolved. Thus the principle of Constitutional Criticism is flexible, and acts which may be criticised as unconstitutional at one time may be acceptable as entirely constitutional at another. The advantages of flexibility are clear. On this score, of holding elections, they were foreseen by Locke,[1] and the corresponding disadvantages of a rigid requirement were experienced by the United States, notably in 1864, 1916, 1942 and 1944, when the need to hold Presidential or Congressional elections, and the consequent possibility of a change of policy, fell at awkward junctures in national affairs. The disadvantages of flexibility are twofold: first that it is often debatable whether a particular act is unconstitutional, and secondly that even if it is, there is no legal remedy left by which it may be undone or put right.

The chief general importance of the principle of Constitutional Criticism—as opposed to particular criticisms which may on occasion be of fundamental importance—is that it shows that it is logically permissible to talk of *abuse* of authority on the part of the supreme authority, and it indicates the grounds on which such an accusation may be based. Contrary to the first thesis of Unlimited Sovereignty, which asserts that the authority of the sovereign is unlimited, so that it does not make sense to talk of its being abused, the Constitutionalist maintains that it does make sense, and in particular cases can be established by argument. This contention is difficult to make clear because there are many different types or ranges of argument we use, and a systematic ambiguity in certain crucial terms. Many thinkers will allow that we can talk of *moral* abuse of authority on the part of a sovereign, but not *legal* abuse. They would concede that not all things were lawful to the supreme authority in the moral sense of the word 'lawful', but maintain that all things were lawful to the supreme authority in the legal sense of the word 'lawful', as a matter of logical necessity. There is one sense of the word 'lawful' in which we may concede that it is a tautology that all things are lawful to the supreme authority, namely that in which 'lawful' means 'conforming to the formal criteria of validity for Positive law'; as we have already said, laws, even unconstitutional laws, enacted according to the correct procedure by the Queen-in-Parliament are valid laws; and in this sense it is a logically necessary truism that all things are lawful to the supreme authority. The difficulty is that not only is the legal sense of the word

[1] *True End of Civil Government*, Ch. XIII, § 156.

'lawful' confined to a purely legalistic sense, but the moral sense is often, according to many modern theories of morals, confined to an entirely subjective sense. Each individual makes his own autonomous approbations or disapprobations of political acts, and one man may consider as wrong any or all of the following political acts: a decision to open cinemas on Sundays, the conviction of an author for obscenity, the retention of capital punishment, the possession of nuclear weapons, the suspension of Habeas Corpus, an Act of Attainder, the abolition of the House of Lords, the abolition of the House of Commons, the establishment of a fascist *régime*. Any of these could reasonably be regarded as morally wrong: all might be effected in a lawful, in the legalistic sense of 'lawful', manner. No interplay between morality and legality is possible: the only argument is a resort to violence. The right of rebellion is the uniform remedy for Resistance fighters against Hitler, demonstrators against Nuclear Disarmament, and members of the Lord's Day Observance Society alike.

Against this, I maintain that there are not two types of argument, legal and moral, with nothing in between them, but a whole spectrum of arguments ranging from purely legalistic arguments about Positive law to the individual aspirations of personal morality. The solicitor advising his client has a different concept of law from the legislator deliberating on what laws to enact, and we can usefully distinguish public from various private moralities, the latter being both more optional and more stringent than the former. I may, as a Christian, believe that it would be morally wrong for me to devote all my talents to making money for myself: but I am talking in a different mode of discourse when I say that money-making is morally wrong from when I say that murder or lying are morally wrong. Thus when I say that *not all things are lawful to the supreme authority*, I mean it neither in the sense that some decisions of the supreme authority may lack legal validity—which is self-contradictory—, nor in the sense that some decisions of the supreme authority may be morally wrong in the way that I think money-making is wrong—which is true, but trivial—, but something in between.[1]

The reason why not all things are lawful to the supreme authority is that a decision procedure can exist only against a background of values held in common by members of the community.[2] It follows that these essential shared values provide the basis on which constitutional criticisms can be founded. These may be basic moral

[1] See further below, §§ 71, 73, 74.   [2] See further below, § 73, p. 324–25.

principles: thus we condemned the legal provisions for genocide enacted by the nazi authorities: and thus we would condemn an arbitrary Act of Attainder—if the Queen-in-Parliament were to enact, say, that all fat clergymen whose surnames began with the letter F were to be hung, drawn, and quartered, we should criticise and condemn it on moral grounds, not some highflown private morality about which there might be reasonable differences of opinion, but the most basic and essential public morality, which no rational agent could reasonably dissent from. Shared values need not, however, be moral values. If the Pope of Rome were to pronounce the views propounded by the Bishop of Woolwich in his book *Honest to God* to be dogmas of the Roman Catholic Church, his pronouncement, although irreversible, would be open to the criticism that the Roman Catholic Church existed on the basis of, among other things, shared beliefs which were inconsistent with the Bishop of Woolwich's views. Similarly the criticism which would be made of an Act extending the life of Parliament beyond 1964, would not be a simple moral criticism, that such an Act was contrary to the law of Nature, but rather that such an Act ran counter to certain other ideals—of accountability, of the possibility of peaceful change of government, of not altering the rules in one's own favour—which were part of our common heritage and were an integral part of that mutual understanding which constituted us one community and nation. In brief, Constitutional Criticism takes its stand on those common values which constitute the community as the community that it is.

The principle of Constitutional Criticism thus provides a point of entry into political argument whereby we can *criticise* the decisions of the supreme authority, although we can have no recourse to any legal remedy. The fact that an authority is the supreme authority does not mean that its decisions are above criticism, that criticisms are logically irrelevant, in the way that its decisions *are* beyond appeal, and that it is logically impossible to upset or reverse or quash them. We have, as it were, a foothold for argument, though not for action. A Melian dialogue[1] is possible with the supreme authority as well as with the supreme power, and it is possible for the Melians to win the argument, even though the authority, which has the final say, may refuse to hear them, and even though the Athenians, who have the power to control events, will win the fight.

[1] Thucydides, V.84–116.

SECTION 10

CONSTITUTIONAL LIMITATION

THE alternative to the principle of Constitutional Criticism is that of Constitutional Limitation. Although it has its disadvantages, it has the two great merits of not leaving it debatable whether a particular act is unconstitutional, and, in the American version at least, of providing a remedy against unconstitutional action on the part of the government.

Since we cannot specify exact limits to the lawful exercise of authority, a constitution must set outside limits. It follows that there will be many acts which lie within these outside limits, but are none the less unlawful for that. They will be constitutional in as much as they fall within constitutional limits, but unconstitutional in as much as they are open to legitimate constitutional criticism. The danger is that the two senses of the word 'constitutional' will be confused, and that because the act lies within the limits of the constitution it will be concluded that it is not open to legitimate criticism, on the score of constitutionality, at all. Gerrymandering is a peculiarly American vice. In face of this danger, constitutional draughtsmen are tempted to impose more and more stringent limitations, until the Constitution becomes absurdly detailed.[1] If, on the other hand, they resist this temptation, not only will the Constitution fail to rule out many possible abuses, but often it will be framed in such vague terms that its application in any particular case will always be unclear. Most European constitutions have contained a recital of highflown principle, without any further provision for applying it or giving it effect except in so far as legislatures and executives choose to observe it.

The Constitution which avoids both these pitfalls and goes furthest in securing effective limitations upon authority is that of the United

---

[1] e.g. that of Oklahoma. The ninth article of its constitution contains the following provision: "No railroad corporation or transportation company, or transmission company shall, directly or indirectly, issue or give any free frank or free ticket, free pass or other free transportation, for any use, within this State, except to its employees and their families, its officers, agents, surgeons, physicians, and attorneys-at-law; to ministers of religion, travelling secretaries for railroad, Young Men's Christian Associations, inmates of hospitals and charitable and eleemosynary institutions and persons exclusively engaged in charitable and eleemosynary work." (Quoted from A. D. Lindsay, *The Modern Democratic State*, Oxford, 1943, p. 227.)

States of America. This admirable creation is detailed enough to leave nobody in much doubt about the proper procedures of government, without, save in a few minor respects, being so detailed as to prevent the natural change of the content of government from one generation to another: and it includes enough statements of general principle to communicate to any reader the spirit of the Constitution, while ensuring, by means of judicial review, that the other organs of government cannot disregard the general principles it has set out. In this way, the Constitution lays down limits, which are clear enough in normal circumstances, but which, if a new situation does arise where the application is not clear, can be given an authoritative interpretation.

The combination of Constitution and Supreme Court has proved in practice an effective check upon the powers of the other organs of government in America. The question then arises about the role of the Supreme Court: if the Supreme Court is the sole authoritative interpreter of the Constitution, it will be argued by proponents of the various doctrines of sovereignty that in the United States sovereignty is vested in the Supreme Court. So far as lawyers are concerned, the Constitution is what the Supreme Court says it is. It, and it alone, is guardian of the Constitution; *quis custodiet ipsos custodes?*

Two considerations may be urged in support of this view. The first is that the Supreme Court has always been required to adjudicate on questions of substance as well as of form, and in particular to determine whether the content of an enacted law is consonant with the principles of justice and liberty laid down by the Constitution or vaguely implicit in the Constitution. The scope of the latter is very wide. The Supreme Court has become in effect the expositor of Natural Law after the manner of mediaeval courts of justice. The Supreme Court is august, and is accorded a respect not given to Congress, because the Supreme Court is felt to be the mouthpiece of the moral law, whereas Congress is merely the arena of politics.

The reasons why the balance of respect has tilted away from Congress and towards the Supreme Court are historical reasons concerning procedure and the distribution of congressional seats, and do not concern us here: but the effect has been to develop the Supreme Court into another House of Congress, and from being merely a negative check on legislation into being the spearhead of legal change. Most notably in recent years on the question of the rights of Negroes, the Supreme Court has effectively altered the law, where Congress has been impotent. Without discussing the merits of this or other decisions, two points must be conceded: the interpretation placed by the Supreme Court on the Constitution goes beyond, and in some cases is clearly contrary to, what the framers of the Constitution had in mind when they formulated it in words; that is to say, the Supreme Court takes a generous view of its interpretative powers, and does not feel restricted to determining the semi-historical question of what the words of the Constitution were meant to mean when they were adopted: and secondly, the decisions of the Supreme Court are effective; not since Andrew Jackson has any organ of the Federal government dared to ignore the Supreme Court's ruling.

In spite of these arguments, it does not follow that the Supreme Court is the Sovereign Body of the United States. To make a minor point first, the Supreme Court can only adjudicate disputed cases, and cannot promulgate laws in general application on their own initiative. The restriction to particular cases does not matter, since all inferior courts must follow the Supreme Court's ruling in all similar cases, but the restriction on initiative does confine the Supreme Court's powers to those questions on which the citizens of the United States are not all agreed. A Roman emperor could make his horse a consul, but the Supreme Court is unlikely ever to do more than adjudicate between two candidates, both human, both moderately well qualified, who have at least a faceable claim to the Presidency.

The Supreme Court is restrained not only by its formal procedures as a court from acting arbitrarily. It is also subject to the substantial check that it derives all its authority from its *rôle* as interpreter of the Constitution, and the Constitution can be read by any American citizen. Its powers of interpretation may be wide, but are not infinitely wide, and if the Supreme Court were thought to be abusing its position as interpreter it would lose respect and cease to be effective. There may be room for disagreement on whether the provision of "separate but equal" facilities is consonant with the XVth amendment to the Constitution: and if the Supreme Court rules that it is not, the ruling may be grudgingly accepted but it will be accepted. If however the judges of the Supreme Court refused to admit to their number a nominee of the President appointed to fill a vacancy, or if they started ignoring constitutional amendments (not concerned with the representation of a State in the Senate)[1] duly passed by a two-thirds majority in Congress and three-quarters of the State legislatures, then it would become quite clear that the judges were usurping powers that did not

[1] Art. V, last sentence; see above § 8, p. 30n.

belong to them, and the usurpation would be resisted. It is an error to suppose that because a court interprets the law, therefore the court creates the law; for the court derives its authority from the law, and far from being *legibus solutus*, as a sovereign is said to be, only will be effective so long as it can be seen to be in agreement with the law in almost all those cases in which the law's meaning is generally agreed. The range in which there is room for different interpretations of the law is limited, though not limited exactly, by the many cases where the law is quite clear, and it is only within this limited (though *indefinitely* limited) range that the Supreme Court is effectively supreme. And the fundamental reason for this is that although men are not always agreed —so that we need courts to adjudicate doubtful cases—, they are not always disagreed either, so that the powers of courts are effectively, though not formally, limited.

SECTION 11

EFFECTIVENESS

THE untidiness of the preceding four sections is often avoided by giving a formal, tidy, account of a legal system, but with the gloss that a system will count as such only if it is *effective*. The law of Great Britain is that enacted or upheld by the Queen-in-Parliament: the law of the United States is what the Supreme Court says it is: but in each case, there is an implicit proviso that these bodies have their supreme powers only so long as they behave themselves, and that if the Queen-in-Parliament or the Supreme Court took it literally that they could declare any laws they liked, and started to promulgate arbitrary or wicked ordinances, then they would very quickly cease to be effective. A formal tidiness is achieved for the legal system at the expense of shifting all the untidy qualifications and reservations to the extra-legal notion of effectiveness. It is in effect a doctrine of absolute sovereignty tempered by the right of revolt.

The notion of effectiveness is thus made to bear a great weight; and it is therefore the more important to distinguish carefully the different facets of meaning that it has.

There is first the sense of the word 'effective' in which it distinguishes at this present time the legal systems of Great Britain and the United States from those of the Confederacy, of Hitler, of the Tsars, the Kaisers, and the Austro-Hungarian Empire. There is nothing formally wrong with the laws of *emigré* governments and fallen *régimes*: it is merely that they are of no effect. Any one can devise a formal system for adjudicating disputes, and many people have, but these systems are of no interest to the lawyer unless they are in force, unless their decisions are binding and do alter the course of events.

In times of civil war and revolution there may be difficulty in identifying the effective legal system of a country: careful distinctions between *de jure* and *de facto régimes* are made, and these illustrate certain points of principle. But in normal circumstances there is no doubt about what, in general, the effective legal system of the country is. This is because a single effective method of settling disputes is essential to a community's continued existence. A revolt must either succeed or fail quickly, or else the community is torn into two warring communities or dissolved into general anarchy: and therefore there cannot be—because we cannot afford there to be—any prolonged doubt about which *régime* is the effective one.

The second facet of effectiveness is concerned not with whether, but with how, a system of laws is able to alter the course of human affairs. It is partly, we realise, a matter of coercion: it is partly, we hope, a matter of consent: it is partly, we sense, a matter of obligation. The interplay of these and other factors will be considered in the next section.

The third facet of effectiveness is the way in which the content of legislation is controlled by the need for a formally omnicompetent system to remain in force. Legislators are more aware than lawyers of the fact that many desirable standards of behaviour cannot be enjoined by law, because the law would not in practice be observed and could not be enforced. The story is told of an Eastern monarch who was urged by his Imans to take serious steps to suppress adultery: so he made it a capital offence. But since under Islamic law, a man could be convicted of a capital crime only on the testimony of seven witnesses, the loose-living were as pleased with the new law as were the strait-laced. It is one thing for laws to be enacted, quite another for them to be obeyed. Legislatures are restricted both in their particular enactments and in their general pattern of legislation by the need to secure obedience. If they neglect this limitation on their powers on a specific issue their enactment will be disregarded and they will bring the law into contempt: if they neglect it generally, they will bring about a breakdown of law and order and their own supersession. The Queen-in-Parliament may be the supreme authority in the land, and everything the Queen-in-Parliament enacts may have the force of law: but if the Queen-in-Parliament were to ordain that every one of her subjects was forthwith to take his own life, her sovereignty would therewith cease. Effectiveness is not only a test of which formal legal systems are actually, at a given time, systems of law, but also a limitation on the hypothetical content of any system of law. It thus does lend itself to being an extra-legal qualification to a legal doctrine of absolute sovereignty. We cannot be content, however, to leave it at that. Men are, albeit imperfectly, rational animals. Although often they will obey without questioning and without thinking at all, out of habit, out of loyalty, out of gratitude, and although sometimes they are made to obey willy-nilly, by force, at other times they will think and ask, 'Why should I obey?'. Answers can be given. But each answer not only shows the subject why he should obey but implies some restriction on what the sovereign may ordain. Therefore, instead of having effectiveness as merely an extra-legal qualification on a legal doctrine of absolute sovereignty, we need to make sovereignty less than absolute, incorporating into our account of a legal system itself the various qualifications that the requirement of effectiveness imposes. We need to consider in detail both the various ways in which a system is effective, so that not only does it decide questions but its decisions are in fact carried out; and the corresponding limits (though *indefinite* limits) this places on the decisions that can be given.

SECTION 12

POLITICAL OBLIGATION

THERE are many possible answers to the question, 'Why should I obey the law?' or, 'Why should I obey the decisions of the supreme authority?' Some answers are more applicable to particular laws than the law in general, and *vice versa*. Often several answers can be given at once. Sometimes different answers shade into one another. It is convenient to tabulate them, with examples:

I Prudential considerations:
   a Fear of sanctions (i) Coercive[1] sanctions: e.g. imprisonment.
                    (ii) Non-coercive sanctions: e.g. loss of job.
   b Fear of other consequences: e.g. general breakdown of law and order.

    [1] For definition of coercion, see below, § 15, p. 57, or p. 367.

II Because this particular decision is one I have always agreed to in substance, or would agree to if I were to think about it.

III Because this decision is of a form I have agreed to; that is, I have specifically agreed to abide by the results of this decision procedure: e.g. in entering a golf tournament I signed on my entry form an agreement to accept the decision of the committee of the golf club.

IV Because I have come to agree with this decision in the course of the discussion and argument whereby it was reached: e.g. in a small committee, where after discussion a "sense of the committee" emerges, and afterwards each member defends the committee's decision as his own.

V Because I was consulted, and participated in the discussion and argument, even though not convinced of the rightness of the decision: e.g. a Fellow of a college in Oxford or Cambridge may be out-voted by his colleagues; but he none the less feels more part of the college than a lecturer at a provincial university, just because he has been in on the discussion of policy, and has been able to have a say, even though he has not been able to get his own way.

VI Because it is the decision of a community of which I am a member. Either I must go along with it, or I must go it alone. And the latter is not a viable option: e.g. a sociable hiker who is a member of a rambling club, which wants to ramble in a different direction to the one preferred by him.

These different answers to the question, 'Why should I obey the law?' form a heterogeneous group. No single, all-embracing answer can be given. Different people ask the question in different circumstances and in different frames of mind, and the appropriate answer will depend upon the questioner, his situation, and the law in issue. Since political philosophers vary in their estimates of human nature, they find different answers convincing, and therefore select different motives for political obedience as primary. Speaking with extreme crudity and over-simplification we may say that Ia(i) and Ib, fear of coercion and fear of anarchy, were the motives on which Hobbes based his political thought; that mediaeval theories of Natural Law were centred on II—because the particular decision is one I agree to in substance anyhow—as the dominant reason for obeying the law; that

III—because the particular decision is of a form I have agreed to—
is the rationale of political obedience which Social Contract theories
were trying to articulate; that IV—because I have come to agree with
the decision in the course of the discussion and argument whereby it
was reached—is what gives life to Rousseau's idea of the General Will;
that V—because I was consulted——is the principle upon which
Parliamentary government is based; and that VI—because it is the
decision of a community of which I am a member, and either I must
go along with it or I must go it alone—represents the truth behind
what Hegel and the Idealists have had to say. To put it another way,
Hobbes, faced with the question, 'Why should I obey the law?'
replies, 'You had better, or else', and then amplifies the 'or else' in
terms, immediately, of the sovereign's power to coerce, and, generally,
of our interest in avoiding the state of nature. The mediaeval philosopher answers the question by saying, 'Because you ought to', and
explains political obligation simply as a case of moral obligation. The
Contract theorist says, 'The reason why you should obey the law is
because you promised', Rousseau, 'because that is what you really
want', Burke, 'because you have had a say in making it', Hegel,
'because that is what you really *are*: the you who obeys the law is the
real you; the you who is tempted to disobey is a fleeting irrational
phantom'.

These characterisations, let it be repeated, are crude. But in understanding and assessing them, it is helpful to ask how each justifies our
obligation of political obedience, and how far, if at all, this justification
sets any limits to what authority may lawfully ask us to obey. Natural
Law and Social Contract, in justifying our obligation to obey, clearly
also limit the things that the government is entitled to enjoin upon
us: the justification offered by Hobbes equally clearly imposes no
such limitations. Justifications in terms of the General Will IV, and
of the Organic State VI, have tended not to set any limits to the supreme authority, although it is less clear that they cannot.

The motives under head I—fear of sanctions, coercive or otherwise, and fear of other consequences—are, together with the actual
use of force, peculiarly effective, as we shall see,[1] but on that account
are thought to be regrettable. Their effectiveness is a brute effectiveness; they are intellectually opaque; they may coerce or compel,
but they cannot convince; they are addressed to men as intelligent
animals, not to men as rational agents; and whereas they are effective,

[1] See below, §§ 14, 15.

where they are necessary, with criminals, the worst of men, they are often ineffective, where they are not needed, with martyrs and saints, the best of men. In using coercion or applying sanctions we feel that we not only are taking a low view of men but often are in fact making them conform to that view. Force can brutalise. Where possible, we prefer to avoid the use of force and sanctions, and when we must enforce the law, we prefer to do it indirectly rather than directly. And always when we have to give an intellectually opaque answer to the questioner, we can be asked the further question, 'Is it right to do that to me?' to justify treating him as less than a rational being. In answering *this* question, we have to show both that the man ought to do what the law required for some other reason than the fear of coercion or sanctions; and that the need to secure compliance with the law was sufficiently great to justify the use of sanctions, and possibly even coercion, if the man was sufficiently selfish or unreasonable not to obey for any other reason.

We should also note, under head I, that while the use of coercive sanctions is reserved to the State, the use of other sanctions is not. They are, almost necessarily, as we shall show later,[1] at the disposal of other communities and of individuals. In all cases, their use poses the same problems: they are effective, but rationally opaque, and in need of further justification. We should note furthermore, that Ib, fear of consequences other than sanctions often shades over into some other motive. I may feel that the law is conducive to my long term interests, and that if I disobey the law my example will be infectious, and that the consequent breakdown of law and order will be more disadvantageous to me than the temporary inconvenience of observing the law on this occasion. Thus a motorist might reason that it was in his interests to stop for the traffic lights, even though he could be sure of getting away with it if he shot them on this particular occasion. But the argument of enlightened self-interest is easily extended. For, whenever I am a member of a community, I am likely to feel that the realisation of its values is also the furtherance of my own interests, and that it is up to me to do my part. And this shades over into a communal sentiment of type VI. Ethically speaking, a prudential consideration arises only when we calculate the actual consequences of a particular act of disobedience to the law. We often represent other actions as being done from motives of enlightened self-interest when they are indeed enlightened but not purely self-interested, because, by a curious

[1] § 14, pp. 54–55 and § 45.

inversion of intellectual values, we feel self-interest is intellectually more respectable than any disinterested motive. We feel shy about showing ourselves to be moral, and are ashamed to avow any altruism on our part. Such moral modesty may become a man, but a philosopher needs to know men's motives as they actually are, and not deck out our little unselfishnesses under a specious plea of enlightenment.

The motives under heads II, III, IV, V, and VI, corresponding to the answers 'Because you ought', 'Because you promised', 'Because you want to', 'Because you were consulted' and 'Because you must if you are to fulfil your real self' are more rationally transparent, but correspondingly less effective in securing compliance from an unreasonable man, than the threat of sanctions. One cannot argue with threats; but nor can one be convinced by them; whereas one can be convinced by arguments under the other heads, II–VI. We can see these motives most clearly, if we consider voluntary associations.[1] A rambling club may decide to go for a walk on the Chilterns: but if some members prefer to go to the South Downs, there is nothing to stop them. The members of a purely voluntary association are not compelled, in any sense, to accept its decisions. If they do accept them, it is because they agree with them or think that they ought to abide by them. Both these are very powerful motives. As we have seen, human beings often do agree—if they did not, there would be no communities, neither States nor voluntary associations nor anything else; even when they do not agree at first, they often reach agreement after discussion; and even when a man disagrees with the prevailing view, he often feels that he ought to go along with it, his own views notwithstanding. The fact that men are sometimes sufficiently reasonable to be able to reach agreement in spite of initial disagreement is what gives colour to the doctrine of the General Will. In a very small group—sometimes in a committee—a general view really does emerge, which is not simply the sum of the initial views of the members separately, but has been developed by the process of argument[2] out of the interplay of debate. This can happen, but it can happen only if the parties concerned are willing to modify their views, and not determined to stick each to his own opinion at all costs. A certain intellectual modesty and unselfishness is required if men are to resolve their disagreements by discussion and argument; without it, people

---

[1] For definition, see below, § 14, p. 55, or p. 367; see further § 64, p. 278.
[2] See further A. D. Lindsay, *The Modern Democratic State*, Oxford, 1943, pp. 240–4.

will prefer their own opinions, because they are their own, to any others whose sole recommendation is that they are true, and discussion will degenerate into sterile debate, animated by intellectual *amour propre* rather than any spirit of sweet reasonableness. This is the point behind Rousseau's distinction between the wills of all and the General Will. The wills of all, separately, are taken to be intellectually selfish and self-willed, unmodified by the pressure of reason and argument; whereas the General Will is taken to be essentially reasonable, intellectually unselfish and moral. But the distinction is not always like that: corporate decisions are often selfish: an individual dissentient may be malleable by reason and not at all self-willed, only unconvinced by bad arguments, and right where the others are wrong.

Where a man has engaged in argument out of which an agreed conclusion has emerged, there is no question why he should accept it. Even though he did not agree to begin with, he has come round and been convinced by the argument, and has made the conclusion his own, which he fully consents to. But arguments often do not end in agreement: even when everyone is possessed of all the relevant information and is trying to be reasonable and intellectually unselfish, differences of opinion often remain. Yet even if the dissentients do not agree with the views of the majority, they may appreciate their position and see their point of view. Political argument, as we have seen,[1] is a two-sided affair, and by having engaged in it we may come to appreciate the force of the arguments on the other side; and without either having convinced the others of the rightness of our views or having been convinced by them of the rightness of theirs, we may nevertheless have been convinced of their sincerity and the respectability of their views. Thus to have participated in the process of producing a communal decision will sometimes make a man ready to accept it, even though he does not himself agree with it.

On other occasions a man may be totally unconvinced—sometimes rightly—by the arguments adduced, and participation, far from having induced in him any degree of acceptance, may only have served to demonstrate to him the invincible unreasonableness of the others, and the unmitigated wrongness of the decision. Yet even here a dissentient may feel obliged to acquiesce in the other view, and act against his better judgement, and go along with the rest. Nor is this unreasonable. If we recognise that human beings not only have imperfect information but fallible judgement, we realise that it is in the nature

[1] § 6.

of human associations sometimes to reach wrong decisions: just as, in view of his imperfect information, a man who wishes to consort with his fellow men must be prepared sometimes to obey and not always to make up his mind entirely by himself, so in view of fallibility, a man cannot expect always to find agreeable the conclusions on general issues which have been reached after discussion and argument. To insist that one must never act against one's own judgement is to refuse to associate with other fallible, imperfect men at all. Even if one discounts the possibility of ever being wrong oneself, one must admit the possibility of other people being wrong, sometimes of everybody else being wrong; and then if one places any value upon associating with other people and doing things in common, one is committed to not always having everything exactly one's own way, even though one's own way, may appear to be, and possibly is, the right way.

We could even go one stage further, and say that it is incoherent to think that one could be a member of a community without having any obligations. For that would be to have all the other members of the community subservient to one's own will: and then they would not be colleagues and equals, but slaves. Therefore one cannot be a *member of* a community without obligation, but only a *tyrant over* it. To have the sole say about what shall happen is to be isolated. An autocrat is cut off from the give-and-take of social life, because for him it is all take and no give. It is logically possible to wish to be a self-sufficient despot: but it is not logically possible to combine that with a social existence. In as much as a man regards himself as a social being and desires a social life, he gives up the solitary supremacy of his own will, and concedes that what is to happen is not to be determined by his will alone. He must either subject himself to obligations, or else suffer the logical loneliness of the man without ties.

SECTION 13

CONSTITUTIONAL CRITICISM

THE different arguments justifying political obligation generate different principles of Constitutional Criticism. The mediaeval theories of Natural Law held that rulers ought only to ordain that which was morally right, or, at least, that which was not morally wrong. In any community many of the decisions yielded by the decision procedure can be justified, independently of the procedure whereby they were reached, on the grounds that they instantiate in particular cases common values held generally by members of the community. And arguments which can be used to justify some decisions, independently of the procedure whereby they were reached, can by the same tokens be used on other occasions to criticise other decisions, which, although validly arrived at by the decision procedure, nevertheless run counter to the common values of the community.

Natural Law arguments are thus in principle fundamental. Nevertheless in practice they are unsatisfactory. They are fundamental, because they represent the principle of Constitutionalism *par excellence*. They are unsatisfactory, because they are vague, and because they are static. They are vague because the common values of a community are seldom made explicit. They afford arguments of Constitutional Criticism rather than formulations of Constitutional Limitation; and, happily in our society, there are few decisions taken which are clearly, beyond doubt, clean contrary to our common values. Many of the decisions taken in accordance with our procedures are wrong: but few are so wrong that no arguments can be adduced in their favour, and that we can all be quite sure not only that they are wrong but that they are altogether outrageous. We defer until later fuller consideration of the doctrines of Natural Law[1] and of the extreme circumstances, fortunately rare, in which arguments for political *dis*obedience are conclusive.[2]

Natural Law arguments apply only to those decisions which the subject has already agreed to in substance. But although often there is basic antecedent agreement (though usually only implicit) to communal decisions, often also it is unrealistic to speak of any *antecedent* agreement. Until a particular question arose, people had not considered it, and could not have agreed on any answer beforehand. Nevertheless, the question once posed, we are fairly confident that a reasonable man will reach some particular decision. And therefore, if the decision procedure yielded such a decision, we could again defend it independently of its having been reached by the decision procedure: and *per contra*, we could criticise other decisions reached by the decision procedure, if we were sure they were totally unreasonable. Such arguments are closely akin to Natural Law arguments, and have often been considered under that title. But I want to distinguish the requirement that decisions be reasonable (or to be exact, that they should not be

[1] § 74.   [2] § 73.

unreasonable[1]) from the requirement that they be moral (or rather, not immoral), and, as we shall see in due course,[2] many consequences flow from our adopting an ideal of rationality to guide our decision-makers in making their decisions,[3] and on this basis we shall develop the principle of the Rule of Law.

The Contract theories meet the question, 'Why should I obey the law?' with the answer, 'Because you promised' and invoke the Social Contract to determine also what rulers may legitimately ordain. As a principle of Constitutional Criticism the Social Contract is less valuable than the Rule of Law.[4] But particular political compacts provide the standard means of generating specific Constitutional Limitations, and every time we settle an unresolved dispute by recourse to an agreed decision procedure, we can be construed as contracting with each other to submit our dispute to arbitration. Contract theories are thus useful in constitutional practice, but for the reasons given in Sections 7 and 10, they are inadequate as comprehensive theories of Constitutionalism, and have led to a distorted view of the State,[5] and could be invoked to justify deeply unconstitutional practices.[6]

The fourth and fifth answers, 'Because you really want to' and 'Because you were consulted', lead to constitutional principles of a quite different kind. These answers apply only to people who are not only parties to a dispute, but participants in the process whereby the decision was reached. The manner and extent of the participation are not fully determined. It never can be that the participant has the sole say and himself decides the question without deferring to anybody else. It sometimes is the minimal sense of knowing, or being able to know, after the event, the arguments and considerations which led up to the decision. In this sense we all participate in parliamentary debates, and assist (in the French sense) the administration of justice. All adults (other than aliens, peers and lunatics) participate in another way in parliamentary elections. In a different way again, parties to a legal dispute being adjudicated by the law courts, have special rights of participation through their being represented by counsel. The departments of State are felt to be under some duty, when drafting bills to be presented to Parliament, to consult with "interested parties" who will be affected by the proposed legislation.[7] In a different way again, some people assist (in the English sense) the administration

---

[1] § 28.   [2] § 27, pp. 124–9.   [3] See generally, §§ 24–31.
[4] See below, § 66, pp. 285–6.   [5] § 67.
[6] § 66, p. 286; § 67, p. 290.   [7] See below, § 53, p. 227.

of justice often and voluntarily as magistrates, others occasionally and compulsorily as jurors.[1] Among our political ideals, we have not only that of the Rule of Law, that decisions reached shall be, so far as our imperfections allow, rational and right, but that of Political Liberty, that our decisions shall be reached, so far as the practical exigencies of the situation permit, in such a way as to involve each individual, and enable him to feel that the decision is *his* decision, or at least that the process whereby it was reached was one in which he had been able to play his part.

Hegelian doctrines similarly argue that the individual should conform to communal decisions on the grounds that they are, really speaking, his decisions. Only, here it is not in virtue of the individual's having had a say in the decision-making process, but simply in virtue of his being a member of the community. His participation is only a general one, in that he participates in the life of the community generally, not a particular one in any decision-making process. This sense of participation, although dilute, is pervasive. Since we are social animals, almost all our doings are done in the society of our fellow men. We want social intercourse and need it. Solitary life is likely to be nasty, brutish and short, and necessarily cannot be continued from one generation to another. Even in our inmost thoughts we pay tribute to our social nature by formulating them in language, itself a social phenomenon. Conscious of ourselves as individuals though we often are, we achieve our sense of our own identity, in part at least, by finding some *community-*[2] or *group-*[2] identity, and considering ourselves each as a *member of* a certain community or group, as an Englishman, an Oxford man, a doctor, a pigeon-fancier, a Christian, a father, a member of the local cricket club. Without a sense of belonging to some community or group, a man feels lost, and may feel that he does not properly exist at all, but is merely a piece of flotsam in the tide of human affairs. A man feels he does not really know who he is unless he can not only name himself but describe himself to himself; in Greek, he wants to be able to answer not only ὅστις ἐστι but ποῖος ἐστι. He needs to give an account of himself, and for many this can be done only by describing himself under some community- or group-description that is meaningful for him. Very often the State is one such community; it is an essential part of some men's

---

[1] See below, § 20, pp. 84ff.

[2] For definitions see above, § 3, p. 11 and below, § 64, p. 276; or below, p. 366.

view of themselves that they are members of that State, and therefore they cannot refuse to regard its decisions as binding. Very often, but not inevitably. If men are to identify themselves with a community, a community must stand for something, must stand for something men can value, must be a community a reasoning man can be proud to belong to. The modern view that the State should be "value-free" and should confine itself to the minimum tasks of keeping law and order and providing drains is ruled out: one cannot identify oneself with a public utility company.[1] Also, a community which is to be valued by its members must value them in return. It need not invite them to participate in its decision-making processes, but it must show by one means or another that it recognises their existence and their services. It is partly a matter of mass-psychology, which the dictators have understood far better than the liberal societies of the West: but it is also a matter of rational principles of Constitutional government. The principle of Humanity that every man should be treated as a man, humanely,[2] and the principle of Fraternity, that in spite of all the divisions and distinctions between members of a community, they should treat one another as fellow members and individuals in their own right, are two such. More generally, we often need to be on our guard against arguments of Freedom leading to conclusions of Indifference. Our society should be a free one, but not an uncaring one. We confer Freedom on people, for good reason, and allow them to make wrong decisions: but should not seem to think that what they do does not matter, or refuse to recognise good deeds on principle.[3]

SECTION 14

ENFORCEMENT AND SANCTIONS

ALTHOUGH there are many arguments which may be addressed to a rational agent to show him why he should obey the law, these arguments are not always effective with mortal men. Men are neither sufficiently reasonable nor sufficiently unselfish always to be prepared to obey the law, all the arguments of the last section notwithstanding.

[1] See below, § 67, pp. 292–3. [2] See below, § 28, pp. 132–3; and § 57.
[3] See further below, § 32, p. 145, and § 75, pp. 346 and 348.

All of us sometimes, and some of us always, are bloody-minded. We will not comply with the decisions of authority from any motive of enlightened self-interest, Ib, nor for any of the reasons II–VI. Only coercion or the fear of sanctions will bring about our compliance.

In as much as there are bloody-minded men about, and we are all on occasion bloody-minded, the decision procedures of voluntary associations are not effective. Not only are their decisions not always carried out, but we always know that they may not be carried out, and therefore cannot confidently rely on their being carried out. Therefore voluntary associations, important though they are both to us in our ordinary social life and to the philosopher in his analysis of the community, are felt to be ineffectual. They depend too much on the goodwill, and often the whim, of their members: we feel we cannot entrust important matters to their care, knowing ourselves and believing other people to be, at least not always, untainted by bloody-mindedness. We think that voluntary associations ought to be more effectual, and we strive, with some success, to bring it about. But it remains for the most part an ideal, and for serious business we need communities whose decisions are binding, which will, that is, be carried out willy-nilly. Decisions must be enforced, and authority cloaked with power.[1]

A decision is directly enforceable against a party when it can be carried out against his wishes and in spite of any obstruction he may offer. A decision is indirectly enforceable if it can be arranged that if he does not co-operate in carrying it out or acquiescing in its being carried out, then he shall either have carried out against him further measures which he would like to, but is unable to, resist, or be prevented from doing some range of things he would like to do.

Decisions which are enforceable but not directly enforceable are enforced by means of *sanctions*; a sanction is an alteration in a person's position carried out against his will and itself enforceable directly or indirectly. Any community that allows any measure of liberty to any of its members, enables those members to take some sort of sanctions against others: I can withdraw from an unwelcome visitor permission to be in my house: I can refuse to do business with a dishonest tradesman: a club can refuse to admit a bounder to its membership. Since in fact as we shall see later,[2] almost all communities must allow some

[1] 'Authority' and 'power' are used in the sense defined in § 4, pp. 16–17. For list of definitions, see pp. 366ff.
[2] § 45.

measure of liberty to almost all its members, it follows that almost everybody will have some sanctions—even a child can take away its custom from a sweet shop. These sanctions are often not effective in adapting other people's behaviour to our wishes, but sometimes they are, and often they are not wholly ineffective. The whole aspect of society is changed by the fact that although usually the direct enforcement of decisions is exclusively in the hands of the officers of the law, there is no such monopoly of indirect enforcement. In particular, once granted the background of direct enforcement of the law by the State, it is possible for there to be many other communities, not themselves States, but able to impose decisions on their members that are, in virtue of certain sanctions, binding. Clubs, universities and trade unions are such communities. The sanctions at their disposal are sometimes so effective as to make them appear quasi-states. If I am expelled from a trade union, I may well lose my livelihood. The simple distinction often drawn by writers on political theory between coercive communities, or States, on the one hand, and voluntary associations on the other can be misleading. Some associations are purely voluntary, but many are not; we cannot consider only the State, and refuse to recognise the importance of any other community on the plea that it is merely voluntary, because the coercive machinery of the State provides, so to speak, a skeleton on which other communities can build up systems of sanctions which make their decisions almost as enforceable as those of the State. We need to make a tripartite classification of communities: those communities which have coercive power are *States*: those which have sanctions, but not coercive ones, at their disposal are *associations*, but not voluntary ones: those which have no serious sanctions at their disposal are *voluntary associations*, in a strong sense of the word 'voluntary'.[1] The decisions of voluntary associations are not enforceable at all. The decisions of other associations are indirectly enforceable. The decisions of States are indirectly and directly enforceable. Voluntary associations pose no problem of power: if people like to carry out their decisions, they do so, in some important sense, of their own free will, and they cannot complain that power is being exercised wrongfully over them. Other associations do raise the problem of whether power is being rightfully exercised, and whether its use can be justified. And this is pre-eminently so with the power of the State, which rests ultimately on coercion.

[1] See further below, § 64, p. 278.

SECTION 15

COERCION

THE concept of *coercion* and the related concepts of *force, violence, pressure,* and *sanctions* are difficult to elucidate; and it is easy to use these words in shifting senses. We do not distinguish in our customary ways of talking the different degrees of restraint we may feel on free actions. We have a reasonably clear idea of physical violence, but tend to use metaphors of force and compulsion in many cases where there is no question of physical violence. We talk of being *bound*, not by chains, but by obligations: we find arguments *cogent, compelling* or even *coercive*, though no argument yet has been able to frog-march me through the streets: the pressure of public opinion no doubt is effective in shaping men's behaviour, but it is a pressure very different from that of a dagger in the small of the back. Such metaphors are natural, and without them we might find it difficult to convey our meaning: but they do not make for clarity in political philosophy. Our characterisation of a community as having a method of settling disputes other than by force, is intended to exclude, not settlements achieved by force of reason, but only those by force of arms: in freeing men from the pressure of the dagger of the bandit, we must not be thought to be offering them freedom from the pressure of public opinion. There are many fears, many threats, many ties, many compulsions in civilised society: civilisation even creates its own fears, threats, ties, and compulsions. In establishing a civil community we are not providing a guarantee against all fears and threats, all ties and compulsions. We are not establishing some new Utopia, in which man will be absolutely free and unconstrained. It is enough that we are offering certain limited, but definite, freedoms, security against certain simple but devastating fears, threats, ties and compulsions.[1] We therefore do not count it as a case of coercion if I am compelled to do something on pain of losing my job, nor do we count it as a case of force being used by one person against another when the one prevents the other from achieving his objects simply by a refusal to co-operate; for example, when we talk colloquially of a woman forcing a man to leave the army by refusing to marry him unless he does. The sensitive soul may wish to be no man's enemy,

[1] See further below, § 34, p. 149.

and to conduct himself so that all shall wish him well: he then would be *vulnerable*[1] to any man's ill will, and might find himself *forced* to modify his proposed course of action, if he did not wish to be *hurt* by incurring another man's displeasure. But again, these senses of the words 'vulnerable', 'force' and 'hurt', though perfectly legitimate, are not the senses we wish to use here. We wish to use the words in their minimum sense, applicable to *almost every* human being, insensitive and unambitious as well as sensitive and full of high aspiration. The reason is that we are concerned with the *enforcement* of decisions: we are considering the conditions under which decisions will be carried out regardless of the recalcitrance of the bloody-minded. We therefore define *force* in terms of bloody-mindedness, of what happens irrespective of how recalcitrant a man is, of what happens to him willynilly. Force, then, we say, is being used against a man, if in his private experience or in his environment either something is being done which he does not want to be done but which he is unable to prevent in spite of all his efforts, or he is being prevented, in spite of all his efforts, from doing something which he wants to do, and which he otherwise could have done by himself alone. A man is being *coerced* when either force is being used against him or his behaviour is being determined by the threat of force.

Force is thus the ultimate means of enforcement, and coercion the ultimate sanction; as the Kings of Prussia averred when they inscribed upon their cannon the motto, '*ultima ratio regium*': we, however, have made this not a contingent, cynical observation of *Realpolitik*, but an analytic truism, following straight from our definition of force, cynical only in as much as we maintain that some people are sometimes sufficiently selfish and sufficiently unreasonable to be bloody-minded and recalcitrant to reason and unamenable to argument. With them there can be no argument, but only non-argument—which I call coercion—, force and the threat of force.

States are communities whose decision procedures are made effective by means of coercion. The use of coercion by the State is not simply, as some have supposed, a regrettable accident: that kings who can, will. The need for coercive power on the part of the authorities of the State is the consequence of its non-selectivity of membership. Other communities can be selective in their membership—they do not have to have just anybody who happens to be there as one of their subjects. In a monastery there is no need for coercion, because only those

[1] As above, § 1, p. 4.

people join monasteries who are prepared anyhow to obey the orders of their Superior. Similarly, Plato, in setting up the Ideal Community in the *Republic*, does not have to consider coercion, because only volunteers in the first place are to be members of it, and thereafter he believes, perhaps wrongly, everyone will be so well educated and so enthused with the Ideal Community, that no one will ever seriously want to be out of line. We have already seen how in voluntary associations even when dissentients are not completely persuaded, they may yet be sufficiently persuaded to toe the line without the use of sanctions. Expulsion, even when ineffective as a sanction, remains, necessarily, effective as a remedy. But a State lacks this safety valve. It cannot expel a member without recourse to coercion. And so, if a State is to be able to enforce its decisions uniformly upon all those unselected members who happen to be members at any one time, it must be able to use methods of enforcement which are going to be effective against anyone. Thus from the fact that a State is an unselective community, together with the fact that people, some always, all some times, are selfish and unreasonable,[1] it follows that if the decisions of the State are to be enforced, the State must have at its disposal not only sanctions, but some *sure-fire* sanctions or methods of enforcement. And this is what we mean by coercion. The argument from sanctions, Ia, is effective with those who are not amenable to arguments addressed to them as rational agents—it requires only, as we have seen,[2] that they should be intelligent animals: while the actual use of force does not require that men are intelligent or even animate (and so does not appear in the list as any sort of motive for political obedience at all); but is none the less effective for that, in carrying out the decision of a court.

Provided we are to have communities which are unselective in their membership, we need to be able to enforce decisions against the recalcitrant: and therefore are concerned with the minimal senses of the words 'force', 'coercion', 'hurt', and 'vulnerable', which are applicable to all human beings, thick-skinned and thin-skinned alike. Almost every human being does not want to be flogged, tortured, wounded, or killed:[3] being frog-marched, being imprisoned, being made to suffer great pain, or being killed, effectively prevent any human being from doing almost all the things he wants to do.

The concept of force is applicable in the specific way it is, because of certain contingent features of human nature. If the thumbscrew

---

[1] § 1, p. 2, B(i) and B(ii).   [2] § 12, pp. 45–46.
[3] See further below, § 41, pp. 172–3.

gave as little pain as the odour of violets, or if men seriously thought that pain was unreal or death to be welcomed, we should have little reason to fear the evil-doer, and the structure of our common life would be different. Or, again, if we were effectively invulnerable like tortoises. It is only in view of men's general agreement that pain and death are bad things, and the relative ease with which we can hurt one another, that we place such value on the maintenance of law and order, and can use the methods we do use, to ensure that the decisions of the courts are in fact carried out.

Our common dislike of pain and death determines the form that our concepts of force and coercion take, but is not, as we saw earlier,[1] a necessary condition of our having those concepts at all. Even a community of tortoises could use force against a recalcitrant member in preventing him from going where he wished. Or, again, if men were isolated on separate South Sea islands, and their sole communication was by means of wireless, it would be possible to "coerce" a recalcitrant islander by jamming or threatening to jam his wireless, so that he would be unable to transmit or receive any messages. Jamming his transmitter would be like imprisonment: it would make him unable to do anything that he might want to do in the public world, namely the aether, common to members of that community. Jamming his receiver would be like, only less like, the infliction of pain. It would be less like because it is less specific. To prevent the recalcitrant islander from receiving messages, it would be necessary (leaving aside possibilities of directional jamming, which are irrelevant to this example) to jam all wavelengths and prevent any one from receiving any message. Everyone would have to cut off his nose in order to spite one renegade's face. This illustrates the point made earlier[2] that while it is a necessary fact that human beings should be vulnerable, it is a contingent one that they should be vulnerable in the specific way that they are; namely that by operating on a man's body we can cause pain to that particular man, and can bring about an irruption into his private experience, which is of a sort that is disliked by everybody but which in this particular instance is experienced by him alone.

The only condition which can be imposed on one individual agent specifically, and not on any others, and to which agents are necessarily vulnerable, is impotence. Agents operating in a common public world must be able to thwart another's actions: for anything that one may do, another may undo or may spoil: else they would not be acting in a

[1] § 1, pp. 4–5.   [2] § 1, pp. 3–4.

common world at all, but each in his own isolated domain. Hence it is specific. And impotence must be regarded as an evil, something to which he is vulnerable, by any agent who wants to do anything at all. It is for this reason that I claimed[1] that imprisonment is the paradigm form of coercion. Men are only contingently killable and torturable, but are necessarily susceptible to imprisonment or something like it. Even if it were not regarded as a penalty, it would still be effective in frustrating the efforts of the recalcitrant to prevent a judicial decision being implemented. And so imprisonment plays a crucial part in our judicial system. It may be feasible to dispense with the death penalty, as we have already with all forms of torture, mutilation, and corporal punishment: but we have not dispensed with, nor could we conceivably dispense with, imprisonment as an ultimate sanction against the recalcitrant, and as the ultimate means of securing the enforcement of the law.

It is for this reason also that in English common law peculiar importance is laid upon the personal liberty of the subject. As long as a man is not incarcerated, he is able to do many of the things that he wants to do, and in particular to take all sorts of steps to secure remedies for any wrongs he may have suffered. Habeas Corpus reflects the especial importance of imprisonment in our scale of values as being necessarily an evil, which we are all susceptible to in view of our inhabiting a common world in which we interact and want to do things.[2]

We have shown that if there are to be unselective communities with effective decision procedures, then in view of characteristic B(i) of human nature, that we are inadequately altruistic, and perhaps also B(ii), that we are not completely rational, some coercion is necessary; and that in view of characteristics A(i) and A(ii), coercion is possible. We have not yet shown why there need be unselective communities at all, and although to most people it is obvious that there must be, it is worth disentangling the different reasons why.

If there were no coercive sanctions there would be no sanctions, or at least no serious sanctions, at all. Although many individuals and associations can exercise non-coercive sanctions, they can do so only against the background of the coercive sanctions of the State. If I fail to comply with one of its decisions I may be expelled from a club, and thereby cease to be entitled to frequent the club premises. This is an effective sanction only because were I to continue to frequent the club

[1] § 1, p. 5.   [2] See further below, § 20, pp. 86–87.

premises, the club could bring an action for trespass against me, and invoke the law of the land to enforce their sanction against me. In the absence of such a law, I could continue to occupy my seat in the smoking-room just as before. Similarly, the sanction of sacking a man operates only against a background of earning, owning, and spending money, which in turn depends upon the law for its maintenance. There would be no point in having a job, if contracts were completely unenforceable and theft unpunishable. Thus, although it is true and important that there are many non-coercive sanctions at the disposal of bodies other than the State, they exist only because the coercive power of the State provides the framework on which they can obtain purchase. Thus if there were no coercion, there would be no sanctions, except that of bare expulsion, with no legal consequences flowing from it; and all associations would be voluntary associations.

Would it matter if all associations were voluntary ones? Although voluntary associations are often felt to be, and sometimes are, in-effectual, they need not necessarily be so. The bare threat of expulsion is a powerful sanction with many people: characteristically, Churches are in a position to use this weapon, but no other; and the threat of excommunication has proved an effective threat for securing obedience. Could we not arrange it that this was always so?

We know that as a matter of fact the threat of excommunication has not *always* been effective. Not only are there some people who do not care about the Church, or do not believe that if they are excom-municated they will go to Hell, but there have been people—in the Middle Ages—who did care, and did believe, but still were not prepared to knuckle under to the ecclesiastical authorities. Behind the historical fact lies a general principle, that individual agents are *inde-pendent* agents, and can do many things in the common public world without the co-operation of any other agent. A man can often say, 'I shall do this' or 'I did it', and not merely, 'We shall do this' or 'We did it'. If it were not so, men would not be conscious of themselves as individuals at all: but since it is so, the bare fact of exclusion from a community does not destroy a man's capacity to act in the common public world, and to interact with other men, and therefore to do things which they do not want done. It is a public world, a world unselective in its inhabitants: it may be inhabited by anyone, and any inhabitant may be minded to do anything, and often will be able to do it on his own. If men were less vulnerable than they are, so that the amount of harm a dissident could do did not greatly matter, or if men were more vulnerable, so that the mere fact of being excommunicated from some voluntary association, the mere fact of standing ill in another body's estimation, was felt to be unbearable, then we could have only voluntary associations. But these extremes of vulnerability are neither necessarily true of men as interacting but independent agents, nor actually true always of men as we know them. Man cares too little and is too easily killed, for all associations to be purely voluntary, and therefore some communities must be coercive. Coercion is the off-spring born to bloody-mindedness by vulnerability.

SECTION 16

VIOLENCE AND THE STATE OF NATURE

WE HAVE argued the need for coercive communities from the bare fact of having communities at all, and therefore decision procedures, which, if they are to be effective, must be enforced, and can be enforced only by the use or the threat of force. Coercion on this showing is the necessary concomitant of communal life among men. We can, however, use another, more traditional, argument, contrasting "civil society" with the "state of nature", or, in our terminology, a dispensation in which disputes between two parties are settled by a decision procedure, as contrasted with one in which the two parties resort to force. In the traditional approach the emphasis is on violence and the avoidance of violence, rather than on communites and procedures for reaching decisions which are, if need be, enforced.

The state of nature is, paradoxically, an artificial concept. Philosophers imagine what life would be like if certain features of civil society were absent. But since men are social animals, they cannot live completely unsociably, and we cannot picture human life with all features of human society removed. Whichever features we imagine away, many others will remain, and the resulting state of nature will turn out to resemble in striking and implausible ways the civil society it was supposed to be contrasted with. The traditional approach is full of pitfalls, just because we cannot think of human beings who are never members of any community, and therefore cannot make them the starting-point of our enquiry. Nevertheless, although we are necessarily sometimes members of some communities we are not at most particular times necessarily members of any particular community; whereas we always need to avoid violence. And therefore the avoidance of violence, rather than membership of communites, has seemed of paramount concern to political thinkers. We shall survey this alternative approach, showing how human beings, as characterised in Section 1, need to form communities if they are to avoid violence.

If there are agents inhabiting a common world or capable of interacting with one another, there will be *conflicts*. A conflict arises when such agents are taking steps to bring about incompatible states of affairs. A conflict is the analogue of a dispute, only whereas a dispute is defined with reference to a community, a conflict is not. A dispute is about how a community shall decide a question—though often the question at issue is whether the community shall authorise one, or the other, party to get his own way. A conflict exists when two individual agents, not necessarily members of the same community, are each trying to get his own way, when it is not possible for them both to have their own way. In such a case there are two possibilities. Either at least one of the parties to the conflict uses every means within his power that he thinks will be effective for getting his own way or both of them abstain from some means which they could use and which they think would be effective. In the former case we call the conflict a *violent* conflict, and speak of the party or parties as *using force*, or of their having *resorted to force*, or *resorted to violence*. In the latter case, whichever party wins the conflict and succeeds in getting his own way, the other party is abiding by the result and giving up the opportunity of bringing about the state of affairs that he wants, while the option is still open to him to take further steps, which might yet prove effective. He therefore is accepting, if only tacitly, the outcome of the limited conflict, in which not all effective means are used, as deciding the original, potentially unlimited, conflict. And therefore in the latter case, the parties do have some other way of settling their conflict than by resort to force; they have some sort of decision procedure.

The definition of force given here is a more active one than that given in terms of enforcement, which was from the victim's point of view only. Force, we said,[1] was being used against a man, if in his private experience or in his environment either something is being done which he does not want to be done but which he is unable to prevent in spite of all his efforts, or he is being prevented, in spite of all his efforts, from doing something which he wants to do, and which he otherwise could have done by himself alone. In a conflict, since the states of affairs the two parties are trying to bring about are incompatible, at least one of the parties is having something done which he does not want to be done but which he is unable to prevent, or is being prevented from doing something which he wants to do. And if the conflict is violent, the loser is losing in spite of all his efforts, and therefore, according to the passive definition is having force used against him. The two definitions come to the same thing, as we should expect, since in a violent conflict, where at least one party is using force, at least one must be having force used against him.

One further qualification is needed: the two parties must be comparable in power. Once a prisoner has been overpowered and incarcerated, although he may be still trying by every means in his power to prevent his gaolers from preventing him from escaping, there is no longer a violent conflict, nor indeed any conflict at all. For a conflict to be a conflict, its outcome must still be open. Once the issue is settled, or if the issue can be in no doubt, there is no actual conflict, however much ill-will there may be. And therefore if there are to be conflicts, the parties must be of comparable strength.[1] It is important for our notion of law-enforcement that the parties are not comparable, and that the power of the State is incomparably greater than that of the subject, so that there can be no doubt but that the decisions of the courts can be enforced. For then force plays no part in settling conflicts or deciding their outcome, but only in ensuring that the decisions reached by the decision procedure are in fact carried out. The distinguishing mark of a civilised community is not that it avoids the use of force altogether, but that it confines its use to officers of the law acting on the instructions of a legal functionary. Force does not decide disputes: disputes are decided by the law, and force or the threat of force is used only to make sure that decisions are carried out, without any further question or doubt, even though one of the parties is recalcitrant. To this extent, Leviathan is rightly so called.

With these definitions and qualifications, we can say that recourse to a decision procedure and resort to violence are mutually exclusive and jointly exhaustive modes of settling a conflict. Either there is a

[1] Compare above § 1, p. 2n., and H. L. A. Hart, *The Concept of Law*, Oxford, 1961, pp. 190–1. The limits between which the parties to a conflict must be equally matched are so wide that it is best not to talk of even an approximate equality.

procedure which will produce a decision which is binding on both parties, or each party will try by *every* means in his power to get his own way. Even the apparent counter-example of Ordeal by Combat will fit into this dichotomy: for, first, it is usually not any sort of fight, but a fight subject to some sort of rules—for example, the Queensberry rules; and secondly, and crucially, because it is a fight with a *terminus*, after which the issue is decided, and the losing party, if he attempts to reopen it, will bring into play the whole panoply of the law against him; the trial by combat therefore is essentially different from the vendetta, and so, paradoxically, does not count as a resort to force; for a resort to force involves the use of *every* means within a party's power.

We then are faced with the logically exclusive alternatives of either having conflicts settled by some method, the results of which are binding, and can be enforced—and this means having coercion and the State—, or of having conflicts all become violent conflicts, settled only by resort to force. Therefore, if I attach any logical or rational merits to avoiding violence, and believe that it is important that conflicts should be settled by means of some rational and orderly method, and not any old how, then I must accept with this preference for rational and orderly methods the need for some coercive machinery of State to ensure that conflicts really are settled according to some method, and are not in the event left to the haphazard arbitrament of force. This is, as it were, a purely logical preference, and angels and tortoises and wireless operators on South Sea islands might all on these grounds accept the desirability of organising some system of coercion, and constituting civil society.

With human beings, however, there is more than logical preference for wishing to avoid the state of nature. Not only are human beings peculiarly vulnerable but they are much better at attack than defence or counter-attack. The peaceable human being has much to fear from the bandit, whereas the bandit has little to fear, because he can play tip and run. The state of nature, intolerable between men, has proved tolerable, although unpleasant, between States. Moated castles in the Middle Ages and Second Strike in our own Nuclear Age have weighted the scales enough to deter the aggressor from always attacking. For attack is not always successful, and even when successful in inflicting damage, may still result in an unacceptable amount of damage being inflicted in return. So the state of nature between nation-states is not necessarily a state of war. For States are not only, like men, vulnerable, but, unlike them, immobile. They are easy to identify, and are sitting targets.

In short, if separate wills can act in the same world at all, there is a possibility of conflict: if separate wills operate in a common world and have any aspirations in common, it is possible for one or more of them to set about systematically frustrating some others of them and *vice versa*; and it will constitute a resort to force or violence when one party attempts to frustrate by every means possible what the other party is trying to do, which he could do without the co-operation of the first party, and which he continues trying to do by every means possible. Thus the possibility of violent conflict is, apart from the ease of hurting one another, a concomitant of our being separate agents sharing the same world and to some extent the same values. If, furthermore, separate agents not only act in the same world but can act directly on one another, and these interactions or interferences are evaluated in much the same way by all men, and some are thought by all to be undesirable, then the problem of violence becomes much more acute, and it becomes of paramount importance to prevent our conflicts becoming violent conflicts, or our disputes settled by resort to force.

SECTION 17

COERCIVE COMMUNITIES

JUST because a community has its decisions enforceable by force, it has two other characteristics. It must, in a certain sense, have a *monopoly of coercive power*: and its decision procedure must, in a certain sense, be *omnicompetent*.

We argue first that since the State is a community which exercises coercive power, it is the *only* community which exercises coercive power. For if there were another community also able to coerce people, having, that is, at its disposal a sure-fire means of enforcing its decisions, then when the State tried to enforce a decision on a particular individual, it might be the case that the other community would subject the same individual to coercive pressure not to comply with the State's decision. And if that pressure was coercive, it would necessarily (by our definition of 'coercive') be effective, and the individual could not comply with the State's decision, which therefore would not be enforceable, and the State would cease to be a State.

Thus when the State authorities in Sicily *subpoena* a witness, and say, 'You must tell the truth in court, or else . . .', if the Mafia can at the same time intimidate the witness and can say, 'If you tell the truth, we shall shoot you' or 'shoot your wife' or 'burn your crops', and this is no idle threat, then the State's power to enforce its decisions and maintain law and order is going to break down. The coexistence between the civil authorities and the Mafia is necessarily unhappy. There is necessarily a state of war between two communities both claiming to exercise coercive power over the same people in the same area at the same time. If there is interaction between two communities, and each is claiming coercive power over the same man, there is no possibility of settling a conflict between the two communities about what that man shall do, except by resort to force. And this is the state of war. Hence we are led from the fact that the State must exercise coercive power to the further fact that the State must *alone* exercise coercive power.

Writers on jurisprudence often say that the State "has a monopoly of coercive power"; and we can accept this phrase provided we are careful to distinguish it in two different senses, namely

(1) Coercive power should be exercised only with State authorisation;
(2) Coercive power should be exercised only by State officials.

It is in the former, not the latter, sense that we have shown that the State must have a monopoly of coercive power. We can, even in a modern legal system, cite a few cases where coercion may be legitimately exercised by a private citizen, even, where the occasion demands it, without explicit antecedent authorisation. Thus under English common law, if I see a serious crime committed, I am under an obligation to arrest the criminal by every means at my disposal, even though I am a private citizen; and if I have got to use force, then I must use force. Similarly, if I am assaulted, in general I should try and run away, but if I cannot get away, then I am entitled to hit back. Thus even in English law we have rule (1) "only with State authorisation" not rule (2) "only by State officials". In other systems, the distinction is much clearer; for instance, under Jewish law at the time of Our Lord, the Sanhedrin could pass sentence of death, but could not execute it;[1] only Pilate could do that. The Jews, however, were quite

---

[1] John xviii. 31. See also A. N. Sherwin-White, *Roman Society and Roman Law in the New Testament*, Oxford, 1963, Lecture II.

prepared to let the guilty be stoned, although they were unable officially to execute sentence of death. So with the woman taken in adultery,[1] and more notably with Stephen. According to the account of his trial in Acts,[2] we have a public judicial process carried out by the High Court of the Jewish State, followed by, as it were, private enterprise for carrying out the judicial sentence. It used to happen more than it does now: under English law in the Middle Ages, if one secured a court order that one did own and was entitled to possess a certain property, one was entitled to go and repossess it oneself, using such force as was necessary.[3] But for very good reasons, whenever possible we centralise the use of coercive power, and now, if a man gets a court order for the possession of a certain house, he is not entitled to go and turn out the interloper by force; only bailiffs—who are State officials—can use the force that is required. By so doing, we avoid the danger of lynch law, we are likely to avoid some violence, and we may gain greater respect for the law and the officials of the law. These are strong arguments for reserving a monopoly of coercive power to State officials, but they are arguments of expediency, not arguments which flow from the essence of the State. It is essential to the existence of the State that coercive power should be exercised only with State authorisation. It is expedient, furthermore, that whenever possible coercive power should be exercised only by State officials. But the latter requirement can be dispensed with, and can never be completely stringent, as there will always be some occasions when in the nature of the case the court is not going to be able to give the innocent protection against violence and irreparable damage: and then even English law, which leans over as far as possible towards having parties refer their disputes to court, must allow the private citizen to use force in his defence, since by the time the court is able to act, the damage will already be done.

We have already shown[4] that the decision procedure of a community is omnicompetent in the sense that the supreme authority of a community *can* decide on any question, without there being any definite limits to its competence laid down or determined by some higher authority. I now want to argue that the State is omnicompetent in the further sense that it *must* be prepared to decide any question

---

[1] John viii. 1–11.   [2] Acts vii.
[3] Hobbes, *Leviathan*, Pt. 2, Ch. 21, ed. Michael Oakeshott, Blackwell, 1946, p. 143.
[4] § 9.

that arises, although not necessarily in the terms in which it is posed. The omnicompetence of the State in this sense follows from the State's having a monopoly of coercive power. For if the State alone has coercive power, the State alone is ultimately able to enforce its decisions, and therefore all disputes will get referred, ultimately, to the State authority, since only what is sanctioned by the State is, ultimately, effective, and only decisions reached under the aegis of the State's decision procedure are really binding. Hence it is that authority follows power, and we refer disputes to the arbitration of the powers-that-be, because only their judgement is effective. And hence also, every dispute that arises is referred ultimately to the powers-that-be, and their support invoked by every party to any dispute, their decision sought on every issue.

Much weight rests on the word 'ultimately'. It is the mark of a wise government and a happy State, that the State authorities avoid pronouncing on many issues whenever possible. But it is a mistake to think that power can refuse jurisdiction altogether. The clearest example today is provided by the peace-keeping operations of the United Nations. Once the United Nations uses force to maintain peace, it has to decide, if only by default, what sort of peace is to be maintained, and in disarming law-breakers is committed to deciding the law. An M.P.'s letter to *The Times* is worth quoting:

Sir,—Your leading article on Monday on the United Nations in Cyprus rightly says that the role of the United Nations force "ought not to be going to Cyprus to act as an auxilliary of the Cyprus Government". But it does not say what the United Nations force should do beyond have some powers to search and call in arms, if it is to be effective. This last point is taken a bit further by your correspondents of the Parliamentary Group for World Government and by Dr. Bowett, in his letter yesterday, who insists that the United Nations must give its force a mandate to disarm potential law-breakers or those obstructing the force in the exercise of its mandate.

Such a function by the United Nations—and I am in favour of it—would mean that certain problems have to be faced: there would be disputes and there would have to be rules by which the United Nations forces must act. There might have to be detention of individuals found guilty of contravening the rules. But what judiciary would adjudicate on such disputes in accordance with these rules? Should not Her Majesty's Government urgently raise at the United Nations the need for a judiciary for this purpose, to accompany the United Nations forces in Cyprus? This could be a valuable move towards making the passive peace-keepers of the United Nations into active policemen, who are able to enforce world security law on everyone in the territory concerned.

I am, Sir, yours, &c.,

DICK TAVERNE.

House of Commons, March 19, 1964.

The point made by the letter is that it is not enough for the United Nations to decide to use force: it must also decide how the force is to be used in a large number of disputed issues with an indefinitely extended range of topics. If a United Nations "policeman" finds two people quarrelling, it is not enough for him to tell them to stop quarrelling or he will shoot them both: he must hear the rights and wrongs of the case, that one man was trespassing in the other's garden or that one man has stolen the other's motorbike; and he, or some judicial superior, must decide which man is to be told to go away, or to which man the motorbike is to be given. If the "policeman" refuses on principle to get involved in the dispute, and merely stops the people quarrelling at pistol point, without himself deciding the quarrel, the quarrel will break out again as soon as his back is turned. Even the United Nations cannot be omnipresent, and suffers from imperfect information. And so, since it cannot keep its eyes on everyone always, it must be prepared not merely to suppress quarrels as they arise, but to settle the conflicts and decide the disputes which are causing the quarrels. And we cannot lay down antecedently any limit on the sort of topics that may be disputed. And therefore the State, since it has a monopoly of coercive power, and cannot allow men to settle their conflicts by resort to force, must be prepared to adjudicate on these topics. If it is going to stop people fighting, it must hear their complaints and provide decisions of their disputes.

This extreme, and apparently totalitarian, conclusion is subject to an enormous qualification. Although the decision procedure of the State has to be prepared to provide an answer for every issue that arises, it does not have to decide it in the terms posed. If I maintain that $\pi = 3\frac{1}{8}$ and you maintain that $\pi = 3\frac{1}{7}$, no court will adjudicate between us: the courts will merely allow me to assert for my part that $\pi = 3\frac{1}{8}$ and you to assert for your part that $\pi = 3\frac{1}{7}$. Provided that I do it at home, or so as not to disturb other people, I shall be allowed to go on saying $\pi = 3\frac{1}{8}$, whatever you say. Only if we start trying to shout each other down and create a disturbance, will the law intervene, and then not to say which of us is right, but only which, if either, is entitled in that place and at that time to vent his views. The legal system of a State needs to be omnicompetent in this limited sense that it always provides enough of an answer to prevent recourse to violence. How narrow these limits are depends on the particular case in question. Sometimes the courts have to determine the truth of what was said—as in cases of libel or fraud. Sometimes courts have gone further, and have taken it upon themselves to settle the truth of falsity of general propositions of science, metaphysics, or divinity. But it is not necessary, if a legal system is to be complete and omnicompetent, that it should pronounce on every intellectual and theoretical issue: all that is necessary is that whenever *A* wishes to do *X* and *B* does not want him to, the courts should be able to settle the matter, one way or the other, and not leave it to them to fight it out.

The way in which the legal system of the State is drawn in to adjudicate disputes far outside the normal province of the courts is illustrated by the Scottish Free Church case.[1] By the Act of Union of 1707, the Queen-in-Parliament makes no claim to ecclesiastical jurisdiction in Scotland, and the civil authorities try to play, over ecclesiastical questions in Scotland, the same inactive *rôle* that Congress plays over ecclesiastical matters in the United States. In 1904, however, a case was brought up to the House of Lords, arising out of a scheme for reunion between certain Presbyterian sects. For the trust deeds by which certain property was vested in trustees on behalf of the Church, laid down exactly what the doctrine and constitution of the Church was to be: and hence there was a question of whether the trustees could properly allow the Church to unite with other Churches, or whether it must be held for the few dissentients who kept to the "original doctrines" of the Church as laid down in the trust deeds. And this was an issue that the courts did have to decide. Lord Haldane was able to speak at great length on the Hegelian doctrine of corporate personality in arguing the case; and Lord Halsbury, the Lord Chancellor, found it necessary to cite (in Greek) the decrees of the synod of Jerusalem in giving his judgement.[2]

More recently, the High Court pronounced the doctrine of separation held by the Exclusive Brethren to be intolerable, and on this ground assigned custody of a child so that she should not be brought

---

[1] *Free Church* v. *Overtown and others* (1904).

[2] For an account of the case, see *Law Quarterly Review*, xx (1904) pp. 415–26; for criticisms of the judgment as being unnecessarily theological, see *Law Quarterly Review*, xxi (1905) p. 1, and xxii (1906) p. 126. But whichever way the House of Lords had decided, it would have been adjudicating on what were the essential doctrines of the presbyterian Free Church.

up in accordance with the doctrine. Although Mr. Justice Pennycuick thought it was not the function of the court to pronounce on moral matters, nevertheless the principle of separation was, in his view, to a high degree detrimental to the infant, and she should, therefore, go to her father[1].

Thus in construing trust deeds, determing what constitutes the welfare of an infant, in patent law, in cases of foreign marriage and foreign divorce, the court may have to involve itself in disputes on which it could not normally be regarded, nor would regard itself, as competent to pronounce. On occasion it may have to hear argument and evidence on highly technical points of Calvinist theology, of moral welfare, of organic chemistry, South American law, or even of high metaphysics, and have to decide as best it can; though if it is wise, it will endeavour to avoid being sucked into such disputes as these. But the State cannot avoid these embarrassments, or the charge of totalitarianism, by simply refusing jurisdiction in all cases that turn on points of religion, morality, chemistry or metaphysics. As with the range of what the State can decide, so with the range of what the State must decide, we cannot solve our problem by laying down clear and definite limits. Rather, we have a tension, a two-sided argument. We have to accept the ever present possibility, and the occasional need, of the State laying down the law on unsuitable topics, and to counter it by giving reasons why the State should wherever possible avoid doing so, and by developing institutions and procedures which will prevent the State from being embroiled in unnecessary disputes, and which will enable such questions to be discussed and settled out of court. Totalitarianism is to be avoided not by refusing responsibility but by parcelling out authority, influence, and power.

SECTION 18

LEVIATHAN

HOBBES was much more impressed with the power of the sovereign of a State than with his authority: his sovereign was, indeed, the supreme authority, *legibus solutus*, entitled to do anything; but much more important, the sovereign was the supreme power, able to do anything. And it is this second thesis of Unlimited Sovereignty, that in any coercive community it will always be possible to point to some

[1] 31 July 1964; reported in *The Times*, 1 August 1964.

person or persons who has or have supreme power, that is, whose word is always obeyed, and whose power cannot be controlled by any means whatever,—it is this, the assertion of unlimited power that has seemed to be the most pressing problem of modern politics.

The two theses of Unlimited Sovereignty lend support to each other; and it is partly because there are two, that the position seems so strong. If we attack the thesis of Supreme Power, a defender can fall back on that of Supreme Authority, and in view of the considerations adduced in Section 12, he who has authority, does also have power: and if we attack the thesis of Supreme Authority, a defender can fall back on that of Supreme Power, and in view of the considerations adduced in Section 17,[1] he who has power has authority. In showing in Section 8 that it is not quite true that in each community there is some body with supreme and unlimited authority, we have thus weakened the second thesis that there is a body with supreme and unlimited power.

We may also make against the second thesis of Unlimited Sovereignty the point we made against the first, that it is one thing to say that for everything that can be done there is some body who can do it, and quite another thing, and not at all following from it, to say that there is some body who can do everything. As before[2] $(x)(\exists y)F(x,y)$ does not imply $(\exists y)(x)F(x,y)$. For any project x which is physically possible to a community, there is some body, not necessarily a single person, who can put that project into effect. Great Britain could, if it had really wanted to, have sent a rocket to the Moon in the years 1945–70: as it did, in the years 1940–5, stand up to Hitler. One can state what the conditions are for the implementation of either project— how much we should have to be willing to be taxed, what sacrifice of lives we should have to be prepared to make, how far we should have to give up other uses of scarce resources: and one can state who are the people who could effectively make these conditions hold good—perhaps the leaders of the majority party in the House of Commons, perhaps the leaders of both parties acting in concert, perhaps many more than this. But this is not say that the leaders of the majority party in the House of Commons, or of both parties, or any other specifiable set of persons, can do anything they like. The Emperors of Rome were unable to prevent their subjects becoming Christians, the Princes of Europe were unable to secure conformity to their own religious views, the French Army in 1923 could not make the

[1] See also below, § 26, pp. 119–21.   [2] § 8, p. 30n.

miners of the Ruhr dig coal. And although, since the boundaries of what is possible in practice are indeterminate, it might be argued in any particular case that those in power could have achieved their object had they been prepared to use all means whatsoever, yet at least these examples show that it does not follow from the fact that if there is anything which can be feasibly desired there is some body or bodies who can bring it about, that therefore there is just one body which can do anything it wants.

Hobbes' doctrine of Sovereignty gained some strength from the fact that persons, but not procedures or laws or ideas or principles, can be pointed to, literally, with one's finger. And although, as we saw,[1] this was an invalid argument for the first thesis of Unlimited Sovereignty, it does carry some weight in favour of the second. It is very natural, on arrival in a new country, to ask, 'Who is in charge here?', 'Who is the boss?', and expect to have someone pointed out as the man who has the last word, the man who really counts. Some people have been so firmly convinced that there must always be a boss, that when they have been able to find none, as in Britain or the United States, they have invented him, and have started on a vain search for the man-behind-the-scenes, who really occupies the seat of power. But although only a believer in some hidden conspiracy can maintain that there is a sovereign person in Britain or the United States, it is very reasonable to maintain that General de Gaulle (or in time past Napoleon or Louis XIV) is sovereign of France; or that most African or South American States are in the control of a single man.

Even where the government is an autocracy, however, and where it is reasonable to point out one man as having supreme power, his power is not really unlimited. Dictators depend not only, as we saw earlier,[2] for their authority, but for their power, upon their being felt to embody some aspiration or ideology. If General de Gaulle grew a walrus moustache and started wearing check tweeds, and took to giving lectures to the French people on the merits of John Locke, and, instead of kissing the mayor of the village he was progressing through, suggested that the two of them should adjourn to the local for a tankard of beer—then General de Gaulle would not stay in power long. Similarly, if Colonel Nasser built himself a residence in the Scottish Baronial style, became a Master of Fox Hounds, took to reading the Second Lesson at Mattins on Sundays, and afterwards giving his guests Christmas pudding and port, and urged the inhabi-

[1] § 8.   [2] § 7, pp. 28–29.

tants of Egypt to play cricket, then he would cease to represent to them the ideal of Arab independence, which is the source of his power.

Thus even with dictators, who are the best examples of Hobbesian sovereigns, it is not true that they can do anything they want. They can often do very much more of what they want than can other people, and other rulers of other countries, but they can do what they can do only because they are felt to be the sort of person who will do certain things and who will *not* do certain other things, in particular because they embody certain ideologies. Even when sovereignty can be located in a single person's body, it is not simply to be identified with that body, but is constituted in part also by that person's actual and hypothetical behaviour in time past and in time to come. There are many limitations that the practicalities of policies impose on the possessors of power. Sovereigns may be supreme over their subjects, but they are characteristically the servants of circumstance and the slaves of their own ideologies.

We thus see that the second thesis of Unlimited Sovereignty is false in much the same way and for something of the same reasons as the first thesis. The man, if there is one, who has the supreme power, like the possessor of supreme authority, has it with strings attached. He has it only because there is some consensus of opinion that his judgement is to be preferred to other peoples'. The arguments, however, are not going to be exactly the same in the two cases, because power is not a matter of procedures, but of organising things so that one has one's orders obeyed. The power to coerce others that a single man can exercise by himself, is limited. Not even Goliath could defeat single-handed a whole army; and even a Samson must sleep. Hume made the point well, using the word 'opinion' where I should use the word 'influence':[1] "As force is always on the side of the governed, the governors have nothing to support them but opinion. It is therefore on opinion only that government is founded: and this maxim extends to the most despotic and most military governments, as well as to the most free and most popular. The Soldan of Egypt, or the Emperor of Rome, might drive his harmless subjects, like brute beasts against their sentiments and inclination. But he must, at least have led his mamelukes or praetorian bands, like men, by their opinion."[2] I shall

---

[1] See above, § 4, pp. 16–17, or below, p. 366.

[2] *Essays*: Essay IV 'of the First Principles of Government' para. 1; quoted by A. D. Lindsay, *The Modern Democratic State*, Oxford, 1943; p. 199. I am indebted to Mr. J. D. Mabbott for the original reference.

call this the Mameluke argument. It shows that although some people may be coerced, not all can be. There must be in any community larger than a family more than one person doing the coercing, and those who are doing the coercing are themselves uncoerced. The possessor of supreme power may be able to use coercion against most of his subjects, but still needs to have the free co-operation of a minority—maybe a fairly small minority, but not a vanishingly small one—of his subjects, those who actually carry out his orders. And therefore his power is not absolute or unlimited.

Besides the Mameluke argument, which refers only to the Party, in the Marxist sense, there is another argument against the unlimitedness of power which applies to the people at large. Even if there are Mamelukes to man the coercive machinery of the State, the effectiveness of a legal system cannot be secured by coercion alone. There must be a minimum degree of acceptance of it by the bulk of the population or they will not resort to it for the settlement of their own disputes. Men being finite in their capacities, rulers are not omniscient, and will not know of every dispute unless at least one of the parties to it informs them of it; and people will not invoke the law unless they think they will obtain justice. An occupying army has at its disposal all the resources for coercion that any civil power could have; but unless it is studiously "correct" in its behaviour towards civilians, it will secure only as much compliance from them as it is able to extort by threats. Only when an administration is established which observes some principles of justice, will the conquered people bring their disputes to their conquerors for adjudication. Suppose an Eastern Monarch does not like being disturbed from his nocturnal activities in Araby by the tedious business of giving Solomon-like judgements, and therefore promulgates a rule that he will always clip off litigants' ears. He will save himself a lot of trouble—people will not come to him for the resolution of their disputes. But by the same token he will largely divest himself of his power—he will cease to be the Supreme Decider of his community, and people will have to find some other way of resolving their disputes. They will establish their own jurisdictions, as the Jews did under the Romans, the Christians under the Turks, and again the Jews in modern Europe. The Ghettos were sub-states, with their own procedures for resolving their disputes, which procedures were more or less effectively enforced by more or less coercive sanctions; communities which were not completely independent of the paramount power, but able to get their way in most things. Pilate wanted to release Our Lord.

The reason why sub-States come into being is that the authorities of the State, who normally would have the power, are not prepared to exercise it justly, and therefore lose jurisdiction. And this is a reflection of one of the facts of human nature, B(iii), Imperfect Information. Leviathan is not, *pace* Hobbes, a mortal God, because God is omniscient, and no man, nor any number of men, can be. And therefore unless the subjects at large will bring their disputes to the sovereign for resolution, the sovereign will not know what is going on. His information is always limited; but if he is not just, his information will be very much more limited than it otherwise would be. This is why, as Hume pointed out, "Every form of Government must be founded on some principles of equity and natural justice". The subjects do not have to like everything that the sovereign does, but they do have to like *some* things that the sovereign does, else they will tell him very little. They will then cease to be subjects in the ordinary sense: they may become victims; and in so far as they live at all they will be in a separate community with its own rules. Their life will be opaque to the gaze of the sovereign, in a way in which it is not where the sovereign uses his power in a manner thought to be just. The relationship between the sovereign and his subjects is *not* one simply of naked force, but a form of *symbiosis*. Although there is essentially an element of force in the relation between the sovereign and his subjects, it is not merely force. The subject recognises his sovereign not only as a person whose commands he must obey, but also as the person who will protect him, who will act *justly* in deciding disputes between him and his neighbour.

We may call this argument the Ghetto argument. The Mameluke argument and the Ghetto argument each prove that the supreme power in the State is nevertheless unable to do anything it likes. As in the case of the supreme authority, we cannot lay down exact limits to what the supreme power can do. We can however say some things which the supreme power ought not to do and cannot do. Even Hobbes admits[1] that a sovereign neither is entitled, nor is effectively able, to have his subjects all kill themselves: and we can think of other examples of what the sovereign is not entitled to do, or is not capable of doing.

To sum up against the two theses of Unlimited Sovereignty which together constitute Hobbes' doctrines of Leviathan: against the first

[1] *Leviathan*, Pt I, Ch. 14; Pt. II, Ch. 21.

thesis, of supreme authority, we argued that since it is only by virtue of our being able to agree, that we are able to have a decision procedure at all, it must be possible for us to agree on occasion that the decision procedure is not working and is no longer worthy of respect. And against the second thesis, of supreme power, we argue first that since it is only by virtue of some people giving voluntary obedience that we can have coercive machinery at all, it must be possible for them on occasion to be unwilling to obey, so that no one can be coerced; and secondly, that since men are possessed of only imperfect information, the government will always be the less well informed, and hence the less able to control events, the less it secures the respect of the governed. Therefore we deny both theses of Unlimited Sovereignty, and say instead, first *not everything is lawful to the supreme authority*, and, secondly, *not everything is possible to the supreme power*.

SECTION 19

THE TAMING OF LEVIATHAN

HOBBES was wrong on both counts. It does not follow from the nature of the State that we have to have a Hobbesian sovereign; neither an absolute prince who is *legibus solutus*, entitled to do anything, nor a boss who is in fact able to get away with everything. It makes sense, therefore, to talk of the abuse of authority, and it is rational to plan the control of power. 'Abuse of authority' is not, as we have seen,[1] a meaningless concept; nor, as we shall now see, is it a hopeless endeavour to contrive means to control power.

The means by which we can control power are not clear-cut. As with securing authority against abuse, we can lay down rules, but they are never adequate, and sometimes inapplicable. What is applicable in one country in one set of circumstances is inapplicable in another country in different circumstances, and methods of control which were effective at one time are likely to lose their effectiveness over the course of years. Although we need to have rules, rigid rules which we abide by rigidly, we must not be rigid in thinking about them. Other rules may serve the purpose equally well. All rules have their defects. We need always to be on the look-out to see if our own safeguards are becoming defective and in need of amendment.

[1] § 9, pp. 35–37.

Other rules may serve the purpose equally well. I shall be insular in my exposition, but do not wish to claim that the institutions of England or the English-speaking world are either the only good ones or necessarily the best. Trial by jury has much to recommend it, but the Dutch manage perfectly well without it, and it is an unsuitable procedure in many social conditions; even in England and America it does not always work out for the best. Englishmen are apt to make a sacred cow of their institutions, and imagine that if only they can export sufficient quantities of cricket and Erskine May, all will be well with the rest of the world. This is not necessarily so. Institutions can flourish only against a certain social background, which may not obtain in other countries. What is important is not simply the institution, which has been developed in the course of English history to meet problems with resources which may be peculiar to England, but the *rationale* lying behind that institution.

All rules have their defects. Rules are rigid, and cannot take account of the infinite complexity of human affairs. However well we frame them, we cannot anticipate all the eventualities that may arise, and there will always be some situations in which, considered by themselves, it would be better to act otherwise than as the rules prescribe. If we have the rule that a man is presumed innocent until proved guilty, many guilty men will escape, and law and order will be less well maintained. If we allow to Senators unlimited time for debate, and secure to every State equal representation in the Senate, we enable a small minority to frustrate legislation, and pay the penalty of having laws that are out of date, and inadequate to modern needs. If we fetter Leviathan by the Separation of Powers, and various other devices, we pay the price of loss of efficiency. Give one man absolute power, and he can get on with the job, and be answerable for any failure: parcel out the power, and you divide the responsibility and there will be opportunities for passing the buck.[1] There may be overriding arguments for not risking the dangers of dictatorship, but there *are* arguments on the other side, which a Frenchman or an African could reasonably adduce. There is not one ideal system, the English or the American, by which all others are to be judged according as they conform to it or not, but rather a number of arguments, against, as well as in favour of, any set of rules, and we have to strike a balance, as best we can, between them.

The means by which we keep Leviathan under control are: the

[1] See below, § 26, pp. 119–21, and § 49, p. 210.

Separation of Powers; the Assignment of Responsibilities;[1] Remedies for Wrongs; Answerability for Actions; Process of Law; and the Rule of Law.

The Separation of Powers is traditionally understood to mean the division of the functions of government into legislative, judicial and executive, with different organs performing the different functions. As a first approximation, the classification of functions is helpful, but the classification cannot be carried through completely,[2] and it may be confusing rather than helpful to try and force governmental functions into this mould. It certainly has never been put fully into practice. In Great Britain, the supreme judicial court is the House of Lords: in the United States the President has a circumscribed legislative function as well as executive ones. Nearly always the chief executive magistrate has some legislative and judicial authority as well. In Great Britain the Legislature has ultimate authority over the other organs of government: in the United States, subject to a number of qualifications,[3] the Judiciary has. We must therefore approach the traditional doctrine of the Separation of Powers warily. It has its value, particularly in the separation of the Judiciary from the other branches of government; but it demands careful thought. A weaker doctrine of the Separation of Powers is worth asserting, particularly in conjunction with that of the Assignment of Responsibilities. It is a great safeguard against the misuse of power, if different persons or bodies have to co-operate before the power can be exercised. We give two men keys to nuclear weapons, both of which have to be turned before the weapons can go off. One body—the police—catches the criminal: another—the court—hears the case: a third—the prison authorities—carries out the sentence. The ill-will, incompetence, or venality of one official cannot effect much harm; nor even the more insidious corruption that mistaken zeal often induces in a whole body of men.

The Assignment of Responsibilities not only assigns different responsibilities to different men, but defines the responsibility assigned to each. The jury is not called upon to say whether the accused is a

---

[1] Later, in § 26, pp. 117–18, we define the word 'office' to mean the same as 'responsibility' here.

[2] Compare the *Federalist*, ed. Max Beloff, Basil Blackwell, Oxford, 1948, p. 179, No. xxxvii,: "Experience has instructed us that no skill in the science of government has yet been able to discriminate and define with sufficient certainty its three great provinces, the legislature, executive and judiciary." See further below, § 46, pp. 199–202.

[3] § 8, p. 30 n.; § 10, pp. 39–41.

worthy citizen or a scoundrel deserving punishment, nor whether a certain type of behaviour ought or ought not to be forbidden by law, but only whether the accused has or has not done what he is accused of having done. This makes it much easier to establish standards for the correct discharge of a responsibility, to tell whether an official is doing his duty properly and to provide remedies if he is not.

The Separation of Powers in its minimal sense of assigning different responsibilities to different, individual or corporate, bodies, provides a safeguard against the selfishness we take to be inherent in human nature under assumption B(i).[1] And it is practicable only if, again as we assume in B(i), men are not completely selfish (nor completely unreasonable, as we assume in B(ii)), but can work together for some common goal. The community of purpose between the separate holders of separate powers must be enough for them to resolve their differences and co-operate, else the whole system will break down. The Mameluke argument[2] is thus transposed into a new setting. Just as every coercive community depends on there being within it another non-coercive community, founded entirely on obligation and consent, and constituting as it were the backbone of the State, so a State which does not want to give itself over entirely into the hands of a Leviathan to provide an effective decision procedure for its other-wise unresolved disputes, depends on there being within it other less contentious communities, whose members can resolve their disputes by discussion and compromise, without recourse, or without very much recourse, to a decision procedure. These communities constitute in the strained sense of Section 2, secular Churches or "establishments" whose members are, to a lesser extent than other men, subject to limitations B(i) and B(ii). Every State must have its Mamelukes, to wield coercive power; and should have its Establishment men—its moral Mamelukes—to control it.[3]

It is worth noting here an entirely different argument for having the Separation of Powers, an argument based on the dialectical nature of practical reasoning.[4] There are often two sides to a case, and it is well that the different sides should be put by different mouths, and that different officials should be charged with the duty of presenting them as strongly as possible. This is pre-eminently so in a court of law:[5] but Humanity similarly requires that there should be probation

---

[1] See above, § 1, p. 2. [2] § 18, pp. 75–76.
[3] See further below, § 22, p. 96, and § 72, pp. 321–2. [4] § 6, pp. 22–23.
[5] See further below, § 28, p. 131, and § 46, p. 199; but see also § 48, p. 208.

officers as well as warders, welfare officers as well as bailiffs. It is sometimes complained that the State speaks with many voices, so that the citizen is confused: but it is really an advantage, because then amid the many voices the citizen will hear someone who is speaking to him and for him, and with whom he can himself talk.

The Assignment of Responsibilities in its sense of assigning a definite responsibility to each official, reflects the third human limitation, B(iii), of imperfect information, and, to a lesser extent, the second, B(ii), of fallible judgement. An official cannot take into consideration all facts and all arguments which are relevant to what would be the best thing to do on a particular occasion. By limiting his task, we make it possible. A judge cannot tell what would work out for the best for all the parties to a dispute; but he can hope to tell whether the case falls under a certain law or not, and on that other judges will usually agree with him. An inspector of taxes cannot determine whether it would be better to tax a particular tax-payer and build an extra room in a government office, or to leave the tax-payer prosperous and the office smaller; but he can assess the tax-payer's liability for tax in accordance with the Finance Act. A prison warder cannot, and does not have to, decide whether a prisoner is guilty or not, but only has to see that the sentence of the court is carried out. These definite assigned tasks, because they are definite and assigned, give much less scope for abuse. A policeman commissioned with the indefinite task of upholding law and order, and suppressing vice, would have many excuses to hand if accused of oppression or brutality; some criminals need suppressing with a firm hand, and who is to say that the complainant was not such a one? But if we restrict the responsibility of the police, we restrict also the excuses that can be reasonably put forward, and thus the possibility of abuse.

Even with limited spheres of responsibility, officials may go wrong. Judgement is fallible, B(ii). But human judgement is not hopelessly fallible, and therefore although mistakes will be made, it is possible for them to be recognised as mistakes, and corrected. The hierarchy of courts, appellate courts and the court of ultimate appeal, is the lawyers' remedy for the possibility of judicial error. Other wrongs need other remedies, which we shall not particularise here.[1] All that we need do now is to emphasise that with any scheme of government, things may go wrong, and that one should always consider not only how schemes are intended to work out, but how they may in fact go awry, and what

[1] See below, § 49, pp. 208ff.

steps then need to be taken, what procedures need to be available for those who are aggrieved.

Things may go wrong. Part of our task is to establish procedures for setting them to rights again, but part should be to discourage officials from allowing things to go wrong. Officials should be answerable for their actions. There should be some body entitled to ask them the question 'Why did you act in that way?' to which they are obliged to give an answer, and render an account of what they have done, and why. It is a powerful safeguard against abuse, especially if the sphere of responsibility assigned is a limited one, so that there is not much room for dispute over what ought to have been done. Again, we shall not particularise here, but only remark that Answerability for Actions is needed because of men's selfishness and fallible judgement, B(i) and B(ii), and is possible because of men's judgement not being hopelessly bad, B(i) again, so that when an official is called upon to explain his actions, we can assess his explanation, and decide whether he had good reasons or not for acting as he did.

The last two in the list of safeguards against Leviathan are more obviously restrictions. Process of Law is a restriction on the exercise of coercive power: the Rule of Law is a restriction on the competence of legal authority. We may regard these two as the pre-eminent bastions against the two theses of Unlimited Sovereignty.

Process of Law is an instruction to those in power not to use coercion except with legal authorisation. Thus the Fifth Amendment (1791) to the Constitution of the United States lays down: "No person . . . shall be deprived of life, liberty or property, without due process of law." This in itself might seem a trivial restriction, as the Supreme Authority could always authorise whatever it wanted. It is not a trivial restriction, however, in conjunction with the Rule of Law, which restricts what the authorities may authorise. Exactly what the restriction is that the Rule of Law imposes upon the authorities has been understood differently by different thinkers. Sometimes it has been simply the principle of Constitutionalism, *not everything is lawful to the supreme authority*; sometimes some doctrine of Natural Law; but chiefly it has been taken in conjunction with the traditional doctrine of the Separation of Powers to restrict the authority of the judicial, executive and legislative branches of government in characteristic ways. As with the doctrine of the Separation of Powers, there are difficulties in carrying through the Rule of Law, thus understood, completely and rigorously. Nevertheless it is an important and easily intelligible ideal. We therefore state the Ideal Rule of Law[1] as imposing on each organ of government its appropriate restriction, namely:

(i) The Judiciary must apply existing law, not make up new laws.
(ii) The Executive must act only on the instructions of the Judiciary in applying coercion.
(iii) The Legislature must enact only *general* laws, not Acts of Attainder, nor retrospective laws.

SECTION 20

PROCESS OF LAW

PROCESS of Law is an instruction to those in power not to use coercion except with legal authorisation. The problem is how to make sure that the instruction is obeyed. How is it possible to control those who control coercive power? The answer is that it is possible under certain conditions, such that we can know whether or not those in control of coercive power are behaving themselves, and can do something to remove their power if not.

We have first the problem of knowledge: how to know whether or not those in control of coercive power are behaving themselves. And we can use here, as we did for the settlement of disputes in a community, the fact that we can agree on procedures even when we cannot agree on questions of substance. Our instruction to those in power is resolved into a set of instructions about *procedure*; because it is quite clear whether the correct procedure is being followed. Opinions may differ on substantial issues—on flogging, on capital punishment, on whether a particular man was really guilty or not, on whether a particular sentence was excessive or not—, but we can all agree that a thug is not to be flogged in a police station while awaiting trial. Provided it is a question of procedure, putative abuses can be brought to light, effectively investigated, effectively remedied, and the perpetrators punished. We need first to consider the ways in which the law does authorise the use of coercion and secondly the ways in which it provides safeguards against its unauthorised use.

[1] See further below, § 26.

The paradigm case of coercion being authorised by law is when it is authorised by a court. A court order is made whereby a judicial official instructs an executive official to take a particular, named man, and do something to him—keep him in prison for a specified period of time, hang him, flog him,—whatever the court has determined. The executive official has no discretion, but simply has to carry out the sentence of the court.[1] All the discretion is in the hands of judicial officials, who can argue and talk, but never wield a truncheon, who are characteristically old men with weak muscles, who abhor the idea of violence and would never themselves be tempted to use force, or to beat up a recalcitrant prisoner in the cells. The men who might feel this temptation, whose strong arms actually convey criminals to the cells, put their wrists into handcuffs or their heads through the noose, and who are naturally tempted to use strong-arm methods, are given no discretion. Their instructions are precise: it will be quite clear whether they have obeyed them or disobeyed them.

The paradigm case is not the only case, nor could it be. Criminals must be apprehended and brought to court, before the court can order them to be punished, and this in turn may require coercion. Moreover, as we have already seen,[2] even the private citizen is sometimes authorised to use coercion. We therefore need to set out a complete list of the circumstances in which the law authorises the use of coercion against a civilian.[3] Coercion may lawfully be used or authorised by

(i) a private citizen; only in the clearest possible cases, either in self-defence when it is impossible to run away, or to prevent a serious crime being committed or to arrest the criminal, and then only until the police have arrived.

(ii) a policeman; in addition to the above, only on reasonable suspicion on a stated charge, and then only for arrest, for less than 24 hours.

(iii) a magistrate; only on information supporting a *prima facie* case; only for remand until trial; bail to be given whenever possible.

---

[1] Except for the quasi-judicial authority of pardon, reprieve or remission of sentence, vested in the Crown. This can only reduce, never increase, the sentence; and is not at the discretion of the officials actually carrying out the sentence.

[2] § 17, pp. 67–68. [3] Military law is, necessarily and rightly, different.

(iv) judges;[1]   the paradigm case; wide discretion, but often
                          limited by statute, particularly with respect to
                          the maximum penalty.

(v) gaolers;   in self-defence; in order to carry out a sentence
                          of a court; in circumstances specified by the
                          Prison Code.

What the law authorises is clear: but other things may happen. If
coercion is used unlawfully, how do we come to know about it? And
what then can be done? One person will know that force has been used
or threatened—the victim; unless, indeed, he has been killed, against
which other safeguards are required.[2] If the victim is alive, he will
know. How then can we make sure that he can communicate his
knowledge to others who will be able to take effective action? The
answer is to secure to every one a right of access to the Judiciary, who
are the people to hear complaints and provide remedies. So far as the
ordinary use of violence by ordinary citizens goes, there is no problem.
The victim can go to the courts and bring an action for assault and
battery. If, however, the victim is held under arrest he cannot go to the
courts and make his complaint. Therefore the first requisite is to bring
any and every person detained in custody before a member of the
Judiciary, so that he may state his case to him in person. We have two
provisions to secure this: Habeas Corpus and the twenty-four hour
rule.

A writ of Habeas Corpus can be obtained on behalf of any person
detained by anyone, public official or private citizen alike. It is an
instruction from a Judge to those holding a person in custody to bring
that person into the presence of the Judge, and to show the Judge what
authorisation they have for keeping the person in custody. It may be
that there is a perfectly good reason: the governor of a prison keeps
many persons in custody; and he can show the Judge the court order,
issued by another Judge, instructing him to keep the person named in
custody, and that will satisfy the Judge. Or it may be that the custodians
claim that they are not keeping the person in custody at all, but that it
is a purely voluntary seclusion; as might be maintained by the Mother

[1] Including magistrates trying cases which fall under their jurisdiction. For
the sake of brevity, in this section, when English law is being discussed, 'judge'
with a small 'j' will include magistrates and juries, and 'Judge' with a capital 'J'
will be confined either to full-time, permanent, paid adjudicators (including
County Court Judges and Stipendiary Magistrates) or to Judges of the High
Court alone, as the context requires.

[2] See below, p. 88.

Superior of an enclosed order of nuns, if a writ of Habeas Corpus were obtained on behalf of a novice. In that case the Judge can himself talk to the person, and decide whether she is being coerced or not, and if he decides that she is, he can order the court officials to escort her from the court a free woman.

Habeas Corpus is a wide-ranging remedy, but it suffers from two defects: the victim cannot himself obtain a writ, because he is in no position to do so. It must be done on his behalf by somebody else, a solicitor, a relative, or a friend. Moreover, a writ of Habeas Corpus must be addressed to someone, and often it is difficult to discover where a man is being imprisoned and who are his gaolers. The twenty-four hour rule suffers from neither of these defects. Neither the victim nor his friends have to do anything to initiate action under the twenty-four hour rule, nor is it necessary to discover by which public official, and where, a prisoner is being kept under arrest. For the twenty-four hour rule is a general, standing instruction to all public officials to bring before a judicial officer—a magistrate—every person they may happen to have in their custody, who has not been placed in their custody by the order of some judicial officer, within twenty-four hours of his losing his liberty. This ensures that "arrest" is what the word means, a temporary stopping, while the case is tried, not a permanent incarceration.

The twenty-four hour rule does not provide any remedy for a person kept in custody by private citizens, who are not public officials; and, being general, is less peremptory than a writ of Habeas Corpus, addressed, in the second person singular, to a particular man. Nevertheless, in present circumstances, it is a more powerful safeguard than Habeas Corpus. Habeas Corpus has its place in the affections of Englishmen, because of the part it has played in the history of the fight for the liberties of the subject. But this fight won, it is the twenty-four hour rule that keeps the liberties of the subject secure from official erosion.

Habeas Corpus and the twenty-four hour rule are powerful safeguards for the innocent. An Englishman at peace with his conscience can sleep soundly, not fearing the nocturnal knock, and a sudden and silent exile to Siberia, to the gas chambers, or to the firing-squad. He knows that if by mischance he falls into the hands of those who have the handcuffs, he will within a day have the ear of a humane and considerate man who will effectively secure for him liberty and justice. But even the guilty have rights; and we need to ensure not only that every man shall be brought before the Judiciary at first, but that even those convicted and condemned shall remain within view of the Judiciary, so that they can see that the convict is not treated more harshly than the court has ordered. We need therefore to establish *judicial supervison of prisons.* We already have it in principle through Habeas Corpus, which enables any Judge to pick any prisoner out of any prison, and interrogate him to satisfy himself that the prisoner is being lawfully detained. More effective supervision is secured by the fact that prisons are regularly visited by magistrates who arrive unheralded at the prison gates, and must be shown over whatever part of the prison they wish to see. If prisoners were often beaten up by warders, or if there were torturings or floggings, it would be discovered sooner or later in the course of a spot check by someone quite outside the prison system and independent of its *ethos,* who would be under no covert pressure to keep quiet, who would suffer no sanctions if he spoke out, who would know that what he had witnessed was wrong, and that he was under a duty to say what he had seen, and who was of such standing and repute that his word would be believed. Thus we can be sure that unless there is a vast conspiracy of silence, totally at variance with what we know of the character of friends and acquaintances, there are no Dachaus or Buchenwalds in England.

The dead speak not. We have relied on victims being alive so that we can know of the violence they have suffered. But what opportunities there must be in Pentonville or Brixton of doing away with a dangerous witness and stopping his mouth for ever! Against this the law provides some safeguard, and some degree of judicial supervision. No exception is made for corpses in prisons to the rule that every corpse before it is disposed of must either be certified by a doctor as having died of natural causes or else be made the subject of a coroner's inquest. It seems a ghoulish and unnecessary provision that after a judicial execution, a coroner must go to the prison and view the body and certify that it has been lawfully hanged: but there is this point to it, that it brings in a judicial officer at the last stage of the application of coercion against an individual, as well as at the first feasible one, and that this procedure makes sure that if an unauthorised killing takes place either a judicial officer will get to know of it or many people will know that something fishy has taken place. The absence of a death certificate, just because it is a universal requirement, will warn everyone who has a hand in disposing of the corpse, that he is doing wrong. Sooner or later conscience will compel someone to tell.

We have secured that if anything goes wrong in the use of coercive power it will come to the notice of the judiciary. We now have to consider what legal remedies there are, what instructions the Judiciary are authorised to give in the event of coercive power having been unlawfully exercised.

The first and most important remedy is to prevent the wrong continuing. Since the paradigm form of coercion is imprisonment, the paradigm remedy is release. Habeas Corpus enables a Judge to set a man at liberty immediately. He walks out of court a free man, without any further delay while bureaucrats put the necessary documents into the pending tray or keep the matter under active consideration. Similarly under the twenty-four hour rule, if the magistrates then or on a subsequent hearing decide that there is no case to answer, the prisoner is immediately discharged. And so too if, having been lawfully arrested and lawfully remanded in custody and committed for trial, the prisoner is in the end found not guilty.

It is not always enough merely to remove the grievance: it is sometimes necessary also to redress the balance of right. Where a man has been arrested on reasonable suspicion, but his guilt has not been proved beyond reasonable doubt, it is enough that he should be released. There has been no abuse of coercive power, and although the prisoner has been inconvenienced, there is nobody, except possibly himself, who has acted wrongly, against whom a remedy ought to lie. But where there has been an unlawful use of coercion, it is right that both the victim should be recompensed and the perpetrator punished. If a private citizen has used force against me, without my first having attacked him, or having committed a serious crime or being in the act of committing a serious crime, I can sue him for assault and battery. So too, if a policeman uses more force than is necessary to overcome my resistance and arrest me. If a policeman arrests me without having reasonable suspicion that I have committed a stated offence, I can sue him for wrongful arrest. Once I am at liberty, I can do these things, and the remedies provided by law will be effectively at my disposal.

If a private citizen or an executive official makes a mistake and uses coercion unlawfully, he will suffer for it; zeal is no excuse for exceeding authority. The fact that an official is engaged in carrying out his official duties, does not exempt him from the duty to observe the law himself, or make him immune from legal action if he fails to observe the law. There is no "diplomatic immunity" for officialdom. The fact of his being an official will of course often affect the application of the law to a man: a policeman who does have reasonable suspicion is not liable for wrongful arrest; and the governor of a gaol keeping a convict in prison on the order of a court is in a different legal position from a Mother Superior keeping a recalcitrant nun fretting in her cell. But the fact of being an official only alters and does not suspend the application of the law. Officials, like ordinary citizens, are legally answerable for their actions, although the answers that may be acceptable to the court are likely to be different. In view of the fact that officials, like ordinary mortals, are sometimes wrong in their judgement and not necessarily disinterested, it is of prime importance that they shall be answerable for their actions: for then they will have a powerful incentive to exert themselves to act reasonably and disinterestedly, and to avoid committing errors of judgement or lapses from integrity. Therefore, in particular, the prerogative of pardon must be sparingly exercised, and not used to provide a *de facto* blanket immunity for all the servants of the Crown. To dispense all executive officials from being answerable to the Judiciary, and to leave them answerable only to the chief executive, is a major step towards tyranny, and when King James II claimed a general Dispensing Power as part of his prerogative, he was rightfully dethroned.

Nevertheless there is a tension in determining to what extent officials shall be subject to legal penalties if they act in error. Men's judgement being fallible it is inevitable that officials will make mistakes: if we say we shall punish these mistakes mercilessly, men will not become officials. While we need to give officials, being only men, an incentive to act honestly and competently in the discharge of their official duties, we must not demand of them, being only men, a more than human standard of excellence in their official actions. If a man undertakes a task which is hazardous and full of pitfalls, we can demand a reasonable standard of performance, but must not be extreme to mark what is done amiss. Our solution is to assign definite responsibilities to each official, and in particular in this case to confer narrowly limited discretion on those officials who are most tempted to abuse it, and make them subject to sanctions if they overstep the mark, and to reserve the discretion, whenever we possibly can, to the Judiciary, who are relatively free from temptation, and whose errors are relatively easy to detect and correct. Policemen and warders have, like private citizens, very little discretion to authorise coercion, and if they make a mistake, even in good faith, they will suffer for it. Judges are left with a wide discretion; but if they make a mistake, although there is a legal remedy—appeal to a higher court—, it will only correct the court's error—quash the conviction or alter the sentence—and will not subject the erring Judges, provided only that they acted in good faith and not corruptly or maliciously, to any penalties for their mistake.

SECTION 21

THE JUDICIARY

In Process of Law large discretion is conferred on the Judiciary, and therefore we depend upon there being judges capable of discharging judicial functions well. There must be at least a minority of persons capable of being judges, imbued with a love of law and liberty, and conditions must be such that those who actually are judges shall be able to discharge their functions without fear or favour. We have so arranged things that it is the judges who may make mistakes without being brought to book for it: it is important therefore that the mistakes shall be few.

The Judiciary needs to constitute within the State a sub-community which is an Areopagite society,[1] in which though judgement may fail and information may be inadequate, yet men are not sufficiently selfish to prefer their own way to the right way, and in which, therefore, no sanctions are required. This makes certain demands both upon the natural abilities and propensities of the men concerned and upon the environmental conditions under which they live. For some judicial purposes more than average intelligence is required: and in all judicial functions a degree of disinterestedness is required which is not easily come by. The need for intelligence and disinterestedness has inegalitarian overtones.[2] A State that values justice, law, and liberty, will be an unequal one in the important sense that in it judges must occupy positions of power, and not everyone is capable of being a judge. Objection is sometimes made on egalitarian grounds to the present system of selecting jurors and appointing judges. It is alleged that it would be more democratic to select jurors by lot, as in Ancient Athens, and to elect and re-elect judges by a popular vote, as in some

---

[1] See above, § 2, pp. 7–8; and below, § 70, pp. 308ff.
[2] See further below, § 58, p. 255.

American States. It should, however, be clear that the paramount consideration in choosing people to be judges ought to be the good administration of justice, and not any social or political dogma. For if the judges are not worthy and capable of power, power will fall into other hands, and we shall all be equally defenceless before the men who wield the truncheons.

We need safeguards against fallibility and selfishness. Against fallibility we have the safeguard that judges are bound, by and large, to apply existing law, and not each decide cases on his own;[1] and where there is room for serious disagreement with a judge's decision, the dispute can be settled by an appeal to a higher court. Against selfishness we have a variety of safeguards: juries are a chance selection of men, who are unknown and therefore unbribeable before the trial, and are un-get-at-able, often literally so, during the trial. Any private interest or prejudice that one of them may have is unlikely to be shared by all twelve. Granted only a limited level of reasonableness and unselfishness, individual interests will cancel out, and a jury does not exist as a body long enough for any corporate selfishness to develop. These provisions offer good security that the verdict of a jury—the highest common denominator of the individual judgements of the jurors—will be reasonable and disinterested.

The judges do not have the random anonymity of jurors. It is a matter of great moment to ensure that they are effectively un-get-at-able. Historically the most important achievement was to make the judges irremovable by the Crown. This deprives the government of its most powerful sanction against a judge who will not toe their line: and while it is difficult for a man who knows that it may cost him his job to decide fairly and justly between Sovereign and subject, it is not so difficult for a man to be disinterested in his decisions if he knows that he personally stands to lose nothing, whatever decision he gives.

It is also important that he should stand to gain nothing; and this in the modern world has an important corollary. Many people now have security of tenure (always, of course, during good behaviour) in their jobs, and cannot be dismissed at pleasure, but still depend on favour for promotion. It is important that no judge can reasonably expect to be promoted, or fear that he may be passed over if he fails to watch his step. Else his independence is undermined; as happened in the Middle Ages, when the custom grew up of translating a bishop from one see to a better; whereby all those in less lucrative ones were made

[1] See below, §§ 27–34, and § 51.

subservient to Pope or King. Therefore a county court judge, when appointed, must expect to remain one to the end of his days, and not entertain any fond hopes of the High Court, and if ever it becomes necessary to establish stipendiary magistrates throughout the country, they too ought to be un-promote-able, and to be a stipendiary magistrate must be made to be an acceptable "career grade".

Judges who are irremovable and un-promote-able will be independent of the government. They must also be independent of possible litigants. Therefore they need to be so rich that they are unbribeable. For many years in England the judges were above the reach of temptation, but with the great inflation in the years during and after the Second World War, they were brought down to a level where ordinary financial considerations operate. No case even of attempted bribery has been reported, but Sir Winston Churchill was right in deciding that judges must be paid enough not only to be incorruptible, but to be obviously so. Parliament objected to his proposal to make their stipends free of income tax, perhaps rightly; but should have used other means to secure the same result, so that no judge should be subject to financial pressure of any kind, and so that no judge should ever have to consider whether he might, on retiring from the bench, augment his pension by going into business.

Financial pressures, although the most obvious, are not the only pressures that may be brought to bear to influence a man's judgement. Indeed, just because they are so obvious they are easy to recognise and often to resist. Social and personal pressures are more insidious. It is a great merit that Justices proceed in eyre, and are strangers in assize towns and not local dignitaries. They are aloof, and so far as local society is concerned, anonymous. The wig and the robes are the badges of a real anonymity, and it is unlikely that the judge will know anything of a case except what he is told in court, or that he will ever, in his personal capacity, have done business with any litigant, or been to dinner with him, or met his uncle out shooting. It is sometimes argued that the North of England needs a permanent Crown Court established in York, with resident judges. But the arbitration of strangers is to be preferred.

Granted these, or other similar, conditions, the Judiciary will constitute a sub-community or set of sub-communities within the State, in which, thanks to our being selective in our choice of personnel, and thanks to our having stacked the cards appropriately with respect to environmental conditions and the pressures arising therefrom, we have been able to modify limitation B(i)—Some Selfishness—on human nature sufficiently for the sub-community to be an Areopagite society, operating without sanctions. The metaphor of *symbiosis* is again appropriate. The coercive community, if it is to be a Constitutional Free State, needs the existence of judicial communities which are not only without coercive sanctions, but which are pretty well without sanctions at all—voluntary associations.[1] Judicial communities similarly can exist only within the framework of a coercive community which provides a corner where there is an environmental sub-climate in which virtue prospers and disinterestedness is a practicable policy, and from whose unselected citizenry the select membership of the Judiciary can be chosen.

SECTION 22

CONTROL OF COERCION

THE procedures enjoined by Process of Law are clearly effective against isolated abuses of coercive power. They have, as a happy historical fact, proved effective in preventing any general abuse of power on the part of those who control the coercive machinery of State: but we have yet to show why they have been effective, and under what conditions they will continue to be so.

Coercive power is not the only power. A man has power[2] if it results from his saying, 'Let X happen' that X does happen. His power is coercive if, should the person whom he addresses be utterly unwilling to bring X about, nevertheless that person's behaviour will be determined either by force or by the threat of force so as to bring X about, his own unwillingness notwithstanding.[3] But men are often not utterly unwilling, and therefore there are many people possessed of power, but not coercive power, and hence we can found the State not on force alone, but primarily on reason, consent and obligation. So long as men are not all utterly unwilling and bloody-minded, they will do some things they are asked to do because they think they ought to or because they are persuaded that the things are good things to do. Therefore a person who has authority, as I have defined

[1] Compare above, § 19, p. 81.
[2] See above, § 4, pp. 16–17; or below, p. 366.   [3] § 14, p. 57.

it,[1] will also have power; moreover, there will be some people with influence,[1] and hence also power.

The recipe for Constitutional Freedom is that the coercive machinery of the State should itself be based as much as possible on authority and influence, and as little as possible on sanctions, and not at all on coercive sanctions. This will provide a built-in clutch, which will engage so long as those in control of the coercive machinery are using it rightly, but will "slip" if ever they attempt to abuse their position. The Home Secretary controls the coercive machinery of State, but with the aid of magistrates, who are voluntary, and judges, who are un-get-at-able. In the course of exercising coercion against criminals, the Home Secretary needs the co-operation of magistrates and judges, which is forthcoming if he wants to exercise coercion lawfully, but not if he wants to exercise it unlawfully. Chief Constables are not appointed by the Home Secretary nor are removable by him at will. They will be greatly influenced by what the Home Secretary says, but only so long as it is not contrary to the procedures laid down in Process of Law: if the Home Secretary asks a Chief Constable to make a special effort against drug-trafficking, prostitution, or speeding, the Chief Constable is likely to comply; but if the Home Secretary were to direct a Chief Constable to have all the prostitutes in his area shaved and branded, he would not comply, nor would he lose his job for not complying. If a Chief Constable told his subordinates to "frame" a particular suspect, they might do it, particularly if they were themselves convinced that he was a criminal, and fabricate evidence and perjure themselves in court to secure his conviction: and if a policeman refused to pay his part in "framing" a man, he might suffer for it; he probably would not lose his job, but he might lose promotion, or be detailed to perform unpleasant duties. But at the worst, he could only lose his job: he could not himself be imprisoned, fined or executed for disobedience to orders. Such an offence does not exist in civilian law. In the army, disobedience may constitute mutiny, and may be punishable by death; and few men would risk martyrdom rather than take their place in a firing squad carrying out an unlawful execution. But the martyr's crown is padded for civilians, and although it may be difficult to stand up for Justice, and may cost dear, it is not *that* difficult, and the cost is not *that* great. Comparable buffers separate the Home Secretary from the warders who operate the gallows and keep the cells locked. Neither the Prison Commissioners nor the

[1] See above, § 4, p. 16, or below, p. 367.

governor of a gaol are likely to co-operate in helping the Home Secretary to put away a troublesome subject, and if they do not co-operate, there is not much he can do about it. He cannot bring many sanctions to bear on them. Even if he were able to get rid of them, it would be difficult to find replacements who were more complaisant to his will. And a Home Secretary unaided is likely to be an incompetent gaoler and ineffective executioner.

Naboth's life would have been safe in England. If Jezebel had sent letters to the judges or the local justices of the peace, they would have sent copies to *The Times*, and would have found Naboth "Not Guilty": if to the Chief Constable, he would have consulted his Watch Committee, who would have told him to do nothing: if to the governor of the local gaol, the mere appearance of his warders trying to arrest Naboth, and drag him off, would have produced an outcry and a writ of Habeas Corpus. Even if the police had been willing to perjure themselves—as sometimes in England, most regrettably, they are—, they would not have been prepared to frame a man they knew to be innocent; and if a wicked Chief Constable could find two members of his force evil enough to do his dirty work, they would still be subject to cross-examination by defending counsel, and Naboth would be able to give his own evidence before a judge and a jury who were both beyond Jezebel's reach.

Finally we should notice that the Home Secretary not only has to rely on influence and authority, rather than power based on sanctions, to get his wishes carried out, but depends for his being Home Secretary on influence and nothing else. If a majority of the members of the House of Commons will not support him with their votes, the government of which he is a member, cannot continue. The party system, with all its defects, institutionalises the principle of Influence, not Force, as the basis of Power; and our Parliamentary Mamelukes are, for sound historical reasons, sensitive to any abuse of coercive power, and ready on that account to withdraw support.

The institutions of Freedom will only work under certain more general conditions. We have arranged, as it were, for the clutch to slip if ever those in control of the coercive machinery of State attempt to misapply it. But for this to be feasible, the clutch must slip neither too readily nor not at all, nor must the coercive machinery of State be overloaded.

To take the last point first. It has been possible in England to have little resort to coercion, because there have been relatively few criminals so desperate as to need coercing at all. The great majority of the populace are law-abiding: even when they break the law, it is enough normally to summon them to the magistrates' court, for them to come at the time stated, uncoerced: and even those criminals who will not come voluntarily, are not prepared to use fire-arms to avoid arrest. And therefore it is a practical policy to have the police unarmed too. And therefore the police are impotent against the whole people. If, however, the crime rate continues to increase, and criminals become more dangerous, the case will be altered. Law and order must be maintained. If peaceable citizens cannot go about their lawful occasions without reasonable certainty of not being set upon by thugs, they will demand stronger action against criminals, or else must take the law into their own hands. In order to secure more effective action against criminals, the safeguards against the coercive machinery of State being misused will be dropped. Shopkeepers in seaside resorts will demand that they be protected from teen-age hooligans: passengers in buses will demand that they shall not be delayed by C.N.D. demonstrators lying in the streets: and measures devised against these law-breakers will be available in future against law-abiding citizens who may wish to demonstrate lawfully against unconstitutional behaviour on the part of the government.

In a similar way, if criminals take to carrying arms, the police will have to be armed too, and not only armed but entitled to shoot first— it is neither reasonable nor feasible to require policemen not to shoot until one of their number has been maimed or killed. But if policemen are armed and entitled to shoot first, they may make mistakes; and few men, however much they were in the right, would risk being at the receiving end of a gun fired by mistake. At present the worst risk the law-abiding citizen runs in view of the fallibility of the police is that he might be arrested—perhaps by mistake for someone else; if this should befall him, within a day he will have been able to protest his innocence to someone outside the police force—a magistrate—and will be released. And knowing that this is the worst that can happen, a law-abiding citizen can argue with a policeman if a policeman seems to be abusing his power, and can, for example, take the policeman's number and report him for misconduct. One would feel less confident about arguing with a man, even a policeman, with a gun; it might go off, and there would be no one then to say that you were not behaving in a suspicious manner, like a criminal who might be armed and attempting to resist arrest.

The emergence of the highly mobile, motorised criminal gang again poses a problem for Freedom. One way in which we have drawn the teeth of the coercive machinery of State has been by decentralisation. If I suspect that the Chief Constable of Hampshire has got his knife into me, I can go and live in Dorset, where there will not be the same *animus* against me. At present it is a fanciful hypothesis, but if the Home Secretary and the Chief Constable of Hampshire were both communists, and I were an active anti-communist, I might well then feel that Dorset was a more salubrious base for my activities. Such a hypothetical contingency carries little weight against the actual activities of criminals who steal a car in one county, use it to hi-jack a lorry loaded with tobacco in another, leave the lorry in a third and dispose of the tobacco in a fourth. Against highly organised and mobile criminals we need to have a highly organised and nation-wide police force. But this constitutes a centralised coercive force which could be used effectively not only against criminals but against the liberties of the people.

So too, on a juristic level, a presumption of innocence is workable only if most people are in fact innocent. If the guilty are only a very small proportion of the populace, then by allowing those guilty men to escape whose guilt cannot be proved beyond reasonable doubt, we shall not cause a serious increase of crime or threaten the maintenance of law and order: if however most people are unruly, and in the habit of breaking the law, we cannot afford to allow them a presumption of innocence. And so in countries where the people suffer from too Latin a temperament, or where there has been an earthquake or a revolution, draconian measures have to be applied—the imposition of a curfew, the shooting of looters at sight—in order to re-establish law and order, the *sine qua non* of civil society. Nor is this only a measure of practical necessity: it is one of logic also. A legal presumption of innocence becomes un-workable, because incredible, when there is a rational presumption of guilt. We know that most motorists habitually break the law: we just do not believe their protestations of innocence: nor do the courts, which while formally maintaining the presumption of innocence, in fact will find a man guilty on fairly flimsy evidence, and will acquit him only if his innocence can be proved beyond reasonable doubt. In the application of the law about H.M. Customs and Excise, where again a presumption of innocence would be un-realistic, it has in some cases been formally removed; and a man found in possession of a watch, on which Customs duty has not been paid, has to prove his innocence, rather than have his guilt proved.

In these different ways, a general law-abidingness on the part of the great majority of the people is a necessary condition of constitutional liberty. *Legum idcirco* OMNES *servi sumus, ut liberi esse possimus.*[1] Other emphases express other truths. It is necessary, if we are to be free, that most people serve the laws not barely by obeying them but in a more positive sense. Criminals must not only be few in number, but isolated. Most citizens must be prepared to co-operate with the police in a passive way, by giving information whenever they can, and evidence in court when required. For if people do volunteer information freely and give evidence when it is needed, they have something to withold if ever the forces of law and order should seek to abuse their power and overthrow the law. If people "prefer not to be involved in court proceedings" then criminals will be convicted only on police evidence, and the temptation and opportunity of perjury on the part of the police will both alike be increased. The Ghetto argument[2] is two-edged, and subjects who withhold all co-operation with the forces of law and order make themselves victims rather than citizens.

'*Servi*' is a strong word; a man is a slave of the laws not merely if he obeys them and occasionally co-operates in bringing law-breakers to justice. The co-operation implied is much more active than that. It is not strictly true that in a free society every one must be a Mameluke—or rather, admirable though this would be as an ideal, no actual society composed of men, characterised as they are by selfishness and fallibility could reach that degree of voluntariness, so that if 'free' is to be applied to actual societies, it cannot mean that; but it is a characteristic of a free society, that far more people than in any other form of society, do, and must, play an active part in running it, in which they willingly submit themselves to requirements not of their own choosing.

A voluntary acceptance of heteronomy is a necessary condition of Constitutional Freedom. If we are to be free from the danger of abuse of power, the coercive machinery of the State must be manned at vital points by people who can refuse to carry out instructions which they deem unlawful. Their complying with instructions must in some sense be voluntary. But if the coercive machinery of State is to be effective, the people who man it must act together, and this will not happen sufficiently surely and often to be effective if each acts as seems best

---

[1] Cicero, *Pro Cluentio*, 146.   § 19, pp. 76–77.

to him. The magistrates are voluntary, in that a man may choose whether to become a magistrate or not, and will not lose anything financially if he ceases to be a magistrate; but while he is a magistrate he must administer justice not as seems to him most equitable and just but as the laws lay down. An Anglican or Roman Catholic judge may think that divorce is contrary to the will of God, and wrong; but he must not refuse to grant decrees *nisi* on that account; nor may a humanist sitting on the bench refuse to pass sentence of death upon a convicted murderer for conscience' sake. It is not that divorce and capital punishment are not wrong—they may well be: it is that civil society essentially depends upon each man not setting himself up as supreme arbiter of right and wrong, and that Constitutional Freedom depends upon many men discharging to the best of their abilities the definite and limited responsibilities assigned them. As a juror I am not called upon to decide whether the amiable defendant must needs go to prison or not, nor whether prison sentences are the right penalty for drunken driving, but only whether, beyond reasonable doubt, the defendant was drunk or not while driving a car on the date stated. If juries will not convict the guilty, their jurisdiction will be transferred to magistrates who will: if religious and humane men will not become judges, less sensitive souls will, who will not merely not find distasteful duties distasteful, but will be less discriminating in cases in which the judge is required to exercise discretion. Nor is it only the crude argument, "If you won't, worse will." Rather, it is that Constitutional Freedom depends on the Assignment of Responsibilities to men who will discharge them voluntarily, and if each man decides not with reference to the duty assigned to him, but with regard to all the consequences which may result from his decision and his personal moral evaluation of the total resultant, chaos must ensue.

It follows then that conscientious refusal to carry out official duties or to enter into the service of the laws is something never to be undertaken lightly and if at all only with extreme reluctance. One must be convinced not merely that the laws are wrong—which is necessarily often the case, in an imperfect world peopled by imperfect men—but that they are so wrong that they are beyond remedy, that there is nothing good about them, and that the good life cannot be lived under them. It is possible for these conditions to be fulfilled. Socrates refused to carry out an unlawful order of the Thirty, Socrates who valued civil obedience so highly that he allowed himself to be unjustly put to death by the legitimate legal process of Athens. But it is not to be supposed that all systems of government are evil or constitute a betrayal of the State. And if the system of government under which one lives is not irremediably bad, even though it is undoubtedly bad at some points, and even may be wicked, then one may well be under a pure moral obligation to participate in it actively in some fashion. For only by people participating in it willingly can the power of the government be restrained from being abused. He who contracts out forfeits all say in the course of events.

The exact point at which a conscientious man should resign his official commission we cannot determine in abstract. It depends too much on particular circumstances. Sometimes a dramatic resignation may be effective in bringing an issue to public attention, and then, contrary to the tenor of the foregoing argument, it may be the right thing to do. Sometimes refusal to carry out one's duty may be tacitly recognised as a lawful safety-valve—for instance that a jury may refuse to convict even on the clearest evidence, if Parliament has allowed the law to get too far out of step with public opinion. Sometimes a man may be selective in what duties he undertakes. These and other considerations can be usefully discussed and assessed only in the light of concrete situations. The one general point is that, contrary to much modern thinking, the possession of an ultra-tender conscience is not a virtue, but a vice. Or, rather, we ought to have consciences, and tender ones, but must expect them to be bruised. It is often maintained, under the name of autonomy, that a man cannot be acting rightly if he is acting on orders, and that the necessary and sufficient condition of being moral is to think that one knows best. If to this doctrine of Private Judgement is added the doctrine mentioned earlier,[1] that law and morality are totally divorced from each other, and that law is totally external to the moral man—simply a matter of unpleasant consequences if he fails to comply with its requirements—, it is natural to conclude that the path of morality is always that of conscientious objection, and that to the many compromises of public life, and the distasteful, immoral and even wicked facets of the framework of our unselective community, the fastidious man of integrity must respond by saying "*ohne mich*". And this is wrong. The laws for a moral man, are not external, but internal: hence the conflict. And although I, and I alone, am ultimately responsible for the decisions I make, and am in that sense autonomous, this does not mean that I, a finite and fallible being, should never act against my better judgement. Nor

[1] § 9, pp. 35–36; see also § 71.

should I, living together with other finite and fallible beings, deem it
my duty to be a law unto myself, and to do only that which is right in
my own eyes.[1]

SECTION 23

THE CONTROL OF ARMIES

BRITAIN has little to teach the world about the control of armies.
The fortunate fact of being an island during the formative years of our
constitution enabled us to dispense with a standing army altogether.
The Navy was enough: and navies are no use for suppressing native
citizens. Other lands have been less lucky. They have had to have
strong armies, or be overrun by foreigners. And with an army, unlike
a police force or prison service, efficiency is the paramount consideration, and concessions to constitutionality cannot be afforded if the
cost is the difference between victory and defeat. An army must have
a centralised command, and there must be no weak links in the chain
of command, so that obedience must be guaranteed by the possibility
of sanctions, if necessary of coercive sanctions. Military law tends[2]
towards the opposite extreme to civilian law: it embodies the smallest
concessions to Justice, Equity, and Humanity that must be made if
human beings are to work together at all, and where there is doubt,
these considerations must give way to purely military ones.

An army thus has concentrated and effective coercive power which
could be turned against the native citizens, and in particular against the
legally constituted civil authorities. Every State that has an army needs
to consider this danger, and devise safeguards against it.

The danger of disaffection among officers is greater than that of
disaffection in the ranks. For first, mutinous men without officers may
do some damage but do not have the organisation, and are unlikely
to improvise it, to be able to constitute an effective coercive force or to
establish an effective government. Moreover, only extreme ineptitude
on the part of the civil authority will provoke the men to mutiny
against it. Provided they are well fed and regularly paid, soldiers do
not want to mutiny against the civil government. But officers, having
the habitual obedience of their men, are likely to be obeyed even in

---

[1] See further below, § 72.
[2] Only *tends*. In times of peace, and in countries whose safety is not seriously
threatened, more concessions can be, and often are, made.

unlawful enterprises, and an army, properly led, is *ex hypothesi* an effective instrument of coercion. Moreover, officers are not so easily contented by food and pay. They may have other aspirations and ambitions, which civil government may not have been able to satisfy. And so it is that generals in ancient Rome and colonels in modern Arabia have often been tempted to turn their arms against their government, and often with success.

We may make the general observation that most governments that have been overthrown by a *coup d'état,* have been weak and inept governments, which have already shown themselves unfit to rule and unworthy of respect. It is a counsel, too obvious to be useful, to a civil government anxious to safeguard itself against a *coup d'état,* to tell it to be good. Other, more specific, safeguards are worth pointing out. Officers should be largely drawn from, and identified with, the ruling class: for then they will, in general, have little temptation to upset the *status quo.* If officers are to be drawn from the ruling class, some members of the ruling class must be willing to serve as officers: it was because the landed gentry of England were willing, themselves and their sons, to serve their King in the field, however much they might resist his prerogative at home, that such armed forces as there were could not have been used by the King to subvert the constitution. Any nation or government or group which despises the profession of arms, so that none of its own members will undertake it, and so that those who do undertake it do not feel at home there, is inviting the loss of its liberty. Colonel Blimp should not be too much contemned, or he may change his name to Nasser.

The profession of arms should be esteemed, but not too highly. Rome lost her liberty not only because her citizens were unwilling to serve as soldiers, but because her careerists were all too willing to seek military command.[1] If the army provides a path to political power, it will attract people who want political power; and it is dangerous to put coercive power in the hands of those who want political power, because if they get it, they will have too much power, and if they do not, they will be tempted to rebel. Service officers should be honoured, but not promoted to political power—unless they are well and truly retired from the services—in much the same way, though for different reasons, that ecclesiastics are honoured, but debarred from political

---

[1] Cicero, *Pro Murena,* § 30, said that there were two paths to the highest offices in Rome, military command and oratorical skill, and, himself an orator, allowed that the former was more pre-eminent.

office. There will always be ambitious men who will aspire to politica
power; but let other avenues lead to it. Cicero in the Senate, o
Crassus in his counting-house were less dangerous to the Roma
Constitution than Caesar in command.

Other sociological considerations are too detailed to be discusse
here. But sociology apart, even if an army is tempted to rebel, it ma
find it not feasible. An army is not a viable community on its own. I
needs, in many different ways, the support of those it is designed t
defend, and cannot survive unless it can continue to command certai
essential services.

The most obvious is money. And here the case is greatly altere
since Roman times. Then money was entirely in the form of gold an
silver, and it was feasible by coercive power alone to extract rapidl
from a civil population a sufficiency of bullion. A Roman commande
could threaten a city in Asia with fire and sword unless they hande
over a stated quantity of gold and silver; and if they resisted, he coul
carry out his threat, and at the end of the operation, since gold an
silver are fire-resistant, collect all that the city had contained. Th
Colonel of the Coldstream Guards cannot use such short and shar
methods on the manager of Barclays Bank at Berwick with success
When the French army in Algeria revolted in 1958, it could do so onl
with the connivance of the French Treasury which continued to conve
the necessary financial credits. At an earlier stage in our constitutiona
history, in the infancy of credit, when money still characteristicall
took the form of seizable coins, it still proved possible to control th
coercive power by controlling its supply of money.

What gave steam to the principle of Taxation with Representatio
was that the taxes which Parliament had voted, the tax-payers reall
were willing to pay. These taxes could be collected easily and in
expensively, whereas any further levy would have been resisted, an
would have been difficult and expensive to collect, even with the aid o
coercive force. Thus even though the King might be tempted t
dispense with Parliament and rest his power on the army alone, suc
a course was inexpedient, because the army was not good at collecting
taxes, whereas a parliamentary vote did make them forthcoming; an
this in turn depended on the relative willingness with which tax
payers would pay those taxes which they felt they had, through thei
representatives in Parliament, themselves agreed to.

Such a principle of taxation no longer holds good. Parliament is now
felt as the sovereign, or as the electoral college appointing the sover-

eign, rather than as the representative of the tax-payer, and taxes voted by Parliament are felt as levies imposed by a sovereign rather than as contributions promised by one's representative on behalf of oneself. The change in attitude on the part of the tax-payer has been particularly rapid in recent years, partly as a result of the greatly increased level of taxation. In order therefore to collect taxes, less and less reliance has been put on the willingness of the tax-payer to pay, and more and more on methods of enforcement based ultimately on the coercive machinary of the State. The element of consent enters much less into the paying of taxes now than hitherto (though this is a matter of degree only; taxes never were voluntary, nor could they have been), and this safeguard against usurpation has been lost. Although a modern army cannot raise funds for itself by pillage, and we are to that extent safer against military rebellion than our ancestors, a combination of the Army and the Treasury, or at least the Army and the Commissioners of Inland Revenue would be viable, and could, so far as this argument goes, be dangerous.

There are, fortunately, other securities. Military weapons have become much more sophisticated, and demand much more technical skill for their servicing, and depend upon a large technological base for their maintenance. Writers sometimes complain that the invention of the machine-gun strengthened the hand of the tyrant, and destroyed the musket-carrying citizen army which was the basis, in *Realpolitik*, of democracy; but they forget the increased dependence on ordnance and munitions factories, on mechanics and engineers and electricians and signals men; on metallurgists and chemists, nuclear physicists and cyberneticians. The modern army has developed an enormous "tail", and the tail drags the dog, and would prevent him turning and devouring the body politic he is supposed to guard. Once Hephaestus had used his skill to forge a sword, that sword could be used without further recourse to him, against his will and even against his person, to coerce and exploit him. The wielder was superior to the workman, and could exploit him and discard him at will. Not so the pilot of a Spitfire his maintenance men. And with a Thor, a Minuteman, or a Jupiter, there is no pilot, no romantic officer, no swords, no pistols, no machine-guns, but only a host of technicians and hundreds of factories. The distinction between the military and the rest of the community is becoming too blurred for the army to be a separate organisation which might be turned against the rest of the community. The army has become so much part of the community that it must accept the same decision procedures as the rest of the community, or else destroy its own effectiveness. Moreover, with the development of nuclear weapons, the army has become, constitutionally speaking, much more of a navy: in pursuit of greater effectiveness against the enemy, its weapons have become unusable against the citizens at home. Many officers in the Pentagon might be members of the John Birch society and might wish to overthrow the power of the President and Congress: but could hardly do so by dispatching an H-bomb to the Capitol or the White House.

SECTION 24

THE RULE OF LAW

Process of Law safeguarded a coercive community against the abuse of coercive power by laying down a set of procedures governing the use and alleged misuse of coercive power, so that if there were any abuse, the fact would be known, and if it were known, many people up and down the country would withdraw the co-operation that was necessary for the effective working of the coercive machinery of State. Process of Law had to be a procedure, because only a procedure could be clearly enough defined and antecedently agreed upon, for it to be quite clear to everyone, beyond possibility of argument, when an abuse of power was taking place: upon questions of substance rather than of form we can neither always obtain antecedent agreement nor formulate general laws which will cover all cases unambiguously.

Our procedure left wide discretion to certain specified officials—judges—to authorise the use of coercion, and to determine whether coercion in the past had been legally or illegally used. The discretion of the Judiciary had to be very wide, in order that the procedure could be purely procedural and formal, so that *if* there were an abuse of coercive power there could be the maximum possible agreement that it had occurred, so that in turn there should be a concerted withdrawal of co-operation by many different, independent persons up and down the country. We have thus secured effective control of coercive power at the cost of giving wide discretion to certain authorities, and therefore, in the absence of further safeguards, laying ourselves open to the abuse of *authority*. We have already spoken of the need to select carefully those in whom authority is to be vested, and to secure them against some of the cruder pressures and temptations: but this is not enough. Even with the cruder temptations removed, there are many other, more insidious, ones. And even with the best intentions, and perfect self-knowledge, judges and legislators can make mistakes. We therefore need to supplement the set of sharply defined procedures which constitute Process of Law by further procedures, divisions of authority, limitations on discretion, critiques of the exercise of discretion, in order to guide and safeguard those in authority, and to enable their decisions to be criticised. These we shall call the Rule of Law.

The Rule of Law has been differently understood by different writers. By some it has been taken in a sense which includes, rather than supplements, Process of Law: by some it has been used in the same sense as Natural Law. We shall understand it as a restriction on how the authorities may reach a decision and what they may authorise. Not everything is lawful to them. They are not entitled to make any decision they please. Their decisions are open to rational assessment and criticism, by subjects as well as by themselves, upon the basis of human rationality and shared values that are the prerequisites of any community's existing. The Rule of Law restricts the way in which the authorities reach decisions and what they actually authorise in order that their decisions shall not be justly liable to unfavourable criticism. It applies chiefly to the authorities of the State, because they wield coercive power, and it is inherent in their position that their decisions will be enforced upon a recalcitrant party, willy-nilly, and therefore upon one who has in no sense participated in the decision-making process. For this reason, however much we try to arrange coercive communities so that every member does participate in their decision procedures, and should feel the force of the fourth, fifth, and sixth arguments of Section 12 (the arguments from the General Will, from consultation, and from self-identification with the community),[1] it is inherently in the nature of a coercive community that its members may be non-participants. Hence the hard external aspect the State sometimes assumes. And hence also the need for the authorities of the State to be guided primarily by considerations which are independent of the decision procedure actually in force.[2] The Rule of Law must guide the authorities into making decisions which are reasonable (or at least not unreasonable), so that if a recalcitrant party refuses to accept a decision of theirs as binding, we can still feel that it is a decision he ought to accept, in spite of his never having committed himself to it by being

[1] Pp. 44–45. [2] See above, § 13, pp. 50–51.

involved in the making of it. We want to be able to say that the decision is one which he should not flout, and would in fact obey if he were reasonable and not bloody-minded. For then we can expect even a non-participant to accept it, and if he does not, and we have to use force, we have an answer to his further question, 'Is it right to do that to me?'[1]

In coercive communities, therefore, the Rule of Law must be the chief guide. It cannot, of course, be expressed by any simple formula. Although we shall attempt to formulate certain aspects of it as precisely as possible, it is more a style of argument than a set of slogans. We argue on the basis of the reasonableness of men, all the time setting up safeguards against possible error. We believe that men can be rational, can be disinterested, can be adequately informed; but we know that their judgement is fallible, that they are often selfish, that our information is often inadequate. Because of our beliefs, we can believe that society is possible, that men can coexist in communities: because of our knowledge we need always to be taking practical precautions. And therefore we shall, all the time, be guided by an *ideal* of *rationality*, heavily qualified by *counsels* of *imperfection*.

The Rule of Law will alter its aspect as we consider it from the point of view of the authorities or from that of the subjects. The authorities need guidance: what questions to be decided by whom? how to set about deciding them? what decisions to reach? The subjects need the protection of limits and definiteness: to provide them with a basis for predicting the authorities' decisions so that they can make their own plans; to afford them some security and assurance that the authorities will not overstep the limits; and to give them some arguing points for when they need to criticise the authorities' decisions. Subjects need to know where they are with regard to Leviathan, understanding what things they may or may not do, confident that Leviathan will not hurt them so long as they do nothing wrong, and able to engage in rational argument with Leviathan, and form rational views about him.

We shall consider the internal aspect, that of guiding the rulers, first; that is, we shall consider what are the marks of a right or wrong exercise of authority, and defer until later[2] the consideration of what restrictions need to be placed on the exercise of authority if the subject, who might be at the receiving end of a lawful order, is to be able to lead a livable life.

[1] See above, § 12, pp. 45–46.   [2] §§ 34, 35.

In considering the exercise of authority from the inside, we have an ideal of rational responsible action. Every decision of an authority ought to be a rational one. But the decisions that ordinary men naturally make are often not rational. We seek therefore to make the decisions of the authorities as open as possible to the influence of reason, and as immune as possible from natural tendencies—selfishness, inattention—making for unreasonable decisions. To this end, we divide authority between different persons or bodies; we hold authorities answerable for their decisions; we lay down limits on the discretion that each authority has; we have a number of rules of procedure; and we formulate, although only in vague and general terms, the principles that are to guide the authorities.

We divide authority. It is partly for the same reason as we have for the weak doctrine of the Separation of Powers.[1] The self-interest of one man is unlikely to lie in the same direction as that of another, nor are two mistakes likely to be in the same direction. If one official reaches a wrong decision on account of self-interest or by mistake, the other one is unlikely to co-operate in carrying out the first official's self-interested plans, and may well query any mistake. By dividing authority we make it much more difficult to abuse. Rational decisions can still be made, but irrational ones are likely to be filtered out.

The division of authority has the further merit of requiring the one official to think what his reasons are and state them, in telling the other one what he wants done. If authority is divided, people have to co-operate to exercise it: and since we do not naturally happen to act together in the required way, we have to communicate in order to achieve co-operation. And some rationale of the action proposed is almost always implicit in asking a man to undertake it. And therefore, merely in having to co-operate there is some pressure to say what the reasons are, and this in turn makes people think what they are. The letters and files are in part a device for articulating the rationale of decisions; which in turn helps to ensure that the decisions are rational.[2]

We can secure the same end further by making officials, as far as is feasible, Responsible, or Answerable for their Actions. That is to say, they may have to answer the question, 'Why did you do it?' Sometimes we always require reasons—as in the law courts.[3] Sometimes there is only a possibility that the official may have to justify his actions. But even the bare possibility is enough to encourage him to think in

---

[1] § 19, pp. 80–81.   [2] See above, § 6, p. 20.
[3] See below, § 26, p. 121; § 30, pp. 136–7, and § 46, p. 196.

advance what reasons he can, if challenged, adduce in defence of his decision. And thus Responsibility is another factor making for rationality.

We lay down limits on the discretion that each authority has. This makes it easier to establish standards for the correct exercise of the discretion. A man deciding what the Public Interest requires can hardly be faulted as definitely wrong, whatever his decision. But called upon to decide only whether a certain widow does or does not qualify for a pension, he is much more open to question if he gives a grossly wrong decision. By having only a limited discretion in one type of case, he will become subject to certain pressures towards consistency,[1] and will become more expert in reaching right decisions in cases of this type. Each question will thus have to be decided by those best equipped to decide it well. The temptation to abuse authority will be small, since the power that a limited authority confers is itself small, and such errors as do occur will be easier to remedy, by appeal or by a writ of *certiorari*. The possibility of the charge of acting *ultra vires* has been a powerful deterrent against abusing one's authority.

The Rule of Law lays down many rules of procedure for those in authority: that they should hear both sides of the case; that they should consider all the relevant factors, and not consider any irrelevant factors; that they should not be biased by fear, or favour, or private interest. These, and other more particular procedures, prevent some of the worst mistakes. The exact form that a procedure takes is often open to criticism. There may be disadvantages as well as advantages in a given procedure. The procedures of the criminal law have the disadvantage that many criminals escape justice, but we weigh against this the greater importance of ensuring that no innocent man suffers coercion unjustly. Often in fixing on a procedure we have to balance advantages against disadvantages. The Rule of Law does not require that exactly the particular procedures we actually have should be followed rigorously, but only that there should be some procedures, exemplifying the values or securing the purposes that ours do, and that these, whatever they are, should be scrupulously observed.

Finally, the Rule of Law is expressed in certain vague principles— Freedom, Justice, Humanity—which we formulate,[2] and which should guide the authorities, in cases where they are applicable. These principles do not lay down exactly what is, or is not, to be decided in

---

[1] See below, §§ 29, 30, pp. 133–4; 136.
[2] See further below, §§ 32, 38, 55, 57.

particular cases. They are heads of argument, rather than rigid rules. Nevertheless, since those exercising authority are rational, they can obtain guidance from these general principles, and if they fail to, can be criticised by other men, also rational, for having failed to.

The Rule of Law is thus an articulation of the principle of Constitutionalism,[1] less rigid than the principle of Constitutional Limitation,[2] less vague than that of Constitutional Criticism.[3] It contains some principles of Constitutional Criticism, but in addition lays down rules of procedure, which determine the manner of decision-making but not the content of the decisions made, and lays down more definite restrictions still, limiting what may be decided by whom. But it does not quite become a principle of Constitutional Limitation. It does not set rigid—but undecidable—limits to lawful authority. Rather it is a principle of *limited* limitation. We cannot limit authority altogether. But we can limit it in limited respects. We can, at a certain cost, institute rigid and rigorous safeguards over the life and liberty of the subject. We cannot extend such rigid safeguards to all the interests of every subject. But we can have other procedures which although affording less stringent safeguards nevertheless constitute some security against some sorts of error and abuse. To deprive a man of his livelihood is less bad than to deprive him of his life; but bad all the same. It would be unreasonable to have the whole apparatus of the criminal courts, with their formal procedure, restrictive law of evidence, heavy onus of proof: but it would be unreasonable also to say that therefore we could take no cognisance at all of arbitrary dismissal.

We cannot secure that no injustice will ever be done. We cannot construct dams to block the tide of events and prevent authority ever overflowing its limits. But we can choose that some injustices will be done rather than others. We can construct sluices which will divert the floods from the most precious pastures. Life, limb, and liberty are the central interests of man; they are the interests immediately threatened by coercion, as we have defined it.[4] Therefore, just as in Process of Law, we elaborated stringent controls over the power to coerce,[5] so the Rule of Law fences about the authority to authorise coercion by rigid limitations, as well as many rules of procedure. Authority over the coercive machinery of State therefore is the most closely guarded authority, and only the Judiciary in the traditional sense of the word, may directly authorise coercion. We shall[6] elucidate the con-

[1] § 9.   [2] § 10.   [3] § 9, pp. 35–37; § 13.
[4] § 15, p. 57.   [5] § 20.   [6] In §§ 30, 31, 34.

siderations which should govern the authorisation of coercion and with regard to this limited, but crucially important, sort of authority lay down stringent limitations. Authority in respect of authorising coercion, however, does not stand by itself. It leads on to other sorts of authority. Much as the concept of life leads on to liberty,[1] so the concept of liberty leads on to that of property.[2] Property is a central, though less central, interest of men. Property rights need to be safeguarded, though neither in the same way nor so stringently, as liberty and life.[3]

The rights of property in turn give rise to many other interests. Most of these are relatively modern. Driving and wireless licences could not have been conceived before the twentieth century. Only in a modern industrial economy are jobs and pension-rights more important than the ownership of land or of the other means of production. And therefore while the adjudication of disputes about property has, for the most part, been vested in the judges in the traditional sense of the word, who have worked out many procedures and principles to embody the Rule of Law, the decision of disputes concerning more recently developed interests has been assigned haphazard to administrative officials to decide on an *ad hoc* basis, without proper consideration of the requirements of the Rule of Law. After we have considered how the exercise of authority vested in judicial officials in the traditional sense should be governed by the Rule of Law, both in its internal and in its external aspect, we need to go on to consider its application to administrative[4] as well as to legislative officials.[5]

SECTION 25

THE IDEAL RULE OF LAW

ALTHOUGH the Rule of Law cannot be satisfactorily formulated in a simple way, it often has been taken, in conjunction with the traditional doctrine of the Separation of Powers,[6] as a principle of Constitutional Limitation. It is not an adequate formulation, but it is an easily intelligible ideal, and therefore has proved of great value, if only as an approximation; and, where it is inadequate, its inadequacies are illuminating.

[1] § 32, p. 143–4.   [2] §§ 43, 44.   [3] §§ 53, 61, pp. 226–7, 263–4.
[4] § 46.   [5] §§ 52, 53.   [6] § 19, p. 80.

The Ideal Rule of Law presupposes the traditional doctrine of the Separation of Powers, which is itself only an approximation. It lays upon each organ of government its appropriate restriction, namely:

(i) The Judiciary must apply existing law, not make up new laws.
(ii) The Executive must act only on the instructions of the Judiciary in applying coercion.
(iii) The Legislature must enact only general laws, not Acts of Attainder, nor retrospective laws.

These provisions clearly leave the Judiciary no room for abusing its authority; and the Executive either is acting on the Judiciary's instructions, and so is given no room for abuse, or has at its disposal only those sanctions and means of applying pressure that other bodies, associations, and private individuals have. It has the sanction of dismissal against its own employees, and can secure other people's services by buying them, but it cannot force them or threaten them with imprisonment if they are not willing. The Legislature is less trammelled: indeed the restrictions imposed by the Ideal Rule of Law on the Legislature are inadequate as well as impracticable. But at least the Ideal Rule of Law provides the important safeguard that the supreme legal authority may not authorise coercion against any particular person. Only the Judiciary may do that, after hearing the defence and finding the case proved. *Nulla poena sine* JUDICIO. The Legislature may make the laws, but that is not enough to secure that a particular man should be coerced, nor that any one man should be, unless a whole lot of others too. Only on the orders of a judge can a man be coerced, and the judges will make such orders only in accordance with a law, which the subject can find out beforehand, and take care not to contravene. Moreover the subject can be sure that the authorities will not pick on him, and discriminate against him individually in the exercise of coercive power. He therefore need not be subservient to Leviathan or to those in authority. He has to obey the laws, but in an intelligible sense, he can be said to be governed by laws, not men; and in that sense free.

Unfortunately, the Ideal Rule of Law is an ideal only. We cannot always have it that the different organs of government act only in the manner prescribed. In part it is because the traditional doctrine of the Separation of Powers, presupposed by the Ideal Rule of Law, is itself inadequate. But, this apart, the Ideal Rule of Law is impracticable. Even the judges cannot comply with its requirements completely.

In applying the law they often have to interpret it.[1] In some legal systems, Judicial Interpretation may be given so wide a scope that we may describe it better as Judicial Innovation. The Supreme Court of the United States has acquired authority to interpret the Constitution of the United States with great latitude, and without even being bound by its own decisions. Even in England the common law appears to admit of Judicial Innovation in dramatic, though exceptional, form.[2] We should also note, thirdly and briefly, that judges are granted sweeping authority over the behaviour of people actually in court—I can be sent to prison for contempt of court more or less at the judge's arbitrary command.[3]

In these three ways the restrictions stipulated by the Ideal Rule of Law are not imposed on the Judiciary in practice. As regards the Executive, there is a terminological difficulty. If we mean by the 'Executive', the Police, the prison service, the Armed Forces, together with a few diplomatic officials and the private secretaries of Cabinet Ministers, the Rule of Law is both applicable and adequate. But the word 'Executive' is commonly extended to cover all people who are paid by public funds to perform services, except for judges and Members of Parliament. About the activities of this large number of administrative officials the Rule of Law says nothing. This is unsatisfactory. To refuse to give a man a motor licence or a pension is not to exercise a coercive sanction against him: but it is a sanction all the same, and those who have such sanctions at their disposal possess power and need to be guided in their use of it. Again, while an administrator is unlikely to be tempted to deprive a man of life or liberty, administrators are very apt to cast covetous eyes on private property, and have devised various procedures for acquiring it against the owner's will. Naboth, had he lived in England, would not have lost his life, but he would have lost his vineyard none the less.

Administrative officials have authority, and, unlike the executive officials we have been considering, discretion in its use. There is a possibility therefore of its being abused, and need of principles and procedures to secure its right use. It is often maintained that it is enough to make officials answerable to their superiors, and their superiors answerable to Parliament, and that apart from this the

---

[1] See above, § 7, pp. 24–26, and, more fully, below, § 31, p. 140, and § 51, pp. 214ff.

[2] See below, § 51, pp. 215–16.

[3] See further below, § 28, pp. 131–2 and § 46, p. 199.

discretion of the Executive ought to be left unfettered. But this is to be misled by words. Administrative officials wield power, although not coercive power, and Parliamentary supervision, valuable though it is, cannot constitute adequate guidance for its use or safeguard against its abuse in a multitude of individual cases.[1] For reasons which will emerge later,[2] it cannot be maintained that the non-coercive power wielded by administrative officials is just the same as the non-coercive power which, as we shall see later,[3] many associations and private individuals exercise. To be refused a car licence or a passport is not like being refused permission to fish on a certain stretch of water. A civil servant dismissed is in a worse case than a salesman out of a job. A compulsory purchase order may be legally valid, but deprive me of my property as unjustly as an Act of Attainder would deprive me of my life. The Ideal Rule of Law fails to cover any of these cases, because it takes over an inappropriate classification of functions of government, and fails to consider State power which is not coercive power. In due course we shall develop principles which constitute the Rule of Law for the Administration:[4] for the present we need only to see that the Ideal Rule of Law, although perfectly adequate for the Executive in the narrow sense of the word, is deficient in preventing the unlawful use of authority by the Executive in its wider sense.

The Ideal Rule of Law is confessedly weakest in the restrictions it places upon the Legislature. It is evident that laws can be enacted in quite general terms and yet be wicked. Against this, there is some safeguard in that legislators will not enact laws to other men's detriment if the laws must work to their own detriment also. It might seem tempting, at least to a philosopher influenced by Kant, to hold that laws should be couched in entirely general or universal terms, and not name any particulars; and that then the self-interest of the legislators would prevent any really bad laws being passed: tempting, but quite impracticable, and even if practicable, ineffective. How, for instance, could any Railway Act of the last century have been phrased in entirely general terms? Particular contingencies arise which demand particular remedies, and Parliament has to pass a Private Bill, authorising specific measures, referring to particular places or persons or institutions. Moreover, the formal requirement of being couched in entirely general terms is not enough to secure genuine generality. It is possible, with sufficient ingenuity, to phrase a measure in general

[1] See further below, § 49, pp. 211–12. [2] § 46, p. 196.
[3] § 45, p. 192; § 66, p. 278. [4] In §§ 46, 49.

9—P.P.

terms but so as in fact to apply to only one case. The formal requirement of generality or universality does not preclude a covert parti-
cularity of application, which entirely defeats the spirit of the Ideal Rule
of Law. A German customs tariff in 1902, in order to avoid a most
favoured-nations obligation, provided for a special rate of duty for
"brown or dappled cows reared at a level of at least 300 metres above
the sea and passing at least one month in every summer at a height
of at least 800 metres".[1] And philosophers who have pursued Kant's
principle of universalisability will be able to construct many other
examples. The Ideal Rule of Law in its restrictions on the legislative
organ of government is thus inadequate as well as impracticable.

Locke failed to face the logic of Hobbes' argument. Locke thought
that in securing the supremacy of the Legislature, he was ensuring that
the governance of England would no longer be a *dominium regale*, as
the Stuarts had sought to make it, but a *dominium politicum et regale*.
He thought of the Legislature as a Parliament, a forum of Constitutional
Criticism, which would limit the power of the Crown, and secure that
it acted πολιτικῶς, constitutionally. He did not see, as Hobbes had,
that if the Legislature be supreme, then it would not limit the sovereign,
but would become itself the sovereign; and that all the problems of
sovereignty which had arisen with the King in the seventeenth
century could arise again with Parliament in the eighteenth. The Civil
War and the Glorious Revolution unseated the monarch, but not the
sovereign: and the Americans had to fight further and think harder to
bring Leviathan to his knees.

The Ideal Rule of Law fails as a complete formula of Constitutional Limitation. Nevertheless it is a valuable bulwark against
tyranny. If Acts of Attainder are barred, the life and the liberty of the
ordinary citizen are safe from Leviathan. The Americans felt that their
property was not secure against the fiscal demands of a sovereign
Parliament in which they were not represented, but Parliament laid
no claim to any prerogative power of arrest or of summary jurisdiction, and the five members would have felt safer in Philadelphia
in the eighteenth century than in Westminster in the seventeenth. The
Ideal Rule of Law does not provide the whole answer to the problem
of securing the right exercise of the supreme authority, but if it can be

[1] G. Haberler, *The Theory of International Trade*, London, 1936, p. 339.
Quoted by F. A. Hayek, *The Constitution of Liberty*, London and Chicago,
1960, p. 489.
[2] Cf. Sir John Fortescue, *The Governance of England*, ed. Charles Plummer,
London, 1926, p. 109.

ıodified enough to be applicable, it will provide an answer to the roblem of securing the right exercise of the authority *to authorise ıercion*. It then will be one principle of Constitutional Limitation, not ıe only one, but the first one, the one which safeguards the citizen gainst the unbridled use of coercion. This is not all that we want, ut it is the condition of everything else that we want, and onstitutes, as we shall see, the first and most basic form of ʾreedom. It draws the teeth of Leviathan, though it does not tame ım or make him amenable to reason.

The Ideal Rule of Law fails as a complete formulation of the Rule f Law for the same reasons for which the principle of Constitutional ̦imitation fails. It is partly a matter of language, partly our inability ɔ agree on all questions. Because language is not crystal clear in its pplication to all cases, we can never dispense with some measure of ıdicial Interpretation:[1] and laws, if they are to receive universal onsent, cannot deal with contentious matters, and if they do deal with ontentious matters, will not only be objected to by some, but may be ıtirely unjust. We therefore need to reconsider the arguments which ̤d to the Ideal Rule of Law, so that we can concede all that is due to the rguments without fixing on an unworkable formula; and give ɛalistic guidance to officials, as well as effective safeguards to subjects.

SECTION 26

OFFICIAL RESPONSIBILITY AND DISCRETION

ʌN OFFICIAL is a person or a body entrusted with some duty or task ʾr commission, granted some authority to carry it out and respon ̦ble for the exercise of that authority. The word 'official' is used ̣ colloquial language primarily of public officials, but the sense ere given is wider, and covers representatives of private persons r bodies, trustees, executors of wills, etc. Like an employee, an fficial has some duty, task or commission assigned to him or under ̣ken by him, and is responsible for carrying it out: but, unlike some mployees, an official has some authority; his *ipse dixit* creates or ́ters obligations or releases people from them. The executors are ̣e owners of the deceased man's goods and property: they can sell ̣em, or hand them over, or assent to their being vested in a named

[1] See below, § 51.

person: the judge's decision instructs and entitles the prison official
to keep a named convict in prison for a specified length of time: th
decision of the Pension Board puts the Exchequer under an obligatio
to pay, and entitles the pensioner to receive certain specified sums o
money.

In modern life we very often act as officials, or *in an official capacit*
as I shall term it. It is what we characteristically do *in* offices, in th
modern sense of the word, in which it designates a place, a buildin
or a room. We can also use the word 'office', or 'trust' o
'commission'[1] as an abstract noun to designate the combination o
duty, discretion, authority, and responsibility (at least in the genera
sense) which an official can be said to hold. In spite of some awkward
ness, I shall use the word 'office' in this rather than the modern sense
'Commission' has too military a connotation, 'trust' too legal an
financial.

A man who holds an office is in some sense responsible for what h
does (or fails to do) acting in his official capacity. For to hold an offic
is to be entrusted to discharge some function, and therefore anythin
done in an official capacity should be connected with the functio
entrusted to the official, and therefore it is at least logically proper t
ask what the connexion is.

To be responsible, as the etymology of the word shows, is to b
answerable. The question that a responsible man is able or obliged t
answer is 'Why did you do it?'—or 'Why did you fail to do it?'
Since an official's actions are, or are supposed to be, connected with th
office he has undertaken to discharge, it is logically proper to as
him, of any particular official action, why he did it, in order to elici
what, in his view, the connexion is. He is responsible, that is, in
stronger sense than that in which all sane adults are able to answer fo
their actions, for he has to be able to give an answer of a certain sort
namely an answer showing how the action in question is connecte
with the office that he holds.

Anyone may ask anybody any question he likes: but he may no
obtain a satisfactory answer. The ways in which answers may fail to b
satisfactory are of great importance to political as well as to mora
philosophy.

We have first a set of answers that are, essentially, non-answers
Asked 'Why did you do it?' a man replies, 'It was not me' or 'I di

[1] Also the word 'responsibility' as on pp. 80–82 in § 19 above; but I wan
to keep the word to its literal meaning, elucidated here.

not do *that*' or 'That is not what I did' or 'I could not help it' or 'I did not mean to'. All these are non-answers: they do not give reasons why the man did the action in question, but, if accepted, make the question, 'Why did you do it?' unaskable. If I can truthfully say, 'It was not me' or 'That is not what I did' or 'I could not help it' or I did not mean to' then the question, 'Why did you do it?' no longer arises, and if it is still addressed to me, I no longer have to answer it. I am not responsible, in the literal sense. I may have to answer some other question ('Why did you do whatever it was that you did mean to do?' or 'Why did you not take more care?'), but I do not have to answer the original question in the form in which it was asked.

The form of non-responsibility which has been of concern to moral philosophers has been that corresponding to the plea, 'I could not help it', as a non-answer to the question, 'Why did you do it?' In political philosophy, by contrast, the question is, 'Why did you fail to do it?' and the non-answer is, 'I was not able to'. A man cannot be blamed for not doing what he was unable to do: a necessary condition of responsibility is power. Indeed, we often use the word 'responsibility' to mean 'power', as when a man says he wants greater responsibility. In political affairs the plea, 'I was not able to', assumes especial importance, because it arises not only when the respondent actually lacks the power (in my sense)[1] to accomplish what was expected, but equally when he lacks the authority—has not been "empowered" as it is revealingly put. In any constitutional government we seek to limit both the power and the authority of the government, and often may succeed in limiting the latter more than the former. People often ask why the government does not do this that or the other; abolish poverty, ignorance, drunkenness, crime. The answer, that the government is not responsible for these things, is felt to be a non-answer. If it is taken as meaning that the government does not have any obligation in these respects, it makes the government appear to be uncaring and unconcerned with the welfare of its subjects. If it is taken as meaning that the government does not have the power to do anything about ameliorating the condition of the people in these respects, it is patently false—the government may not be able to bring about a perfect state of affairs, but it could do more than it is doing now. The real answer, that there are cogent reasons for limiting the government's authority which makes it rationally, though not physically impossible, for the government to carry out the requisite measures, is obscured under the

[1] See above, § 4, p. 16; or below, p. 366.

disclaimer of responsibility. The government is, both in the general and in the formal sense of the word, responsible, but has adequate answers to the question, 'Why do you not do something about it?' It may be a specific one—that the evils engendered by prohibition are worse than those of allowing people to get drunk: it may be the more general one, that in a constitutional State the government's authority is limited, and that other persons and bodies have the authority and power to bring about the desired change. Universities, colleges, schools and parents are the authorities for disseminating knowledge and dispelling ignorance. The government may be able to help them, but cannot supplant them. It may co-operate with them, but not act in their stead. Poverty could easily be abolished, provided people were not free to choose their own jobs or spend their money as they liked: but once we allow, as we do in a constitutional State, that individuals, not the government, shall decide what work a man undertakes, or what goods he shall buy, the government no longer has the authority or the *lawful* power, to direct our lives so as to ensure that no one shall be in want. This, of course, does not mean that there is *nothing* the government can lawfully do: it may still be able to institute schemes for National Assistance, Sick Benefits, Old Age Pensions, and the like: but these are likely to be palliatives, not remedies, because the government, of set constitutional principle, is not in complete control of events, and cannot ensure that everything will be just as it should be. So again with crime, which the government unquestionably has an obligation to prevent, the government could do a lot more to suppress it, by having a national, centrally controlled, police force; by reversing the burden of proof, so that the accused were guilty unless they could prove themselves innocent; by authorising the police to use torture to extract information from reluctant informers; by allowing suspects to be detained on suspicion, pending further enquiries, or until they had satisfied the police of their inoffensiveness. All these methods would be efficacious in reducing crime: each of them is open to serious and weighty objection. The government has a good answer when it is taxed with not employing these means to abolish crime. It is responsible for doing what it lawfully can, but for very good reason we will not give it the authority or the lawful power to finish the job properly. We cannot, consistently with Freedom or Constitutionalism, have the government in complete control of events: and therefore we cannot, consistently with Freedom or Constitutionalism, blame the government if everything is not as it should be. We forget that the government is, not only of its own nature, but of our own devising and desiring, not omnipotent and not all-authoritative, and that there are many things it cannot do and even more that we do not really want or trust it to do. A great deal of politics is bad theology. But the government is not God, nor a mortal god; we will not even let it be Leviathan.

The question, 'Why did you do it?' may fail to elicit a satisfactory answer because it is given a perfectly respectable non-answer. But it may fail in other ways. It may be given an answer, not a non-answer, but an unsatisfactory one. Or it may not be given an answer at all. Anyone may ask anybody any question he likes: but he may not be vouchsafed any sort of answer whatever. Prominent people may be too busy to answer all the questions we should like to ask them; and if as sometimes, their reasons are too discreditable to stand scrutiny, they have a further reason for refusing to answer. We therefore need to place on officials a limited legal obligation to answer for their actions to certain people. They are not just responsible, but responsible *to* someone. Administrators are responsible to their cabinet ministers, and these in turn to Parliament. The parliamentary question is the tool for compelling those who are responsible actually to respond. We thus have a further, formal or legal sense of the words 'responsible' and 'responsibility', in which a man may be responsible *to* someone else for some of his actions or inactions, in virtue of a specific duty he owes him, or a commission he has undertaken or an office he has been assigned.

Not every man can be responsible *to* everybody else. Time forbids. The structure of formal responsibilities must therefore be incomplete. Sometimes we lay on officials, e.g. judges, a duty of stating their reasons publicly, but no further duty of answering questions from anyone. Sometimes we have a chain of responsibility, subordinate officials being responsible to superior ones, and they to superior officials still, and so up to the supreme authority. The supreme authority, because it is supreme, is not responsible *to* anybody: but, we maintained, it was still responsible in the general sense. This was the principle of Constitutionalism.[1] There may not be any body which can call the supreme authority to account for its actions, but we all can criticise them, and are entitled to do so. Rulers are, in my sense of the word, officials; officials whose duties and authorities are not exactly defined, but who share with minor officials the characteristic feature of having their actions open to critical assessment and appraisal. We

[1] § 9.

may not be able to say precisely what the duties of the government are, or what the limits of their authority are, because all the residual imprecision of human affairs remains at the top, even if we have been able to assign definite duties and authorities lower down. Nevertheless, as we have argued earlier, this does not mean that the authority of the government is completely unlimited. Contrary to what the Roman lawyers maintained, and in so far as the analogy between public and private law is not misleading, to possess the government is not like owning a piece of property but like holding a trust.

Whether formally or only generally responsible, an official answers for his official actions by giving reasons for them. These reasons have to be of a certain sort. It is not enough for an official, as it would be for a private individual,[1] to say simply, 'I wanted to'. An official is responsible, not merely in having to give reasons why he did, as a matter of fact, make the decision in question, but in being obliged to have reasons why he *should* have acted as he did. He has not only to explain his actions, but to justify them. He has to give the reasons why he did them, which were also reasons why he should have done them, and which would be reasons why anybody else similarly situated should act similarly. These reasons, however, may not be conclusive. They may not even be sound. Characteristically, there are arguments for and against every course of action, and often the arguments are fairly evenly balanced, and it is difficult to decide which are weightier. We may disagree with the man's judgement, and find the arguments on the other side more convincing: but even so, we are not on this score alone entitled to reject his account of his actions or to blame him for them. For human judgement is fallible. It may be that we are wrong, and he is right. Even if we discount this possibility, we cannot blame a person who exercises his discretion reasonably, though in our considered view, wrongly. For if we are not prepared to excuse a *bona fide* error of judgement, we ought not to have given him any latitude or discretion, but ought to have laid down ourselves what it was that we wanted him to do. Therefore it is not enough to condemn a man, giving an account of his actions, that he has not completely convinced us that they were the right actions for him to have done, or that we should have done the same thing in his place. We must be less exacting than that.

How much less exacting we should be depends on circumstances; on what office the man had been entrusted with; the risks and rewards

[1] See below, § 38.

of the enterprise; the cogency of the reasons he acted upon; how far a reasonable man could discount the force of the arguments on the other side. We expect a higher standard of judgement from those entrusted with great offices of State than from those undertaking minor enterprises: if a man has only flimsy arguments to justify his actions, or if he has overlooked obvious and fatal objections, we are ready to impute blame, but where the arguments are very nearly balanced we cannot be extreme to mark what is done amiss.

However much less exacting we are, there is a certain minimum which we demand in any account of the exercise of discretion. Discretion must not be exercised arbitrarily or corruptly, or from fear or for favour. A man must not decide for no reason or for reasons of self-interest or because he is frightened or because he has a personal liking for somebody or other. If a man does any of these things, or if he fails to exercise a certain degree of competence, depending on the circumstances, he is failing in the trust reposed in him. Even if he is not responsible to anyone, and not legally answerable for his official actions, he is still responsible in the general sense and open to Constitutional Criticism for his failure even to attempt to reach the right decision.

SECTION 27

RATIONALITY AND UNIVERSALISABILITY

THE Rule of Law is intended in its internal aspect as a guide to the authorities on how they shall exercise their authority, and in its external aspect as a basis for criticising and appraising their decisions. Authority is vested in persons because the judgement of a person is a better way of deciding a dispute than any other procedure, better because more likely to be reasonable and right.[1] Authority is therefore vested in persons with the idea that they shall use it rightly, and it is the idea of the right decision and the reasonable exercise of discretion, which guides us in seeking to guide those in authority. We cannot in general say what the right decision is—if we could, we should have no need of arbitration to adjudicate our disputes— but we have some idea of what the right decision must be like; or at least, what right reasoning is like, and hence what a series of right decisions must be like, and the sort of arguments an authority would adduce if it was trying to reach the right decision.

[1] § 5, pp. 17–19.

Arbitrary decisions cannot be reasonable; and if, on a particular occasion, an arbitrary decision happens to be the right one, it is so only by coincidence. We saw earlier[1] that arbitrary decisions were not satisfactory because they were neither predictable nor stable. We see now that they are unsatisfactory for the further reason that they cannot be reasonable, nor, for the most part, right. If a judge decides a case purely on whim, or from fear, or for favour, we know that he has not reasoned rightly and that his decision is no better, and in many respects worse, than that yielded by the toss of a coin. In one sense of 'please' *quod placuit principi* is just what does not have the force of lawfulness, for in that sense of 'please' it is confessedly irrational, and if the decisions of a *princeps* were all totally irrational, we should have gained nothing, and lost a lot, by setting him in authority. It was only because of the essential non-arbitrariness of arbitrators that they could play a useful part in decision procedures, and we can therefore reasonably demand that they shall not be arbitrary but reasonable in arbitrating our disputes.

Many men have despaired of demanding that our judges should be reasonable or just. They have felt that if they cannot tie them down completely, they cannot tie them down at all. Reason for them is all or nothing. If they cannot be sure of convincing another, or at least of confidently convicting him of error, every time, they cannot hope to convince him ever, and it is simply not worth making the attempt. Such an attitude entirely misconceives the nature of reason, and, for good measure, commits the logical fallacy of confusing contraries with contradictories. Without going into a lengthy discussion of what it is to be reasonable,[2] let me bluntly state, what I have assumed from the outset,[3] that some men are to some extent reasonable some of the time, although it is not the case that all men are altogether reasonable (in the sense of 'infallible') all the time. Were it not so, we could have no community, no decision procedure, and certainly no arbitrators.

It is intelligible therefore to lay down certain general rules for the guidance of those in authority, even though we cannot specify fully what decisions are the right ones. The judicial oath, to administer Justice "without fear or favour" is meaningful; for even though it does not say precisely what Justice is, or what constitute just decisions,

---

[1] § 5, p. 18.
[2] For a discussion of this, see J. R. Lucas, 'The Philosophy of the Reasonable Man', *The Philosophical Quarterly*, 1963.
[3] In B(ii) in § 1, p. 2.

it does say some of the things that Justice is not. We can imagine cases in which we should have no hesitation in saying that the judge had broken his judicial oath. Therefore the oath is meaningful; and, as we know full well, of great importance.

We can rule out certain types of reasoning or non-reasoning as contrary to what those in authority are commissioned to do: we can stipulate that they shall not allow themselves to be swayed by arguments of fear or of favour; that they shall not decide without considering any arguments at all; and that they shall not be swayed by any considerations of self-interest. All these are negative characterisations of right reasoning—we are saying some of the things that right reasoning is not. We can also, in a more positive approach, say some of the things (although not all the things) that right reasoning is.

Right reasoning is rational, relevant, and universal. It is non-egocentric and, unlike tastes and interests and prejudices, should be the same for one man as for another, for speaker and for hearer alike—this is why the jury-box is a usable filter to separate out what has been reasonably proved from the private interests, personal prejudices, and the idiosyncrasies of the individual jurors. Right reasoning is susceptible of interpersonal assessment and criticism, because it claims to be rational. Although I may, as a matter of fact, be in a better position to judge than anybody else, and may indeed be a better judge than anybody else, I am not in a logically privileged position, as I am when I am reporting my own feelings, sensations or perceptions. Subject to some qualifications, I know what I like, I know what I am feeling, and I know what sense-experience I am having, better than anybody else, and necessarily better than anybody else, just simply in virtue of being me. I am logically privileged in these cases in a way I am not logically privileged when I make a value-judgement or claim that I have reached a right conclusion. In these latter cases, although I may be *legally* privileged, as a legislator or a judge is, in the sense that what I say goes so far as the law is concerned, I am not *logically* privileged. That is, it is meaningful to *impugn* my decision (*say* that it is *wrong*) even if it is not feasible, in the given legal system, to *reverse* my decision (have its authority annulled).[1]

Right reasoning is relevant. Any conclusions I claim to have reached by right reasoning I must be able to support by adducing some facts in its favour, and it cannot be true that any fact would be as good as any other fact; for then my conclusions would be quite

[1] Compare § 9, p. 37.

arbitrary.[1] Therefore non-arbitrariness implies some standard of relevance. It is not, however, possible to formulate exact criteria of relevance or irrelevance.[2] But we can make the one point that where we are having to decide a particular issue, whether *this* man should go to prison, or *this* car be licensed to use the public highway, we must ascertain some facts about this man or this car, and base our judgement on them. Else our reasoning, whatever its other merits, will not be relevant, and our conclusions will not be applicable to the particular case in question.[3]

Right reasoning is universal. This is commonly understood in a number of different ways. It may mean simply that right reasoning is non-egocentric, as we have seen above.[4] Another, related, way of more immediate concern to us, in which right reasoning is universal is that although it is in one sense particular, as we have seen in the preceeding paragraph, it is in another sense non-particular: in reasoning about this topic, this situation, this problem, our arguments should be based on general features, characteristics or circumstances, not on the bare fact that the topic, situation, or problem is *this* one. Although we do often reason about particulars, it is always in virtue of the particulars possessing certain characteristics, not (if the words are intelligible) of their being simply themselves. For us to be able to argue or even talk about it, the τόδε must be a τοιόνδε, and it is in virtue of a particular's being a particular τοιόνδε that we can talk or argue rationally about it at all. For while I can refer to this τόδε by means of a token-reflexive word, such as the word 'this', I cannot, without the use of general terms, say anything about it; and if I am to argue about it rationally, since rational arguments are ideally non-egocentric, they must be formulated in non-egocentric terms; and therefore without the use of token-reflexives, which are essentially egocentric, as Russell's illuminating name "egocentric particulars"[5] shows. Λόγοι, even more when they are arguments, reasons, *rationes* than when they

---

[1] In saying this, I do not mean that the conclusions can be *deduced* from the facts, or that the facts *entail* the conclusions. Right reasoning need not be deductive reasoning. I maintain only that if it is concerned with human affairs at all, it must be based on, among other things, some facts about the human affairs in question. For an elucidation of the concept of a fact, see J. R. Lucas, 'On Not Worshipping Facts', *Philosophical Quarterly*, 1958, pp. 144–56.

[2] See further below, § 55, pp. 236–40, and § 56, p. 245.

[3] See further below, § 28, p. 132, and § 55, pp. 234ff.   [4] p. 125.

[5] B. Russell, *Enquiry into Meaning and Truth*, Allen and Unwin, London, 1940, Ch. VII, p. 128, or *Human Knowledge; its Scope and Limits*, London, 1948, Pt. II, Ch. IV, p. 100.

are *verba*, words, are inherently applicable and re-applicable on different occasions to different particular instances of some general form or type.

With persons and particular situations in human affairs there is a difficulty, if, as I maintain, they are infinitely complex. For then we cannot completely specify the features that characterise a person or situation, and however fully we have specified it, we may always have left out some relevant feature. Hence the dialectical nature of argument in the humanities. Hence also the belief of some philosophers that political reasoning, like that of history and the other humanities, is concrete rather than abstract. No finite set of "abstract" characteristics can exhaust either all that can be truthfully and relevantly said of a person or a human situation, or all the infinite facets of a personality, or the infinite complexity embodied concretely in a particular person or a particular situation. Nevertheless, although no finite set of characteristics characterises a person or a human situation without remainder, when we argue about situations or problems in human affairs, it is in virtue of some of the general characteristics or features of the case that we adduce the arguments that we do.

The conclusion, therefore, of a rational argument, although it may be about one particular topic, and may be formulated with the aid of token-reflexives, which refer to particulars egocentrically, and not in virtue of any general characteristic, is, if not already in universal terms, *universalisable*. A man who claims that a particular picture is a good picture, but allows that another picture might be like it in every respect, except that it was not good,[1] shows thereby that he has not been reasoning rationally, and that his putative value-judgement 'This is a good picture' is not a value-judgement, because not a judgement at all. Similarly, a historian discussing some counterfactual conditional, e.g., 'If Hannibal had marched on Rome, he would have taken it', would be convicted of a serious irrationality if he then went on to allege, however, that there could have been another situation exactly like that of Rome in Hannibal's time in all respects, and another commander, exactly like Hannibal in personal qualities, resources and all other respects, and yet this other commander would not have taken this other Rome. We may therefore lay it down as a necessary condition of an argument's being a rational one that it is based on universal characteristics of the topic argued about, and as a necessary condition of a conclusion's being the conclusion of a rational argu-

[1] This example is taken from R. M. Hare, *The Language of Morals*, Oxford, 1952, II.5.2, pp. 80–81.

ment that it should be in some sense universalisable. Some philosophers
have suggested that it is also a sufficient condition of at least a value-
judgement's being a value-judgement. This seems doubtful. For our
purpose, a necessary condition is enough.

The sense in which rationally arrived at conclusions must be
universalisable has raised many difficulties. One, which is important
for our present purpose, is whether the universalisability is a practical
universalisability, such that the speaker should be able, on demand, to
universalise his conclusion, stating exactly and completely what the
relevant universal characteristics are; or whether the universalisability is only in principle, so that *if* there were a case exactly the same
in all relevant (but unstated) respects, then the same conclusion would
follow. The requirement of universalisability in the former sense is a
more stringent one. It requires that the speaker should be able to
specify an *infima species* all the instances of which are qualitatively
identical so far as the argument is concerned, and therefore with the
some conclusion holding of them all. The latter sense requires only
that if different conclusions hold in two cases, there must be some
relevant difference between the cases to account for the discrepancy.
We can, once again,[1] use quantifiers to make the point clear, and
express the difference between these two requirements of universalisability in terms of a reversal of the order of the two quantifiers (x) and
$(\exists y)$.[2]

It is in fact only the weak requirement of universalisability that we
have shown to be a necessary condition of a conclusion's being the
conclusion of a rational argument. The picture enthusiast was proved

----

[1] Compare § 8, p. 30n.

[2] In this case we need the higher-order predicate calculus so that we may
quantify over characteristics. Let x range over particular cases, and G range over
characteristics (including conjunctions of characteristics) of cases, and let $C(x)$
be the conclusion that x is C (e.g. x is a good picture). Then the strong requirement is

$$(\exists G)(x)[G(x) \supset C(x)]$$

and the weak is

$$(x)(\exists G)[\sim C(x) \supset \sim G(x)]$$

which is the same as

$$(x)(\exists G)[G(x) \supset C(x)]$$

In the strong requirement there has to be a set of characteristics G, such that every
case x which is a case of G is also a case of C. In the weak requirement we only
need that if any x is not a case of C there is some relevant characteristic G which
it also lacks. We cannot formalise criteria of relevance, which are none the less
of the greatest importance in the application of the principle. See below, § 29,
p. 135, § 30, pp. 136–7, § 55, esp. p. 235. See also J. R. Lucas, 'The Lesbian
Rule', *Philosophy*, 1955, esp. pp. 202–13.

irrational not because he could not specify fully and precisely those characteristics the possession of which will make a picture good—few of us could—, but because he was prepared to deny that another picture was good although he did not allow that there was *any* respect in which it differed from the picture that, he maintained, was good. If, as many philosophers believe, there are only a finite number of relevant characteristics, the two requirements of universalisability differ only in approach, and come to the same thing in the end. If, however, as I maintain, human affairs are infinitely complex, then the two principles of universalisability are radically different. Even in the former case the end is so far distant that the different approaches have importantly different consequences.

The reversal in the order of the quantifiers, which makes the difference between the strong and the weak requirement of universalisability makes also the difference between finite and infinite. In the strong requirement, in which the order of the quantifiers was $(\exists G)(x)$ we have to specify the relevant features—G—before the occurrence of a particular case x; and although G may be a conjunction of features, it cannot, if we are to have our language perfectly precise, be more than a finite conjunction of features. In the weak requirement, however, in which the order of the quantifiers was $(x)(\exists G)$ we do not have to specify the relevant feature until after the occurrence of each case x, when it may be any one of an infinite list of features, and although in each case G may be only finitely specified after the event, it may be a different G for each x, and the range of x is infinite. Thus the strong requirement, because it requires us to specify the relevant features first and to have completed our specification before any cases arise, ties us down to only a finite number of features that we can mention as relevant: whereas the weak requirement, in allowing us to have our say after the occurrence of each case, leaves us free always to pick out further features of the case in question as relevant; and in giving us the last word on what is relevant, leaves the list of potentially relevant features infinite.

SECTION 28

RULES OF NATURAL JUSTICE

RIGHT reasoning cannot be completely characterised, and therefore, if we are to be definite, we have to concentrate not on saying what it is, but on saying some of the things that it is not. In the face of human imperfection, we articulate the Rule of Law partly in terms of procedures designed not to secure that absolute Justice will be done but to be a safeguard against the worst sort of injustice. Injustice rather than Justice "wears the trousers" in political philosophy, because, being fallible, we cannot say in advance what the just decision will always be, and, living among selfish men, we cannot always secure that it will be carried out. So, for the sake of definiteness, we adopt a negative approach, and lay down procedures to avoid certain likely forms of injustice, rather than aspire to all forms of Justice.

The rules of Natural Justice are general rules of procedure designed to prevent certain sorts of injustice, particularly in individual cases. They have been formulated with legal adjudications[1] in view rather than any other sort of political[2] dispute, but they should not be restricted to disputes that are decided by the courts of law.

The rules of Natural Justice require that no man shall be judge in his own cause; that the judge shall hear both sides of the case; that the judge shall give full consideration to the case; that the judge shall exclude all irrelevant considerations from his mind while reaching a decision; that like cases shall be decided alike; that cases once settled shall not be reopened, though, according to some authorities, there should be some right of appeal; that not only shall justice be done but that it shall be seen to be done; that the judgement shall include not only the bare decision, but the reasons which led to it.[3]

These rules guard against certain, although not all, defects which may afflict our decision procedures. The rule of precedents, that like cases shall be treated alike, and the rule of finality, that cases once settled shall not be reopened, are, as we have seen,[4] necessary conditions of any decision procedure. Provision for appeals recognises the fallibility of human judgement, even that of the most judicious of judges. But, as we saw in Section 5, not all decisions can be subject to appeal. The requirements that proceedings be in public and that reasons be given for decisions is primarily a safeguard against the authorities abusing their position by taking decisions for the wrong, and particularly for corrupt, reasons;[5] it also, though only secondarily, reflects our ideal

---

[1] See below, § 29.   [2] In the wide sense of 'political'. See above p. 20n.

[3] I am indebted to Mr. Robert S. Summers, of the University of Oregon, for some of the rules here cited, and for much valuable discussion.

[4] § 5, pp. 18–19. See also § 27, pp. 127–9, and § 29.

[5] See below, § 31, pp. 136–7. See also the Franks Report on *Administrative Tribunals*, 1957, Cmnd. 218, §§ 24, 76.

of Political Liberty, that everybody should be free to be, in some minimal sense, "in on" all decisions made by the body politic, if only by being able to know what they are, and to follow the reasoning by which they were reached. We can, alternatively, view this as a precondition for the effective operation of Constitutional Criticism. The requirement is not an absolute, although a general one: sometimes even in court cases, the proceedings are not public, to protect the intimate interests of the individual concerned from adverse publicity, and sometimes even Parliament goes into secret session. These are exceptional cases, where the circumstances warrant our making exceptions. There are, however, more general arguments in favour of secrecy, or at least privacy,[1] and these lead to a general conflict of goods, and provided we can have other securities against abuse, we may be prepared to compromise the minimal extent of public participation afforded by publicity of proceedings for the sake of efficiency and enterprise. One general type of such security is the requirement of Responsibility discussed in Section 27.

The rule that *no man shall be judge in his own cause* is a particular case of the requirement that arbitration shall be impartial; which in turn is a particular case of the requirement that a decision, if it is to be reasonable and right, must be based only on relevant considerations, and not on irrelevant ones. Considerations depending merely on the personal interests of the arbitrator are irrelevant, because egocentric and not universal.[2] Therefore partial reasoning cannot be right reasoning, and cannot, except by coincidence, lead to a right decision.

The principle is easy to apply in its traditional field of application— in "causes" which have been brought to a court of law for adjudication; for these the concept of *interest* is reasonably determinate, and it is reasonably easy to secure that a non-"interested" party shall have authority to arbitrate. But the general concept of *interest* is indeterminate, and liable to expand in unexpected directions.[3] Is a judge, committing for contempt a man who has flouted that judge's orders, really a disinterested party? He has no pecuniary interest, true. But if his *amour propre* is involved, is he not really as interested as if he had some financial stake in the outcome?[4] What of a Minister of the Crown, listening to objections to schemes put forward by his own Ministry? As a politician seeking political success, he has a great interest in the success of his Ministry's policies. A disinterested zeal

---

[1] See below, § 39, pp. 163–6.   [2] See § 27, pp. 125, 126–7.
[3] Cf. the concept of *harm*, § 42.   [4] See above, § 26, p. 114.

for the public good and an interested concern in self-advancement merge beyond disentangling.[1] The concept of interest can be expanded until it becomes vacuous. All good men are interested that right, as they see it, shall be done, and truth, as they believe it, shall prevail. Although we can distinguish disinterested interests from interested ones, it is too difficult a distinction to draw for us to be able to use in a rule of procedure. We can only specify certain sorts of interests, and debar those who have such interests from taking certain sorts of decision where those interests are involved.

The rule that the judge shall hear both sides of the case, *audi alteram partem*, is based on three principles: first incomplete rationality and incomplete information; secondly respect for the individual; and thirdly Political Liberty.

There are many considerations which an authority will not have entertained, many facts which it will not know; among them may be crucial ones, which, if only they were brought to the authority's attention, would lead it to decide the issue the opposite way. The person most likely to have thought of cogent considerations, and to know the relevant facts, is the person whose interests are in jeopardy, that is the party opposing the decision. Therefore we shall avoid bad decisions best if we ensure that each potential decision, before it is finally decided, is exposed to what is likely to be the strongest possible criticism of it. By subjecting each potential decision to the most stringent test under the most adverse conditions, we shall weed out all those that will not really stand up. If, having heard the best case that the other side can make, an arbitrator decides against him, his decision is not likely to be wrong simply because he failed to notice some weighty considerations, or was not apprised of some crucial fact.

Besides this recipe for avoiding injustice, we think we owe it to a man as a human being to engage in argument with him, and allow him to engage in argument with us, rather than take decisions about him behind his back, completely disregarding, as it were, his status as a rational agent, able to appreciate the rationale of our decisions about him, possibly willing to co-operate in carrying them out. So a judge, before passing sentence on a convicted prisoner, asks him first if he

---

[1] See the Franks Report on *Administrative Tribunals*, 1957, Cmnd. 218, § 25: " . . . But the Minister, ⟨in deciding the cases . . .⟩ is committed to a policy which he has been charged by Parliament to carry out. In this sense he is not, and cannot be, impartial." Compare the Donoughmore Report on *Ministers' Powers*, 1932, Cmnd. 4060, pp. 78–79; see also below, § 46, p. 199 and note; and § 48, p. 208.

has anything to say; for even a convicted prisoner, although altogether subject to the coercive power of the State, is still a human being, not a sack of potatoes; and a judge should talk to him, and let him talk back in turn, and not merely talk to others about him, as he might about an inaminate object.

The argument from Political Liberty, that a man has a right to be heard, in order that he may have the opportunity of shaping the decisions of State in the direction he wants, is a much wider-ranging argument. But it is not primarily concerned with Natural Justice, and therefore we defer it until later.[1]

SECTION 29

EQUITY AND LEGALITY

THE two principles of universalisability generate two ideals, which I shall call Equity (or Justice)[2] and Legality. The ideal of Equity corresponds to the weak principle of universalisability, that of Legality to the strong. The ideally equitable decision is purely rational, taking into consideration all the relevant factors of the case:[3] the decision altogether in accord with Legality is purely deductive, basing itself only on the finite number of features antecedently specified as relevant by the statute. If we adopt the weak principle of universalisability, the only restriction upon the decisions which might be rationally reached by the judges is that similar cases shall be treated similarly, that is, the rule of precedents of the common law. By the rule of precedents, a judge is obliged either to decide the case before him the same way as similar cases in the past, or to "distinguish" it, that is, to find some feature of the present case not possessed by previous cases which justifies its being decided the other way. The logical form is of the case arising first and the principles applying being stated afterwards. If, on the other hand, we adopt the strong principle of universalisability, the only way in which judges can give decisions which are rational is to give them in accordance with a code. The code may be a

---

[1] § 62, pp. 269–271.

[2] The concept of Justice has many facets, and is discussed later (§ 55, pp. 233–43). The just decision in a *particular case* I call equitable. Equity thus is a part of Justice, particular Justice, Justice in particular cases.

[3] For a further, negative criterion—that *only* relevant factors of the case should be taken into consideration—see below, § 55, pp. 235–6.

complete system of statute law enacted by the legislature, like the Code Napoléon; or it may be judge-made law, but antecedently promulgated, like the Praetorian Edict. But, however authorised, it has the logical form of the principles being stated first and the cases arising afterwards.

We can also use the two principles of universalisability, with the associated distinction between finite and infinite specifiability, to define the pure cases of adjudication and legislation. Adjudication is concerned essentially with the particular, legislation with the general. An adjudication, if it is to be rational, must be universalisable in the weak sense, not necessarily in the strong sense: whereas legislation constitutes a principle, universalised in the strong sense, covering an indefinite number of particular cases; in the language of the logicians, adjudications are concerned with "closed" classes of named persons, legislation with an "open" class of un-named but only specified persons.[1] With adjudications, there is no antecedent specification of what constitutes a relevant factor; though, of course, if we give a justification it must be a finite one, and only refer to a finite number of factors as relevant; but the justification is given *ex post facto*, and we do not have to lay down in advance of the actual situation what is to count as a relevant factor. In legislating, however, we are essentially specifying in advance what features are relevant, and how cases characterised by them are to be treated. Adjudication is concerned with only a definite number (usually only one) of named particular persons, but with an indefinite number of un-named factors being possibly relevant: legislation is concerned with an indefinite number of un-named persons, but with only a definite number of specified factors being relevant.

If an adjudication is to be reasonable and right, it must be reached by argument, itself based on the *past* actions[2] of the persons concerned; else it is still possible that they might act so as not to be characterised in the way required for the argument to apply. If legislation is to be

[1] 'All ravens are black' (about the open class of all ravens) means not only, 'If anything is a raven, it is black' but 'If anything were a raven, it would be black': 'All the engines at Bletchley have engine numbers that are prime numbers' means only, 'If a number is the number of an engine at Bletchley, it is a prime number' but not 'If a number were the number of an engine at Bletchley, it would be a prime number'. The class of engines, and hence of engine numbers, at Bletchley is a "closed" class: we could replace it by a list of particular engines, or of particular engine numbers, without having to specify any class in general terms.

[2] In a wide sense, including qualifications obtained, place of residence, etc.

properly so called, it must be about the legal consequences of the *future* actions of people. For only these constitute a genuinely open class.

The pure cases of adjudication and legislation do not occur in practice. An adjudicator cannot help legislating once he starts recording his decisions. For although he decides a case after the event, and is not tied down by any criteria of relevance promulgated beforehand, if once he states his decision he states it in only finite terms, and this statement is antecedent to future possible cases. The judge has therefore committed himself to deciding future cases which are the same in all relevant respects in the same way as this case; and hence, a judge, by recording his decision does lay down how an indefinite number of similar cases will be treated, and this *is* legislation (albeit on only a very small scale) in our sense.

Legislation also cannot help but adjudicate. However forward-looking it may be, since men form their plans on the basis of their expectations, a future alteration of the law may affect a man's present situation and alter or undo the effect of his past dispositions. Moreover, even the most general measures cannot but apply to particular persons, and legislators cannot help having a fairly shrewd idea of some of the particular people who will be affected by their general enactnents. It is only because particular people will be affected that there is agitation for a change of law. Therefore, quite apart from difficulties about the interpretation of statutes, which we will discuss later,[1] we must allow that every piece of legislation should also be regarded as being partly an adjudication too. We can distinguish the adjudicative and legislative aspects of a decision, rather than classify every decision as being either the one or the other.

SECTION 30

THE FOUR JUDGES

WE CAN illustrate the interplay between the ideals of Equity and Legality, and between the adjudicative and legislative aspects of decisions by recounting an imaginary tale of four judges, Judex I, Judex II, Judex III, and Judex IV.

Judex I is the ideal customary law judge. He is a good man who

[1] § 31, pp. 139–41.

lives in his tent and judges Israel righteously. Every morning he goes
to the gate of the city, and there hears all the disputes the children of
Israel bring him; and after having heard what either side has to say
gives his decision, for the one party or the other, as the Lord saith
unto him. And then goes on to the next case.

Judex I has a second cousin, Basileus, who lives in Greece, and
gives *Themistes*, awards to his people as seems best to him. *Themistes*
are divinely inspired, separate, isolated judgements in particular
cases.[1] If Basileus had been as good a man as Judex I, all would have
been well, but unfortunately the old Adam in him got the upper hand,
and his *Themistes* remained separate, isolated judgements in particular
cases, but were no longer divinely inspired, and in due course his
people came to suspect that he was abusing his authority, and replaced
him by Judex II.

Judex II is the original common law judge. Judgement is still
divinely inspired, and so much so that a judge cannot articulate at all
the motives of the spirit that moves him. But when he decides a case,
he says what he has decided, although he does not say why. His
decision is recorded, and it is agreed that similar cases must be decided
in the same way, although when a new case arises, Judex II, after
having conceded that it does seem *prima facie* to resemble some case
he has decided previously, may go on to say, 'But there is a further
feature of this case which makes all the difference'.

In course of time Judex II gives way to Judex III, the judge of the
law reports. Judex III not only says what he has decided, but also, to
the best of his ability, why. Various considerations led to this. It was
partly that Judex III found that having to put his reasons in writing
aided clear thought. It was also that he wanted to subject his reasoning
to the critical appraisal of others, both in order that he might learn
to do it better, and that a common consensus of judicial opinion might
be established, so that the many different judges, of whom Judex III
was now composed, could keep in step. It was also that subjects and
litigants liked to be given reasons.[2] Not only was it a help to them in
anticipating what Judex III might decide next, but they had found the
bleak 'what' of Judex II's decisions not altogether satisfactory. They
had not always been convinced of the relevance of the differentiating
feature. Some cynics had said that they were no better off than under
Judex I, because if Judex II was minded to give an unjust decision,

[1] Sir Henry Maine, *Ancient Law*, Oxford, 1931, pp. 4, 7.
[2] See above, § 12, and § 24, p. 108.

then no matter how clear the precedents, he could always manage to distinguish the new case by saying, 'But it was on a Tuesday in August in Dover', or some such. If the object of the exercise was to ensure that Judex reached his decisions rationally, the obvious demand to make was that he should state what his reasons had in fact been. And this Judex III was asked to do.

Judex IV is trusted even less. No divine inspiration there. All he has to do is to look at the regulations, and see what the answer is. He is the ideal legal code or statute law judge. He does not have to be wise or more than minimally good. His function is merely to certify that a certain regulation applies to this case, and make the appropriate particular order.[1] The subsumption of the particular case under the general rule is entirely "mechanical" and can be checked by anybody, including the parties to the dispute; so that it would be quite clear if the judge were going wrong.

Judex IV is a humble man, conscious of his human failings and fallibility; and is glad that his Assignment of Responsibility makes it more or less impossible to go wrong. Many modern judges have Judex IV as their ideal, and many subjects, in the ancient world as well as the modern, have deemed this the only satisfactory way of administering Justice. But, as Judex comes down from his pedestal, it is necessary for Law-giver to ascend to the throne; and as the one becomes more mortal, more human, more humble, the other becomes more Olympian, more divine, more pre-eminent. Moses and Hammurabi, Solon, the Decemvirs, Justinian, and Napoleon cast long shadows down the course of history; some spoke with God; some claimed divine inspiration; some were accorded divine honours; all were elevated above the common run of humanity, and needed to be, if they were to carry out their task. And in fact, not actually being divine, their efforts at law-making left a lot to be desired. For the complexity of human affairs makes them not only impossible to describe with complete precision but impossible also to prescribe for with complete fairness; impossible at least in practice, and perhaps also in principle. For if human beings and human affairs are infinitely complex, while their capacities to know and to think are only finite, no human being, not even a Law-giver, can envisage all the possibilities there are, or provide for each one separately in advance. If his language were absolutely precise, so that he could lay down general, but exact, provisions for the future, about whose application to any particular case there could

[1] See §§ 47 and 48 of Introduction to the Prussian *Landrecht* of 1794.

be no doubt, there would still be many combinations of circumstances which he had not considered, and which if he had considered he would have decided in the opposite way from that laid down by the general provisions he had enacted. "And because the dangers of a State can never be all foreseen by any company of men, by reason of the infinite circumstances of humane actions and accidents, therefore they cannot be all caution'd in Positive Laws."[1] *Dolus latet in generalibus.* No man can generalise safely. For men's generalisations, being the generalisations of finite beings, contain only a finite number of characterising terms, and are therefore, in the pejorative sense of the word, abstract, unable to do justice to what the full complexity of the concrete situation demands. Judex I, Judex II, and Judex III may therefore declare a more just decision in the individual cases they consider, than Judex IV can, completely fettered as he is by Law-giver, who, however much wiser he is than Judex, has to divide his attention over all cases in general, instead of concentrating it on only a few cases in particular, and therefore may well, as regards these few particular cases, be wrong. Only an infinitely wise Being, God, can be an adequate Law-giver, being a perfect Law-giver and a perfect Judge, laying down laws that were just in all cases, and giving judgements that were just in each.

Mortal men, not being God, nor having God available in this life, either as Judge or as Law-giver, in the sense of words here used, must compromise. No man is good enough or wise enough for us to be entirely happy to have him either as Judex I or as Law-giver giving laws to Judex IV. So far as the ideal of securing right decisions reached by rational argument goes, we are best served by Judex III, subject to the usual safeguards of appellate courts, and perhaps with the added authority (which the Supreme Court and, now,[2] the House of Lords have) of reversing the palpably wrong decisions of his predecessors. But there are other arguments which lead us to Legality as the chief bulwark of the Rule of Law.

SECTION 31

LEGALITY: THE INTERNAL ASPECT

LEGALITY provides both guidance for the rulers and protection for the ruled. Historically, it was for the sake of both of these together that

[1] A. Ascham, *A Discourse*, London, 1648, p. 66.   [2] Since 27 July 1966

Legality was demanded. Judex I became corrupt, and therefore was replaced by Judex IV to whom no latitude was allowed.[1] Happily now, we no longer need Legality as a safeguard against corruption: and against errors made in good faith, the courts of appeal are equally adequate and in many ways better. Nevertheless, it is often felt that Legality is the only principle an official can adopt if he is not to be a law unto himself, and that therefore Constitutionalism itself demands strict adherence to the principle of Legality.

Although we have distinguished two senses of universalisability, many philosophers do not draw the distinction, and think that there is only one principle, the strong principle, and that this is the hallmark of rationality. To be rational a decision must be in accordance with a rule, and the only alternative is to be entirely arbitrary.[2] Reasoning then is construed to mean solely deductive reasoning, and all valid arguments, if set out in full, are thought to be deductive arguments, in which the conclusions follow from the premises in virtue of the *meanings* of the *words* involved.

Closely linked with this theory of reasoning is a theory of language, that the application of language is always either completely automatic or else entirely arbitrary. These two theories give rise to the doctrine of *mechanical legalism*, which holds that a judge must decide particular issues by *subsuming* them under some law (so that the decision follows *deductively* from the law cited), because otherwise he would be acting entirely irrationally; and that a law must lay down exactly what a judge is to decide in all circumstances, because if it grants the judge any discretion at all, it gives him no guidance whatsoever, and leaves the issue to be decided at his whim.

The theory that all reasoning is deductive reasoning is false,[3] and so is the theory that the application of language is always either completely automatic or else entirely arbitrary. We have already[4] seen that

[1] See, e.g., Mariana, *De Rege et Regis Institutione*, Toledo, 1599, Bk. I, Ch. ii: "kings were expected at first to rule equitably by their own discretion; laws were introduced later, when men became suspicious of the king, to secure equal treatment for all." Quoted by J. W. Gough, *The Social Contract*, 2nd ed., Oxford, 1957, p. 62.

[2] See Franks report on *Administrative Tribunals*, 1957, Cmnd. 218, § 29, p. 6. "The rule of law stands for the view that decisions should be made by the application of known principles or laws . . . On the other hand there is what is arbitrary. A decision may be made without principle, without any rules. It is . . . the antithesis of a decision taken in accordance with the rule of law."

[3] See J. R. Lucas, 'The Philosophy of the Reasonable Man', *Philosophy*, 1963, pp. 97–106; and 'The Lesbian Rule', *Philosophy*, 1955, pp. 195–213, esp. pp. 200–2.   [4] § 7, pp. 24–26.

language is not completely precise, so that however carefully we formulate a law there are still some cases to which its application is not clear or automatic: so that Judex IV, in spite of his ideals, must on occasion interpret the law, and not merely apply it.[1] And therefore even he must on occasion exercise discretion, for to interpret is to exercise some sort of discretion. Every judge must have *some* discretion—obviously, for that is why we have them. It is in fact perfectly feasible to give directives to judges on how they are to use their authority, while not tying them down completely; as, for example, when Parliament directs that the penalty for certain motoring offences shall be disqualification unless there are "special circumstances". It is left to the judges to decide whether there are special circumstances; but it is quite clear to them that they may not deem any circumstances to be special circumstances, and that they may not let a man off more lightly merely because disqualification is in their view too severe a penalty.

Language is richly provided with words and phrases that give guidance without completely withholding discretion; as is only to be expected, seeing that language is a means of communication between *rational* agents, every one of whom may be expected to be able to use his *nous* to some extent. Even the simplest everyday instructions—'Go to the grocers and buy half a pound of butter'—do not prescribe the exact pattern of physical behaviour, and leave the hearer some discretion in the way in which he carries out the commission. The greater discretion vested in a judge is nothing out of the ordinary. It is only, though on a larger scale, the latitude that is inherent in most language; and what is to be expected if human beings are rational agents rather than computers or automata. Hence laws need not be formulae which are either rigidly applicable or else useless. They can, and in fact do, contain many policy-directing words and phrases which tell the judges how they are to give their decisions, although they will still need to use their own judgement in each particular case: 'reasonable', 'foreseeable', 'without due care and attention', 'without due consideration of other road-users', 'in good faith'—it would be absurd to maintain that these, and many other words and phrases, were meaningless, or that laws containing them could not be applied, except purely arbitrarily; but such words and phrases do not always apply themselves, in the way in which some philosophers feel descriptive language ideally should, and we may on occasion, perhaps on

[1] See further below, § 51, p. 214.

many occasions, raise the question, 'Who is to say?' whether such and such behaviour is reasonable, such and such consequences foreseeable, etc. To make the question answerable on every occasion on which it arises, we need to have a judge to give an authoritative application of the word or phrase on that occasion. But this does not mean that the word or phrase has no meaning apart from the judge's interpretation, or that he could in any case whatever give whatever interpretation he liked to it.[1]

Contrary, therefore, to the doctrine of mechanical legalism, that discretion must be either non-existent or else absolute, it is both possible and necessary that judges should be granted some discretion without their thereby being given a completely free hand. Judex IV is not, so far as logic goes, the only alternative to Judex I. There are other arguments for Legality, but we cannot argue on logical grounds from the nature of the concept of adjudication that the ideal of Legality is, simply, identical with that of Rationality, and alone is opposed to irrationality and arbitrariness. Judex II and Judex III can exist as fairminded and rational judges reaching right decisions by right reasoning.

Legality is thus not the same as rationality or Constitutionalism. It is not to be equated with the Rule of Law. There still are reasons for assigning only limited responsibilities with limited discretion to officials,[2] and, in particular, to judges:[3] but these do not require us to make Legality into an absolute; and, indeed, there are many reasons why we should not. For Legality, where it differs from Equity, will be less just, and this is bad, even from the internal point of view of the officials who administer the law. After all, the whole object of the exercise is to produce right decisions. It may be wise to qualify that ideal by counsels of imperfection, but hardly to replace it. Moreover, even the score of expediency, inequitable decisions should be avoided. For the law will be effective only if it is generally regarded as just by the public at large. It will forfeit their respect if it departs too far from the values which the members of the community cherish in common. As Hume said, "Human nature cannot by any means subsist without the association of individuals: and that association never could have place were no regard paid to the laws of equity and justice."[4]

---

[1] See further below, § 47, pp. 203ff.   [2] § 19, pp. 80–82; § 46, p. 197.
[3] § 51, pp. 418ff.
[4] Hume, *An Enquiry concerning the Principles of Morals*, ed. L. A. Selby-Bigge, Oxford, 1902, Sect. iv, § 165, p. 206.

Judges in practice pay great regard to justice, much more than many of them like to admit. Many judges see themselves in the *rôle* of Judex IV, and all judges consider themselves bound by the rule of precedents. Nevertheless when faced with a law, whether statute or some previously decided case, which outrages their sense of justice, they tend to "interpret it away". They seize on any feature they can of the case before them which they can use to "distinguish" this case from those where an unjust decision would, according to pre-existing law, have to be given. Thus, paying lip-service to Legality, judges often succeed in advancing the cause of Justice. There are advantages in maintaining always the semblance of Legality, even while deciding the case on its substantial merits,[1] but clearly they are not being guided by Legality alone, and Legality therefore is not for them the sole and sufficient principle.

Judges are not alone in loving Justice. Not only the citizenry at large, but officials of the executive arm of government, are moved by considerations of Justice and Mercy more than by a strict regard for the letter of the law. And therefore, if the law is inflexible, and the judge has no discretion to mitigate its asperities where Justice or common sense requires it, those persons who are actually in a position to exercise discretion, even if they are not in theory authorised to do so, will. People insist on being reasonable, and if judges cannot be, then executive officials must. Thus the police in respect of the Traffic Acts. If exceeding the speed limit is made an offence with no excuses allowed, then if a man really has a good excuse—e.g. rushing a patient to hospital—the police will not prosecute. Similarly with many parking offences, too little discretion on the part of the magistrates has resulted in too much on the part of the police.[2] In the end, Legality is self-defeating. The whole point of having judges is that decisions cannot be given according to the rule-book, and someone must have discretion: and the principle provision of Process of Law is to put the

---

[1] See below, § 51, pp. 216–18.

[2] There is no effective defence against a charge of obstruction. But very often the police agree to allow a car to be parked, that is, they agree not to prosecute. The Oxford police issue the following instructions and labels to persons attending certain conferences in Oxford.

"If you wish to park your car overnight without lights in Mansfield Road or Saville Road, this LABEL MUST BE FIXED to the windscreen of your car. DO NOT OBSTRUCT GATEWAYS, DRIVES or the ENTRANCE TO ANY PROPERTY. The Police are liable to prosecute owners not complying with the terms of this notice." (Copied from windscreen label of car 897 SPA in Mansfield Road, Oxford, on 22 September 1964.)

discretion in the hands of the Judiciary. But if we then, in deference to Legality, try to remove discretion from the Judiciary, we are defeating the whole object of the exercise. The Rule of Law cannot be reduced to the principle of Legality. Legality is a form of Constitutional Limitation which although often useful as a safeguard against abuse, cannot be always adequate. So far as the internal aspect of the Rule of Law is concerned, Equity rather than Legality is the hallmark of rationality, and while, in view of the imperfection of rulers and judges, we may on occasion regard Legality as a safer guide, it is always one of limited application only, and we must be ready to rely on other principles and procedures to secure our decisions against various sorts of error.

The Rule of Law, however, is concerned not only to give guidance to the rulers in taking decisions, but to give protection to the ruled, who are also human beings, also fallible and finite ones. They need the protection not only of limits and definiteness, but of intelligibility and manipulability, so as to enable them to make and carry out their own plans, as well as providing them with arguing points for when they need to criticise the rulers' decisions. These needs give a different aspect to the Rule of Law—its external aspect. We view the State from the many different points of view of private citizens, those who are not officials, or not acting in an official capacity. Whereas the unifying theme of the internal aspect of the Rule of Law is Rationality, that of the external aspect is Freedom. Freedom yields further arguments for Legality: Freedom plays an integral part in our structure of legal rights and duties: and it is on Freedom that our notion of property is based. Although considerations of Freedom sometimes run counter to those of Rationality,[1] Freedom and Reason complement each other: Freedom is a good only for rational agents; and only for free beings does the possibility of rational action arise.

SECTION 32

FREEDOM

THE concept of Freedom is difficult to elucidate. As we shall show later,[2] it is necessarily two-faced, one man's freedom being opposed to

---

[1] See below, § 35, p. 152, and § 76, pp. 351ff.
[2] § 36, pp. 157–8; § 39, pp. 167–8.

other men's, and at different times different emphasis has been put on different aspects. Also it is a word with strong emotional connotations, and in many different conflicts in the course of history, protagonists have sought to annex the word 'freedom' as a slogan for their side. 'Freedom' has thus acquired many different senses, and often we can best determine what exactly is being meant, by considering what is *not* being meant; what the word 'freedom' is being opposed to. Nevertheless, Freedom is not simply a negative concept. There is a common strand running through all its uses, and it is because of this that we value it, and regard it as a great good.

The central sense of Freedom is that in which a rational agent is free when he is able to act as seems best to him without being subject to external constraint on his actions. Freedom is a necessary condition of rationality, of action, of achievement. Not to be free is to be frustrated, impotent, futile. To be free is to be able to shape the future, to be able to translate one's ideals into reality, to actualise one's potentialities as a person. Not to be free is not to be responsible, not to be able to be responsive, not to be human. Freedom is a good, if anything is.

From this centre, the concept develops in different directions: we may consider some intention I might form, and ask whether I am free to carry it out, or whether anyone can bid me nay; freedom here is being contrasted with prohibition. This is the sense in which a man who is not a slave is free: he does what he wants, not what another tells him to. Equally important, however, is freedom contrasted not with verbal prohibition but with the pressure of factual circumstances. I cannot act effectively if I am in great pain. We are not only rational agents but sentient beings, and as such are in various ways *vulnerable*. Some of these weaknesses, like susceptibility to pain, are almost conditions of sentience. Others, like susceptibility to hunger, or injury, are perhaps merely contingent conditions of human life as it actually is. But for any being who *cares* about what happens—and therefore for any rational agent who might hope to achieve anything—there must be some states of affairs that he wants to happen, and therefore some others that he does not want to happen, and which he will seek to prevent. Avoiding action always may have to be taken, and may conflict with acting in other desired ways. Therefore it is a general condition of being able to act as one desires that one is not having to take avoiding action, that one is *free from* the necessity of taking avoiding action. And so we may regard Freedom as being chiefly freedom from pressures, freedom from pain, from hunger, from ill health, from fear, from want, from arbitrary arrest, from public opinion. We may define a man as being *free from* some real or apprehended evil, if the evil neither happens, nor would happen nor would be likely to happen, were he not to take any otherwise superfluous avoiding action.

There are many other senses of the word 'freedom'. In mechanics we talk about degrees of freedom; and in other sciences we talk of free energy, free radicals, free variables. Psychologists discuss freedom, and contrast it with the inner compulsions to which a man may be subject. Philosophers are much concerned with the freedom of the will. These are all legitimate and intelligible uses of the term and are natural extensions of the central sense. But I shall not discuss them, because they are not relevant to freedom in its political and legal senses, all of which turn on the two aspects of freedom which I have outlined, freedom to and freedom from.

In all political and legal thought, the two aspects of Freedom are linked. They are linked in two ways. First, my actions may have consequences others wish to avoid; so that my freedom to act as I wish may conflict with their freedom from suffering harm. Secondly, it is characteristic of legal rules, and of all political affairs, that they are backed by sanctions; the restraints enjoined by laws and ordinances must be observed if one is to be free from the pressure of constraints one would most certainly wish to avoid. At one level of crude calculation, the reason why I am not free to break the law is that if I do I shall not be free from those pains and penalties which are prescribed as punishments. And so we are tempted to argue conversely that to be free to do something means to be able to do it without fear of the consequences. But it does not follow, and, indeed, if we take consequences in a wide sense, it cannot be true that to be free is to be able to act without consideration of consequences; for then we should be free to act only in matters of indifference. This is the sense of the word in the phrase, 'You are free to choose as you please', when it is tantamount to saying, 'I do not care what you do'. But the freedom of indifference is not the freedom men have fought for. Therefore, although legal and political freedom to act are essentially linked to freedom from the pains and penalties of the law, the two must in our minds be kept distinct.

Let us consider Freedom in the sense where it is contrasted with prohibition. A man is *free to* perform a particular action if he is not forbidden by an identifiable rule or person, that is authoritative; if, supposing he were to formulate his intention in words, 'I am going to do X', it would not conflict with any applicable rule or injunction, 'Nobody is to do X' or 'You are not to do X'. I am free to walk down the street, to sing the National Anthem in my bath, and, if my employer gives me permission, to leave the office early: I am not free to manufacture heroin, to move a pawn backwards, or, if my fiancée disapproves, to go to a dance with another girl. In each sentence we can replace the word 'free' by the phrase 'at liberty'. I am at liberty to walk down the street, etc. In the latter cases, however much I might want to do the deed in question, I could not, and could quote, as my reason for not being able to, a rule or person forbidding me. We contrast these cases, where I cannot do what I want to do because of some prohibition, with other cases where my inability is due to some physical impossibility or lack of control of my circumstances. We sometimes dream of being as free as a bird. In the present century writers have sometimes maintained that one is not really free to go to the South of France unless one is rich enough to afford it. These are intelligible uses of the word 'free', but somewhat strained. More naturally, we should wish that we were *able* to fly like a bird, and regret that we could not *afford* to go to France. In economic matters, the word 'free' means either more than the sense presupposed by the protagonists of "economic freedom", or less. If I was told I could go to the South of France free, I should expect to be able to go *without paying;* that is, the normal prohibition on taking goods or accepting services, other than those one had paid for, was in abeyance. Thus we have free samples and free passes; and with these, I should feel aggrieved if I was told that they were free because I was in a position to pay for them. On the other hand, when we talk of free trade, a free market, freedom of movement, freedom of employment, or a free port, we do not mean that goods are to be had without money, or that anybody is in a position to afford exactly what he wants: all we mean is that there are no prohibitions of a certain type, no customs duties, no immigration controls, no Control of Engagements Order. Economic freedom is not comparable with legal freedom or political freedom. It is comparable more with the metaphorical use of freedom when we speak of a mountaineer who had been wedged in a crevasse at last regaining his freedom. A man who is so poor that he never has any money at his disposal after the necessities of life have been bought is in the same sort of situation as the man unable to move at all. But the mountaineer, after having freed himself from his crevasse, cannot legitimately

complain of his lack of freedom in being unable to scale a particular
precipice; nor should the man who can only afford to travel to Wembley
complain that he is not free to go to the South of France. His trouble
is not a lack of freedom but a lack of money. Poverty can be an evil,
and great poverty is a great evil: but it is a different evil from lack of
freedom.

SECTION 33

FREEDOM TO AND FREEDOM FROM

FREEDOM in the sense of freedom *to* do something, where we can
do whatever it is that we want to do, without there being any authoritative rule or person to tell us not to, I shall call liberty, to distinguish
it from freedom in the sense of freedom *from* some real or apprehended
evil, which I shall call security or immunity. The words 'liberty',
'security', 'immunity', have often been used to mark off these different
aspects of Freedom, but not always. The Liberties of the Middle Ages
were often also Immunities for the reason that in them the two aspects
of freedom were almost coincident. The mediaeval Liberties were
liberties of communities to order their internal affairs themselves, and
not at the behest of some feudal overlord, a bishop or a king: they
were therefore to be immune from his arbitrary interference in their
internal affairs, though still under his general suzerainty. Liberty
granted by an authority, freedom to do certain things, involves immunity from that authority's power, freedom from the authority's
punishing anybody who does those things.

The mediaeval sense of liberty, although applied originally to
communities, applies equally to individuals. An individual will be
free, *vis-à-vis* his ruler, if he is not subject to his arbitrary behests, and
if he can be sure that provided he does not contravene his ruler's
non-arbitrary prohibitions, he will not be punished by his ruler's
coercive power. The second condition is necessary, because it is the
control of coercive power that makes the ruler authoritative so far as
the individual is concerned, and therefore if there is no freedom *from*
punishment, there is no freedom *to* act independently of the ruler's
specific commands, and the subject is in the position of a slave. The
minimum condition of being a free man is a two-fold restriction, on

the ruler's authority to issue arbitrary injunctions, and on the ruler's power, or at least practice, of imposing punishment.

SECTION 34

FREEDOM UNDER THE LAW

" . . . laws wherein all men might see their duty beforehand, and know the penalties of transgressing them." Richard Hooker, *The Laws of Ecclesiastical Policy*, Bk. 1, Section 10.

THE two aspects of Freedom are combined in the notion of Freedom under the Law. The subject is free to do what the law permits him to do: and in doing what the law permits him to do and in not doing what the law forbids him to do he is free from the pressure of coercive sanctions. The law is authoritative and in a position to lay down what the subject is free to do and is not free to do, just because it controls coercive power and is able to secure freedom from coercion to those who abide by what it lays down. A legal system which is no longer enforceable is no longer authoritative, for it fails to secure to those who obey it freedom from coercion; as is shown by our speaking of laws being no longer "in force", which means both that they are not enforced and that they are not authoritative. To this extent, Hobbes and Austin were right. The effective enforcement of a legal system is a necessary condition, and very largely also a sufficient condition,[1] of its being authoritative: for only then will the liberties, the "freedoms to", that it confers be effectively secured by immunities, "freedoms from" the fear of coercion.

Historically, immunity from coercion was the first-felt need. For without that immunity, the orders of the ruler, however arbitrary, however unlawful, cannot be resisted. And whether or not a ruler was actually prepared to enforce his unlawful orders by means of coercion, it would be a brave man who would dare disobey, unless he could be certain that he was entirely secure from the exercise of coercive power by a wrathful ruler. Immunities must be guaranteed, so that subjects can know for certain that they have nothing to fear from their sovereign's frowns, and that it is not the potentate's displeasure that is dangerous, but only disobedience to the laws. It is for this reason that

---

[1] But see below, § 73, pp. 326–8.

the emphasis over the years has been on Process of Law rather than on limiting the scope of the supreme authority. Provided coercive power can be kept under proper control, we can discuss the limits of lawful authority: but if we are not free from the threat of coercion, we cannot be fearless in criticising the conduct of the coercers, or in any of our doings. Therefore freedom from the fear of coercive sanctions for law-abiding citizens is the first freedom we must have if we are to be free at all.

We must be careful not to over-state this requirement. It is freedom from coercion in the strict sense, that we need, not freedom from every pressure whatever. People often feel that freedom from coercion is not a real freedom unless it is also freedom from every fear or threat, every tie, and every compulsion, and therefore they are tempted to inflate the demand for freedom and not be content with anything less than some ideal freedom, in which men will be absolutely free and unconstrained. Apart from the logical impropriety of extending the meanings of words illegitimately, such a demand is incoherent. For the only condition in which we could fear nothing would be that in which we valued nothing. To have values is to be vulnerable: to be absolutely free from all pressure is to be in a vacuum, in which events have no purchase on us, because we have no concern for events.[1] Therefore we cannot seriously want to be free from all pressure, much as we dislike being subject to some of the pressures that actually bear upon us. What we are concerned with here are those pressures that effectively incapacitate us from resistance—that is, coercive pressures. Other pressures may seem to us to be overwhelming: we may feel compelled to alter a course of action by the threat of dismissal from our jobs: but these are not coercive pressures in the strict sense. One *can* stand out against them, and accept the consequence of losing one's job; and even if one is not prepared to accept the loss of one's job, it is a sort of pressure different from the threat of death, torture or imprisonment. We may want to protect people from these lesser, but none the less effective, forms of pressure. It is a need that has been very much felt in recent years, especially with the growth of the administrative branch of government. But these lesser securities are different from the prime one, security from coercion, which is the first condition of the subject's being a free man, able to make his own plans and lead his own life.

Process of Law is effective in preventing the illegal use of coercion

---

[1] See above § 1, p. 4.

and in giving every law-abiding subject confidence in the face of the wielders of coercive power. 'You cannot touch me,' the citizen can say to the policeman, 'I have done nothing wrong.' But Process of Law, as we have seen, needs to be supplemented by considerations of the Rule of Law, to ensure that authority is not abused. The citizen needs to have confidence not only in the face of the policeman, but in the face of the judge, and even in the face of the sovereign, if he is to be really free. He needs to be able to say to his judge or his sovereign, 'You cannot punish me: I have done nothing wrong.'

Hence the first argument from Freedom to Legality. However good an equitable judge is, however fair and reasonable his decisions, he states his reasons *ex post facto*; the subject cannot argue with Judex I on a level footing, because he has no hold on him at all, nor with Judex II and Judex III, because he can never be sure that they will not pounce on some feature of his case to distinguish it from all the others, or think up some new reason for not treating it in the way he had expected.[1] The principle of Equity gives the judge the last word in the argument: but if the subject is to be free from fear of coercive sanctions, he needs to feel that the judge does not have the last word, logically speaking, for fear it be turned against him. Even though the equitable judge is entirely fair, and will not in fact discriminate against the subject, the subject cannot be sure of this beforehand: and therefore cannot feel secure under the rule of Equity, but must demand Legality so that the judge shall be as subject to the law as he is, and so that he can address him on a level footing and with confidence.[2] Under Equity the subject may in fact be secure: but only under Legality can he feel absolutely secure.

The principle of Legality confers on the subject security, so far as coercion is concerned, *vis-à-vis* his rulers. If we have the principle *nulla poena sine lege*, a subject can know what the law is, and that he has not contravened it, and that therefore the authorities cannot get him, no matter how much he is *persona non grata* to them. Although I may be in the authorities' bad books, with or without good reason, I can still be sure that I shall not go to prison, provided only that I have not broken any law in the statute book. The law-abiding citizen need not fear the knock in the night: he knows that he cannot be exiled to Siberia or slaughtered in Buchenwald.

In granting to the subject an ever present security, the principle of

---

[1] See § 30, p. 136, and § 51, p. 216.
[2] See also below, § 58, pp. 254–5.

Legality grants also a liberty for the future. A man who knows what the law is, not only knows now that he is not liable to any legal penalty, but knows what he can subsequently do, without laying himself open to penalties, that is to say, what he may (legally may) do. He can plan his actions so as to keep within the law. Although, of course, he is not free to do anything he likes, he knows what it is that he is not free to do, and knows that he is free to do everything else, everything, that is, that the statutes do not forbid. The finitely formulated statutes lay upon him a limited legal unfreedom, but leave him legally free in all other, indefinitely many, respects. Legality means not only that the subject knows where he is, but that he also knows where he can go: he knows where he stands *vis-à-vis* the judge, and he knows how he can move with respect to the laws. Although they are restraints, they are limited and predictable ones. Legality assimilates the laws of the land to the laws of nature, which, although they prevent me from doing some things, can be known and can be reckoned with, and can often also be used and manipulated. Legality makes it possible to know the law in advance, and to accommodate one's actions to it: for Legality requires that laws be formulated in a finite number of general terms in advance of the event; so that the subject can know what the laws are before he makes his plans, and can be sure that nothing not prohibited by existing law will turn out to be a crime. *Nullum crimen sine lege.* This is the second argument from Freedom to Legality.

The combination of immunity from coercion for the law-abiding subject with liberty to do anything that has not been prohibited by a law, we may call Constitutional Freedom, or Freedom under the Law. It is the first and most basic form of Freedom. It defines the Freedom of the subject *vis-à-vis* his ruler, not *vis-à-vis* his fellow subjects. It concerns the liberty of the subject, and his security against the arbitrary use of the power of coercion, as seen from the subject's point of view. We want the subject not only to be free, but to know that he is free, so that he may act as a rational autonomous agent in full consciousness of his freedom. Hence, quite apart from the danger of error or abuse on the part of the ruler, we have the need for Legality in order to secure to the subject *chartered* freedoms. We crudify our ideal of complete rationality, by reversing the order of argument, and by limiting in advance the factors that may be counted as relevant. Justice becomes rougher, but easier to reckon with; less exact, but less exacting; less perfect, but safer for imperfect men to live with. The laws remain, but under them we are free.

SECTION 35

LEGALITY: THE EXTERNAL ASPECT

"The certainty of laws involves an obscuring of reason, in so far as in them reason is supported merely by authority. And this makes us experience the laws as hard to obey, and yet we are constrained to obey them because of their being certain". Vico, *Scienza Nuova Seconda* (1744), I, ii, Ch. CXI.

THE arguments from Constitutional Freedom to Legality are both arguments of imperfection, the imperfection of the ruled. We argue for Legality because we are imperfect, finite, fallible, selfish creatures. Its very demerit is its merit. It fails to do justice to the complexity of some hard cases because of its finitude. A law, however complicated, is only finitely complicated, and can specify only a finite number of characteristics as relevant to a case. This means that with some cases the law will enjoin a decision not in accordance with the merits of the case, because it takes into consideration only some and not all of the features of the particular case in question, which we should regard as relevant. But it also means that a finite human being, with only finite capacities and only finite time available for study of the law, can discover what the law is, what are the features of a case that are relevant in the eyes of the law, and what will be the legal consequences of his acts.

Even if judges were perfectly just, and gave decisions that were entirely equitable, those concerned with the law from the outside would still not be content. For they want to know what the law is in advance, so that they can avoid breaking it inadvertently, and avoid being punished. If men were perfectly informed and infallible in their judgement, they might be able to know exactly what a just judge would decide in every case; but they would not then be men. It certainly is so that men are neither perfectly informed nor free from error in their reasonings, and perhaps it is necessarily so, that there should be some matters of indifference if different beings are to inhabit a common world. At the very least we need to have conventions on issues in themselves indifferent, where it does not matter what we do, so long as we all do the same thing; for example, the Rule of the Road. But even on issues not completely indifferent,—the enforceability of contracts, the law of Landlord and Tenant—it matters less to the subject *what* decisions would be given than that he should *know* what decisions will be given. For if he knows, he can plan accordingly, while if he does not know, he cannot arrange his actions rationally so as to secure the goals he has set himself. If the laws of the land which will be enforceable by the State are known in advance to the subject, he can take them into account in his calculations in the same way as he can take laws of nature into account. Forgery and phosgene are both to be avoided by the man who values his liberty or his life. It is a condition of the subject's freedom and independence that the laws of the land shall be certain and knowable in advance. And therefore the subjects will want their judges to be as like as possible Judex IV.

Men can fail not only in their knowledge of what is right, but in their will to do it. Men are incompletely unselfish,[1] and often want to achieve their own ends, irrespective of whether they are right or not; and it is, as we shall see,[2] a mark of a free community that we do not systematically set out to prevent men from forming and carrying out all plans that are at variance with what we believe to be right. Individuals, we believe, ought to be permitted to exercise their own, private, judgement about what they shall do, subject to only a limited number of legal restrictions. They ought to be able not only to know the law, in order to avoid inadvertently contravening it, but to calculate on it, and even to some extent against it, and to avail themselves of it, and even to manipulate it for their own purposes.

Human limitations thus lead us to trade Justice for certainty. *Durum sed ita scriptum est*, but it is only because the law is hard and rigid that we know where we are with it, and can avoid it and use it and rely on it, in the same external way as a law of nature. We therefore reverse the quantifiers, and set up Legality, with the strong requirement of Universalisability, in the place of Equity with its weak requirement. It means that Justice becomes less rational but more knowable, less moral but more dependable, less internal but less restricting. Justice ceases to be something which, if only we were better informed and were possessed of a sounder judgement, we could have worked out for ourselves: but becomes something on which we can accept a competent lawyer's advice with confidence. Justice will sometimes be unjust: but will be less often censorious. One will feel less pressure to endorse the verdict or the sentence of a court of justice as one's own: but equally the court will enquire less into one's own inward motives and attitude of mind, and there will be a veil of privacy between the judge and oneself, behind which one will be able to think one's own

[1] § 1, B(i), p. 2.   [2] § 38, pp. 166–7; § 68, p. 299; § 76, pp. 351–4.

self-interested thoughts, and come to know oneself as the selfish but genuine self that one is.

The goddess of Justice is often represented as blindfolded, weighing the arguments in her scales. The figure can be taken in two ways: it can be taken, and was perhaps originally intended to be taken, as an ideal of Equity: the eyes are blindfolded so as not to see *irrelevant* features, corrupt considerations of fear or favour; Justice, like God, is no respecter of persons, and will give her decision solely on the merits of the case. And so she does not see the persons, but only weighs the arguments. But equally we may regard the goddess as representing Legality, into whose scales may be put only those factors deemed relevant by law. The dispenser of Justice does not allow herself to look beyond the text of the law, and only takes into consideration what the law lays down. Not only does she not consider the persons of the litigants, she does not consider their personalities, their attitudes, their moral merits or their real deserts. Justice is morally blind as well as uncorrupt and impartial, and a man can approach the courts as he can an automatic vending machine with the assurance that it will dispense justice without regard to any personal defects or weaknesses of his, or of any other factor whatever, save only those laid down by law beforehand. The uncouth, the eccentric and the selfish can approach Legality as well as the respectful, the respectable and the righteous, and can, provided only they tender the coin demanded by statute in the way of proven evidence, be sure of winning their case. Legality is the bad man's charter.

These arguments from the external point of view, like those from the internal point of view, have force but do not lead inescapably to absolute Legality. They are all arguments from imperfection, and imperfect though we are, we are not that imperfect. Even the demand for predictability and manipulability can be pitched too high. While we want to avoid uncertainty, we do not need, nor can we hope to have, absolute certainty about every question, in law any more than in nature. It is enough to know that the sun will rise tomorrow: we do not need to know, nor can hope to know, that it will certainly not rain. Similarly it is enough to know that provided I commit no murder or treason I shall not be hanged, and that if I make a straightforward contract it will in the ordinary course of events be enforceable at law. If a man sails close to the windy side of the law and gets unexpectedly caught, or if in some unforeseen contingency a contract is held to be unenforceable, it may be a good, or it may be a bad, thing; but it does not destroy the knowability or the reasonable certainty that the law must have for the ordinary man of good faith, if he is to order his affairs freely and rationally.

SECTION 36

LEGAL LIBERTY

IT IS clear that there is more to the notion of Freedom than the Constitutional Freedom secured by the Rule of Law. I may live under a system of laws which are entirely general, and be secure from any arbitrary exercise of power on the part of the rulers; but still be hemmed in and restricted in all my doings, seldom able to do what I want, nearly always obliged to act in a way laid down by law. Although, in one sense, law is the guarantee of liberty, in another, it is the negation of liberty. Cicero says "*Legum idcirco omnes servi sumus ut liberi esse possimus*":[1] but Salmond says, "The sphere of my legal liberty is that sphere of activity within which the law is content to leave me alone";[2] and both seem to be right. We therefore need to go beyond the Rule of Law in the sense of Constitutional Freedom, Freedom under the Law, and consider the problem of Liberty within the Law. We consider first the definition of a formal concept of legal liberty, in order that we may then discuss what the laws of a free country must be like.

Our concept of liberty or freedom to is defined by contrast. We are free to do X when we are not forbidden to do it, either by an identifiable rule or by an identifiable person, regarded by us as authoritative. Similarly we are free not to do X when there is no authoritative rule or person forbidding us not to do X, i.e. commanding us to do X. If we are living in a community, for every X that I might want to do, somebody else might want me not to do it. For the community to be a community there must be a common decision procedure, either allowing me to do X or not allowing me to do X. If I am allowed to do X we may say that I am legally free to do X: if I am not allowed to do X, we may say that I am under a legal obligation (or, that I have

[1] *Pro Cluentio*, 146. See also, *De Lege Agr.*, Bk. II, 102: *Libertas in legibus consistit.*
[2] Salmond, *Jurisprudence*, 11th ed., Glanville Williams, 1957, Section 78, p. 271; quoted by Jerome Hall, *Readings in Jurisprudence*, p. 529.

a legal duty) not to do X. From the point of view of the other person who objects, or might object, my legal obligation will be viewed as his legal right. If I am under an obligation not to do X, then he can be said to have a right that I should not do X. This terminology, which is due to Hohfeld,[1] is illuminating, in that it shows how rights and duties are merely different aspects of the same legal relationship. We should be cautious, however, in that the word 'right' is used in many other ways, which can easily cause confusion; in particular, 'right' often means 'liberty', for reasons which will shortly become apparent. With this *caveat*, Hohfeld's analysis is extremely valuable. We have, as it were, a Square of Obligation, which enables us to describe both outcomes of a dispute from both points of view.

Suppose there is a dispute about a particular action X, which has been done, or is about to be done, by a particular man A, to which another man, B, objects. The decision procedure of the community is invoked; that is, the two parties go to court. The court will give its decision, based on certain general characteristics of the action X, the man A and the man B. The court will either decide in favour of A's doing X or against, and it can be looked at from A's point of view or from B's. We now classify:

If the court rules:	In favour of A's doing X	Against A's doing X
From A's point of view	A is free to do X	A is obliged not to do X
From B's point of view	B has no-right that A should not do X	B has a right that A should not do X

Hohfeld coined the word 'no-right' to fill the space in the left-hand column of the bottom row; and he uses the words 'Privilege' and 'Liberty' as alternatives for the left-hand column of the top row. The left-hand column is the contradictory of the right-hand column and *vice versa*. The top row is equivalent to the bottom row, and *vice versa*. In order to bring out the equivalence, we need to include in the

---

[1] W. N. Hohfeld, 'Some Fundamental Legal Conceptions', 23 *Yale Law Journal*, 1913, pp. 16–59; and 'Fundamental Legal Conceptions as Applied in Judicial Reasoning' 26 *Yale Law Journal*, 1917, pp. 710–70. Reprinted in W. N. Hohfeld: *Fundamental Legal Conceptions as Applied in Judicial Reasoning and other Legal Essays*, ed. W. W. Cook, New Haven, 1923, pp. 35ff., Yale Paperbound, New Haven, 1964, pp. 35ff. For an earlier statement, see Salmond, *Jurisprudence*, Section 77, pp. 269–70 in 11th edition.

statement from A's point of view to whom he does or does not owe a duty. Let us, therefore, retabulate:

If the court rules:	In favour of A's doing X	Against A's doing X
From A's point of view	A is at liberty, with respect to B, to do X	A is under a duty to B not to do X
From B's point of view	B has no-right against A that he (A) should not do X	B has a right against A that he (A) should not do X

This is Hohfeld's analysis,[1] on the basis of which we can build up a definition of *formal freedom*.

It is not enough for the decision procedure of a community to produce decisions. It must produce decisions which are effective. If A wishes to do X and B wishes that A should not do X, and the dispute is referred to a court which decides in favour of A, then it is not enough for the court merely not to forbid A from doing X; it must also forbid B from trying to coerce A, having failed to get a court order against him. Otherwise, the decision procedure has decided nothing. If it is to be a substitute for the appeal to force, it must not decide only the principal issue in question, but some subsidiary ones as well. Thus if the court decides that I am at liberty to do X, despite your objection, it must also lay upon you the duty of not preventing me by force from doing X. Else, it has not substituted its own decision for the arbitrament of force. If for example, the court decided that I was at liberty to do X, but failed to rule against your using force to stop me, there would be the further question whether I might use force to prevent your attempt to stop me doing X from being successful. If the court says that I may in my turn use force, then it has abdicated its position as an arbiter between disputants, and it would be a waste of time for us to go to court, and we shall have simply to fight it out, literally, between

---

[1] To be exact, Hohfeld puts forward *two* squares of obligation: the one given above, and one based on his concept of *power* (as opposed to *disability*), and its equivalent from the other man's point of view, liability (as opposed to *immunity*). Hohfeld's distinction between, e.g. a power and a right, is that if A possesses a power with respect to B, then A can by a voluntary action of his alter one of B's legal relations, for instance, A can bring it about that B has a certain duty towards him: whereas if A possesses a right with respect to B, then B already had the corresponding duty towards A. But in view of the fact that A's and B's mutual rights and duties depend, among other things, on their actions, Hohfeld's distinction is not a fundamental one.

ourselves. If, on the other hand, the court says No, and lays it down that
you are allowed to stop me by force from doing X, but I am not to try
by force to prevent you from stopping me, then this is what we
describe as my *not* being at liberty to do X, but being under a duty
towards you that I should not do X. Hence it is, that for every liberty
possessed by one person there must be laid upon the other party a
set of subsidiary duties not to use force to prevent the one person from
exercising his liberty. That is, looking at it entirely from the one
person's point of view, each of his liberties needs to be supplemented by
a set of subsidiary rights (in Hohfeld's sense) against would-be
interferers that they should not interfere.[1] My liberty to walk down
the road would be vain if it were not supported by a Hohfeldian right
against any man who would stop me. This is why in common parlance
the word 'right' is used indiscriminately of Hohfeldian rights *and*
Hohfeldian liberties.

There are certain exceptions to the concomitance of Hohfeldian
rights and Hohfeldian liberties: in a boxing ring for example, the pro-
tagonsts are at liberty to hit each other (so long as it is above the belt),
but have no right that the other should not prevent them by force.
Under international law a neutral is at liberty to ship contraband to a
belligerent. Other belligerents have no-right that he should refrain,
but they too are at liberty to seize the contraband. The neutral is at
liberty to run when sighted, but if he disobeys a signal to heave to,
the belligerent is at liberty to sink him. Both these exceptions are
peculiar: they stand half-way between a normal system of laws which
decide every case, and the law of the jungle, which is no law at all, and
in which every conflict is settled by force. Some things are not allowed
in boxing or international law: hitting below the belt, or sinking a
stationary neutral ship. But most issues are not decided by the rules:
he who can, may. With such, defective, incomplete systems we are not
concerned: their only interest is as illustrating, by contrast, the normal,
complete system, which provides a decision, other than by resort to
force, for every issue that arises.

Every normal and complete legal system therefore must support
the liberties it confers with ancillary rights. If I am to be free, so far
as you are concerned, to do X, then I must also have *some* right of your
not preventing me *by force* from doing X. The limitations implicit in
the italicised words are important. I may well be entitled to do X while
you are entitled to prevent me from doing X if I attempt to do so in

[1] But see below, § 75, p. 348.

an unreasonable or unseemly manner: and although you may be forbidden from *using force*[1] to prevent me from doing X, you may well be entitled to use *some* sanctions to prevent me. An uncle may threaten to cut his nephew out of his will if he becomes a bookie: a girl may "force" her fiancé to give up his motor-bike[2]: but though these are restrictions on freedom in one sense—an important one to the man concerned—, they are not restrictions on the man's legal freedom. So far as legal liberty goes—freedom in the formal sense we are concerned with here—the man is free to become a bookmaker, is free to keep his motor-bike; and neither his uncle nor his fiancée is free to stop him absolutely, though they are free to do some things which may well in fact deter or prevent him. If he really wants to, the young man can become a bookie or keep his motor-bike, and accept the consequences of his uncle changing his will or his fiancée breaking off the engagement. He is free so to act—there is no law against it—and they are free to carry out their threats—there is no law against that either: whereas he is not free to forge his uncle's signature, or hit his fiancée; and his uncle is not free to have him put in prison to prevent him being a bookmaker, and his fiancée is not free to sell or destroy his motor-bike in order to prevent him using it any more. In assigning legal liberties, a legal system, even a normal and complete legal system, does not guarantee that a man will be free to exercise them without anybody bidding him nay, and without his being subject to any pressure not to do what he is entitled to do. All that is required is that the system of rights and liberties is so arranged that the parties never have to resolve their disputes by force or violence or the threat of violence.

So far we have spoken always of duties or liberties or rights, of one man with respect to another. This is because there are necessarily two parties to a dispute, and it is only with reference to actual or hypothetical resolutions of a dispute that the concepts of duty, liberty, and right originated. Nevertheless we tend to think of duties, liberties, and rights as very often falling upon, or belonging to, only one man. My freedom to go upon the Queen's highway is not a freedom with respect to you particularly: it is a freedom with respect to more or less anybody: as Austin terms it, "the world at large". In such cases there is no point in specifying the large, indefinite class with respect to whom I have some liberty or right. We just say that I have the

---

[1] See above, § 16, p. 63, or below, p. 367.   [2] See above, § 15, p. 56.

liberty or right in question; if pressed, we should say, at a first approximation, that I have it with respect to everybody else; and only if pressed further will consider whether there are any exceptions—e.g. policemen—to the rule that nobody is to prevent me going as I please along the highway.

With duties we are more ready to ask the question, 'To whom is the duty owed?' But often, even with duties, it is a little unnatural to attach them, as owed, to any particular person; they are owed, if owed to anybody at all, to everybody. The duties laid upon the subject by the criminal law, or by taxation law, are not felt as duties to any*one*, not even to everyone, but rather to the community as a whole. Criminal prosecutions are brought in the name of the Queen, in whose name also the case is decided. We need to walk warily, therefore, when we claim that duties, rights, and liberties always concern not one person but two: for the second one may be difficult to identify, difficult to specify exactly, and sometimes may not be an individual at all. Nevertheless, there always are two parties to a dispute: and if nobody existed, neither private individual nor public official, who could object to one's doing an action X, no question of whether one was legally free to or not could ever arise.

SECTION 37

PRIVILEGE AND ACCOUNTABLE DISCRETION

WITHIN the Hohfeldian concept of legal liberty, an important distinction must be drawn between those liberties which arise from the accountable discretion entrusted to an official[1] and those which are absolute and are not in any way a trust.

The discretion granted to an official is accountable. He has authority to decide certain questions, but he is responsible for his actions, in the sense that he should have an answer to the question, 'Why did you do that?' and be able to give reasons why a person entrusted with his office should have acted in the way he did.

In contrast to this, the person in whom a privilege is vested is not answerable for his actions in any legal or constitutional way.[2] He does not have to give reasons nor does he have to have them. He may act

---

[1] § 26, pp. 117–18.
[2] This, of course, does not preclude a man's being *morally* responsible for his exercise of a legal privilege.

on whim, he may act out of inclination, he may act in pursuit of self-interest, and, legally, he is quite entitled so to do. A man exercising a privilege is entitled to say, 'I just wanted to', if challenged to explain his actions: an official exercising a discretion entrusted to him is not. Whatever an official decides to do, he must be able to describe it as being what seemed best to him from the standpoint of the trust, not merely as what he happened to want to do. We therefore distinguish within the Hohfeldian concept of a legal liberty the accountable discretion exercised by a man acting in an official capacity, where his decision is, one way or another, open to some sort of legal or constitutional criticism, from the absolute discretion, which I call a privilege, and which more closely corresponds to our everyday concept of liberty within the law, where we are not required to give any reasons for our actions, and the simple fact that we want so to act is sufficient legal justification for our doing so.

The ways in which an official may be required to give an account of his exercise of his discretion are many and various. But there are always, as we have seen,[1] certain minimum conditions which we demand in any account of the exercise of discretion. These minimum conditions provide us with criteria for distinguishing the responsible exercise of accountable discretion in an official capacity from the exercise of an absolute privilege or liberty. There is no objection to my exercising an absolute privilege or liberty arbitrarily or unreasonably, in return for some financial reward, or from fear or for favour: exception will be taken, however, if I exercise official discretion for these reasons. Financial reward, because it is the most definite, is the most useful criterion. There is no objection to my conveying my house, or a car, or a washing machine, to another man in return for money, or to working for him for a wage, or giving him my advice for a fee: but it is a criminal offence to vote for a man in a parliamentary or local election in return for money—which shows that we do regard the vote as a trust rather than a right. For this reason also we regard it as regrettable, although there cannot be a law against it, that some electors cast their votes arbitrarily and vote for the first name that appears on the ballot paper. Similarly we seek to protect voters from intimidation, and look with some disfavour upon nepotism in ministerial appointments. We do not have similar views—unless we are unduly censorious—about "investors" giving their money to the pools, or about a workman seeking to placate an irascible employer

[1] See above, § 26, p. 123.

whose property he has damaged by offering to make good the damage himself in his own time, or about an aunt bequeathing her house to her nephew. An advowson in the Church of England—the right to appoint the parson of a particular parish—is thus not property, in our sense, because there is the offence of simony—appointing a man who has paid to be appointed. Civil Service Commissioners, Degree Examiners, Electors to Scholarships, and innumerable other public and private officials have wide discretion over whom they elect or appoint, but commit an offence if they do so for money: and are sworn not to do so arbitrarily or for fear or for favour. Not so a private employer.

We thus have a useful test of whether a Hohfeldian liberty is an accountable discretion or absolute privilege, in whether it is logically possible to exercise it corruptly or not. It always makes sense to speak of an official acting corruptly, just as it always makes sense (even though there may be no legal remedy available) to speak of an official abusing his authority:[1] whereas it makes no sense to speak of a privilege being exercised corruptly, because the concept of a privilege is such that the concept of its being corruptly exercised cannot apply. This, however, is only a criterion: the essential characteristic of a privilege is that the holder is not, legally or constitutionally, answerable for his exercise of it. A legal privilege is a Hohfeldian legal liberty to act, combined with a further Hohfeldian legal liberty not to give or have any good reasons for one's act. It is the right to act irresponsibly.

SECTION 38

IN DEFENCE OF PRIVILEGE

IT IS often felt that it would be better if there were no private privileges but only public offices; that is, instead of assigning to private persons various legal privileges, in the Hohfeldian sense, according to which they are entitled to do various things merely because they happen to want to, they should be granted only public offices, which would confer on them all needful discretion but would make them formally responsible for the exercise of that discretion. This would leave them free to do all things reasonable, but would eliminate the irrationality and selfishness that disfigures our national life. It is largely through the

[1] § 9, p. 35.

rational and disinterested discharge of official duties that rationality enters into the life of the community, and if all actions were done in the course of official duty, we should make the life of the community rationally transparent, instead of, as at present, rationally opaque. Moreover, many people would prefer it that way. It would make their life much more significant if it was wholly lived under the aegis of public policy rationally conceived and rationally executed. It would provide them with a rationale for existing and a purpose in life, which are lacking if their *raison d'être* is merely themselves, and their object in life is merely to enjoy themselves. And so we demand the abolition of the self, and the consecration of every individual life into a facet of the communal whole, to be lived as part of a public trust.

Such a conclusion is wrong. It fails for three reasons: it is impracticable, it is inefficient, and it is undesirable. It is impracticable because men are selfish. We can control the old Adam in us, especially if we can divert him: but we cannot suppress or abolish him. If we have relatively few offices and trusts, we can require that people, while holding them, shall discharge them unselfishly. For we can be selective in our choice of office-holders, and the office-holders themselves have time in which to lead their private lives, and let off their accumulated head of self-interested steam. If we screw down these safety valves, men will not become totally unselfish. They will continue, on occasion, to serve their private interests as before, but will do so under cover of discharging their official duties. They may even conceal their motives from themselves, and be all the more zealous in increasing their power or enlarging their empire, because they are convinced that they are doing whatever they are doing for the purest love of the public good. Since it is impossible to have separate agents interacting in a common world and having some values in common, without each agent being imbued with some *nisus* towards egocentricity, it is best to license it and legitimise self-interest, in order to distinguish from it, on occasions of need, real disinterestedness. If we legitimise self-interest, it will come into the open, and can be recognised for what it is, and can be controlled: if we attempt to suppress it, it will run underground, often unknown and always unchecked.

The inefficiency of officialdom was borne in on the public by the various experiments in nationalisation and State-control in the years after the war. There are two causes. First, if I am accountable, I must keep accounts. The private trader can take decisions and forget the reasons why: the official must take care to formulate his reasons and file them, in case there is a parliamentary question, or a query from the board of directors. The bureaucrat therefore must spend much time in unproductive justification in the face of questions that may never be asked, while the private trader is getting on with his job. In some cases the loss of "productivity" is justified. The time spent by judges in delivering their judgements is well spent, because first it gives guidance to other potential litigants for the future, and makes the law more predictable and more serviceable to the subjects; and secondly it is of paramount importance not only to prevent judges from abusing their powers but to make it reasonably certain that they cannot. Similarly with public officials who wield great power or who control large sums of public money, the danger of abuse is so great that it is worth accepting greater inefficiency or greater cost in order to have safeguards against abuse. But the argument does not carry over to all our transactions. Trustees and executors waste a lot of time that the beneficial owner is saved.

Accountability is a drag not only on the rapidity of business but on its enterprise. The conscientious official or trustee will not take risks on another's behalf that he would be prepared to accept on his own. The less conscientious official will seek a refuge in inaction, since if a risky enterprise fails he will have to justify having embarked on it, while if it succeeds he will not receive much credit. In either case, there is a premium on safety—which is only to be expected since answerability was first devised as a safeguard. But too much safety is dangerous. A community in which nobody is prepared to take risks or make innovations is likely to perish of inanition.

The fundamental reason why accountability is a drag upon enterprise is that human beings are infinitely complex, but human communications are of only finite capacity. In giving my reasons for deciding one way rather than another in human affairs, I can articulate my arguments only to a finite length and a finite degree of complexity; and often there will be much more I could have said, if only I had had wit enough and time enough to say it. If I am to answer for my decisions, I will make a decision according to the answers I can give; and it may be other than what I really think is the best. This is not to say that what I really think to be the best is not rational. It may well be rational (though of course it may not be): I may have weighed the arguments and have reasoned with myself to the best of my ability, and find myself inclined, by reason, one way, but be unable to state all my reasons, to articulate all the arguments. It is one thing to think, another to be able to formulate one's thoughts in words. The latter is a valuable skill, possessed by judges, civil servants, novelists, and dons; but although connected with the ability to reason through to the right conclusion, is not the same as it. Many people can think but cannot express their thoughts at all well: and, on the other hand, there are some people—including some academics—whose judgement is invariably faulty, but who can formulate their fallacies in the most felicitous phrases. The word 'reason' includes judgements which are felt as well as those which are formulated: Pascal's *ésprit de finesse* as well as his *ésprit de géometrie*. The word 'reasons' naturally applies only to the latter. It often so happens that a man is acting in accordance with reason, but is unable to state in words what his reasons are.[1] If that man is strictly accountable for his actions, with little or no discretion or latitude allowed him, he will have to decide not in accordance with reason but in accordance with such reasons as he finds himself able to formulate. This is, of course, a safeguard against errors, and especially gross errors, of judgement, but it is often also a barrier against his following reason all the way; particularly so when it comes to assessing persons. The reasons we can give why we trust or distrust a certain man often seem unconvincing when put down in black and white: yet it is not the reasons given, but the actual results, which are important. The banker may be able to justify his having made advances to one man rather than to another, but if in the event the first is unable to repay while the latter proves himself a reliable client, the banker may be able to exculpate himself, but cannot recover the money. Similarly in selecting a man for an academic post, similarly in innumerable other transactions, the arguments that can be adduced in incontrovertible form are far less important than assessments of personality. But assessments of personality not only are perilously subject to prejudice and bias, but merge into that very "favour" that officials are sworn to eschew. The banker is right to trust his boyhood friend; in innumerable different situations he has observed him and discovered him to be trustworthy and competent: but if the bank manager gives overdrafts to his friends in preference to others, it surely will smack of favouritism and "the old boy net". A scholar is right to back his pupil for an appointment. He has had opportunity to note his fertility of mind, his intellectual integrity, his industry. He knows that he will put his time and talents to proper use. But

[1] For further discussion see J. R. Lucas, 'The Philosophy of The Reasonable Man', *The Philosophical Quarterly*, 1963, pp. 97–106. See also above § 7.

academic appointments should be made, we feel, on an impartial assessment of merit, not on a basis of personal contacts and likes and dislikes. The favour of a partly rational being, although suspect, is not wholly bad, and is often the best indication we have of merit. If we allow decisions to be made on personal grounds, they will be suspect: if we take care to exclude all suspicion of favour, we often will have deprived ourselves of the only useful guidance we could have had. The goddess of Justice, we recall, weighs the scales with her eyes blindfolded. This, we have seen, can be taken in different ways. But however it is taken, and whatever the arguments for having Justice blindfolded, it clearly makes for inefficiency to have all decisions made without benefit of sight.

We have finally the fact that we do not want to live all our lives as officials. Some people like to be "on their own" all the time: and even if we regard this as a regrettable desire, characteristic of Kulaks or Middle Western Republican businessmen, fairly strong arguments would need to be found before we were justified in denying to these people the right to live non-official lives. And even men who find fulfilment in officialdom, even the most dedicated civil servants, like to have some private life as well. Nor is this merely a liking that men happen to have, like our liking for strawberries. It is part of our respect for human beings as such, that we are prepared to accept the simple fact that a human being wants something to be the case as a good reason for its being so. We cannot of course let everybody have his own way about everything: but if we refuse ever to allow a personal predilection any weight, unless it is backed by an impersonal rational argument, we are not allowing anything to personality as such. It may be rational, but it is less than human. I show my rationality in subjecting my own will to the sway of reason: I show my humanity in subjecting my own will to the will of another whom I love, or respect, or pity, even though it is *un*reasonable. The humility of humanity is greater than that of rationality; more essential to the happy life, more easily overlooked by political theorists. Human beings often are awkward, often do want silly things, often ought to want things which they do not. It is tempting to disregard their unreasonable wants when thinking about what laws to lay down for them: but to disregard what they actually want is to be no longer laying down laws *for them*, but to be seeking, in a roundabout way, to impose our own wills on them: an ancient temptation and a natural one, but not a laudable one; and one that is open to a devastating *tu quoque* from the would-be wilful subject.

Personality, as we have already seen, is too complex to be conformed to the canons of rationality. Faced with the infinite complexity of personality, we cannot expect always to comprehend it, but must simply accept it. We must let other people be themselves: we must have courage ourselves to be ourselves. By this I do not mean that we should never make reasonable demands of other people or of ourselves, and that if a person claims to find self-fulfilment in murdering his friends, we ought to let him do so. I mean, rather, that even when all the rational demands we can formulate have been met, there remains something more. We may reasonably demand of a writer that he should observe all the rules of grammar and syntax: but his style is something more than his observance of all these rules. So in a man's life, there are many rules he ought to observe, and many further particular points where the right answer is reasonably clear: but there is much more in his life than all this, which is not determined simply by conformity to rules or to reason, but which bears the imprint of, or even, according to some authorities, constitutes, his personality. This we value; not only as a concession to human weakness—though often it is chiefly this—but also as being the highest and best and most valuable we can aspire to. And therefore, both as an exercise in human humility, and as a consequence of a proper pride in humanity, we want to give human personality full rein, and room in which to develop. And therefore the good community is not an official community, but a free one, in which 'I want to' is always a good, often a sufficient, although never a conclusive, reason for allowing a man to act in the way which he desires.[1]

SECTION 39

FREEDOM AND PATTERNS OF LIFE

WE HAVE now given a formal account of legal Freedom or Liberty. We have shown that it concerns two parties, and that in any normal and complete legal system, liberty for one party needs to be supplemented by some duty on the other party not to interfere by force. Liberty for the one involves restriction for the other, so that there can be no simple solution to the problem of liberty, but, rather, every

[1] See further below, § 76, pp. 351ff.

solution must be a balance both between freedoms and restrictions, and between liberties and securities.

In the formal, legal, sense of freedom, every freedom is correlative with an unfreedom: there is no question of one system offering more freedom than another, but only of its allocating freedoms better. England is a free country because the police are *less*, not more, free than they are abroad; because other people are less, not more, free to strike me, to enter my house uninvited, to have their views unquestioned by me, to have their wares not undersold by mine. That is, we attach more importance to being able to do some things than others; to being able to go where we will in public than to freedom from crowds, and to being able to enjoy privacy at home than to being able to gratify our curiosity about our neighbours' doings.

Our notion of freedom, therefore, is tied to an idea of human nature, of what men want to do, of what they should want to do. We are often faced with conflicting wants, and have to adjudicate between them, giving one sort of freedom rather than another. Women very often want to choose for themselves to whom they shall give themselves in marriage: parents very often want to ensure that their daughters are married wisely and well. In giving the final say to the bride, provided she is over twenty-one, rather than to the bride's parents, we are spelling out one particular view of human nature rather than another. In this case it might seem obvious to a modern man which way the decision ought to go: but in other cases the decision will go the other way; the right of a man to go whithersoever he will is overridden by the right of a man to privacy in his own house. If I want to go into your house and you do not want me to go into it, it is your want, that I should not do something, rather than my want, that I should do it, which is preferred. Even with marriage, although English law preserves the freedom of the bride, at whatever cost in anguish to her parents or to other suitors, to marry whomsoever she wants, it does not guard so jealously the right of remarriage. The children of a first marriage and the relatives of the dead husband are thought to have more legitimate grounds for objecting to a widow's remarriage than the parents of an adult woman, although not conclusive ones. In this again we are spelling out a certain concept of marriage, and the commitments and loyalties involved.

A more difficult case is that of noise. For many people, particularly the young, freedom is taken to be freedom to make whatever noise one likes: for many others, particularly the elderly, freedom is freedom to be able to hear oneself think. It would be tempting to assign to each individual a sphere in which he could be as noisy as he liked provided no noise penetrated into the spheres of those who wanted to be quiet. But such a division into spheres of influence, however tempting, is completely impracticable. Men do not live in spheres. Men are perpetually interacting with one another. They cannot help but do so, nor would they wish it otherwise. Therefore we cannot solve the problem of noise by insulating men from one another in cells. Rather, we consider what is reasonable for a man to do and to expect others to do. It is reasonable for a man to talk; for children to laugh and shout as they come out of school; for fire engines and ambulances to use alarm bells and sirens; for everybody to sleep at night. It is not reasonable to use a loudspeaker out of doors, except in special circumstances; or to use a pneumatic drill as a musical instrument; or to "rev" a motor-bike continuously; or to make any loud and prolonged noise at night. Instead of assigning spheres, we consider patterns of life: life lived by people who are not deaf, who want to sleep at nights, who want to be able to converse with one another by day; but who sometimes call to their children with a shout, often walk along the streets, sometimes come roistering home late at night, let off fireworks on the Fifth of November, and are summoned to church by the sound of bells. Since the Industrial Revolution, which has made many of the activities in which men may reasonably engage much more noisy than before, and much more noisy than other men may reasonably be expected to bear, the conflict of interests has become much more difficult to adjudicate. The freedom of one man in a railway carriage to hear his favourite wireless programme on his transistor set is irreconcilably opposed to the freedom of another to talk to his neighbour or to read his paper in peace. Men do want to travel fast and use jet aircraft to do so; and these are reasonable wants: but so too are the desires of other men living in houses near aerodromes not to have their sleep disturbed or their nerves frayed by continual ear-piercing roars. We cannot claim that Freedom requires us to decide one way rather than the other. A State in which nobody was able to use jet-aircraft would not be naturally described as more or less free than one in which some were unable to sleep. The issue is not one of Freedom, but of different wants and interests, both reasonable but not both compatible; and the way in which a State resolves such a conflict shows not how great is its love of liberty, but which wants it cherishes most, and which pattern of life it regards as pre-eminently its own.

The pattern of life that a society cherishes changes over the years. It changes partly as a result of a reassessment of the general scale of values, partly under the impact of new scientific and technical discoveries. The ideal of romantic love rates much higher in the modern world than it did in ancient times, and is now set above the ideal of stable family life. The germ theory of disease gives strong grounds for curtailing the liberty of a man suffering from a dangerous infection. Even within the confines of his own home, a man no longer is entitled to do what he likes, if this involves interfering with his neighbours' television. Modern man is free to do many things his ancestors could not do; but is subject to restrictions they never dreamed of.

SECTION 40

THE SUBSTANTIAL CONCEPT OF LIBERTY

THUS far it might seem that Freedom was a purely formal concept. Every politico-legal system has its liberties and obligations, its privileges and restrictions, its rights and duties; and if we increase freedom at one place we necessarily diminish it at others. But although this is true, we nevertheless regard some systems as more free than others: some formal freedoms are more important than others. And although in marginal cases, the ideal pattern of life in a society will determine which freedom is more important, it is not simply a conflict between different patterns of life; for among different patterns of life we can pick out some that are more concerned with freedom than others. The purely formal characterisation of freedom is not enough: nor is it sufficient merely to refer to patterns of life, important though these are in giving content to our idea of freedom. We must therefore give content to our idea of Freedom first by contrasting with it certain other political ideals we may have, and secondly by analysing more closely the connexion between freedom and action in a pattern of life.

A free society can be contrasted with an orderly one, a just one, an equal one, an efficient one, a united one, a rigid one, a secure one. These ideals cannot all be achieved at once, and we inevitably have to compromise. The extent to which we sacrifice other ideals to that of Freedom indicates how far our society is a free one. Thus in the administration of justice, we sacrifice Effectiveness to Freedom in insisting that a suspect must be cautioned on arrest and brought before a magistrate within twenty-four hours; or, in civil cases, in requiring writs to be served personally, and in taking no effective steps to prevent defaulting debtors from "disappearing". More generally, we hamper the efficiency of the government by securing individuals against arbitrary arrest or dispossession of their property. This can be viewed as a sacrifice of Efficiency to Freedom, though it can also be viewed as a sacrifice of Efficiency to Legality.

Similarly for the sake of Freedom, we sacrifice fairness, as when we allow a man to cut his children out of his will and leave his property to his secretary; or Justice, as when we allow a guilty man to escape on a technical point of law; or Equality, as when we allow a man to make himself rich without sharing his riches round the rest of his fellow men; or Uniformity, as when we allow Roman Catholics to stay away from services in church; or Security, as when we allow women to buy what hats they please, and thereby expose milliners to the risk of penury if fashion goes against them. On each of these issues we could have drawn the line between what is and what is not permitted differently. A free society is one where in order to have men acting according to their own wishes, we are prepared to forgo other political ideals. But it is always a compromise: it is always a matter of more or less. Absolute Freedom, like Absolute Justice, Absolute Equality, Absolute Uniformity, is an ideal impossible of attainment.

In deciding between my wanting to do X and your wanting me not to do X, a large number of considerations may be adduced. We intuitively equate freedom with my being able to do X; but as we have seen, in any complete system, to give one man freedom to do X involves denying other men freedom to stop him from doing X. We therefore cannot simply equate freedom with an absence of legal restriction. Nevertheless our intuitive sense is a good guide: the distinction ordinary language makes between doing X and stopping another man from doing X, although difficult to formulate, is often easy to apply. And then a love of Freedom will incline us to safeguard a man's right to do X rather than another man's right to stop him doing X. More precisely, if a man's action can correctly and naturally be described by an intransitive verb, then in a free system, he will be entitled to do that action, and other men will not be entitled to stop him, unless there are good reasons otherwise. That is, the onus, in a free system, is on those who would stop a man from doing something, to show why he should not be allowed to, rather than on him to show why he should be allowed to. Moreover, in a free society, a strong case has to be established before we will say that a man ought not to be allowed to do the action in question.

The difficulty is to give the correct description of a particular action on a particular occasion. Our concept of action is elusive, and depends as much on what the agent would have done if circumstances had been different as on the bodily movements that actually occurred. Many legal disputes are about the correct descriptions of particular actions, and call into consideration the context of action and the standards of behaviour current in society. I shall not enter into these disputes, but shall consider only those cases in which there is accepted a description of the action in terms of an intransitive verb, or a transitive one which does not have a person as its direct or indirect object; descriptions such as 'I was walking', but not such as 'I was hitting him' or 'I was throwing a stone at him'. For such an action there is in a free society a *prima facie* case for the agent's being entitled to do it: but this *prima facie* case can sometimes be defeated, and we have to discuss what considerations will defeat it.

SECTION 41

LIBERTY AND HARM

THE intuitively most obvious reason why a person should not be allowed to do a certain action is that the action would cause or would constitute a harm to some other person; since we are considering actions described in a somewhat minimal way, it will be the consequences of the action thus described, rather than the action itself, that will be harmful.

To be harmful, a thing must be something that most people do not want, and which we think that they are right not to want. It is part of our common set of values, which we are prepared to affirm, irrespective of what any particular person wants or claims to want. The paradigm cases are death, bodily injury, and imprisonment. Most people not merely want to avoid these evils, but are convinced that they are evil, and will not be persuaded otherwise. No matter how much a man protests that so far as he is concerned he does not mind whether he is killed, mutilated, or incarcerated, we do not take him seriously, and we continue to regard it as harming him if he is killed, mutilated or put in prison. There are good reasons for regarding death, injury, and imprisonment as *entrenched* evils, evils entrenched in our whole conceptual structure.[1] Indeed, unless there were some things commonly regarded as harms, there would, as we have seen, be no basis for any community at all. A number of men whose sets of values had nothing in common, could have no common passions, no common sympathies, no common life. Each would indeed be an island.

There must be some concept of harm, and some things regarded as harmful if there is to be any community at all. Men being constituted as they are, they invariably regard death, injury, and imprisonment as harmful, but not only these. A man is harmed by being exposed to infection, by having his reputation blackened, by being sacked from his job, by being kept in ignorance, perhaps even by being corrupted morally or spiritually. What is regarded as harmful depends upon the common values of the community and the ideal patterns of life cherished by it: to interfere with the neighbours' television was not to cause harm in the Middle Ages; nor is it in twentieth-century Britain to cast a spell. The concept of harm is thus an elusive one, although the paradigm cases are clear. It is therefore a dangerous one for the political philosopher to use. The paradigm cases give it a spurious air of certainty and definiteness, while the extended ones are in fact uncertain and indefinite. When Mill asserted his "one very simple principle", that "the only purpose for which power can be rightfully exercised over any member of a civilised community, against his will, is to prevent harm to others"[2] he assumed that harm had a definite and limited sense, and that he was arguing for the limited Minimum State of Locke and the English Whigs.[3] But almost at once he has to extend the sense of harm, if his principle is to be even remotely plausible, to cover cases of *failing to* give evidence in a court of justice, *failing to* bear one's fair share in the common defence, failing to save a fellow creature's life, and failing to protect the defenceless against ill-usage— "things" Mill says "which whenever it is obviously a man's duty to do, he may rightfully be made responsible to society for not doing".[4]

---

[1] See § 1, pp. 1–4; and § 15, pp. 58–60; see also P. R. Foot, 'Moral Beliefs' *Proceedings of the Aristotelian Society*, LIX, 1958–9 pp. 83–104, esp. pp. 89–91.

[2] J. S. Mill, *Essay on Liberty*, p. 73 (Everyman edition). Compare a similar formulation in terms of the word 'hurt' in the *Model Penal Code*, of the American Law Institute, tentative draft No. 4, p. 277: "the protection to which every individual is entitled against State interference in his personal affairs when he is not hurting others", quoted by H. L. A. Hart, *The Morality of the Criminal Law*, O.U.P., 1965, p. 36.

[3] See further below, § 67 pp. 287ff.   [4] p. 74.

But this definition of harm in terms of obvious duties (or, equivalently, of obvious rights) is a very wide definition, and depends, at least in respect of what duties are obvious, on the culture and the values of the society in question. The whole of Mill's *Essay on Liberty* is vitiated by the ambiguity in his use of the word 'harm'. Nor is this merely a weakness in argumentation. It makes his simple principle at once too narrow and too wide. On the one hand, the libertarian State, according to Mill's prescription, is precluded from doing many things that many lovers of Freedom may reasonably want their States to do: on the other hand it gives too little a safeguard to the individual for the exercise of liberty. For even if we do not extend the sense of harm unreasonably, there remains a large number of courses of action which we normally expect a free man to be entitled to take, which nevertheless cause some harm to some other person. If I compete successfully for a scholarship or a prize, I am in all probability doing somebody else out of it: if I buy my groceries from one shop rather than from its rival, I am depriving its rival of the profits it would otherwise have made: if I tell the truth about a blackguardly politician, I may wreck his political career. Yet in none of these cases do we regard the undoubted harm that a man's actions will cause another as a sufficient argument for restricting his freedom. More generally, we may observe that almost all of a man's actions that are significant are going to affect other men, and usually some for the worse. If men then are to have any significant freedom of action, it cannot be defined in terms of not causing harm to others; else the principle of Freedom will have contracted into the principle *de minimis non curat lex*.

The concept of harm is at once too narrow, too wide, and altogether too vague to provide a criterion for freedom: rather, it describes *an argument, a* reason for restricting freedom, though not a conclusive one. If we start with the question, 'Why should he not be allowed to do it?' the answer, 'Because he will thereby harm somebody else' is an answer; only, it is possible to accept the fact alleged, of his action being harmful to another, and nevertheless continue to maintain that he still ought to be allowed to act, the harmful consequences to another notwithstanding. The general reason for this is that we regard men as *agents*, active beings, rather than as *patients*, sentient suffering beings; and therefore regard freedom of action as a greater good than security against suffering; as indeed is witnessed by our paradigm cases of harms—death, injury, and imprisonment—which are pre-eminent evils only if it is pre-eminently good to be able to act. We have a non-anaesthetic, non-analgesic view of life. Life is vivid, vivacious, full of vitality; a doing, not an anodyne. And therefore in general we do not regard it as a sufficient reason for stopping a man from doing something that he will harm someone else by doing it. The balance still tips in favour of Freedom. We will not purchase security for ourselves at the cost of being slaves to other people's sensibilities.

We therefore reject Mill's "very simple principle". If we take 'harm' in a limited, definite sense, there are other reasons for restricting liberty besides harm: Public Interest for example, Equity, the maintenance of public standards, perhaps the maintenance of morality. Although it might be contended that each of these could be considered as being really founded on the need to secure some person or persons against some sort of harm, it makes for clarity of argument if we separate these arguments from those where a definite harm is being done to a definite person. We therefore say that the prevention of harm to others is not the only purpose for which power can be rightfully exercised. We also say that the prevention of harm to others is often not an adequate justification for exercising power against a member of a civilised community. In all cases, except the paradigm cases—death, injury, imprisonment (together with physical pain, which is analogous to, though less permanent than, physical injury)—the argument from harm is not conclusive: it gives *a* reason, but the argument can continue, and the prevention of harm may, on balance, be deemed an inadequate reason for imposing a certain restriction. This is not to say that we never decide to restrict men's freedom in order to ensure their fellows' security against harms other than the paradigm ones, but only that the argument is complicated, and many considerations are involved.

SECTION 42

RESTRICTIONS ON FREEDOM

THE prevention of harm to others, although the most obvious, is not the only reason for restricting Freedom. We also restrict Freedom, and sometimes rightly, on grounds of general public utility, on grounds of Equity, for the purpose of establishing conventions of meaning, in order to extend men's control of their social environment, in the course of collective activities, and for the realisation of corporate moralities.

Let us consider first a case that falls under all these heads, and is central to the possibility of there being a community governed by law. As we have already seen,[1] it is essential that the decision procedure of a community should be recognisable. A community is a body which can reach a common mind about what shall happen, which is able to decide between the different views held by its different members. Since men's judgement is fallible, they will not always reach a common mind in the sense that each and every member of the community agrees to a course of action. It is therefore necessary to have a decision *procedure*, so that everybody can agree how a decision is to be reached, even though he may not agree with the decision. It is necessary then to secure the procedure against any possibility of there being disagreement about whether it is the procedure or not: that is, everybody must be able to recognise the agreed decision procedure *as* the agreed decision procedure. And therefore in every society which is not so small that every man can recognise a judge by personally identifying him, the decision procedure must be made recognisable to members of the public by some *conventional* symbol of authority: in Hobbes' words:[2] "Nor is it enough the law be written, and published; but also that there be manifest signs that it proceedeth from the will of the sovereign. For private men, when they have, or think they have force enough to secure their unjust designs, and convoy them safely to their ambitious ends, may publish for laws what they please, without, or against the legislative authority. There is therefore requisite, not only a declaration of the law, but also sufficient signs of the author and the authority."

These sufficient signs are necessarily conventional. They identify for us that process of law which we all agree to be *the* method of settling disputes. They therefore can be counterfeited: and if the conventions are to be preserved, men must not be free to use these conventional symbols just as they please, but must be forbidden from so doing under penalty of law. In England it is an offence under Section 10 of the Police Act, 1919, to wear uniforms resembling those of a police force, and in 1964 Security Organisation Ltd. was convicted under this act for having had three of its employees wearing dress with the appearance of the Wolverhampton police force uniform. There was no question of the security guards doing harm to anyone by wearing police uniform. The Magistrate said, "I do not think there is anything

---

[1] See above § 4, pp. 14–16.
[2] *Leviathan*, Pt. 2, Ch. 26, ed. Michael Oakeshott, p. 178.

sinister about this whole matter in any way at all"; but nevertheless imposed a fine of £15 with 10 guineas costs.

The Magistrate's decision was right. It can be defended on many grounds; but not that of preventing harm to anyone. Any supporter of Mill's "one, very simple principle" should consider the case of *R. v. Security Organisation Ltd.*, and whether we are obliged, in the name of freedom, to permit men to wear police uniform, fly the Royal Standard, or to print documents purporting to be issued "By Authority". Prohibitions of this type are entrenched in the fabric of society. They are essential if the community is to continue to exist; but not because otherwise any definite individual would suffer any definite harm.

Considerations of Public Interest can be adduced not only to determine the balance between freedom and harm, but by itself to justify the restriction of freedom. The laws of copyright, for example, restrict men's freedom of speech and of writing and of musical performance, because by doing so we enable authors and composers to obtain financial advantage from their labours, and this in turn encourages them to devote their energies to these rather than to other occupations. This, the most usual justification for copyright, is a pure utilitarian one: we may, in addition, feel, on grounds of Natural Justice, that it is only fair that authors and composers should be given some right of property in the fruits of their labours. But in neither of these cases can it be plausibly maintained that copyright laws protect people from harm that would otherwise be inflicted on them. The laws of copyright are not created to protect an antecedent good, but protect it in order to create it. And it is only against the background of these laws that we can conceive of authors' and composers' interests either existing or being harmed.

Many restrictions on Freedom are devised in order to extend men's control of their social and legal environment. The fact that I am not free to break my contracts is what makes contracts contracts: if contracts did not bind me, I should not be free to enter into binding contracts. It is conceptually impossible to be free both to make and to break promises. And similarly, I cannot be free to dispose of my property unless I can cease to be free to use it as I will; and if men and women are to be free to divorce each other by mutual consent, then they are not free to enter into lifelong binding commitments to each other.

This consequence of Freedom loses its air of paradox if we consider the parallel in the natural world, which we are able to control only by virtue of causal laws which can themselves be formulated in terms of impossibility. I am able to switch the light on only because it is impossible, granted certain conditions, for the switch to be down and the bulb not to give out light. I can lever a stone out of the soil by reason of the impossibility of the one end of the lever going down without the other going up. If there were no natural impossibilities, there would be no natural necessities (for this is but a verbal difference—'it is necessary that p', means the same as 'it is impossible that not p'), and if there were no natural necessities there would be no causes and effects, and therefore no way of effecting anything at all. In practice we can put our wishes into effect because we can play upon natural impossibilities so as to rule out the non-occurrence of that which we desire. And just as we are able to control natural phenomena by reason of natural impossibilities and natural necessities, so we want to be able to control human affairs by means of impossibilities and necessities humanly imposed. From one point of view they are restrictions: from another they provide the fulcrum whereby we obtain purchase on the course of events.

We sometimes restrict Freedom in the name of Equality, in order to secure equal treatment for everybody. If, for example, I engage in trade, I may be required not to refuse any customer who tenders the purchase price of goods I have in stock. The railways, in Britain, are common carriers: they must carry every consignment, in proper condition and properly paid for, that is presented to them for carriage. An innkeeper cannot turn away a traveller, unless he is dirty or drunk or disorderly. We may go further, and require that the same price be charged to every man for the same article or same service. Nobody is obliged to engage in trade: but if he chooses to do so, he is not free to pick and choose his customers, but must treat all comers equally.

These requirements of Equality could be justified on other grounds. Often we can demand Equality on the ground that otherwise any person discriminated against suffers harm: if the baker refuses to supply me alone with bread, I may not be able to find any alternative source of supply, because there will not be enough demand, in view of his readiness to supply everybody else except me. We can also argue that the general utility of knowing that one will not be discriminated against outweighs the slight loss of freedom required: if one could not be reasonably confident that on arrival in a strange town one could find a place to spend the night, travel would become a much more risky and tedious business: a French housewife who haggles in the market may sometimes secure a better bargain than her English counterpart who sees the goods priced and must either take them or leave them; but the Englishwoman is saved much wear and tear, and if she sometimes does not get the best of the bargain, she never gets the worst of it, nor ever need fear that she has been diddled.

Nevertheless the demand for this sort of Equality is not based merely on the fact that it secures some people against some harm and secures to all some advantages. It is, rather, an assimilation of public acts to official acts, and subject to the same requirement of Equality before the Law.[1] The rationale of the assimilation is given by the part played by *money* in the transaction. Money is a *conventional* token of value.[2] The State, in issuing coins, provides us with units, qualitatively identical and numerically distinct, and in suppressing forgery it guarantees the value of the coinage. A trader in accepting coins, relies heavily on this facility provided by the State, and can fairly be required in return that just as he can be sure that one coin is as good as another, so he shall regard one man's money as being as good as another's; and just as he can rely on the value of the money he accepts, others shall be entitled to rely on the acceptability of the money they offer. Money would be of no value to the trader if he had no safeguard against forgery: money would be of no value to the customer if he could not be sure that he could use it to buy goods. Hence, where all that one party to a commercial transaction does is to receive money, he is under an obligation to accept money tendered without discriminating between the people offering money; but only where one side to the transaction is purely monetary, on a cash basis. A trader is not obliged to offer credit to customers equally readily or on equal terms; nor is he obliged to treat all comers equally, if their side of the bargain is not to be discharged in purely monetary terms. A school can properly refuse a pupil, who offers good money, if they think he will be unruly, or un-teachable: a landlord may choose as tenant the man who will take the greatest care of his property: a customer may buy in one shop rather than another, because he likes its wares better. And we can go further than this: the grounds of discrimination need not be relevant ones. A school (unless it is a State-school, under a special duty of non-discrimination) can choose pupils not because of their teachability,

---

[1] See below, §§ 58, 59, pp. 253ff.
[2] Aristotle *Nicomachean Ethics*, Bk. V, 1133a29. Compare *Politics*, Bk. I, 257a39, b10.

but because of their great-uncle's connexion with the school: a land-lord may choose for his tenant not the best farmer, but the most enthu-siastic hunter of foxes: and the customer may buy his wares not at the shop which gives best value for money, but at the one whose manager is a friend. This is Freedom. The rule against discrimination is (for private individuals, not for public authorities) limited in scope; and outside its limits the man who is doing the discriminating is often the sole judge of the relevance of his reasons for discriminating.[1] Only where, thanks to the qualitative identity of monetary tokens, we can reasonably lay down a rigid rule that everybody's money is to be equally acceptable, do we do so. It seems fair to exact this condition when from the nature of the transaction, all that the trader is interested in is the customer's money. But in all other cases, where one man is dealing with others not purely and simply as bearers of coins but as individuals who will perform different duties with different degrees of reliability and competence, he is reasonably entitled to make some discriminations between them; and therefore by us, who love liberty, he is in fact allowed to make almost any discrimination.

SECTION 43

ALTERNATIVES AND HOMES

THE prevention of harm to others, although not the only, is the most important reason for restricting Freedom. Not only is a certain measure of security a *sine qua non* of all human activities, but in balancing the liberty of one man to do X against another man's security that X should not be done, the two facets of Freedom are in direct and inevitable conflict. Freedom here is opposed not to any other political ideal, but to itself.

There is no simple formula for striking the balance between one man's liberty and another's security. It is, rather, a matter of weighing arguments. There are arguments, nearly always, in favour of liberty: there are arguments, nearly always, in favour of security. And in each actual controversy there will be counter-arguments against the main arguments, and further arguments in turn against these. It is im-impossible to lay down rules for conducting, or for settling, such arguments. One very general consideration, however, is nearly always

[1] See more fully below, § 59, pp. 257–8.

applicable, and of great value. It is the consideration of *alternatives*. On the side of liberty, we consider

(i) what other means are available to the agent for bringing about the same desired result,

(ii) what other state of affairs would constitute the same action of the agent, and

(iii) what other actions would be almost as satisfactory to a reasonable man as the action objected to.

Similarly, on the side of security, we consider how the harm feared may be

(i) avoided,

(ii) compensated for, and

(iii) guarded against, and at what price.

We have little compunction in forbidding a man from doing one thing, if there are other things he could do equally well. Nor do we take steps to secure to a man immunity from a harm he could easily avoid. Thus the whole argument between freedom and harm is conducted not simply in the indicative mood, the actions actually done and the harms endured, but in the subjunctive mood, actions that a man could have done, might have done or should have done, and the harms that need not have been endured, could have been made up for, or should have been foreseen. It is an argument of counterfactual hypotheticals rather than of categorical assertions. This is why the argument is indeterminate, and lacks any sort of decision procedure; and it is because we are considering the alternatives open to a *reasonable* man, that our conclusions depend on our view of man, and the ideal pattern of life.

We are, in general, able to resolve the conflict between liberty and security by adducing alternatives, because we have a standard device for providing each man with alternatives, differing only inessentially, in its position in time and space, from the alternative objected to. This is the *home*, in which a man is both free himself to act and secure from other men's unwelcome attentions. Because men have separate homes, we can in general provide a modicum both of freedom and security. Often, what I am not allowed to do in public—e.g. walking about naked—I am allowed to do in the privacy of my own home: and, far more often, if I want immunity from other men's action, I can obtain it by withdrawing into the security of my own home. Homes are, almost literally, spheres of influence. Although, as we have seen, all the problems of human conduct cannot be solved by simply dividing up the world into spheres of influence—in part, because men want to interact with one another, and not to be altogether isolated—, yet the idea is a natural one, and by assigning men their private spheres, we do ease, even if we do not abolish, conflicts between one man's freedom and another man's security, by providing the one or the other with an acceptable alternative.

The division of the world into spheres of influence does not provide a complete solution to the problem of human conflict. It fails, obviously, where actions performed at home harm other people outside the home —television interference for example. It does not apply to all those activities which are not confined to the home. It cannot apply in serious criminal cases, nor in many other cases if the law is to be in the least effective. An Englishman's home is his castle, but not if he murders people there, nor if he runs an illicit still, nor if he harbours fugitives from justice. Nor again will an Englishman's house count as his home if he uses it for the purpose of trade; then it will only be his shop, and as such much more liable to regulation: for then he is acting not towards certain particular persons but towards members of the public in general; and in so far as he uses money—a facility provided by the State—the State, as we have seen,[1] has a further interest in his actions. It is in part the nature of our activities as well as the *locale* that determines whether they are purely private or a matter of public concern; and, especially, the exact description of the other persons concerned, whether they are to be regarded as simply certain specified individuals, what logicians call a "closed" class, or whether they are to be regarded, rather, as falling under a more general description, a chance selection from what logicians call an "open" class.[2] In the latter case, the interests and sensibilities of the general public, the common good, and common ideas about the texture of life, afford reasons for restricting freedom, which do not apply to private actions performed in private; or better, we should take the public as the standard case, from which we except private cases, where we can, through the devices of the home and private property, in order to enable them to have alternatives, both of actions and of safeguards, which cannot be made available to them generally in public.

That the private case is the exception from the public one, rather than *vice versa*, can be seen if we consider that we are often prepared not only to allow in private actions which if done in public would be

---

[1] See § 42, pp. 179-80.   [2] See above, § 29, p. 134, n1.

forbidden, but to allow, where no financial advantage is obtained, actions which would be forbidden if done for money. Our treatment of blackmail affords a clear case. If I discover something disreputable about another man, and disclose it, out of a sense of public duty, or from pure, disinterested ill-will, I commit no offence; an offence is committed only if I try to make money, by threatening to disclose his secret unless he pays me money. There are good reasons why blackmail, and many other profitable activities, should be forbidden: but often what is rightly forbidden if done for profit, may be permitted if done only for fun, and Freedom is thereby enlarged, since the man who really wants to undertake the activity in question, may do so, if he is willing to forgo the profit he might have made. The law allows me to live with a prostitute and be her protector, so long as I live with her purely for love, and not for money.

SECTION 44

PROPERTY

THE institution of private property is analogous to that of the private home, only instead of assigning to each individual a sphere of influence all of his own, it assigns each "good" to some individual or corporate body. Private property is a legal privilege of using and disposing of some good, together with a security (a Hohfeldian right)[1] against other people using or disposing of it. If I own something I am at liberty to use it, and other people have a duty not to use it without my permission: and I have a Hohfeldian power of disposing of some or all of my privileges, that is to say, of authorising other people to use and dispose, and of renouncing my own privileges and powers.

We naturally think of property as land or material objects to which a certain person or body stands in the relation of *ownership*. But this is wrong. For, first, property need not be constituted by land or material objects. The copyright of a certain book, play, or tune is property without being either. We may feel that this is an artificial example, as indeed it is. We have seen[2] that copyright is created by laws forbidding copying without permission. With land or material objects the privative sense of privilege is naturally given—if I am to be free to

---
[1] See above, § 36, pp. 156–7.　　　[2] § 42, p. 177.

use it as I will, you cannot be: with books, plays and tunes, being *universals* rather than *particulars*, there is no natural privation—my singing a tune does not in the least prevent your singing it too—and so we need special laws to enable universals to be owned in the way that particulars can. Thus, while there is a natural tendency for property to consist either of areas of the public world which agents inhabit in common or of material objects in the public world, it need not.

Once we see that property does not consist necessarily of places and things, it becomes easier to see also that ownership is not a simple relation of attachment but a complicated bundle of rights,[1] and privileges. And once we have seen this, we can see further that the different privileges, rights, and powers need not always go together. The mediaeval Church taught that landowners were entitled only to the usufruct of their land, but ought not to sell the land itself. We go further, and restrict the privilege of the owner of land to certain sorts of use only—e.g, agricultural use. Or again, in the Church of England, the parson has a freehold in his benefice, which secures to him the use of the revenues, but does not entitle him to transfer the benefice to another, but only to resign it: while the patron has the advowson, which entitles him to appoint a new parson on the death or resignation of the old one, but cannot touch the revenues. Thus, quite apart from any modern developments, the concept of property is not nearly as sacrosanct as some philosophers have made out. Locke and the Americans over-emphasised the importance of property, partly because of Locke's nominalism, partly because in the yeoman economy the ownership of land secured to a man who was willing to work a livelihood that was independent of all other men. Security of property came next only to that of life and liberty, and was an effective guarantee of Constitutional Freedom. With the change in the economy from a static agricultural one to a dynamic one, the pre-eminent importance of property has been eroded. The tenure of jobs is often felt to be as important as the freehold of land. This is not to say that property is not important: but the case has to be re-examined and re-argued.

The chief argument for property is that it is a form of Freedom. The institution of private property can help resolve the conflict between one man's liberty and another's, in the same way as the institution of private homes. For it is true of most goods that there are other goods which are fairly similar, and so one man's having exclusive rights over

---

[1] In Hohfeld's sense. See note on p. 157.

one piece of property leaves it open for another man to have equally exclusive rights over a comparable piece, affording him reasonably acceptable alternative courses of action and enjoyment. I am free to drive in my car to Penzance, and you in yours to Inverness. It is reasonable to curtail your freedom to drive in my car to a place of your choosing, because it is in general possible for you to acquire a car of your own. And in this way, private property, like the private home, enables men to have some acceptable alternative action open to them, and some acceptable alternative for avoiding the effects of other men's action.

This argument works where we have a number of articles, more or less similar, so that each man may have one, in much the same way as each has a home. Where it is in principle impossible for there to be a second piece of property more or less resembling the first, e.g. with patents for productive processes, we have some hesitation in applying our ordinary laws of property. For the most part, however, the concept of ownership is so widely and well understood, and the institution of property has so many other advantages besides the one adduced here, that we tend to apply the laws of property wherever possible, even at the cost of some awkwardness. In particular, there are strong arguments from Freedom and from Public Interest for the institution of private property.

Property is a freedom—a legal privilege—in using and disposing. Although some times it is good to make men accountable for what they do—how they use and how they dispose—it is neither feasible nor desirable to make men always accountable. The general arguments for Freedom carry over to property. What agents inhabiting a common world are most likely to quarrel about is either the occupation of a certain area or volume of their common world or the handling of some movable object in it. Therefore it is natural to define disputes or potential disputes with reference to particular areas, volumes, or movable objects, and to confer authority to decide what shall happen in these areas or volumes, or to these movable objects, to some person or persons or body of persons. And although this authority can be conferred in the form of an office, so that those who hold the authority are accountable for its exercise, there are arguments, as we have seen,[1] for not doing this as a general rule. And hence there is a general argument in favour of private property.

[1] § 38.

Such a general argument does not show that the rights of private property are absolute, or ought to be unfettered, or that the rules ought to be just as they are now. Since property (or ownership) is not a primitive concept, but is constituted by a complex of rules, there is no reason thus far why the rules of use and of disposal should not be different from those now in force. It might well be possible to alter them for the better. All that we need to bear in mind is that property, like Freedom, is in part a concession to men's selfishness, and rules which impose too much unselfishness are likely to fail in their effect. Just as clever conveyancing clerks were able to find ways round most of the statutes Parliament used to pass about landed property, so now, if we alter the rules we must consider how selfish men, out to maximise their own interests without regard to the intention of the law, will play the rules, and may circumvent our purpose in revising the rules. Nor is this altogether wrong: after all, part of the point of property was to act as a safety valve, and to be something that people could legitimately be selfish about.

The rights of property are not, and never have been absolutely absolute. Always they have been fettered by various legal obligations. The landowner must not deprive his neighbour's land of support, by excavating his own up to the boundary: he must not allow the use of his land to be a nuisance to his neighbours: and the old principle of "ancient lights" has received a great extension under the Town and Country Planning Acts, so that now landowners, very properly, have been deprived of the absolute right to spoil the view. Equally, the owner of a car or a wireless set is not allowed to use it without a licence. The owner of a patent may be legally obliged to grant a licence to use it. The owner of a work of art may not sell it abroad just as he likes. A Scotsman may not leave his property to whomsoever he will, but must give a share to his wife and his children.

All these, and many other, restrictions on the absolute rights of property are feasible, and may be desirable. But they remain minor qualifications on the general principle of absolute discretion in using and disposing. And this is a special case, defined usually with reference to places or things, of the more general principle of Freedom. A man may do as he likes with his own—by definition, for we define his own as that which he may do as he likes with.

The existence of homes and private property often resolves the conflict between one man's freedom to act and another man's security from harm, by giving one party or the other an outlet or a safeguard which will not threaten the security or restrict the freedom of the other. It is a method of evading the conflict rather than of deciding it, and sometimes the method will not be available, and always we shall have to decide in the public sphere whether Freedom or Security is to be preferred.

The argument from alternatives often still applies. In walking along the highway, it is easy for me to alter my course to avoid bumping another man who has stopped to tie his shoe-lace; my freedom is restricted in order to provide security for him: but for longer waits, the position is reversed, and the other man's freedom to remain stationary for long periods is restricted to give me security against obstruction in my passage along the highway. For it is a very small alteration for me to have to alter course or even pause as I go about my business, whereas there is no reasonable alternative to stopping for the man whose shoe-lace has come undone: but it is not reasonable for me to be delayed for a long time, or for a large number of other people to be inconvenienced by obstruction. The balance of inconvenience in such cases is, however, never all one way, and seldom decisive; and therefore we adopt different solutions for different types of case; we are harder on parked cars than on stationary humans; on a clearway or motorway, at the one extreme, we will not allow any obstruction at all, while in a market-place, at the other extreme, not only may people be in the same place for hours on end, but they may be allowed to put up stalls.

Not only does the existence of private property sometimes fail to avoid conflict, but often it generates it. *Meum* and *tuum* may delimit "spheres of influence" in which each one of us in entitled to exercise an undisputed sway, but then there will break out second-order demarcation disputes on where exactly the boundaries are to be drawn. Not all goods are qualitatively identical to other goods. The paradigm example of cars, where because each can have one of the same model, neither need quarrel with the other about the use of either car, is not a typical case. Many goods are qualitatively unique: some because no other article happens to be exactly like it——for example, a particular piece of furniture; some in view of an extrinsic circumstance——there are other fountain pens which are just like this one, but this is the one my father used, and therefore is unique in my eyes; some, as we have seen,[1] because they are of a logical type where to be numerically distinct is

[1] p. 185.

necessarily to be qualitatively different also—if you and I each own th
copyright of a symphony, the symphonies are necessarily dissimilar, an
are not qualitatively identical in the way that two Morris Minors may b

Landed property is necessarily unique. You may own as many acre
as I do, but they are necessarily located in a different place, and it i
by its location that landed property is defined. Landed property there
fore is the sort which poses the greatest problems. The ownership c
land is, like that of a movable object, naturally privative, and not, lik
that of a copyright, only artificially so; and yet land, like a copyrigh
is essentially unique, and not, like a movable object in princip)
reproducible. Since we all always have to occupy some place or othei
and since for most of human history it is only by cultivating land tha
a man has been able to supply his material wants, it is natural that ther
have been more disputes about the ownership and occupancy of place
than of any other sort. In particular, rulers from Ahab to the lates
Minister of Town and Country Planning, have coveted the lands c
their subjects, and subjects from the time of Naboth to the presen
day have sought to preserve their ancestral acres intact.

Disputes about property may arise not only over particular item:
but over the amount of property an individual owns. As soon as w
have money—even before—, we begin to measure wealth, and dra·
comparisons. The poor may envy the rich, the rich despise the poo·
and the middle classes strive to keep up with the Joneses. Mone·
enables many disputes to be resolved, and is a great buttress of Free
dom, but the love of money can cause many further quarrels and ca·
lead to a sort of tyranny.

The great virtue of money is that it widens the range of alter
natives open to an individual at any one time. There are a large numbe
of conventional tokens—coins, bank-notes—qualitatively identica]
each of the same, conventional, value; and therefore my money is a
good as yours, and yours as good as mine, and any third person ha·
the alternative open to him of dealing with me if he does not like you
and *vice versa*: and, similarly, you and I have the alternative of dealin;
with a third person instead of with each other. Moreover, we do no·
have to exchange goods for goods, but can exchange goods for mone·
or money for goods, and can exchange a greater or smaller quantit·
of money for some particular goods; and thus our dealings are greatl·
facilitated, and the liberty of each greatly extended.

We pay two prices for this liberty. The first is impersonality. Mone·
is anonymous. Modern thinkers, especially since Marx, have deplore·

the fact that the cash nexus is impersonal, and yearn for a more complete, cosier form of economic organisation. But total cosiness would be suffocating. If I am always to treat other people entirely as ends-in-themselves and never in the least bit merely as means, then I can never do anything simply for the reason that *I* want to do it. *Per contra*, if any man is ever to be in any way free, then there will be someone whom some time he will be entitled to treat, if only by omission, not fully as a person with a complete set of claims on him, but only as possessing certain minimum rights. My relations with a shop-keeper, business-men, ticket-collector are necessarily to some degree impersonal *because* I am free to go to another shop, deal with another firm, travel by another line to another destination. This is not to say that I am entitled to treat shop-keepers, business-men, or ticket-collectors *merely* as means, and not *at all* as ends-in-themselves. I am not entitled to murder, rob or defraud them: nor ought I to be rude to them. But there is a certain impersonality in my relation to them, which is simply the reverse side of the coin of Freedom. And therefore, although we may complain that modern life, dominated by a money economy, is *too* impersonal, and seek ways of humanising modern institutions, we cannot legitimately complain of its being at least to some extent impersonal, for that is just what we want it to be, in as much as we want to be free, free, among other things, to neglect on occasion the personality—the personal claims and the personal wishes—of others.

The second price we may have to pay for economic freedom is the loss of economic security. It is easy to overplay this loss. The landless labourer of the last century who was forced into the factory to sell the work of his hands was indeed in a bad plight: but so too the landless labourer of all ages, who did not have the wherewithal to keep himself alive. Because of our recurrent needs for food, clothing, warmth, medical attention, we are all vulnerable. Many have been insecure, many unfortunate. Economic freedom does not in general make people worse off or more insecure: on the contrary, it has in general made people better off, and the landless labourer who would have starved in the time of Hesiod is able in an industrial society to find alternative means of securing subsistence. Nevertheless, even though most people may be better off, some are more insecure. Milliners, and other purveyors of female fashion goods, are the paradigm example; but also all those who have come to depend on one particular type of job, and then are thrown out of work by change of demand, technological progress, economic crises, bad management or restrictive trade union practices. Those who value security of employment above all else can obtain it, by entering some walk of life which is shielded from market fluctuations—but usually at the cost of lower wages. It would neither be practicable nor desirable to guarantee to everyone complete security of employment. There could not be a market economy if everybody was completely secure: and the market economy does provide greater liberty, as well as being more efficient, than any non-market system, where there are no alternative options open to each operator. But the price of this liberty is a measure of insecurity, and, in the midst of general prosperity, misfortune and hardship fall selectively on people who have done nothing to deserve it.

The institution of private property and money thus raises problems, as well as solving others. But the general principle of alternatives often still applies. Compensation is one application of it. Where a man is deprived of some possessions, the monetary equivalent is often awarded to him in order to provide him with a security or a liberty of action alternative to that afforded by what was taken from him. Thus many actions for Tort or Negligence in the civil law, thus, more importantly from our point of view, compensation under compulsory purchase orders. Ahab offered Naboth an alternative vineyard, or, alternatively again, the equivalent in money, thus far acting entirely properly, and more justly, indeed, than many modern expropriating authorities. Further discussion of the procedures by which expropriation ought to be controlled we leave until later;[1] but the principle of full, fair, and prompt compensation clearly derives from the doctrine that to provide alternatives goes a long way to resolve a conflict.

A very different application of the principle of alternatives is found in the anti-trust legislation in the U.S.A., and the complaints against monopolies in England in the reign of Queen Elizabeth I. Monopolies, by definition, exclude alternatives. Freedom thereby is circumscribed, and the safeguards provided by competition are lost. There may, none the less, be a balance of argument in a particular case in favour of a monopoly, either of selling, e.g. electricity in Great Britain, or of buying, e.g. milk by the Milk Marketing Board in Great Britain, or, in almost all countries, the services of soldiers. But in general monopolies run counter to Freedom, and where they do exist, special measures are needed to protect the liberty and the security of those who deal with them.

---

[1] §§ 53, 52, pp. 226–7, 223–4.

SECTION 45

PRIVATE SANCTIONS AND PRIVATE POWER

A MAN who possesses a legal privilege possesses some sort of power. There are certain occasions when the bare fact that he indicates that he wants to do X entitles him to do X, and the law will enable him to do X,[1] however unreasonable it is of him, and however much better it would be if X were not done. Sometimes other people will care very much whether X is done or not. A woman in love with a man will care how he acts, and therefore will be vulnerable, and therefore will be under pressure to conform her actions to his wishes, for fear that if she does not, he will do what she desperately wants him not to do. Therefore the man will have, indirectly, a greater power, a power not only over his actions, but over hers. If he says 'Let X happen' where X is some action of hers, X will happen. And this is power.

Fortunately, most men and women are made vulnerable by love only with respect to the actions of a few other people. Lovers, parents, children, brothers, sisters, friends, do care, and can be hurt, and can therefore be manipulated, by those who do not reciprocate all the affection they receive. But, for the most part, we do not care all that what other people do, except where it impinges in a fairly tangible way upon our own interests. It is the possession of private property rather than the affections of our private lives that gives men private power. Private power is not so much a matter of being cherished by others as of having external goods that others covet. And the very utility of money, in making property commensurable and extending the liberty of exchanging property for property, makes more effective the power that property confers.

Although the power of money is great, it is not as great as the coercive power wielded by the State. Money is peculiarly susceptible to the argument from alternatives: if it cannot be obtained from one person it may be available from another. And often, although not always—not if he is starving—a man *can* do without. The power of money, although effective in securing most of the things desired by the man who has it, is *resistible*. The rich man who wants land can purchase it—but not Naboth's. The rich man who wants women can buy them

---

[1] See § 4, p. 16, or below, p. 366.

—but not Lucrece. The power of money, and of property generally, has already some safeguards built into it. This does not mean that we should take no cognisance of the money power at all, and should adopt a principle of extreme *laissez-faire*: but it does mean that we do not need to restrict private powers to the same extent as we need to restrict coercive power. The money economy and the market place may be harsh and heartless, and may cause unnecessary suffering: but money cannot be cruel or malicious, in the way that a wicked ruler can pick on a man, and incarcerate him in a dungeon till he dies. Wage-slaves are not slaves, for they are not slaves *of* anyone. They are obliged to sell their labour to earn their living—almost all men have to earn their living, most by selling their labour—but they are free to seek fresh employment, and often do. They are not committed to any one master, and in that are essentially different from slaves, who are.

Nevertheless, private powers, although resistible, are often not resisted; the sanctions at the disposal of private individuals or corporate bodies, although not extreme, are in fact effective. So much so, that sometimes they seem to be quasi-States.[1] Clubs, universities, and trade unions are able to impose decisions on their members, that are, in virtue of the sanctions they can impose, effectively binding. Such power, like all power, can be abused. We can at least, as always, criticise the decisions of such bodies. And where the sanctions, and therefore the power, are, thanks to the background secured by the State's coercive machinery, very great, we may properly insist that various safeguards should be instituted against some abuses. As always, we cannot lay down a simple formula of demarcation. Neither the rights of private property nor the responsibilities of the State are absolute. There are arguments for leaving things uncontrolled, in the absolute discretion of private persons, as we have seen.[2] There is a further argument from the "Right of Association".[3] There is some justification for some State cognisance of private powers in that it is the coercive power of the State that provides purchase for all other private powers. Sometimes there are further arguments to show that some degree of State supervision is, in a particular case, desirable.

---

[1] See above, § 14, p. 55; and below, § 64, p. 278; § 65, pp. 283–4; § 66, p. 293
[2] §§ 38, 44.
[3] See below § 64, p. 277.

SECTION 46

ADMINISTRATION

No GENERAL rules for administration can be formulated, since administration is not a homogeneous type of activity. Some sorts of administration really are to be compared with the traditional executive activities of government. Some are to be regarded as adjudications. Some are more like legislation than anything else. Often all these aspects are present in varying degrees. Sometimes, therefore, we can extrapolate from the procedures and general principles we have formulated for reaching executive, judicial and legislative decisions, strictly so called. Often, however, we ought to rethink our procedures and principles, and consider afresh in what way our fundamental ideals of Rationality and Freedom can together, so far as possible, be achieved.

From the internal aspect, the first requirement of the Rule of Law is that administrative officials, like judicial officials, shall be able and disinterested. We are fortunate. Particularly in the last hundred years, thanks to Gladstone, Jowett, and the mediaeval universities, there has never been wanting a succession of men duly qualified for at least the secular service of the State. Britain has been blessed with as good administrators as judges. We have, happily, no cases of corruption in the higher Civil Service, nor many of incompetence. But civil servants, although superb, are still, as they themselves admit,[1] fallible. They need guidance, and we need safeguards. As we have already seen,[2] guidance can be given without fettering discretion completely. We are thus not obliged to adopt the canon of Legality for administrators any more than for judges, so far as the internal aspect of the Rule of Law goes. Nor, from the external point of view, is the need for Legality quite so pressing.[3] Although the use of "policies" to guide officials in their decision-making raises some problems of its own, we can in general use "policies" rather than laws to give guidance to administrative officials and secure reasonable consistency in the decisions they make.[4]

Although by means of "policy-words" we can secure conformity between one administrator and another, it is more difficult to secure a general consensus of public opinion about what administrative

---

[1] Compare above, § 2, p. 9. [2] § 31, pp. 139–41.
[3] See below, pp. 197–8. [4] See below, § 47, pp. 203ff.

decisions ought to be taken, because they often involve arguments about the Public Interest. The Public Interest is a difficult concept to elucidate, and even more difficult to apply.[1] We can often—although far from always—agree on the rights and wrongs of a case, where the question is one of Justice; but where it is one of the Public Interest, differences of opinion are likely to be sharper, and less easy to resolve by discussion and argument. The courts of justice are rightly reluctant to allow considerations of the Public Interest to affect their decisions, but administrators cannot keep their deliberations uncontaminated. They need on occasion to consider the Public Interest, on occasion to be swayed by it. But this is not to say that they should have scant regard for Equity, and not be governed by the procedures of Natural Justice.

All officials exercise an accountable discretion. It is always logically permissible to ask him to justify his decisions, and sometimes he is under a legal duty to provide some sort of answer to some sort of person. It might seem desirable to have all officials accountable to the public like judges. Judges have to justify their decisions in public. They have to answer, or rather anticipate, the question 'why?' in respect of every one of their decisions. But it would be impracticable to have all officials accountable in this fashion. Time forbids; and, as we have seen,[2] accounting for one's actions is a drag on efficiency and enterprise. We cannot adopt the solution of converting public offices into legal privileges, as we can with purely private affairs. But we can, on occasion, reduce the number of reasons required to be stated. We can do this partly by having subordinate officials responsible *to* a superior one, so that they have to justify their actions not publicly to all comers but only privately to him, not always, but only when he requires them to.[3] We can also accommodate the difficulty we have in articulating our reasons[4] by reversing the onus of proof. We need not require all officials always to prove that each decision taken was the right one; in some sorts of case we can presume that the decision is reasonable, even if all the reasons are not, and perhaps cannot be, given: only where decisions seem flagrantly wrong need we call them to account. We have a choice. We can have safeguards. Or we can have efficiency and enterprise. We can secure that reasons be given in certain restricted fields, but not in all fields. To require that reasons in writing be given and published for every military decision, every

---

[1] See below, § 48, pp. 207ff.   [2] § 38, pp. 163–6.
[3] See further below, § 49, pp. 208ff.   [4] See above, § 38, pp. 164–5.

appointment to a public office, every contract let by competitive tender, would be to hamstring the process of decision-making. We can protect some things, but not all things. And for everything we do protect, we have to pay some sort of premium in the form of inefficiency, delay, or expense. The only question is what things are worth protecting to what extent and at what cost.

The answer is given by the Rule of Law in its external aspect. Not only the rulers, but also the ruled, are interested in the decisions which the rulers take. The interests men have vary from the highly specific central interest each man has in his own life, liberty and property, to the general, and sometimes rather diffuse, interest all good men have that right decisions shall be taken. We cannot list all interests. But we can identify a number of important ones and arrange them in an order. Life is the most central interest, both because it is the pre-condition of every other interest, and because each man's life is what is most peculiarly his own. Then liberty. Then property, since property is what enables a man to have his own way, without violent conflict, in some part of the public world, and each man's property is, by conventional assignment, his own. These three interests are traditionally and rightly, assigned, with a few exceptions,[1] to the care of judicial, not administrative, officials. The courts of justice are the proper tribunals to dispose of the most individual-centred interests, because Justice is oriented towards the individual:[2] and the procedures of the courts contain many safeguards against error or abuse. With these interests, we are so much concerned with the individual that we have conferred charters of freedom and security on all individual subjects, good and bad alike, so that each may be his own master, and keep his distance from the law.

Even men's chartered interests are not altogether inviolate. Certain sorts of property which are unique, either necessarily, like land or copyright, or contingently, like a steelworks, may be expropriated by a decision which Parliament has authorised an administrative official to take. Many defenders of Freedom have upheld the rights of property as absolute. They forget that property is a form of Freedom, and that no Freedom is absolute, but is always the result of striking a balance between one man's liberty and other men's security, in the light of the alternatives open to them. The doctrine of alternatives applies with particular force to property. Compensation alleviates expropriation. One of the difficulties in making planning legislation work is that

[1] See below, § 61, pp. 261f.   [2] See below, § 55, pp. 234ff.

successive administrations, in spite of the rebuke of the Franks Report,[1] have sought to avoid paying full, fair, and prompt compensation for land compulsorily acquired. This has led to a confusion between the right of property, which each man defends pertinaciously, and the interest, but less central interest, which each man has in his property taking a certain form. A man may well not want to sell some land, some shares, a copyright, or a patent; and has an interest in opposing any such proposal. But if the proposal is going not only to inconvenience but to impoverish him, he will resist it far more vehemently, and will justly demand that the same procedures and principles should apply in his case as apply in the law courts, since his property is in peril. By making modern administrators come up at least to the standard of Ahab, we should distinguish the two interests involved, that of property, strictly so called, which only the courts of justice are competent to dispose, and that of a man's property taking one particular form, which although a real, and fairly central interest, may properly be dealt with by other tribunals.

There are many other interests, especially in the modern world. Some, although not so central as those of life, liberty, and property, are far from peripheral, and should be assimilated to the central interests, although not treated with quite the same tenderness. Others are more peripheral, either because they clearly cannot matter all that much to the person concerned, or because they cannot be said to concern one individual very much more than any other. In such cases we cannot work out the Rule of Law by giving chartered freedoms and securities to all the individuals concerned. But we can enable the subject who is interested to find out where he stands; to make predictions with some confidence about some decisions; to manipulate, within limits and in good faith, the apparatus of State; and to a lesser or greater extent to participate in the process of making decisions.

In issuing licences and passports, in granting patents and copyrights, in awarding pensions or assessing compensation, an official is altering the legal position of an individual citizen. To be prohibited from driving or going abroad, for example, is a serious deprivation in the modern world, even if not as serious as the deprivation of liberty. The citizen concerned has a great interest in the decision reached, and many of the considerations which apply to a judge apply also to an administrator exercising discretion in this sort of case. The

[1] Report on *Administrative Tribunals and Enquiries*, 1957, Cmnd. 218, Section 278.

discretion conferred on judges is secured against abuse in four ways. First, the judges have a limited office: their commission is to administer the law in accordance with the canons of Legality and Equity; they do not have to decide all questions, nor take all factors into consideration, but only a limited range of questions, on the basis of only a limited range of considerations. Secondly, the judges have to account for their decisions in public: their judgements have to be reasoned judgements, made public in court, and subject to the scrutiny of all and sundry, and in particular, of their colleagues learned in the law. Thirdly, the laws which guide the judges' decisions are themselves public, so that the judges' decisions are effectively open to criticism. Fourthly, and to a lesser extent, there is sometimes some provision for appeal. Judicial discretion has been thus greatly fettered, partly as a safeguard against judicial error or abuse, chiefly in order to confer on the subject chartered security and liberty. Going to law in England has been expensive and slow, but predictable and safe. The criminal law, in which the life and liberty of the subject may be in jeopardy, is made so far as possible, "fail-safe": the guilty often escape conviction, but the innocent seldom suffer a serious miscarriage of justice. Administrative discretion likewise needs to be safeguarded against error and abuse on the part of the administrator, and the subject likes to know where he stands in respect of future administrative decisions. But there is not the same need for absolute security and Constitutional Freedom, just because neither the life nor the liberty of the subject is ever at stake. The extremely elaborate, expensive and time-consuming safeguards which protect the subject in the law-courts are not in place in administrative procedures. We have to hedge heavily against the danger of being hanged or imprisoned by mistake: we need to hedge still, but not nearly so heavily, against not being given a pension that is our due.

Those administrative decisions which are primarily adjudications on individual cases should therefore be reached in ways comparable to decisions which are strictly judicial, but subject to fewer safeguards. The individual whose interests are concerned should have the opportunity of stating his case, meeting any case there is against him; he should be told of the decision, and the reasons for it; the arbitrator should both be impartial and seem so; and there should be some right of appeal. Moreover reasonable steps should be taken to make it possible to predict decisions in future cases and to rely upon them. Administrative decisions, however, can differ from strictly judicial ones in that the procedure can be much less formalised, and that the discretion of the arbitrator need not be so heavily fettered out of consideration for Legality. We want to show proper respect for the individual whose interests are at stake: and therefore he should be heard.[1] We want to guard against abuse, bias or error on the part of the arbitrator, and therefore, again, the individual's side of the case should be heard,[2] and the arbitrator should have to state his reasons, and be subject to appeal. But an administrator can be given a wider discretion than a judge to decide the case "on its merits" rather than on any rigid, antecedently-stated, legal rule, just because the life, liberty and property of the subject are not at stake, but only other, less central interests. We do not need to go so far in assimilating these interests to laws of nature, because these, though important, are not the essential conditions of an individual's being free under the law. Strict Legality, as we saw,[3] is the bad man's charter. But while it is right to make it possible for the bad man to live, so long as he keeps on the right side of the law, there is no special reason why he should be entitled to manipulate the whole apparatus of State intended for rela- tively un-bad men. We want to make sure that the ordinary man can get, and can be sure of getting, his pension, his driving licence, or his passport. But there is no call for us to facilitate pension fiddles, or the use of driving licences or passports for purposes for which they were not intended, but which had not been anticipated when the rules were first laid down. The special arguments which justify our qualifying judicial discretion by considerations of Legality do not here apply, and since often administrators are dealing with new fields of activity, there are few well-worn paths which could guide them in framing legalistic rules.

It is enough therefore that an administrator should be modelled on Judex III, not Judex IV. He should be uncorrupt, competent, im- partial, hearing both sides of the case, reaching a decision based on the relevant facts, and deciding similar cases similarly, though not em- barrassed by so great a wealth of precedent as his judicial brother, and perhaps not so rigidly bound by the rule of precedents—he should have greater latitude in finding further facts relevant, so as to distinguish cases. The general principles guiding the various different officials adjudicating the same type of case, should from time to time be formulated, and made public, but they should be, and should be clearly stated to be (as

---

[1] See above, § 28, pp. 132–3; and below, § 62, pp. 269ff.
[2] See above, § 28, p. 132.   [3] § 35, p. 154.

often in fact they are) "for guidance only", and should not be regarded as laws which officials have to apply, like Judex IV, strictly, according to the letter, without any possibility of further argument.

A very large number of administrative decisions are thus comparable to judicial decisions, strictly so called, and should be assimilated to them. These are the cases where fairly central interests of particular individuals are at stake, in circumstances which are *prima facie* similar to those in which a whole class of other individuals are treated in a standard way, and in which there is no element of competition. Decisions in all such cases should be guided by considerations of Justice and Equity, and the procedure should be analogous to that of the law courts, though less formal, and less subject to safeguards, procedural or substantive. In particular, the two *rôles* of the Crown, as representing one side of the case, and as adjudicating impartially between the two sides of the case, should be kept separate, just as in the criminal courts the functions of prosecutor and judge are kept clearly apart.[1]

Adjudications which are competitive can be dealt with shortly. When the Federal Communications Commission is allocating wavebands to broadcasting corporations in the United States, it cannot give every deserving candidate a waveband, but has to choose some corporations to the exclusion of others. Similarly in Britain licences to run bus services are not issued to all comers, but are restricted, in order to avoid some bad effects of excessive competition. In each case, although the decision of the authority alters the legal position of one of the candidates, the situation is inherently unlike that where the authority is issuing a driving licence, or a licence to operate a wireless receiver. In the latter case, the applicants are competing only against a standard, in the former they are competing against one another. In the latter case, therefore, we can have the authority adopt a simple adversative procedure, giving each applicant the opportunity to establish the merits of his case, whereas in the former a simple adversative procedure is inapplicable. Again, where the issue is simply whether a particular individual qualifies for some generally available benefit (licence, pension, passport), it is feasible to require that reasons for refusal be given: but reasons for thinking one candidate more meritorious than the others are more difficult to articulate, and more

[1] Compare in the United States the view of the President's Committee on *Administrative Management in the Executive Branch of the Government*, 1937, p. 40, and the Final Report of the Attorney-General's Committee on *Administrative Procedure* (Sen. Doc. No. 8, 77th Cong., 1st Sess. 1941, p. 208).

embarrassing to publish. The procedure therefore for exercising discretion in competitive cases should be inquisitorial rather than adversative, and reasons should be given, if at all, only to superior officials. This is not to say that no safeguards are needed. We might need to have stringent safeguards against corruption. We may have procedural safeguards such as public advertisement of the opportunities offered, to make sure that each applicant's merits are considered, and that the decision is at least impartial. But the whole exercise is more like a competitive examination than a trial.

Similar considerations apply to cases which fall under the traditional view of the executive function of government, for example where an official is letting out contracts: that is, he is exercising his discretion in choosing with whom the government will enter into mutually advantageous commercial relations. In selecting one competitor, the official is rejecting others. The legal position of the unsuccessful competitors is not in any way altered by the official's action, but their expectations, or at least their hopes, are disappointed, and in this sense their interests have been harmed. They have not any direct claim on the attention or consideration of the official, but they have, along with all other members of the public, an indirect claim, that public money should not be spent incompetently or corruptly. We may therefore lay down a certain procedure, for example that government contracts should always be advertised and tenders invited, so as to secure a minimal level of care and competence. Some authorities go further, and lay down that the lowest tender must be accepted; but often there are objections to this, e.g. with development contracts awarded by the Ministry of Aviation. Provided an official has not acted corruptly or carelessly, and has reasons for choosing one tender rather than another, which he can state, if required, to a superior official, no further check is in general necessary. For, in general, none of the interests harmed by the decision are definite or chartered interests, and disappointed contractors can seek business elsewhere.

Where the government or any corporation, public or private, has a monopoly, discretion may need to be fettered further. For then there is not some alternative outlet open to the disappointed party, so that he has more than the general tax-payer's concern that public money should be spent wisely and well. An official may be disinterestedly biased against me. Provided he is not corrupt or grossly incompetent, I cannot in ordinary cases impugn his action, because it is typically not clear that his prejudice against me is not a "post-judice", a reasonably held low view of me. A building contractor, whose tender is passed over in favour of a rival, cannot reasonably expect to be told why, because it would be an intolerable clog on the administration if reasons always had to be given, and often they would not be conclusive. But a householder, deprived of a telephone or of the electricity supply, is in a much worse position, for there are no alternatives open to him; and although telephones and electricity are not part of the Rights of Man, or the Liberties of the Subject, they are part of the contemporary way of life, and a man deprived of them is cut off from important aspects of normal life. He therefore has a more definite interest in the official's decision and a stronger claim on his attention and consideration.

For these reasons, monopolies, whether public or private, whether of buying or of selling, should be subject to what I shall call "Common Carrier" conditions. "Common Carrier" conditions fetter discretion in individual cases, but not, or not very much, in general cases. A railway company was free (subject to some exceptions) to run what trains and offer what services it liked, but was not free to refuse any particular consignment of goods or to charge an individual customer as much as he could be persuaded to pay. Comparable obligations can, and should, be laid on all public services. The general policy may be left to the officials of the service (though it may not: Parliament may direct, as a matter of national policy, that every household shall have a postal delivery or an electricity supply) but in individual cases they should be bound by their own general rules. Moreover where there is a dispute between a public service and a private individual, it should be settled by independent arbitration. A monopoly has too much of a whip-hand to be left to settle its own disputes.

There are many other cases where it is not yet clear how the ideals of Rationality and Freedom are to be reconciled. Our thinking has been hampered by the traditional doctrine of the Separation of Powers.[1] We have been led to define the judicial and legislative organs of government narrowly, and to lump everything else together as the executive—the hangman, the typist in the Ministry of Agriculture and Fisheries, and the Post Office engineer, along with an Inspector of the Ministry of Town and Country Planning, a Special Commissioner of Inland Revenue, and a Permanent Under-Secretary of State. It is unfortunate that administrators have come to be regarded as making decisions in which the executive aspect is primary rather than the

[1] See above, § 19, p 80.

judicial or, on occasion, legislative aspect. It would have been better if administrators had been thought of as being like judges rather than as being like secretaries. Secretaries are secretive. Whereas judges have erred, if at all, in modelling themselves on Judex IV rather than Judex III, civil servants have been, to outward appearance, like Judex II or even Judex I. It is not that they have been corrupt or incompetent. From their own, internal point of view they have been deeply imbued with the Rule of Law. It is from the external point of view that criticisms are made. We do not know where we are with Whitehall. The deliberations of Parliament and the arguments of the law courts are public, and the outsider can follow them all he wants: but between Westminster and the Strand is a no-man's land whose workings, although vitally important to us, are veiled from our eyes.

The secretiveness of civil servants is defended on the grounds that the Public Interest requires it, and that only by protecting civil servants from publicity can we enable them to give really frank advice to their Ministers. There is merit in both these contentions. Sometimes the Public Interest does require secrecy: some communications should be privileged in order that they may be confidential. Some, but not all. The same arguments as are valid against conferring blanket immunities on public officials in regard to the law[1] are valid in regard to public discussion too. The mis-classification of administration as a species of executive activity has created the wrong presumption. The arguments for secrecy, to differing degrees in different cases, need to be made out, and weighed against the general argument from the Rule of Law that we all should be "in on" decisions of State, at least to the extent of knowing what they are and why they were taken.

We cannot formulate a complete set of rules for administration. So long as secrecy lasts, we often do not know what the issues are. More fundamentally, our concept of *interest* is elastic, and liable to expand from generation to generation. Some decisions which interest us greatly now were of no concern to Montesquieu or Locke. Many interests we regard as peripheral will seem central to our sons. We cannot say in what way and in what spirit questions should be settled until we know how much they matter, and to whom. Therefore I offer few firm conclusions, but only a programme, a programme of making administrators amenable to the Rule of Law, from the outsider's point of view as much as from the insider's. And this is a programme we greatly need to undertake.

[1] See above, § 20, pp. 89–90.

SECTION 47

POLICIES AND LAWS

W E H A V E already seen that it is possible to have *policies* which guide decisions without determining them precisely.[1] We can instruct the body making the decision to attach special weight to certain considerations or certain arguments, without precluding them from overriding these considerations in some particular case, in which they reckon other considerations to be even more weighty. In contrast, a law, ideally, in accordance with the principle of Legality, determines precisely what is to be done in what sort of circumstances. Legality would like it if adjudicators were all like Judex IV, who merely subsumed particular cases under general rules, and proceeded then by deductive argument to the relevant conclusion. The attractions of deductive argument are, first, that it is felt to be subject to a "mechanical" check, and we can be sure of spotting it if Judex IV is in error, and second, that everybody can follow out deductive arguments for himself, so that everybody can know exactly what the decisions of Judex IV will be. We can never completely realise the ideal of Legality, but with certain sorts of decisions—those affecting life, liberty, or property—we go a long way towards it. Law is relatively knowable in advance, predictable, manipulable, available to bad men as well as to good, and is applied by judges who exercise relatively little discretion.

Policies need to be carried out by men who can exercise a reasonable discretion, who have some *nous*, who are not mere language-users, capable only of following out deductive inferences and nothing more. A decision implementing a policy is less predictable, less manipulable than a decision in accordance with a law, although in paradigm cases a reasonable man can be reasonably certain which way the decision will go. But a policy, although weighting some considerations, does not exclude all others, and it is always possible that some consideration may arise which will outweigh even those I am anxious to weight. A doctor may have the policy of "First come, first served", in his surgery, but still will make an exception for an expectant mother with a fractious child. My policy in driving may be "Safety First", but still I will take risks in rushing a dangerously ill patient to hospital.

Policies thus lack the precision and predictability of laws, because

[1] § 31, pp. 139–41.

they do not have the limited criteria of relevance that a law lays down. It is always possible that a case may have peculiar circumstances which will bring other considerations into play which will in turn make the decision go the other way. Nevertheless, policies, although not perfectly precise are not completely indefinite. We can distinguish a policy of Justice, from that of Mercy, or of Expediency, or of Generosity. Although no one decision is incompatible with a given policy, a whole run of decisions can be. Moreover, although a bare decision by itself is not highly indicative of the policy behind it, the reasoning leading to a decision is. Judex III is in this respect very different from Judex II. We can tell easily what Judex III's policies are, because we can assess his arguments and see how much different ones weigh with him.

Policies may conflict. I may wish to be both just and merciful, or to achieve both Equality and Efficiency in economic affairs. In some cases different policies can be reconciled, in others each may be compromised a little in order that neither shall be abandoned altogether, in others again one may have to be sacrificed completely. It is where policies conflict that we have the greatest difficulty in reaching a rational decision or predicting what decision another rational agent will arrive at. If we attach importance to consistency and predictability we may institute a rule of precedents, such as Judex II and Judex III were bound by. We can then demarcate borderline cases by a series of decisions, which, as they accumulate, will gradually convert the policy—a tendency in arguing—into a definite law, applying quite definitely to some cases, and quite definitely not to others. The common law has developed in this way. The common law consists not of "laws" (i.e. statute laws) promulgated and deciding all cases falling under them, but of "policies" —maxims, principles, Latin tags, ancient slogans—embodied in a large number of decisions, which now define the effective content of the common law. But the leading cases of the common law give us guidance only because they do exemplify certain tendencies in arguing, and demarcate between one argument and another. Without the principles which the decided cases exemplify, the bare decisions would give little guidance how any future case, not qualitatively identical with some decided one, would itself be decided. To understand the common law is both to grasp the various "policies" it espouses, and to know the particular compromises and reconciliations which have been decided upon in cases where one "policy" conflicts with another.

The common law is governed by the rule of precedents for good reason: we need predictability and reliability, and are prepared to pay the price of a measure of ossification and artificiality in order to achieve them. In more "administrative" issues, which do not involve the life or liberty of the subject, we do not need so great a measure of predictability and reliability, and therefore are less inclined to sacrifice so much to the ideal of Legality. If we have decided wrongly some case where, say, Liberty and Efficiency conflict, it may be better next time to reach the right decision, than to let the wrong decision stand because everyone then can be sure what the position is. Moreover, where different policies conflict, say Fairness and Generosity, the mere fact that on several previous occasions I have decided one way, may be a good reason on this occasion for deciding the other way. Just because I have often been fair in time past, I can "afford to be" generous this time, and *vice versa*: whereas with cases falling under laws, each must be decided separately, and the fact that previous cases have been decided one way is conclusive argument why in a similar case now the same decision should be given.

We therefore weaken the rule of precedents for "administrative" decisions when policies conflict. This is not to say that we abandon it altogether. Civil servants are notoriously bound by precedents in practice, even though not formally in principle. And rightly. For consistency is a mark of rationality,[1] and it is a requirement of Justice that each case shall be decided on its merits, and not on account of extraneous considerations.[2] Therefore in general the rule of precedents should be observed: for if it is not observed, then at least one of the cases in question must have been decided wrongly, or else in accordance with some other ideal than Justice (perhaps Expediency, perhaps Variety). But, of course, this may have happened. Mistakes do occur. And if it has happened, then there is not a further reason, on the score of predictability, for canonising the mistake, as there is when a judge decides wrongly. To this extent, administrators are not bound by the rule of precedents.

It might seem that an official, deciding a case in the light of some policy or policies, had a discretion which was absolute, and that Judex I had returned with a vengeance. But an official need not himself be laying down the policy he is guided by, nor need his application of a policy be beyond question. His discretion may be limited, although not removed altogether, by a directive on what policy he is to pursue, and he may be called to account for his exercise of discretion in any particular case, to show how his decision does implement the policy

[1] See above, § 27, p. 124, pp. 127–9.   [2] See below, § 55.

he is supposed to pursue. The administrator thus resembles the judge. Only, because the administrator's decision is more open to question on any particular occasion, the distinction between general statements of policy and particular decisions is less sharp than the corresponding decision between legislation and adjudication.[1] Nevertheless, most administrative decisions can be roughly distinguished as general decisions about policies or particular decisions in accordance with policies. The distinction, however, is much less sharp, and therefore it is correspondingly more difficult to work a "Separation of Powers" (in the weak sense)[2] with one official quasi-legislating and another quasi-adjudicating. For if a legislator lays down laws, these have an independent meaning, which can be understood by the layman as well as by the legislator and the judge, so that the law is not merely what "the judge says it is": but when a policy is laid down, it has much less independent meaning apart from the particular decisions which exemplify it. It is difficult to lay down exactly the relative weights to be given to, say, Fairness and Generosity, except by giving particular examples, actual or hypothetical, to show where the claims of one just do, or just do not, outweigh those of the other. Policy-maker cannot talk to policy-applier by means of (relatively) clear and unambiguous words in the way that law-maker can lay down instructions for Judex, but only by means of deciding all the difficult cases himself. And therefore it seems natural to make officials who apply policies the servants of those who make the policies, in a way in which we do not make the Judiciary the servants of the Legislature. In British constitutional theory, "policy" is treated as an indistinguishable whole, unlike the sharply distinguished activities of legislation and adjudication. All the administrative officials of a department are completely responsible to the Minister in charge of the department and their decisions are regarded as his decisions, for which he is responsible to Parliament. Whereas laws are promulgated by Parliament in solemn form, and are applied by the courts arguing in public, policies are decided by Ministers informally, carried out without publicity, and subject only to the checks of parliamentary question and parliamentary censure.

The distinction between laws and policies is neither simple nor clear-cut. It is not simple because many different contrasts are involved: it is not clear-cut, because some of the contrasts are contrasts of degree rather than of kind. It follows that we do not have to have only two types of decision-making, that of Parliament and the law courts on

[1] § 29.   [2] See above, § 19, p. 80.

the one hand, and that of the Minister and his officials on the other. There are many other types, subject to different sorts of control and safeguards. Many "administrative" decisions are quasi-judicial as we have seen, subject to some principles of Equity and Legality, but less fettered by Legality than the decisions of the judges. Other decisions, where policies conflict and have to be compromised if they are to be reconciled at all, are even less subject to the principle of Legality, but still should be in accordance with the principle of Equity and Right Reason. Here we may say that in difficult cases, only the Minister himself should decide. He cannot delegate authority, because in the absence of an authoritative decision by him, different officials would be very likely to decide similar cases differently. Nevertheless, although only the Minister can decide, he should decide judicially, and not, for example, in accordance with certain other ideals, such as "Public Interest" or "Expediency". At other times, however, it may be just these ideals he should have in mind.

SECTION 48

PUBLIC INTEREST

SOME decisions, sometimes of what policies to pursue, sometimes of what laws to enact, are taken "in the Public Interest" rather than in accordance with Justice, or Equity. Whereas only certain sorts of factor are taken into account in determining what is just,[1] a decision "in the Public Interest" takes cognisance of many others too. A judge acts wrongly, for example, if he allows his decision to be swayed by whether it will be popular or not: whereas it may be politic on occasion to court popularity, or at least to avoid taking unpopular decisions. *Fiat justitia, ruat caelum*, the judge must say: he is not to be concerned with the consequences of his action. But there are arguments, intelligible if not always commendable, for compromising Justice a little, in order to keep the sky in its proper place.

Thus when a decision is based on "policy", more considerations are relevant than when it has been based solely on Justice, and these further considerations may outweigh those of Justice. For these reasons, the courts of justice are rightly reluctant to subject "policy" decisions to judicial review. But this does not mean that policy decisions are beyond criticism, nor that we cannot ensure that the claims of

[1] See further below § 55, pp. 235–7.

Justice are given some weight. We can secure some sort of account-ability, and can secure to interested parties a hearing. But we cannot adopt the same procedure as for the typical, quasi-judicial case.

Major decisions are usually decisions of policy: where to build a new town, whether to encourage Comprehensive or Grammar schools. Decisions in cases where various policies conflict are decisions of policy: whether to permit a firm manufacturing for export to expand its plant on its present site, or to insist that no further expansion be allowed in the South-East. By allowing interested parties to represent their side of the case we go some way to meeting the claims of Justice. But we cannot separate the *rôles* of the "prosecution" and the "judge", because we cannot delimit what sort of factors are relevant. For a similar reason we cannot give interested parties procedural opportunity to hear and meet the "prosecution" case, nor account to disappointed parties by giving them reasons for the adverse decision. For the reasons, if given, might have nothing to do with any of the disappointed parties. "I have got to find somewhere to put an overspill town, and I have decided to land it on you" or "We cannot find the staff for many more Comprehensive schools, and I want to have as many of them as possible in the North." We cannot therefore have many procedural safeguards to protect the somewhat nebulous interests which may be affected by this sort of administrative decision. We can give some right of rep-resentation, so that the official will not err by overlooking some rele-vant fact or consideration, but we cannot adopt procedural safeguards to secure openness, fairness, and impartiality. Many of the reasons are difficult to articulate, and might be embarrassing to publish. Other considerations than fairness are involved. And the official, in so far as he is a judge, is judge in his own cause. We may try to keep him accountable, but we cannot tie him down by assigning him only a limited office, with only limited discretion, for we cannot lay down in advance what the Public Interest is, nor even what factors may be relevant to it. The Public Interest could almost be said to be that about which reasonable men may reasonably disagree.

SECTION 49

ACCOUNTABILITY AND CONTROL

THE fundamental principle of Constitutionalism is that the authority conferred on an official is not a legal privilege, to be exercised at his absolute discretion, but an authority for whose exercise the official is accountable. From the bare fact that the official is generally responsible, and should have, and be able to give, reasons for his decisions, certain consequences flow about what procedures should be adopted and what formal properties the decisions should have.[1] But even so, officials may err. We need to supplement the general ideal of right reasoning with specific procedures to eliminate the grosser forms of error.

The chief way of ensuring that an official has reasons is to require him to give them. We may make it a general requirement, that the official is always to give his reasons, or we may give some further official the authority to demand reasons. When the reasons have been given, we may—but may not—have a formal procedure for assessing them. Often where another official has authority to demand reasons, he has authority also to assess them. The first official then is responsible to the second.[2] In this case we may give the second official, in those cases where he finds the reasons given inadequate, further authority to overrule the subordinate official's decision, and sometimes also to reprimand or in some way punish him.

Where a subordinate official is responsible to a superior, who further has authority to overrule, and possibly also to reprimand, we hold the superior official *responsible for* all his subordinates' decisions. This is the doctrine of ministerial responsibility. All the officials of a department are responsible to the Minister, and the Minister can overrule any decision a member of his department reaches, and therefore the Minister is assumed to be in complete control of his department, and responsible *for* all the decisions taken in his name, responsible, that is, *to* Parliament, which can in turn, hold him to account, asking him questions, and reprimanding and even removing him, if the answers are not satisfactory.

The perpetual possibility of a parliamentary question is an effective safeguard against the worse kinds of abuse. Every official reaching a decision has in the back of his mind the thought that it may be questioned in Parliament, and thinks therefore how it could be justified if need be. Completely unjustifiable decisions are not taken. Nevertheless the parliamentary question is no longer an adequate method of control. It is partly that the Administration has grown too big, partly that Parliament has grown too weak. Too many administrative decisions are taken for Parliament to be able to scrutinise them adequately. For

[1] See above §§ 26, 27, pp. 123–9.   [2] See above § 26, p. 121.

every one decision that is questioned, hundreds go unscrutinised. Moreover, the party system ensures that the Administration always has a majority in Parliament, so that unless the answer given by the Minister does not afford even a colourable justification of the decision, he will probably get away with it. Answers to parliamentary questions are often not very informative, and the resources of a government department are usually sufficient to prevent any private Member of Parliament being able to bring an administrative official to book.

The doctrine of ministerial responsibility—that civil servants are completely under the control of the Minister, and that the Minister is effectively under the control of Parliament is a fiction. It was finally exposed as a fiction in 1954 when, after the Crichel Down case, the Minister, who had known nothing of what was being done in his name and was entirely free from blame, resigned, and the civil servants whose actions had been criticised, remained. It is not true, and cannot now be true, that a Minister is in complete control of his department: often, rather, the reverse. The doctrine of Ministerial Responsiblity cannot therefore be defended on the grounds that it represents the actual situation, and in so far as it precludes proper control of administrative officials, it is a dangerous delusion. But it can be understood as expressing, although obscurely, that Parliament, the Grand Committee of the Nation, is not to be fobbed off with non-answers, on any question of policy or public interest. If a Minister could say 'I had no authority to say how that question should be decided' then he could not be asked to account for that decision. Asked a parliamentary question, 'Why did you do it?' he could give a non-answer, 'I had no say in it'. The decisions of the courts thus cannot be questioned in Parliament: and the fear is that if some new method of making administrative officials accountable for the exercise of their discretion, then Parliament would lose the little control of the Administration that it now has. At present, if anything does go wrong, at least Parliament knows whom to blame: with responsibility divided, everyone could disclaim his share of it, and it would be impossible ever to bring anyone to book.

This argument has some force for some—major—decisions. It cannot be completely cogent, or we would entrust all power and authority to one man, and hold him responsible for everything.[1] With the division of responsibility that actually exists between different departments, it often happens that one department, say the Foreign

---

[1] See further above, § 26, pp. 118–21.

Office, is unable to do what it thinks best, because another department, say the Treasury, will not let it. We could go quite a long way towards controlling the discretion, as well as the expenditure, of officials, without making it impossible for Parliament to question the rationale of decisions. Procedural and substantial safeguards against abuse of authority could be adopted without jeopardising the final supremacy of Parliament.

Parliamentary control is desirable, if only as a *pis-aller*, over what general policies are adopted, over particular difficult decisions when two policies conflict, and over particular decisions which are decided "in the Public Interest" rather than in accordance with some more limited canon. For over these three sorts of decision no other method of control is possible. General policies are sufficiently like laws for Parliament to need to have the ultimate say over them as it does over the laws: but general policies are sufficiently unlike laws, for it to be necessary on occasion to adjudicate particular questions in order to determine the content of the general policy. Therefore the first and second cases must be under parliamentary control. With decisions in the Public Interest either we make our officials responsible to, and removable by, Parliament, or we make them like Judex I, conferring on them a discretion which is in effect absolute. We can do no other than make them account for their actions to Parliament because we cannot lay down at all what may constitute the Public Interest, and what are, or are not, sound reasons for one decision's being in the Public Interest rather than another's. The party politics of Parliament will ensure that criticisms will be voiced, even though the party vote will often prevent them from being pressed. Issues will be ventilated, and over the long run, Constitutional Criticism will be facilitated. In individual instances decisions will often be wrong, and Parliament will fail to right them. It would be a highly unsatisfactory system of reaching decisions where the central or near-central interests of individuals were concerned. But where only more marginal interests are involved, it is acceptable to entrust them to the rough-and-tumble of party politics, not because it is an ideal system, or one never likely to go wrong, but because it is less likely to stay consistently wrong than any other, and more likely in the long run to be susceptible to the pressure of rational criticism and debate.

Parliamentary control is not adequate where individual interests are involved. Parliament's concern is too spasmodic—many an individual's case does not command its attention at all. Even where it is concerned, it cannot devote enough time to thrash out the rights and wrongs of the whole case. Except on matters, such as Security, where considerations of the Public Interest are paramount, parliamentary control should give way to the adjudication of independent officials, irremovable, like the judges, and giving their reasons in public; in some cases, also, not responsible *to* anyone, though liable to be quashed on appeal.

Where parliamentary control is retained—and except where some quasi-judicial process is involved, there can be no objection to it—it needs to be supplemented. Often an official, as well as being responsible to a Minister, should also have to give his reasons in public. It constitutes a further control. Parliamentary time being limited, parliamentary control by itself can be effective only over a few issues. And the rest, if they are to be controlled at all, need to be controlled by other means as well.

SECTION 50

LEGISLATION

CONSTITUTIONALISM requires Legality, and Legality requires laws, laws laid down in advance and published, telling officials what decisions to take, and telling subjects what the legal consequences of their actions will be.

Decisions which determine how an "open" class of other decisions shall be taken are legislative decisions, or decisions with a legislative aspect. We might hope that in these cases the decision, since obviously of the greatest importance, should always be the decision which was reasonable and right: but there cannot always be just one, reasonable and right, decision, because human beings lack perfect information,[1] and therefore can act in concert only if they have rationally opaque conventions in matters which are in themselves indifferent, and everybody abides by these conventions. The Rule of the Road, traffic signals, and the *Highway Code* enable imperfectly informed drivers to proceed on reasonably based assumptions about what other drivers will or will not do. It does not matter on which side of the road we all drive, so long as we all drive on the same side. And for this we need agreement only, not the reaching of the right decision by rational

[1] § 1, pp. 1–2.

arguments. Much of legislation is a matter of agreement not argument, to be reached by a legislative convention or assembly, not by court of justice. Much, but not all. Although legislation is often a matter of reaching agreement on what conventions to adopt, and then promulgating and publishing them, laws often can be assessed and criticized as being just or unjust, expedient or inexpedient, sometimes even moral or iniquitous.

The Ideal Rule of Law assumes that legislation is a uniform type of governmental activity, and lays down that it should be performed by a special organ of government, the Legislature. We have seen, however, that we cannot have a simple classification of decisions as legislative, judicial or executive; for the same decision may have both a legislative and an adjudicative aspect.[1] We also may go wrong if we assume that what a legislature does is to legislate. A Legislature sometimes legislates, but often it is concerned with criticizing the government or debating public policy. Sometimes, as in Great Britain, it is the supreme authority, and has the last word on all questions, and in particular it decides who shall form the government. In other countries, the U.S.A., it is a subordinate, not a sovereign, body, and has no (or only very limited)[2] authority to decide who shall or shall not hold government posts. Thus in considering the functions of the Legislature there are two grounds of distinction. The first is whether the adjudicative or the legislative aspect is primary. Private Acts of Parliament then are to be classified as adjudications, in the same way as decisions of the courts of law are. The High Court of Parliament is acting as the Supreme Court of the land, overriding all other courts, and having the last say on how any dispute is actually to be decided, all previous precedents and enactments notwithstanding. Often, however, what strikes us about the Legislature is that it is untrammelled in its discretion, in contrast to the Judiciary, which is bound by the principles of Equity and Legality. It is on this basis that Private Acts of Parliament are classified as a form of legislation, because Parliament is not

---

[1] § 29.

[2] The Senate has authority to veto most appointments, but not to propose its own nominees. The House of Representatives can impeach the President before the Senate, and by a two-thirds majority of the Senate, remove him. Congress can enact a law of Succession over the Presidential veto. The present law of Succession places the Speaker of the House of Representatives (elected by the House) next in succession after the Vice-President. Thus a united Congress could conceivably replace the President by its own nominee. But it never has. The power of impeachment is felt to be quasi-judicial, not completely discretionary. It has only once been invoked, and then unsuccessfully.

bound to justify its decisions as being applications or interpretations of existing law, or at most developments of it according to the principles of Equity, as are the courts of justice. Parliament can decide issues explicitly on other grounds: Public Interest, expediency, public demand. It can quite openly innovate. It poses afresh the problem of sovereignty.

We need, therefore, to disentangle distinctions between different *functions* of the *Legislature*, as it reaches different sorts of decision, from distinctions between different *modes* of *legislation*, whereby decisions with a legislative aspect are reached. We distinguish three modes of legislation: for besides the avowed enactment of laws by the Legislature, every judicial decision has, as we have seen, its legislative aspect, and, furthermore, many administrative decisions are more or less explicitly legislative in force.

SECTION 51

JUDICIAL INTERPRETATION AND INNOVATION

ALL judges make law to some extent. The Ideal Rule of Law, which enjoins the Judiciary only to apply existing law,[1] is impracticable.[2] Although attempts have been made to require judges to model themselves on Judex IV, these attempts have always failed,[3] on account of the inevitable borderline ambiguity of any code of law, however carefully formulated. On many occasions the construction of the Act will be in no doubt, but some times it will be uncertain which way the words are to be taken, and interpreters, and not merely apply-ers or enforcers will be required; and then their decisions will have a legislative aspect, since they will lay down for future judges how the words of the Act are to be taken in cases like the ones decided. Although advocates of Legality often inveigh against judge-made law, it is only a slogan: for inasmuch as Judex IV is an unattainable ideal, the only judge who makes no law is Judex I; and advocates of Legality do not want to reinstate him. If the judiciary is to lay any claim to rationality it must in declaring the law make it; for in settling disputed

---

[1] § 25, p. 113.   [2] § 25, p. 114; § 31, p. 140.
[3] §§ 47 and 48 of Introduction to the Prussian Code of 1794, which attempted this, had to be repealed in 1798. See further, P. Vinogradoff, *Common Sense in Law*, 2nd ed., O.U.P., 1946, pp. 88–92.

cases it settles the law for all similar cases: else it is not rational, but arbitrary.

We are bound to have judge-made law. We cannot maintain Legality as an absolute principle. The arguments for Legality must be weighed against arguments on the other side, and a balance struck, depending on the issues at stake. In the criminal law, where the life and liberty of the subject are involved, considerations of Constitutional Freedom carry greater weight than in the civil law, where, characteristically, only property rights are involved, of one citizen against another. It is more important that the subject should be sure that he will not be sent to prison unless he breaks a definite law, than that his financial arrangements should not go awry.

In England, somewhat surprisingly, the criminal law admits of a dramatic form of Judicial Innovation. In 1960 a man called Shaw was found guilty of a common law crime, although he had contravened no antecedently specified rule.[1] It could be argued here that the common law part of the criminal law is not just a set of external regulations laid down merely as the "positive" enactment of the sovereign authority, but is also the articulation of the common values of the community which are shared by most people and should be known to all. The common law is, in principle, common to all members of the community. Any man who sails close to the wind, knows what he is doing, and must not be surprised if, contrary to his plans, he finds himself actually on the windy side. Shaw knew that he was engaging in dubious activities. He could have steered clear, but chose to do what he knew to be wrong, thinking he could get away with it. But he thought wrong. So the argument runs, and against the extreme exponents of Legality it has force: in a simple community with a rudimentary legal system, we might well wish to leave room for further development of the criminal law, to articulate more adequately the common values of the community. But in England the common law is already highly developed, and where it is still defective, the remedy of statute law is to hand. We do not *need* Judicial Innovation in the criminal law. And therefore, since we can do without it, and there are sound, although not conclusive, arguments against it, we should dispense with it. That is, judges' discretion in the criminal law, should be (as regards conviction, not as regards sentencing) limited as much as possible. They

---

[1] *Shaw* v. *Director of Public Prosecutions*, [1961] 2 A.E.R. 446; [1962] A.C. 223. See also *R.* v. *Manley*, [1933] 1 KB 529; and, for discussion, H. L. A. Hart, *Law, Liberty and Morality*, O.U.P., 1963, pp. 6–12.

should interpret only so far as they must; and, since they need not, never innovate.

The argument from Constitutional Freedom carries great weight, but applies only to that limited field where the life or liberty of the subject may be in jeopardy. Other arguments are more widely applicable, but less weighty. Arguments from Equality[1] and moral agnosticism have been adduced, and more seriously from the Assignment of Responsibilities, and the Separation of Powers.

The argument from moral agnosticism is sometimes represented as the internal version of the argument from Constitutional Freedom. Not only some subjects but all judges should be assumed—and allowed—to be bad men. Judges should not be required—nor permitted—to have moral views; and if they do, they should keep them to themselves. And therefore, in so far as they cannot exemplify Judex IV perfectly, they should confine themselves rigidly, in interpreting a statute, to "the Intention of the Act", and dismiss from their minds any consideration of Equity or Justice with the same rigour as they would exclude all considerations of fear or favour or self-interest. Morality is a bad thing, lawyers say, and not to be muddled up with the law. It is a poor argument. Although often we need to qualify our ideal of Justice by considerations of Legality, Justice remains our ideal; if we did not share any moral values we would not live together in a community at all; and were judges unable to reach decisions which were more or less reasonable, right and equitable, we should not refer our disputes to them at all, but to the impartial arbitrament of chance. There are, indeed, arguments for judges being guided by Legality rather than Equity, but no arguments against their being guided by Equity as such. Where a judge has a personal morality[2] which is notably different from the prevailing morality of his time, he should take care not to be prejudiced by his private, personal moral views. But this is because the morality is private, not because it is moral. We, rightly, do not want legal judgements to be merely moral judgements in solemn form. But we do not therefore have to have them immoral or a-moral[3].

Other arguments against judge-made law are based on the traditional doctrine of the Separation of Powers. Law-making is Parliament's business. The judges should not trespass on parliamentary preserves.

---

[1] See below, § 58, pp. 253–5.
[2] See below, § 71, pp. 317–18; § 72, pp. 320–1; and above, § 22, p. 100.
[3] See below, § 71, p. 314, § 75, pp. 343–6.

As it stands, the argument is a confusion, based on too crude a classification of governmental activities. But behind it stand real arguments, based on real features of different procedures appropriate for reaching different sorts of decisions. Judicial decisions can be reached impartially and consistently because judges are assigned *limited* offices,[1] to administer the law, not to make it, so that within this limited field, there is not all that much room for disagreement. The wider the discretion conferred on them, and the more room for disagreement between one judge and another, the less easy it is for any judge to be impartial. It is expedient, therefore, to concentrate all unlimited, political, discretion in Parliament, where, although it may be exercised wrongly, the wrong will be done openly, subject to the critical procedures of party politics. Subservience to political masters is the price for a non-political, and independent, administration of justice; and this is a price worth paying, because, if mistakes are going to be made, which they will be among fallible, selfish and imperfectly informed men, the individual subject will suffer less if they are made not covertly in the courts of justice, but in the overtly political arena of Parliament.

The example of the Supreme Court of the United States of America shows that if we want to keep politics out of the administration of justice, we must deprive the officials who administer justice of all discretion which might be influenced by political considerations. Else there will be an incentive for politicians to attempt to "pack" the courts with their own partisans. But where the ultimate authority is a non-judicial court or assembly, all we need to ensure when selecting people to be judges is that they shall faithfully apply the laws enacted by the Legislature in all cases to which they clearly apply. It was not necessary to pack the English Bench because the same judges who had decided the Taff Vale case could be relied upon, whatever their political opinions or private views, to apply the provisions of the Trades Disputes Act, which reversed the Taff Vale decision. Provided the judges, like reeds, will bow to political winds in due legislative form, there is no reason for them not to exercise, in the absence of a clear directive from Parliament, their own judgement on what is equitable and just. All that we do demand is that where Parliament has given a ruling, judges should follow it, even against their own judgement, not because Parliament is wiser, more equitable or more just than the judges, but, as we have said, because it is expedient to

[1] See above, § 19, pp. 79–81; and § 24, p. 110; and § 30.

concentrate all political discretion in Parliament, where though wrong may be done, it will be done openly.

A second argument urged against judges entertaining any considerations of Equity is that if they will not, then Parliament must. If the Judiciary will not reform the law, they will compel the Legislature to undertake that responsibility. There is merit in this argument: but unfortunately it does not always work out. Parliament has many other things to do besides legislate. It certainly does not, and perhaps cannot, find time to enact all the many minor improvements that need to be made if the law is to be kept up to date. Some bills are passed "on the nod" without adequate consideration: other inequitable precedents or out-of-date provisions are not remedied at all. Legislation by a sovereign legislative assembly, because it is legally all-overriding, tends to be subject to constitutional checks and therefore not to be effectively available for minor reforms. And *per contra*, it is just when the Legislature is inattentive or timid or hamstrung that judges feel forced to take it upon themselves to innovate and to revise the law. The filibuster in the Senate is the ultimate cause of the Supreme Court's coming to take upon itself what are in effect legislative rather than judicial functions.

These arguments are all arguments for restricting the discretion of judges rather than for attempting to remove it altogether. By restricting it, we secure a fair degree of predictability, we make its exercise relatively independent of the personal prejudices or political predilections of any particular judge, and we reserve the decision of deeply disputed questions, on which there does not appear to be one right answer acceptable to all reasonable men, to a procedure more suited to the decision of contentious matters. But we cannot hope for complete predictability. So long as we maintain the supremacy of Parliament, we do not need to fetter the judges rigidly to prevent them from playing politics. And although the possibility of legislation by Parliament constitutes a valuable safety-valve, should the judges be incompetent or perverse, Parliament does not have time to attend to all the particular points where the law needs to be developed or amended.

It is only in particular cases, those where decisions in accordance with the letter of the law are palpably unjust, that we discover the inadequacies of Legality. *Ita scriptum est, sed durum*. But only in the individual case can we realise how hard it is; and, if we are to realise it fully and take it seriously, it must be an actual, and not merely a hypothetical, case; it is a decision reached after taking all the relevant factors into consideration that may be at variance with one based on only the limited number of factors antecedently specified as relevant in accordance with the canon of Legality. We may therefore want to compromise Legality for the sake of Natural Law, Equity, and Justice,[1] knowing that although hard cases make bad law, excessively harsh decisions also make bad law. As we have already seen,[2] the whole *raison d'être* of the apparatus of law is to yield decisions which are, at least approximately, equitable and just. We want our courts to be courts of Justice, and confer discretion upon judges precisely in order that we may obtain Justice at their hands. Legality alone is not enough. Although we often need to qualify other ideals by Legality on account of the imperfection of men—the imperfection of the judged as well as the imperfection of the judges—it is only a qualification, not an ideal in its own right. Moreover, law-makers are also men, also liable to err. And therefore we should not throw away such safeguards as we can have against error or oversight in the written letter of the law.

Judicial Interpretation and—cautious—Innovation is in practice an important source of law. By judicial decisions the law is developed to cover new circumstances and meet new situations. It can be said to grow like coral, through the decisions of judges, as well as to be deliberately constructed, like a breakwater, by Acts of Parliament. Provided the conditions outlined in the next paragraph but two[3] are satisfied, there is no objection. The criticism is not that what is done is wrong, but that it is often thought to be wrong. Judges love Justice: but protest allegiance to Legality. They model themselves on Judex IV, even when they are being guided by other considerations. Highly inequitable precedents are eroded, not openly, because they are iniquitous, but covertly, by seizing on minor features, and using them, artificially, to "distinguish" new cases from preceding ones. There are disadvantages in a devious justice. The Portia principle can be pushed too far. There is a slight sense of deceit in the judicial process when judges make out that, in accordance with the canon of Legality, they are subsuming a case under a law which deductively entails what the decision must be, when really they are trying to decide it on its merits in accordance with their ideal of Justice.[4] Moreover, the law is little more certain than if judges overtly avowed that they were guided by

---

[1] See below, § 71, p. 314 and § 74.   [2] § 31, p. 141.   [3] pp. 221–2.
[4] See, for example, Jerome Frank, *Law and the Modern Mind*, New York, 1930, esp. pp. 104–5, 167, 230–1, 243, 256–7.

considerations of Justice and Equity. There is, thirdly, the grave disadvantage that the development of the law, because it is motivated by a sense of Justice, but has to be represented as flowing from the logic of Legality, will be unnecessarily untidy and unintelligible. Legal technicalities, which judges have seized upon in particular cases in their desire to do Justice, will be elevated into principles. Pretexts and excuses for evading the harshness of strict Legality will be represented as the *rationes decidendi*, in place of the real, rational, reasons which actually weighed with the judge. And this makes for obscurity, needlessly.

We could secure the general advantages of piecemeal reform without sacrificing anything in the way of predictability by having a special, "Legislative" Court of Equity to which judges could refer cases which for the sake of Legality they had been obliged to decide in a way which seemed inequitable, unconscionable or inexpedient: this court would not be authorised to reverse the decision in the particular case—thus preserving certainty—but would have authority to override the precedent for future cases—thus remedying the law at those points where it was in greatest need of revision, and allowing it to develop in a more natural and rational fashion, since the judges would feel more free to innovate openly. Such a court would be legislative, not adjudicative, in that its pronouncements were forward looking, dealing with any number of cases in the future, rather than with only one particular case in the past. And therefore it would have to specify the relevant characteristics of the cases in advance of the cases arising, and not *ex post facto*; the specification would thus be complete and finished and finite, without the possibility of further features being deemed relevant in the further event.

We do not quite have such a court.[1] Our concern for Justice is more urgent with regard to actual and present cases rather than for hypothetical or future ones. The importance of a judicial decision is, for us though understandably not for professional lawyers, that it decides a particular dispute in a particular way, not that it constitutes a precedent for the settlement of other disputes which may arise in time to come. We have not felt impelled to create a court merely to manufacture precedents and not to give real decisions to real disputes. We find we

---

[1] We do have a committee, set up by Lord Sankey, to which the Lord Chancellor can refer cases, and which can produce a one-clause Bill for Parliament to rubber stamp. But it has accomplished relatively little, because it can recommend only entirely non-controversial changes. Further proposals are now (1966) in the air.

can use our present apparatus of adjudication to make necessary innovations cautiously without a serious loss of certainty. For reason is not solely deductive,[1] and policies, as well as laws, can give guidance.[2] If judges publish their reasons as well as their decisions, we—or at least our legal advisers—can enter into their minds, and work out for ourselves how they should, and therefore probably will, decide the case we are interested in. We can tell the way Judex III's mind is going, in a way we cannot with Judex II, because we are able to view Judex III's decision from an internal point of view, and not from an external one only. Except for the utterly bad man, who has no community of reasoning and no community of values with him, and indeed has in common nothing more than a minimal bare descriptive language, Judex III is almost as predictable as Judex IV. Only in cases where two policies conflict need we be uncertain which way the decision will go: and although such cases are not rare, the standard cases, where there is no doubt how the policy applies, are much more common, and are numerous enough to enable a man to arrange his affairs with a reasonable degree of reliance on the legal consequences of his acts. Justice can be served, while much of what is valuable in Legality is saved, if judges take care to extract the principles and formulate the policies by which they are guiding themselves, so that lawyers and legal commentators can foretell the line of future decisions. Administrators, we have argued,[3] should be more like judges: but equally judges should be more like administrators. Both should have great regard for considerations of Legality: neither should worship it, or attempt to be fettered absolutely by the letter of the law: judges should give the greater weight to Legality, in as much as they deal with the central interests of the subject; but it is a difference of degree, not of kind.

We should therefore sanction a certain measure of Judicial Innovation. The inevitable discretion in Judicial Interpretation need not be confined to the bare minimum; and it need not be guided solely by reference to the Intention of the Act, but also by considerations of Equity and Justice. We still need, however, to give great weight to Legality. Judicial Innovation should be slow, predictable, explicit, intelligible and natural. It can then do a lot to make good the deficiencies of the existing law without seriously jeopardising the values Legality preserves, and without making the remedy worse than the

[1] See above, § 31, p. 139, n3.
[2] See above, § 31, pp. 139–41, and § 47, pp. 203–4.
[3] § 46, pp. 196–9.

disease. Piecemeal innovation on the part of the judges enables the law to develop and keep abreast of the changing needs of society. Provided the changes are made slowly, along lines which are intelligible, for reasons which are explicit, reasonable predictability will be preserved and obsolescence obviated. But judges must be cautious in their innovations. Their discretion, even if enlarged, must remain limited. Where Parliament has spoken, they must obey, even though Parliament be unjust. For Equity by itself is not enough of a guide. If we leave judges completely free to decide as seems to them equitable and just, we make them tyrants or politicians. Equity needs to be qualified, and heavily qualified, by Legality. Legality remains a cardinal principle of constitutional government; but not the only one.

SECTION 52

LEGISLATION BY ADMINISTRATIVE OFFICIALS

ADMINISTRATIVE officials legislate in two ways. Sometimes they are taking decisions which are properly described as administrative, but have a legislative aspect. Sometimes legislative authority is explicitly delegated to them by the Legislature.

Administrative decisions can have a legislative aspect quite unlike that of judicial decisions. Planning decisions, especially those authorising compulsory purchase orders, are to be compared with Private Acts of Parliament. The same considerations apply,[1] except that, whereas parliamentary proceedings are inevitably public, we have to take steps to secure "openness" in reaching administrative decisions.

The essential difference between delegated legislation and the legislation of a sovereign legislature is that delegated legislation has the principle of Constitutional Limitation built into it.[2] Delegated authority is limited authority. It can be exercised only within specified limits, for specified purposes and in a specified fashion. If these limitations are not observed, the courts can say that they have not been observed, and can declare the decision in question "*ultra vires*", null and void. No question of sovereignty is involved for neither the courts nor the officials with delegated legislative authority must be supreme if superior to the other: Parliament can be above both, and can therefore allow the courts to determine the limits of the legislative authority

[1] See below, § 53, pp. 224–7.   [2] § 10.

it has delegated, without thereby constituting the courts as supreme. The courts therefore can be used to apply the principle of Constitutional Limitation, without being open to the difficulties that beset the Supreme Court of the United States. We therefore do not need, with delegated legislation, any other protection against the abuse of untrammelled discretion. With a sovereign Legislature, or even with a Supreme Court, many procedures, many conventions, many understandings are needed, just because the authority there vested is unlimited; and always, however carefully circumscribed the procedure is, we still feel that we have only got the wolf by the ears. But with a delegated legislative authority this problem does not arise; and therefore we can insert fewer checks and balances, and fewer safeguards against the abuse of authority, because the authority which might be abused is only limited and not so dangerous as that of the sovereign body.

Nevertheless, delegated authority can be used wrongly, and some safeguards against error or abuse are desirable. The courts can confine discretion within limits, but within those limits the courts are not appropriate authorities to exercise supervision: for whereas the courts have much *expertise* for deciding whether a particular decision lies within the limits laid down by the letter of the law, they have no experience of deciding whether one decision rather than another, both clearly within the limits laid down by law, is more reasonable, or more expedient, or more politic or more advantageous. The courts therefore take care not to pronounce on "policy", that is, on questions of public policy that have been referred to the authority in question. On such questions, Parliament itself could adjudicate, but Parliament has not time even to supervise all the delegated legislation which is enacted now. It is therefore necessary for certain other safeguards to be provided, not as elaborate as those that fence round parliamentary procedure, but sufficient to give reasonable security against the mistakes most likely to arise.

Even where no particular people are named, their interests are often affected. There is therefore an argument for consulting them, and allowing them to make representations: and the chief argument against allowing particular interests to be represented when a Public Bill is under discussion in Parliament—namely lack of parliamentary time—does not apply. Ministers and other officials exercising delegated legislative authority often do in practice consult interested parties before making a statutory order; Parliament may pass an Act of

Parliament requiring that cars have safety devices: but exactly what safety devices are to be required, and according to what specification is better laid down by a statutory order, after consultation with the Royal Society for the Prevention of Accidents, the motor manufacturers, and other interested organizations. But at present this is often only a practice, not a principle. It could well be made a principle. With actual Acts of Parliament, the procedure of first, second, and third readings, of committee and of report, and the division of the House into government and opposition, secure that Bills are published long before coming into effect, and are exposed to critical scrutiny. Statutory orders need to be subject to procedures to secure prior publicity and some form of critical examination. The adversative procedures of the law courts are appropriate. In many cases, giving interested parties the right to be represented would secure this: in others, a "devil's advocate" might be employed on behalf of Parliament and the public, to probe proposed legislation for weaknesses or unnecessary invasion of individual rights and interests.

SECTION 53

LEGISLATION BY LEGISLATURES

THE restrictions laid upon the Legislature by the Ideal Rule of Law were both too narrow and too wide. Too narrow, because Private Acts, referring only to particular persons, institutions or places, are forbidden altogether: too wide, because many general laws can be wicked, or at least wrong.[1] We need to reconsider.

A Legislature enacting a Private Act is correlative to a judicial court reaching a judicial decision. The discretion of the judges is guided by considerations of Legality and Equity, in order that they may not abuse it, and in order that the subject may know the law and have some moral respect for it. The discretion of the Legislature is not fettered by considerations of Legality at all, nor always by considerations of Equity, and we invoke it in order to override considerations of Legality, or occasionally of Equity. We need on occasion to override considerations of Legality because being predictable and certain, they are inflexible and rigid, and therefore sometimes are unjust and sometimes cramping of the Public Interest. Sometimes therefore we pass

[1] § 25, pp. 115–16.

Acts of Indemnity or Attainder, sometimes Acts, such as Railway Acts, preventing particular people—landowners—preventing works of Public Interest.

All Private Acts contravene the principle of Legality—that is their purpose—and therefore there is an inevitable loss of certainty. But, as we have already argued,[1] the demand for certainty can be over-pitched. It is enough that in general the law should be reasonably certain; but it need not be always absolutely certain. Therefore, provided Private Acts are relatively few, we could argue that the subject's reasonable certainty is not sufficiently weakened to matter. The occasional Private Act, like the occasional thunderstorm, is alarming, but does not make ordinary life impossible.

Although this argument has force, it needs qualification, for it does not discriminate between the degrees of harm a Private Act may do. The expropriation of some land, with full and fair compensation, may be a hardship, notwithstanding the compensation, but it is not one the possibility of which will disturb men's sleep. The possibility of the imposition of the death penalty by Act of Attainder might well disturb many men. So far as life and liberty, at least, are concerned, these are good reasons for not allowing the Legislature to override the principle of Legality, even in the interests of Equity. Far better, we might say, that a wicked man should go unpunished than that any innocent should fear for his life. Occasional thunderstorms can be borne with, but hurricanes and earthquakes do shatter the even tenor of our ordinary ways.

Against this it may still be maintained that there are occasions when Legality should give way to Equity if not to Expediency. Else crimes may be committed under the cloak of Legality, with chartered impunity. Attainder is but impeachment under another name. When a tyrant has been overthrown, he should be brought to book, even if, according to the laws enacted under his *régime*, he was acting entirely within the law in all he did. The Allies in 1945 were not deterred by scruples of Legality from bringing the nazi war criminals to trial: nor should any Legislature be prevented from doing the same.

Such an argument is wrongly adduced in support of Acts of Attainder. Whatever the rights and wrongs of retrospective legislation,[2] it is *general* legislation, not a Private Act; and under it, a court has to try the case, subject to the usual procedural and other safeguards that are characteristic of a court of law. There is interposed

---

[1] In § 35, pp. 154–5.   [2] See below, pp. 227–9.

between the possibly partisan passions of a Legislature and the final authorisation of coercion, the judicial habits of mind of judges, who, even if the principle of Legality is to be overridden, can still observe the principles of Equity and Justice. An Act of Attainder, like any Private Act, needs, and admits of, no trial. The legal position of named persons is altered, definitely and beyond all question. There is no burden of proof. No defence of mistaken identity can be admitted; no appeal for mercy. A man is condemned unheard, without benefit of any of the procedures or presumptions which normally protect the accused from a miscarriage of justice. If Legality is to give way to Equity, at least it should give way to Equity only, and not to public policy or partisan passion. A Legislature, whose discretion is untrammelled, and which we often make subject to pressure groups and public opinion, is not the place where Equity is most likely to be observed. Therefore, if the sacrifice of Legality is to be to Equity and not to Expediency, then the Legislature should confine itself to overriding the restrictions of Legality which normally bind a court of justice, and should not attempt to dispense justice itself. We can, at least as regards life and liberty, adopt this principle of the Ideal Rule of Law,[1] *Nulla poena sine* JUDICIO, and have a strict ban on Private Acts imposing penalties on life or liberty, that is to say on Acts of Attainder.

Acts of Forfeiture, Private Acts depriving people of property rather than of life or liberty, are open to similar, if less strong, objections. It is inherent in the nature of some sorts of property, pre-eminently land, but also copyrights, patents, and concessions, that expropriation may be unavoidable: but expropriation with compensation is not forfeiture. Nor again are taxing laws, which deprive people of money, but are Public not Private Acts, Acts of Forfeiture. Private Acts depriving people of property should in general contain compensation clauses, with provision, in case of dispute, for fair and independent arbitration. There are, however, some occasions where compensation might not be required: first, where the Private Bill presented and accepted by Parliament is a "package-deal", in which the interested parties have reached a bargain satisfactory to all of them. Secondly, there are occasions when a concession, or landed property with mineral rights, has acquired a value far in excess of anything foreseen or intended when it was first conferred. There is some argument then that full compensation need not be paid. It is difficult to

[1] § 25, p. 113.

assess this argument, difficult to leave it to others to assess. Modern governments for the most part take their obligation to give compensation far too lightly: one is tempted to say that all Acts of Forfeiture should be banned absolutely. But such a ban is clearly not so stringent as that on Acts of Attainder. It seems better to say that there should be no Acts of total Forfeiture—there always should be *some* compensation for expropriated property: and compensation should be full, fair and prompt except in very few cases, where the expropriated person or expropriated property occupies a position that is unique and anomalous and where moreover it would be inequitable and unwarranted to compensate in full.

Even if Private Acts of Attainder and of Forfeiture are banned, men's interests, although not their chartered interests, may be harmed by other Private Acts. In so far as the object of a Private Act is to override Legality the better to achieve Equity, it is clear that the interested parties should be given a hearing out of respect for them as people. Even where Equity too, is being overridden for the benefit of expediency, or public demand, there are arguments from administrative efficiency and Political Liberty for giving the interested parties a hearing.[1] We can do this with a Private Bill because it will, if passed, concern closely a definite, limited number of people: and we are likely thereby to make the decision of the Legislature as equitable as possible and as well thought out as possible, and we think we owe it to individuals closely concerned to consult them and to give them some opportunity of participating in the procedure of the community for making decisions which will affect them greatly.

With general laws, Public Acts of Parliament, we can have few principles of Constitutional Limitation—necessarily so, since Parliament is the supreme decision-making authority, and its discretion cannot be formally fettered, and Parliament cannot be made accountable to any other body. Even with Private Acts, we can lay down rigid rules of Constitutional Limitation and expect Parliament to observe them, only because Parliament can achieve any of the ends it wants by means of Public Acts, if it really wants to. We cannot prevent the possibility of authority being abused: all we can do is to ensure that if it is abused, it will be abused by the supreme authority, in the full glare of publicity, and subject to powerful and probing criticism. Constitutional Limitation is impossible: we must therefore make Constitutional Criticism as effective as possible.

[1] See above, § 28, pp. 132–3; and below, § 62, pp. 269–71.

One Constitutional Limitation it does, however, seem tempting to make—that no retrospective legislation imposing penalties should be passed. For Constitutional Freedom demands that a man should know where he stands, so that he can, by not breaking the law, be secure from punishment, and so that he can plan his affairs himself in the light of what the laws are. If the law is changed by ordinary legislation, then, although some of his expectations may be disappointed or his interests harmed, he can still avoid being punished by taking care not to break the new law, and he can revise his plans for the future in the light of the new law. But if the law is changed retrospectively, he may find that he has unwittingly contravened the law and rendered himself liable to punishment, and he can never be sure, in making his plans, what the law in force at that time will turn out to have been. Legislation is, in great part, action-guiding. It therefore must be prospective, and retrospective legislation is logically absurd as the *typical* sort of legislation.

Against this, supporters of the Nürnberg trials will argue that with retrospective legislation imposing penalties, it is only in the name of Equity and Justice they want to override Legality, and never in the name of Expediency, Public Interest, or Public Demand. And while it would be entirely wrong to sacrifice Legality to any of these lesser goods, it is not wrong, and can on occasion be necessary, that Positive law should give way to Natural Law. The argument from Constitutional Freedom, they maintain, is being stretched too far. As with Shaw,[1] so, but immeasurably more so, with Goering. Whatever the Positive law, the nazi war criminals knew that what they were doing was utterly and monstrously wrong. The fact that they had gained control of the German State, and could invest all their deeds with a spurious cloak of Legality, does not give them any defence whatever. The Constitutional Freedom of the subject cannot be invoked to confer on the sovereign a constitutional licence for abuse.

Further arguments of expediency are adduced on both sides. Against retrospective legislation, that it opens too wide an avenue for abuse, and in particular it provides a dangerous precedent for any victorious powers in any subsequent war. In favour of Nürnberg that it did at least give the nazis a fair trial, and that the alternative to trying and punishing them was not letting them go unpunished, but executing them summarily, without benefit of trial. The nazi leaders would not have been allowed to go unmolested. Whatever the dangers of staged trials

[1] See above, § 51, p. 215.

at some future time, they are no worse, and might prove better, than summary executions.

It is difficult to reach a firm decision about the Nürnberg trials. I, with hesitation, incline to the view that they were right, but remain deeply uncomfortable about retrospective legislation. Only when, Positive law apart, the criminal must have known that he ought not to have been acting as he did, and only when the ordinary principle of Legality has for some special and exceptional reason broken down, as in nazi Germany, can we abandon Positive law, and take a stand on Natural Law instead.[1]

With the possible exception of retrospective legislation, we cannot lay down any Constitutional Limitation on the authority of the Legislature. What we can do is to consider procedures which will make Constitutional Criticism effective, and consider heads under which particular criticisms may be levelled.

The various procedures of the Houses of Parliament and of Congress are designed to secure that proposed measures should be scrutinised and discussed, and weak points exposed. To some extent these procedures achieve their ends; but the great pressure on parliamentary time, and the over-rigid structure of the party system prevent Bills in Britain from being properly considered. Many are passed "on the nod". Many criticisms, made by the Opposition whose business is to oppose, are factious, and many others are taken to be so. Much of the real business of discussion and debate is carried on outside Parliament, in Whitehall by the departments involved. Parliament is partly effective, but only partly effective, as a forum of Constitutional Criticism of legislation.

There are many merits, mostly unrecognised today, in having a bicameral Legislature, with the Second Chamber weaker than the First. If both Chambers are of equal strength, constitutional deadlock is endemic. If there is only one Chamber, or if the Second Chamber has no authority, there is the danger that the one chamber will abuse its authority. In order to take decisions at all, the Chamber must have a procedure for coming down decisively on one side of the argument or the other, in spite of all counter contentions; and decisiveness is apt to dull sensitivity to criticism. Moreover, any corporate body meeting as often as a modern Legislature does, will develop an *ésprit de corps*, and will be liable to a form of corporate selfishness none the less dangerous for being corporate rather than individual. Bills passed by

[1] See further below, § 74, pp. 340–1.

the House of Commons have to be passed by the House of Lords (subject to certain exceptions) and given the Royal Assent before they have the force of law. Bills of Congress have to be sent to the President who can veto them. In Britain it is generally, but not formally, agreed that the House of Commons should have the chief say. The House of Lords can review and revise, but should give way to the considered decision of the House of Commons. The Royal Assent has not been refused since the reign of Queen Anne. Nevertheless, the House of Lords can throw out a Bill: the Monarch can refuse to assent to a Bill: and then the Bill does not have the force of law, no court of justice will recognise it as such, no man can be punished for not obeying it. The House of Commons has its prep-school moods: but *quod placuit pueris non habet vigorem legis*. And if the House of Commons were to abuse its discretion in a gross fashion, there are interposed between its *ipse dixit* and the final authority of law, further stages which would provide opportunity for further questions and second and even third thoughts. Although the final say rests with the House of Commons, the last word does not. And this legislative procedure exemplifies the logical structure of political reasoning. Political reasoning, as we have seen,[1] is dialectical. It is a matter of arguments for and against, not of premisses rigorously entailing a conclusion beyond all possibility of doubt. But although there are arguments on both sides, they are not evenly balanced, and we have to weigh them and reach a conclusion as best we can. Yet our conclusion, unlike that of a mathematical argument, is never logically final, and always may be open to further objection. Therefore the best legislative procedure is to have a debate, in which both sides of the argument can be put forward, followed by a vote, which will yield a definite decision, followed by further stages in which gross errors, but not all errors, can be put right. The House of Commons thus almost always has in effect the supreme authority and the supreme power in the land, but its authority and its power is not, even formally, absolutely absolute. Mistakes will be made, and the House of Commons is the place where they will be made, and where they can be most easily shown up to be mistakes. But although the House of Commons is the supreme mistake-making body in the land, its liberty of making mistakes is not a legal privilege, but only the concomitant of its very wide discretion. Its discretion is unlimited, but not absolute. For although in all ordinary cases its decision goes, this does not have, as a matter of law, to be so in all possible cases.

[1] § 6, pp. 22–23.

The legislative procedure of Great Britain depends on the weak doctrine of the Separation of Powers.[1] Three distinct bodies, the House of Commons, the House of Lords, and the Monarch, must co-operate to produce a law. If any one of them misbehaves, the others can stymie it by withholding co-operation. Thus we have an effective way of preventing bad laws being enacted. The difficulty is to ensure that it does not prevent all laws, good or bad, being passed. One unco-operative member of the trio could play the rules to obtain every decision to its own satisfaction. After all, it is only because men are in general uncooperative that we have to have the apparatus of State at all: but then it seems self-defeating to make the apparatus of State depend on men's co-operation.

Men, however, are not utterly uncooperative. If they were, the State, howevery necessary, would nevertheless be impossible. It is not because all men all the time are uncooperative, but only because some men some of the time are. We can, therefore, hope to sustain, within the coercive framework of the State, institutions which constitute non-coercive sub-communities. We can—and it is our chief hope of taming Leviathan—operate the machinery of State by means of voluntary co-operation between men. But the spirit of co-operation may fail—it is one of the signs of the breakdown of a society when men and institutions fail to co-operate in running the state. In particular, it is liable to fail over the operation of the supreme decision-making procedure, for two reasons. First, control of the supreme decision-procedure constitutes supreme power. Corporate bodies as well as men may be tempted to be intransigent in order to secure to themselves the real say. Neither the House of Representatives nor the Senate will give way because each thinks that it should be *the* legislative assembly. Further, non-co-operation is one of the ploys of party politics, and what was intended as a constitutional safeguard becomes a move in the party game. Secondly, even with much good will, disagreement is more likely to occur at the highest level of proceedings than elsewhere, just because the discretion there is less limited than anywhere else. A magistrate and a policeman can co-operate, because each knows fairly precisely what his part in the co-operative venture is: but on questions of Justice and Public Interest there is far more room for non-factious disagreement between men of goodwill acting in good faith.

It is therefore advisable not to depend simply on co-operativeness,

[1] § 19, pp. 80–81.

to ensure that the powers between whom the sovereign authority and sovereign power is distributed actually do co-operate. The accidents of British history have secured that the House of Lords and the Monarch have formally the power of veto, but normally feel in too weak a position to use it unreasonably or for party advantage. Only if they are sure that the House of Commons is very badly wrong, or very badly out of step with public opinion, will the other components of the supreme legislative authority dare to veto the considered decision of the House of Commons. But the possibility is there, and helps protect the House of Commons from the corrupting tendency of absolute power.

SECTION 54

CRITICISM OF THE LAWS

THE Rule of Law lays down for legislation, as for adjudication and administration, various procedures and principles designed both to act as safeguards against abuse, and to make those in authority open to the influence of reason. The Rule of Law does not, however, completely determine what decisions are to be taken. Other principles, other ideals, and other arguments can be adduced, besides those of the Rule of Law, in favour of one specific decision rather than another. In the case of legislation, the Rule of Law requires us to have legislative procedures such that criticism is possible and sometimes effective. We need now to consider what are the grounds on which legislation should be criticized.

There are many grounds on which we can criticize laws and policies. Some, such as Justice, Humanity, Freedom, Equality, lie in the nature of the State, and could be regarded as particular specifications of Rule of Law arguments. Some such as Political Liberty, Natural Law, and Morality, may also be considered as fundamental principles as politics, but, if only for the sake of clarity, are best distinguished from Rule of Law arguments. Other ideals, Individualism, Socialism, Collectivism, Syndicalism, Radicalism, Empiricism, Nationalism, Internationalism, and many other -isms, are to be regarded as ideologies, valid perhaps, but not grounded in the nature of the State.

There is one ideal which we, of course, do not have in enacting laws (apart from those regulating the administration of the law). It is

Legality. For it is inherent in the activity of legislation that the letter of the law, at least, is being changed. We may, on grounds of Freedom or Justice, not depart very far from what Legality would lay down, but we are altering the law. And since the law is the background against which men have interests, it is inherent in legislation that some men's interests will be adversely affected. We can and should take care to protect men's central interests, and we may be tender towards certain other "vested" interests: but we cannot make all the interests of everybody altogether safe; and some interests therefore, must be vulnerable to legislation.

We consider first Justice, then various Equalities, together with Humanity. We then consider Political Liberty, and various problems posed by our love of Freedom, and the tension between it and the various moral obligations arising out of our membership of a community; and also the extreme case where our duty of obedience is over-ridden by a higher obligation to disobey.

SECTION 55

JUSTICE

THE concept of Justice is complicated and often confused. We are prepared to criticize persons, procedures, decisions, laws, and whole legal systems as unjust, and the ground of criticism varies in each of these cases. Often the word 'unjust' is used as the most general word of legal or political opprobrium, and the word 'just' as the most general word of legal or political commendation, so that Justice includes all other political goods, such as Equity, Legality, Liberty, Public Interest, Morality and Natural Law; but while Justice undoubtedly does overlap with some other political goods, there are occasions on which we contrast Justice with other goods—on those occasions, for example, in which we have to make some sacrifice of Legality, say, for the sake of Justice, or Justice for the sake of Liberty. Not everything that is unjust is wicked—not generosity *per se* for example; nor is everything that is morally wrong unjust—homosexual intercourse between consenting adults may be morally wrong, but it certainly is not unjust. And therefore there is some sense of Justice, in which it is not so general as to comprise all other goods within it, although still itself composed of many different strands. Joseph, being a just man, was minded to be merciful towards what he took to be Mary's fault:[1] often, however, Justice does not include Mercy, but is opposed to it.

The ancients thought that the primary sense of the word 'just' was that in which we speak of men being just.[2] Justice was a quality of mind. But this must be a derivative sense. We must say that a just man is one who is trying to reach just decisions rather than that just decisions are those that a just man reaches. For men, even just men, do not reach the same decisions all the time—if they did we should have no need of judges to arbitrate at all.[3] We therefore cannot require of a man, before he can be called just, that he should always succeed in reaching just decisions, but only that he should always try. A man is just, even though the actual decision he reaches is unjust, provided that he is trying to reach just decisions, and is going through the correct procedure to avoid reaching unjust decisions gratuitously: that is, if he gives due and careful attention to the case, takes care to hear and consider both sides, and takes care to avoid being swayed by personal interest, or favour, or bias, or prejudice. With persons, as with procedures,[4] we characterize Justice only negatively and incompletely. But we do have a positive concept of Justice. It is too elusive to give firm guidance or play much part in our account of the Rule of Law, but it remains a goal of aspiration and a criterion of appraisal for both particular decisions and general laws.

Justice, like Freedom, is two-faced. It faces, as we have seen,[5] towards rationality and universalisability, and leads us on that account to consider general features of cases and to be no respecter of persons. But it faces also towards the individual, and bids us orient our minds towards the individual and give full attention to the merits of his case, and not be swayed by any extraneous considerations. Rationality alone imposes some conditions of relevance,[6] but Justice is more stringent still. We fail to *do justice* to a man's case if we, quite rationally, on the score of Legality, exclude certain factors from our consideration, or, on the score of Public Interest,[7] bear in mind arguments unconnected with the case in hand. It often is expedient that one man

[1] Matthew i. 19.

[2] Plato, *Laws*, IX, 859–63; Aristotle, *Nicomachean Ethics*, Bk. V, Ch. I; see also definitions of Justinian and Aquinas quoted on p. 235n. Plato, in the *Republic*, elucidates δικαιοσύνη in the community before δικαιοσύνη in the individual man. But this is an expository device, not, I think, his real view. See *Republic*, VIII, 544d. Moreover, δικαιοσύνη in the *Republic* means integrity rather than Justice.

[3] § 2, p. 8.   [4] See above, § 28, pp. 129ff.   [5] § 27.

[6] See above, § 27, pp. 125–6.   [7] See above, § 48, pp. 207–8.

should die for the sake of the people, but it is not just, unless he has committed a crime worthy of death. It is perfectly rational to visit on a wrong-doer severe punishment for a venial crime: by so doing we may shake him out of his evil ways, or deter others. It may even be right.[1] But our sense of Justice is outraged. Justice requires that every man shall die for his *own* iniquity, and that only those who have eaten sour grapes shall have their teeth set on edge.[2] *Suum cuique*, says Justinian,[3] and Aquinas makes it *unicuique* for further emphasis.[4]

Justice is a rational regard for the individual. Because it is rational it is governed by the principle of Equity. But Equity, as we have defined it yields only a necessary, and not a sufficient condition of a particular decision's being just. If different decisions are taken in cases not significantly different, they cannot both be just[5]: but even if the decision is the same in both cases, it is not necessarily just. It is perfectly possible, and all too often happens, that men are treated alike, but unjustly. If we define Equity as treating similar cases similarly, then Equity must be distinguished from Justice. In normal parlance, however, we do not make any distinction, and the words 'just' and 'equitable' are used interchangeably, and we add to the weak principle of universalisability certain important, but indefinite, canons of relevance. A decision fails to be just or equitable if it fails to take into account all the relevant circumstances or if it does take into account other extraneous, and properly irrelevant, circumstances. The commonest objection to Legality is that decisions in accordance with Legality take into account only some of the relevant factors and fail to give any weight to others, which may be more important, and may bear the other way. A just decision, by contrast, is one which is not determined by the application of limited legal rules, but is taken on "the merits of the case", all the merits, not a partial selection of them.

A just and equitable decision is taken on the merits of the case, but not on other, extraneous, grounds. A decision fails to be just if it is based not only on the circumstances of the case but also on a lively consideration of the judge's own interests. It also can fail to be just if considerations of Public Interest or political expediency are allowed to

---

[1] See below, p. 237.   [2] Jeremiah xxxi. 29, 30; Ezekiel xviii.

[3] *Inst.*, Bk. I cap. 1. *Justitia est constans et perpetua voluntas jus suum cuique tribuere.*

[4] *S.T.*, q. LVIII. *Justitia est habitus secundum quem aliquis constanti et perpetua voluntate jus suum unicuique tribuit.*

[5] See above, § 27, pp. 127–9.

weigh. Caiaphas counselled the Jews wisely and well, so far as their Public Interest was concerned.

Both the inner and the outer limits of relevance are extremely difficult to determine. It is difficult, that is, to say what further factors, other than those antecedently laid down by law, are really relevant; and difficult also to lay down what factors are really extraneous to the particular case, and ought therefore to be regarded as irrelevant. It is partly because we cannot consider an individual case completely in isolation from the rest of human affairs. No man is an island, and all men's doings are done in the context of other men doing other things. We have to take into account what the conventions, customs, habits, and expectations of the parties concerned are, and have to consider the interests and rights of the individual in the light of the interests and values of the community at large. Therefore even to arrive at the just and equitable decision, we may have to invoke considerations of Legality, or Public Interest. Nevertheless we do not always have to, and Justice, as we have noted, can be contrasted with Legality, Public Interest, and the like. We therefore consider cases where the just and equitable decision does not depend on Legality or Public Interest, and may be different from decisions which are in accordance with these other canons. It is easier, on the whole, to show that Legality draws the limit too narrowly than that Public Interest draws it too widely. Legality can be faulted by particular hard cases, actual or hypothetical, in which the criteria of relevance antecedently laid down by law are clearly too much restricted, and some highly relevant factor is not allowed to be given due weight. We feel in such cases that Justice demands that the relevant factor should be taken into consideration, and that Legality is unjust in not allowing it to count. If only the law-giver had thought of this case, we feel sure that he would have made provison for it.

It is less easy to mark off Justice at the outer limits of relevance from, say, Public Interest, just because no individual case can be considered completely in isolation from the rest of human affairs. In the criminal law it is at least as much a matter of Public Interest as of Justice that we inflict punishment for the maintenance of law and order and the suppression of crime. We cannot hope to extrude all considerations of Public Interest from the determination of what is just. But we are sometimes clear that however conducive to the Public Interest a decision might be, it would be unjust and inequitable. The clearest examples are those where although there are arguments of expediency for a particular decision, there are *no* circumstances of the case which could justify it. The killing of hostages: the "punishment" of a scape-goat: exemplary punishments that are out of all proportion to the crime committed. These may be defended by arguments from expediency, sometimes even cogent ones: but Justice has been sacrificed. And therefore it is different from Public Interest.

Thus the ideal of Justice in particular cases is partly dependent upon, partly contrasted with, the ideals of Legality and Public Interest. Even where the ideals are in conflict, we accept that in practice the ideal of Justice needs to be qualified by those of Legality and Public Interest (and *vice versa*), and we are hesitant in stigmatizing as unjust a decision which falls short of the ideal of absolute Justice, but is in accordance with law or the Public Interest. If a judge does give a decision which is in accordance with the law, and is the same as those given in all similar cases, any criticism of the judge or the decision as unjust is a criticism more of the law invoked than of the judge applying it or the particular decision subsumed under it.

Our ideal of Justice for laws differs from that for particular decisions, because laws cannot be assessed on the score of Legality, nor can the weak principle of universalisability apply. But the dual allegiance, to Rationality and to Individuality, remains. We criticize a law as being unjust, if it draws entirely irrelevant distinctions, or fails to take into account relevant circumstances of individual cases, or inflicts penalties without regard to desert, or distributes benefits without regard to merit, or lays upon people unreasonably heavy burdens or penalties in view of the objects to be achieved, or if the objects themselves are utterly unreasonable, and run completely counter to our canons of rationality or our tenets of morality.

A law, like a particular decision, may be open to criticism on the score of injustice, and yet be defensible on other grounds. We may, quite properly, compromise our ideal of Justice in order the better to secure ease of administration, the maintenance of law and order, or for the sake of Freedom, Equality, or Public Interest. Thus whenever the law lays down an age-limit, e.g. for voting or for driving, it may be criticized, because age-limits do not exactly correspond to the abilities to vote wisely or drive carefully; but the criticism may be rebutted by the further consideration that the law needs to be clear and definite, and ages are clear and definite, whereas political wisdom and motoring competence are not. A law may be a better law for being less perfectly just, if it becomes at the same time more definite, or more certain in its application. In each case our sense of Justice is slightly strained, but we recognise that there are good reasons for departing from the absolute ideal. But something is being given up, and it is by examining what it is we are having to sacrifice, that we can discover what Justice, as one among many other political goods, is.

A law is unjust if it draws entirely irrelevant distinctions. A law which gave red-haired persons immunity from taxation, or singled out for execution Wykehamists who were more than six foot tall, would be open to criticism because these features are irrelevant ones. But there are no firm criteria of relevance. What is relevant depends upon the purpose of the law. It is reasonable that only tall men should be eligible for the police force, but not that only they should stand for Parliament. A much more deep-seated difficulty is that many features happen to be commonly associated with other ones, without the connexion being rational, necessary or universal. Youth often goes with exuberance at the driving wheel, age sometimes engenders wisdom. People with German names in Britain, people of Japanese origin in the United States, were, perhaps, more likely to be security risks in the Second World War than other people.[1] Yet it is far from true that no young boy is safe and cautious at the steering wheel, that all men over twenty-one are wiser than any boy under it, that all people of German or Japanese origin were security risks. The characteristic picked out by the law is contingently, so to speak epistemologically, relevant, but not necessarily or rationally. 'What has the sound of my name (or the colour of my skin) got to do with it?' the internee indignantly asks. The answer, that it is a crude but usable guide leaves him unsatisfied, for reasons we shall discuss later,[2] but leaves the legislator with the feeling that he has given all the answer he could be required to give.

Ideally, a law should pick out just the class of person, situation, or action that it needs to pick out in order to achieve its purpose. A law against theft should apply to thieves, a law about shops should apply only to shop-keepers. But, because of difficulties of definition or of application, laws often have to specify other classes than those they ideally should. We then may object that this class is too wide—some people are being "caught" by the law, when it should be leaving them alone; or that it is too narrow—some who are being caught, complain

---

[1] I owe this example, and some valuable argument, to Miss L. M. Gordon, of Somerville College, Oxford.

[2] pp. 239–40.

that others, who ought to be caught, are getting off scot-free; or that it is both too wide and too narrow; or that the concomitance, although a reasonably exact one, is nevertheless objectionable because it is contingent and opaque. Suppose, what is not true, that all black men were stupider than all white men: we might still think it unjust to lay down by law that no black man should enter a university, for we might feel that however reliable a guide the colour of his skin was to his intellectual ability, we still owed it to him as an individual man to assess his intellectual ability, and not take it for granted, even if it were in fact true, that we could be sure he was stupid because he was black.

A second difficulty in deciding what features are and are not relevant arises from the fact that in a free society a feature is relevant if a sufficient number of people think it is. However irrational colour-prejudice may be, the fact that a large number of people are conscious of colour distinctions makes these distinctions relevant. Thus, for instance, it has proved necessary in some parts of America to pass laws laying down "quotas" for black and for white people, simply in order to overcome the colour bar that did, as a matter of fact, exist. Similarly in a society where there are a fair number of Jews, and where there is some anti-Semitism, and corresponding anti-Gentile feeling, a school or a club may need to take into account a person's race or religion, in order to maintain a balance that is fair as between the groups, if not between the individuals. Similarly in England, whether or not a public school education is a relevant factor about a man, it is thought to be, and therefore has to be taken into account, if only on occasion to discount it, by all sorts of people who would not themselves be inclined to regard it as important.

The demand for relevance is thus based on the two features of Justice that it is rational and that it is oriented towards the individual. There ought to be a reason why we have a law which does—as all laws must—lump people together in certain categories; and this reason should show us why these categories are the right ones to use. More-over, the law should be concerned not only with classes of people generally, but with individuals as such. Therefore, ideally, the law should use categories which are not merely in general relevant, but are relevant in every case. But we have to compromise our ideal of Justice for the sake of other ideals. We have to compromise it for the sake of Freedom and Expediency, and recognise that in our existing society, as a result of people's past experience and present prejudices, many distinctions which are not *per se* rational, are nevertheless in their actual social setting, significant and needing to be taken into account by a rational man. And we have to compromise our ideal of Justice for the sake of enforceability, and ease of administration. We therefore formulate our laws in terms of features that are partly or contingently relevant but easy to define or determine, in preference to features that are totally and necessarily relevant, but difficult to describe or in actual cases to apply.

A law fails to do justice to the individual if it will not take into account any of the individual circumstances of the case. Modern statutes which impose "strict liabilities" are objectionable because no mitigating circumstances whatever can be pleaded, and men may be deemed guilty when they have neither done anything wrong nor failed to do anything within their power that they should. The owner of a car which was driven by another man not covered by third-party insurance used to be himself guilty of an offence, even if he had been misinformed by the other man, even if he had expressly made his consent to the other's driving conditional on his having third-party cover.[1] Our sense of Justice was affronted by a law which disqualified one man from driving because of another's deceit. We may on occasion defend "strict liability" on the grounds that it will lead to greater care being taken by those on whom the responsibility is laid, and that the general advantage outweighs the occasional injustice of penalising a man for something which was outside his control and no fault of his at all. But always we feel that Justice is being sacrificed, and often, as in this instance, to an unwarranted extent.

In a similar vein we object to the taking of hostages and the imposition of collective punishments. Both practices are effective. And the object—the maintenance of law and order—is laudable. But to hold an agent responsible for an action that he did not do, could not have prevented, and had nothing to do with at all, is to regard him as not being an individual agent, and strikes at the root of our whole concept of a person. So great is our aversion to vicarious responsibility that we are reluctant to make those who have stood surety for a man who has jumped his bail pay the full penalty they have pledged, in spite of their liability having been voluntarily incurred. Similarly collective punishments can never be justified on the score of expediency alone. We are prepared to countenance them, if at all, only where

[1] Road Traffic Act, 1930 (20 & 21 Geo. 5, c. xliii), s. 35 (1) & (2); repealed by Road Traffic Act, 1960 (8 & 9 Eliz. 2, c. xvi), s. 201 (3).

those to be collectively punished form some sort of sub-community, capable of collective action and to which some sort of collective responsibility can reasonably be ascribed.[1] At the very least, the children's fathers or elder brothers must have eaten sour grapes, before it could conceivably be fair to set the children's teeth on edge; and in fact we feel unhappy in imputing responsibility on those who did not actually do the deed, unless very stringent conditions are satisfied, so that we can say that they were "in on it" and made themselves accessories after the act.

Justice not only limits the *sort* of people who can be singled out for treatment, but also *how* they are treated. Granted that a man has stolen a sheep, and is therefore the sort of man who is worthy of punishment, it would nevertheless be unjust to hang him. His crime was not so great as to warrant that. We should note, however, that here, too, we are prepared to compromise Justice on occasion—after an earthquake or riot, for example—and inflict severe and exemplary punishments, the better to deter others. It may be right to do so—if, for example, law and order is in serious danger of breaking down: but the ideal of Justice is being compromised to these other goods, none the less.[2] We should note also that arguments of Justice here are often to the same effect as arguments of Humanity, though based on a different principle. Unwarrantedly heavy punishments are inhuman as well as unjust. To punish sheep-stealing with death is savage as well as unfair. We can discriminate the two arguments by considering cases where Justice allows what Humanity forbids. For a sufficiently odious crime a cruel penalty is just, though not humane. "Hanging is too good for him", people say of the torturer, sadistic murderer, the drug pedler, the war criminal: and we criticize the disembowelling, the flaying, or whatever excruciating end the speaker has in mind, not on the grounds that the criminal has not deserved it—he has—but on the grounds that *nevertheless* it would be inhuman to exact more than the death penalty, and that as men we owe it to ourselves, as well as to him, not to go beyond this limit, at the extreme, in visiting punishment on a fellow human being, however wicked.

Justice limits benefits and burdens, as well as penalties. It is opposed to Generosity. We think that benefits and burdens should either be

---

[1] See below, § 65, pp. 279–82. Compare above, § 18, pp. 76–77.
[2] See H. L. A. Hart, 'Prolegomenon to Punishment', *Proceedings of the Aristotelian Society*, 1959, pp. 10–12 reprinted in P. Laslett and W. G. Runciman, *Philosophy, Politics and Society*, 2nd Series, Blackwell, Oxford 1962. pp. 167–8.

apportioned by merit, or where no criterion of merit exists or is practicable, equally. We feel aggrieved if the State, by granting a person planning permission, confers on him a windfall he has done nothing to deserve. In the same way the press-gang was unjust, because it picked on some men, while others escaped. The principles of just distribution of benefits and burdens are much debated; they do involve, unlike all other aspects of Justice, some principle of Equality.

Justice itself is not Equality. Aristotle, at the cost of great artificiality, made out that it was,[1] and has been too much quoted and too little criticized. Individuals are not equal;[2] therefore neither is Justice. It is only when we are concerned with individuals not as such but simply as members of a community, that we can regard them as being equal. Distributive Justice, which distributes benefits and burdens among members of a community in virtue of their being members of a community, is the only sort of Justice which requires that people should be treated, in a non-trivial sense, equally.[3]

Justice is not Equity, Equality, Legality, Humanity, Rationality, Public Interest, or the Common Good. Often it takes account of them: sometimes it coincides with them. Often it is compromised for them: sometimes it does comprise them. But it is not to be identified with them. We are tempted to identify Justice with every other political good, and to make it embrace them all, in order to set ourselves one single goal of political endeavour. But conflict between different political goods cannot be conjured away by verbal transmutation. There are occasions, as we have seen, when Justice, in the narrow sense, conflicts with Equity, Equality, Legality, Humanity, Rationality, Public Interest, and the Common Good. If we will not acknowledge the conflict, we may fail to save a valuable ideal. Only if we know what the arguments on both sides are can we strike the best balance between them. Therefore we should distinguish arguments of Justice from arguments under other heads. Moreover, even if we could compound all other goods with Justice, we cannot do so with Freedom. Freedom is radically different from Justice, and we have to compromise Justice, however all-embracing we make it, if we are to have Freedom at all. In allowing men to exercise legal privileges, we allow them to act arbitrarily, selfishly, inconsiderately, unreasonably and unfairly. For Freedom entitles a man to act as he chooses, not as some rule lays it

---

[1] *Nicomachean Ethics*, Bk. V, esp. Chs. II, III, and IV.
[2] See below, § 56, p. 244.
[3] See further below, § 60, pp. 259ff.

down[1]. If I have any liberty, then there are some decisions I am allowed to make on my own; I am free in some cases to act arbitrarily. And if that is so, I may in such cases arbitrarily choose one person rather than another, without there being any grounds to justify discrimination. I may choose Jane, and take her to wife, while passing over Bess, her equally well-favoured sister. This is what it is to be free. Freedom is inherently unfair. If we place any value on Freedom at all, we must to that extent compromise the principle of Justice. We are licensing people to act unjustly, and guaranteeing, by the principle of Legality, the charter of Constitutional Freedom, that their unjust decisions shall stand. Especially with the institution of property, the licensed injustices of generations are likely to be cumulative. Heiresses go and marry rich suitors, instead of endowing some more deserving son of poverty. Wealth breeds wealth, and unearned increments often acrue to property in land. This, in general, the freedom-loving State must accept. It can act justly itself—and in the matter of land development it should act more justly than it does—but it cannot secure that all benefits are justly distributed. It cannot, because it is not all powerful nor all responsible. The supreme power is not able to do anything it wants: the supreme authority is not entitled to do whatever it thinks best. Therefore, even if it wanted absolute Justice everywhere, it is not entitled to have it. Only in the public domain (with many difficulties in determining where the boundary of the public domain is to be drawn) can Justice be the guide: in private domains, so far as the State is concerned, the dominant principle is that of Freedom, allowing private individuals to make their own dispositions, according to their own lights, their own interests, or their own fancies.

SECTION 56

EQUALITY

EQUALITY is a difficult notion in politics and a dangerous one. Outside politics, equality is naturally applied to *metrical* concepts. Only when we have a system of measurement does it make sense to raise the question whether two magnitudes are equal or not. We can talk of equal *lengths*, or *areas*, or *weights*, because these things can be measured. It makes sense to ask whether two things are equal when, and

---

[1] See above, § 37, pp. 160ff.

only when, it also makes sense to ask whether one of them is twice as large as the other, etc.

It is an acceptable extension of the concept of equality to apply it to two members, say x and y, of a set, completely ordered by the transitive, asymmetrical relation R, when $\sim xRy$ & $\sim yRx$. Thus we talk of two substances being equally hard when neither will scratch the other, or of two sounds being equally loud when neither is louder than the other, even though we may have no satisfactory way of measuring hardness or loudness.

Further extensions of the concept of equality are neither helpful nor innocuous. We can apply the concept to things which could not differ in degree but might differ in kind, to mean what we normally express by the word 'same' or 'similar'. The phrase, 'Other things being equal', means 'If the circumstances are the same', or 'in the absence of any differentiating features'. But this is not a helpful usage, for we already have perfectly good words to express the fact that two things resemble each other in respect of a certain feature, and the word 'Equality' is charged with emotional overtones which obstruct clear thinking. Men are apt to be resentful if they are told that they are not equal with somebody else, when all that is being said is the perfectly acceptable truth that they are different. The word 'Equality' is a dangerous one in politics. It would be better if it were never used, but always some clearer, and less emotionally charged, synonym. But in fact it is used, and we must attempt to elucidate its various senses, and use it as clearly as we can.

The first rule for achieving clarity when the concept of Equality is involved is always to ask: 'Equality in respect of what?'[1] A man may be demanding Equality in respect of monetary incomes, or, like Procustes, Equality in respect of height: he may be saying that he feels most at ease in the company of those who are (approximately) his equals in age, or among those to whom he neither gives orders nor renders obedience (his equals in rank). But always the word 'equal' by itself is incomplete. It is like the word 'same'. We need to specify the respects in which things are said to be the same or not. Between any two things, however dissimilar, we can always find some point of resemblance: and between any two things, however similar, we can always find some point of difference. Therefore we never can say that two things are the same, or are not the same, without being ready to

[1] Compare Aristotle, *Politics*, Bk. III, Ch. IX, 1280a21ff.; Bk. III, Ch. XII, 1282b22; Bk. V, Ch. I, 1301a28ff.

specify, at least to some extent, the ways in which they are, or are not, the same. And so too, in the political sense of 'Equality', we can never say simply that two people are equal, or unequal, but must have in mind the respects in which they are equal or unequal. We are all equal in some respects—we all must die. In other respects—the possession of personal peculiarities—every one of us is unequal in comparison with everybody else. Therefore all discussions of Equality will be fruitless unless there is a specification of the respects in which Equality is claimed or contested.

We can, secondly, make discussions of Equality more fruitful if we translate them into discussions of *relevance*. Although, strictly speaking, no two things are the same in all respects, we often talk of two things as being the same if they are the same in all relevant respects. What respects are relevant depends partly on the context of argument, and may partly itself be a matter for dispute. It is much easier to discuss whether a particular characteristic is a relevant one, than to discuss whether two men, or two cases, are equal. Therefore we do well to replace controversies about Equality by arguments about *criteria of relevance*.

It will, in fact, prove useful to go further, and have a two-way discussion, one about criteria of relevance the other about criteria of irrelevance. This reflects the dialectical nature of political argument, which makes it important to distinguish the cases where the onus of proof is on a man who claims a certain factor is relevant from those where it is on him who denies it. But of this more later.[1]

Discussions about criteria of relevance and irrelevance have the further merit of emphasising that the Equalities we claim or affirm are optional alternatives, not conjoint necessities. If I choose to regard one feature as relevant and all others as irrelevant, then I shall have one sort of Equality, either as an ideal or as a fact, but at the price of forgoing other Equalities based on other criteria of relevance. We can give everybody equal access to the courts or even equally good legal aid; but we cannot, and necessarily cannot, equalise the outcome.[2] Justice holds the scales equal; but allows one side to go down and the other up. We can provide equal rations of food for each member of the community, but at the cost of satisfying appetites unequally, leaving boys still hungry, and old women overfed. We can give everybody an equal right to vote in parliamentary elections, but then minority communities or groups may never be represented: or we can give

[1] § 59, p. 257.   [2] See below, § 58, pp. 255–6.

different communities or groups their own representatives, but then we do not give each man's vote equal weight. In the United States, the House of Representatives is constituted according to one principle of Equality, the Senate according to another. Each excludes the other. Neither is naturally right. The Founding Fathers had to *choose* which factors to take as relevant and which to disregard.

Equality is often thought to be connected with Justice, often with Legality, sometimes with Humanity. In a manner of speaking it is connected with each of these, but it is a different sort of Equality in each case. Justice (in particular cases) or Equity could, as we now see, be described, rather misleadingly, as Formal Equality: two cases that are formally equal should be treated equally; that is to say, two cases that are the same in all relevant respects should be treated, in all relevant ways, the same. This is none other than the weak principle of universalisability, the principle of rationality, which we have called Equity.[1] It is a principle of crucial importance, but it carries no egalitarian implications, and to describe it as a form of Equality is but a bad Latin pun. The strong principle of universalisability, which we have called Legality, can also be called Equality *before* the law, which lays down that we should treat each case in accordance with an antecedently promulgated rule, which we should apply to all cases that fall under it, and which thus specifies what features are to count as relevant. Equality of Respect, or Humanity, restricts even further the factors to be taken as relevant. Only the fact that men are human is relevant when considerations of Humanity are urged, and in this respect all men indeed are equal, for assuredly they all are human beings. All these, and some other, Equalities are important. But they are different Equalities in each case, and nothing but confusion can result from regarding all these Equalities as being one and the same. The usual egalitarian argument is just such a confusion. It confuses Formal Equality with Equality of Respect. Both principles correlate human situations with possible treatments of them. Formal Equality lays down for one type of correlation that it should be one-valued; that is, that every distinction which can be drawn between treatments corresponds to some distinction which can be drawn between human situations: but this is always possible since no two human beings are qualitatively identical. Equality of Respect lays down for another type of correlation the fact that it correlates characteristics common to all human beings with characteristics common to all humane treatments. Formal

[1] § 29.

Equality specifies the treatment as fully as any one, egalitarian or non-egalitarian, could want, but in doing this for the treatments, is committed to drawing too many distinctions among the human beings for the egalitarian to stomach. Equality of Respect manages not to distinguish between men, so as to gladden the heart of the egalitarian: but in saying so little about men as not to differentiate between them, it says too little about treatments to characterise them in more than a very minimal way—too little to ensure that they all will be equal in the way that the egalitarian wants. The egalitarian wants a map of the logical possibilities which is very detailed—in order to have everybody treated alike *in all respects*—and at the same time a crude outline sketch—in order to include all men together in only one constituency: but the logical manoeuvres which will give him the one will preclude him from having the other, and *vice versa*. We have no warrant for combining the minimal specification of human beings, which is the only one in respect of which we are all alike, with the maximal specification of the treatments we are to receive, which is necessary if they are all to be thought to be the same.

The central argument for Equality is a muddle. There are two sound principles of political reasoning, the weak principle of universalisability and the principle of Universal Humanity, and each has been described as a sort of Equality, Formal Equality in the one case and Equality of Respect in the other. But they are not the same Equality, nor are they compatible, and they cannot be run in harness to lead to a full-blooded egalitarianism.

Egalitarian arguments depend on not making explicit the criteria of relevance and irrelevance being propounded, so that they can shift in the course of the argument. The logical structure of the word 'Equality' makes this easy. It becomes even easier if to the equivocal word 'Equality' we add the vague one 'Opportunity'. We have no way of measuring opportunities. Often we do not know we have them, unless we take them. Success is the only certain proof of their existence. And we cannot always have success. In the face of failure, we have no sure way of telling whether our failure is due to our not having taken the opportunities open to us, or to our not having had them. Pride inclines us to the latter view. We blame external circumstances rather than our own inadequacies, and find in the failures of life fuel for fires of resentment rather than lessons in the grace of humility. Equality of Opportunity has bred envy rather than endeavour.

Like all bad doctrines, it is a corruption of a good one. It has a part, subordinate but perfectly respectable, in the structure of competitions. Competitions occur when there is some good thing, natural or artificial, in short supply, so that not everyone can have all he wants, and each attempts to obtain some to the exclusion of some others. They are a special sort of dispute.[1] In order that they may not degenerate into conflicts,[2] they are formalised to a greater or lesser extent, and take place according to a set procedure. We may assess the procedure of a competition, and criticise it on the score of its being unreasonable, unfair, inefficient or inexpedient; in particular, a rule or factor which confers an advantage or imposes a disadvantage not connected with the main purpose of the competition is open to the criticism of precluding Equality of Opportunity. In games, where enjoyment is the prime object of the exercise, the fun is lost if the outcome is a foregone conclusion. Therefore we arrange players or teams in "leagues" where they will be more or less evenly matched, or handicap the stronger side, so that the result shall still be open. In the serious business of life, we apply criteria of relevance, and object to irrelevant factors being given an influence on the result. We object if government contracts are awarded on the "old-boy net", because not having been to the same school as a civil servant is not relevant to a contractor's capacity to give good value for money. In order to prevent these and other irrelevant factors from operating, we require that contracts be advertised and tenders invited,[3] thereby giving each contractor an equal opportunity in the relevant sense for this sort of competition, of securing the prize. Similarly in a beauty competition we may require the contenders to wear only bathing dresses, in order that the judges may reach their conclusion in the light of facial charms only, and not any adventitious elegancies of dress. In awarding scholarships and other educational advantages we have doubts about the propriety of taking into consideration a boy's competence at cricket or facility on the flute. But here, just because the purposes of education are many and diverse, it becomes much more a matter of dispute what factors should, and what should not, be considered relevant.

The difficulty becomes intractable when we generalise from education to life. We are not agreed on what the good life is, nor on what constitutes success in life, and therefore we cannot lay down what factors should be relevant, and what ought not to be allowed to count.

---

[1] See above, § 3, p. 11, or below p. 366.
[2] See above, § 16, p. 63, or below p. 366.
[3] See above, § 46, p. 200.

We are equally uncertain when the race begins and where the finishing post is. Divorced from its proper context, Equality of Opportunity becomes viciously vague. Every contest ends in some contender winning and others not. But if every contest is succeeded by another contest, the strict egalitarian may object to the result of the first contest being allowed to have any influence on the outcome of the second. Those who pass the eleven-plus have an advantage over those who fail, when they come to compete for places at the university. So egalitarians, who were loudest in their support of the eleven-plus in the 1940s, on the ground that it gave children Equality of Opportunity, clamour for its abolition, on the ground that it denies children Equality of Opportunity.[1] Nor is it merely a matter of their taking a different time as their starting-point. Every competition must result in some being successful and others not: and therefore, if the competition proceeded on a rational basis, it not only creates a new inequality, but reveals an antecedent one. A competition in which there is Equality of Opportunity is one in which the best man wins, and therefore one in which the winner is deemed to have been the best man, and in that, crucial, respect unequal. The egalitarian takes exception to this form of discrimination, and, shifting his ground, demands that it too be eliminated. The objective, he says, should be Equality, not Equality of Opportunity.[2] This change of front reflects neither dishonesty nor outstanding stupidity on the part of egalitarians, but the internal inconsistency of their ideal, absolute Equality. We can secure Equality in certain respects between members of certain classes for certain purposes and under certain conditions; but never, and necessarily never, Equality in all respects between all men for all purposes and under all conditions. The egalitarian is doomed to a life not only of grumbling and everlasting envy, but of endless and inevitable disappointment.

Equality, and more especially Equality of Opportunity, are treacherous concepts. This is not to say that no egalitarian conclusions ever hold good, nor that we must canonise inegalitarian meritocracy. It is, rather, that we should reformulate all controversies about Equality in other less emotive and less absolute terms. We need not slogans, but

[1] "The central and irresistible argument against the 11-plus lies in the denial of social justice and equal opportunity which this implies." Mr. Crosland at Harrogate, 7 January 1966.

[2] So Mr. Brian Simon, Reader in Education in Leicester University, addressing the Confederation for the Advancement of State Education, as reported in *The Times*, 27 September 1965.

detailed arguments about criteria of relevance and irrelevance. Being arguments they are naturally two-sided, and one side may be right without the other being unreasonable, and an opponent may be wrong without being necessarily wrong-headed. In the detailed assessment of argument we shall see the important truth which the idiom of egalitarianism conceals, that on most political questions we are presented with a balance of argument rather than a simple black-and-white issue. Our arguments, therefore, will yield conclusions that are more solidly based, yet more tolerant in tone. Some, but not all, the conclusions the egalitarian yearns for can be maintained on non-egalitarian grounds, better established, but less censoriously affirmed.

SECTION 57

HUMANITY

ARGUMENTS from Humanity are based on the fact that men are human, and ought to be treated in certain ways (or better, ought not to be treated in certain other ways) in virtue of the fact that they are human. Because men are men, they ought not to be killed, tortured, imprisoned, exploited, frustrated, humiliated. Human beings, perhaps because they are sentient centres of consciousness, perhaps because they are rational agents, ought always to be treated not merely as means but also as ends-in-themselves. The exact content of the doctrine of treating men, in part, as ends-in-themselves is unclear, but at least two things are clear: that all men are entitled to such treatment; and that their entitlement derives from their possession of certain features, such as sentience and rationality, which are characteristic of the human species. And therefore it is proper to view this argument as one which starts from the universal common humanity of men—that all men are men—and ends with an injunction about how men are to be treated— that all men are to be treated alike, *in certain regards*. This argument has little to do with Equality, although it is often brought forward under the title "Equality of Respect". It is, rather, an argument of Universal Humanity that we should treat human beings, because they are human beings, humanely. To say that all men, because they are men, are equally men, or that to treat any two persons as ends-in-themselves is to treat them as equally ends-in-themselves is to import a spurious note of egalitarianism into a perfectly serious and sound argument. We may call it, if we like, the argument from Equality of Respect, but in this phrase it is the word 'Respect'— respect for each man's humanity, respect for him as a human being—which is doing the logical work, while the 'Equality' adds nothing to the argument and is altogether otiose.

The argument, however, has often been thought to be really egalitarian. It is expressed by the words, "After all, all men are men" "A man is a man for a'that". From this it is argued in some such way as this:

> All men are men
> ∴ All men are equally men
> ∴ All men are equal

It is not a cogent form of argument. That it is fallacious is shown by the parody which can be obtained by replacing the word 'men' by the word 'numbers'.

> All numbers are numbers
> ∴ All numbers are equally numbers
> ∴ All numbers are equal.

An implicit and illegitimate extension is being made of the respects in virtue of which the men (or numbers) are being said to be equal; it is being assumed that because they are equal in some respects—in possessing those characteristics in virtue of which they are said to be men—therefore they are equal in all. And this does not follow.

Considerations of Humanity will produce some egalitarian conclusions, less fallaciously but less far-reachingly than the frivolous argument above. Whenever inequality results in some people having *too little*, the humanitarian will protest as well as the egalitarian. Human life cannot be properly lived in very straitened circumstances, and we do not show respect for human beings as such if we do not try to alleviate such conditions. Moreover wealth and poverty are, in part, relative terms. It is not just that there is a certain minimum requirement of food and fuel—true though this is; there is also a varying, and in our age rising, level of normality in each particular community, and to be too far below this will preclude a man from participation in the normal life of that community. The pre-war poor scholars in Oxford did not usually suffer from undernourishment: but their poverty did prevent them living the normal life of an undergraduate, and could be objected to on those grounds alone. Not only bread, but Nescafé and books are necessaries of university life—of social existence rather than bare physical subsistence.

This argument, the argument of the rising minimum as I shall call it, seems to me to be by far the most pervasive and persuasive argument for Equality in political thought today. It is a telling argument, but it is open to abuse. It may be a good thing that nobody should be without a television set: but it is only one *desideratum* among many; it does not have, though it sometimes pretends to have, the compelling force of the claim that nobody should go without food.

The argument of the rising minimum ought not only to be tentative in its forcefulness but moderate in its claims, and ought not to set its sights too high. We may say that people ought not to fall too far below the average: we must be careful not to be led into saying that people must not fall at all below the average. This latter would entail a strict equality: but it cannot be justified on any argument from humanity, however much extended. This can be proved by the following consideration. There are differences too small to make any substantial difference—e.g. if I can afford to invite only thirty-nine people to a party, whereas the average is forty. If negligible differences are to matter, it must be because comparisons are being made, not because their consequences are important. People are feeling put upon *not* because they cannot join in normal activities, but because they *mind* that they have got less than other people. But then the argument has ceased to be an argument from humanity plus, and has become an argument from envy; an argument strong no doubt in many breasts, but a different one, none the less, and of a different degree of cogency.

The argument from extended humanity cannot set the minimum acceptable level too close to the average. It therefore cannot require that there should not be any people getting more than the average, and in particular, that there should not be some people getting much more than the average. This is the acid test for distinguishing the true egalitarian from the humanitarian. The true egalitarian will object on principle to any one man having much more than any others, even if, by reducing the one man's possessions, the others would obtain only a negligible benefit, or none at all. The humanitarian has no such objection in principle. He may on occasion play Robin Hood, but only if he is convinced that the beneficiaries are in real need and will be substantially benefited by redistribution, and that the arguments against intervening are less weighty than the arguments for. Equality of Respect will produce some but not all the conclusions the egalitarian desires, not the peculiarly egalitarian ones.

SECTION 58

EQUALITY BEFORE THE LAW

EQUALITY before the Law differs from Formal Equality in the reversal of the order of the quantifiers, and in the consequent restriction on the number of factors that can be counted relevant. In claiming Equality before the Law, we are making not the absurd claim that any two persons must always be treated exactly alike—in which case the courts could never decide in favour of one party rather than the other, and it would be necessary to mete out to the innocent the same penalties as are imposed on the guilty—, but the important claim that the grounds for deciding between two persons should be only those laid down by law, and not any legally extraneous ones, whether reasonable grounds of moral sentiment or Natural Law, or unreasonable ones of private caprice. Equality before the Law goes further than Formal Equality in restricting the considerations that the court can be guided by. If there were arguments from Natural Law or public morality for treating two people differently, it would be no contravention of Formal Equality if they were treated differently: but it would be a contravention of Equality before the Law, unless the law had laid down that such arguments could be considered in such a case.

Equality before the Law does not guarantee equal treatment by the law but equal access to the law, and consideration only of those factors laid down by law as relevant. Nobody is so lowly as not to have recourse to the courts, nobody is so mighty as not to have to answer to the courts: anybody can invoke the courts' aid, everybody must render them obedience: and the courts will decide disputes, after hearing arguments on both sides, fairly and impartially, without fear or favour. Thus much, both Formal Equality and Equality before the Law. But Equality before the Law goes further, and specifies what arguments the courts may attend to. It adds to Formal Equality a sweeping canon of irrelevance. Every factor is irrelevant unless the law has specified it as relevant. It secures, in effect, that not persons but cases are heard, and that all other considerations, however relevant they may seem, shall not be allowed to discriminate between cases which are, according to criteria laid down by law, the same. A man exceeding the speed limit in order to rush an injured person to hospital must be convicted, because the law does not make exception for private ambulance work, in the way in which it does for the drivers of official ambulances. It is simply the principle of Legality, seen this time not just from the point of view of the subject *vis-à-vis* his rulers but *vis-à-vis* his fellow subjects. The subject need no longer be envious of his fellow subjects as persons, for it is only cases, and finitely specified cases at that, which the courts decide. It sometimes seems hard, and sometimes even unjust: but it does provide a guarantee of non-discrimination, and does preclude the possibility of improper considerations creeping in. I cannot feel, face to face with Judex IV, that he might pick on me. If he condemns me, it must be in virtue of certain stated circumstances of the case, and he must be willing to condemn any other person similarly circumstanced: and, apart from the stated circumstances, it does not matter what other characteristics I possess, however obnoxious to the judge, or to the community at large. I can be sure that these will not influence Judex IV at all. With Judex II and III it is not so easy to be sure. In the region of uncertainty, there is room for discrimination. Judex II and Judex III can take into account further factors, not antecedently stated as relevant, and this may upset the bad man, whose badness is taken into account, so that he feels less free to be bad than he thinks he ought to be: and it may upset the suspicious man, who suspects that the judge has decided against him not on account of the factor cited, but for some further reason, unstated. Shaw[1] might feel that he had been "got at" on account of his disreputable activities, and that England was not a free country, because if you were the sort of person "they" did not like, they could get you, even though there was no law against what you had done. And a man with a chip on his shoulder will never be certain that Judex II did not decide against him on account of his Australian accent, his long hair, or eccentric clothes.[2]

The argument from non-discrimination, as such, does not carry much weight. Equity alone, without Legality, will instruct a judge not to discriminate unfairly. All that is lacking is the certainty of not being discriminated against. But this is a much less important certainty than that of not being decided against. Moreover, the requirement laid on Judex III to state his arguments should afford some satisfaction to the suspicious man, that Judex III is not engaging in special pleading against him. Beyond this, the argument from non-discrimination is an argument of Freedom,[3] not of Equality. The bad man feels insecure

---

[1] See above, § 51, p. 215.
[2] Compare § 31, p. 139, n1.
[3] See above, § 34, p. 150.

when judged in accordance with Equity rather than Legality, because he knows that there are facts about him which if taken into consideration would tell against him. With the limited number of factors antecedently laid down as relevant in accordance with the canon of Legality, he knows where he is, whereas with Equity he can never be sure that his sins will not find him out. So far as the criminal law is concerned, we may, at least in England where we can afford to, give the bad man the security he desires. But this because we love liberty, not on any egalitarian account.

The real egalitarian argument is different. It does not so much suspect discrimination as object to the logical form of adjudications of Equity. Equity gives the judge the last word, in a way that Legality does not. However sewn up a case may be, there is always the logical possibility that Judex III may interpose a final 'But . . .', where Judex IV would have no alternative but to give judgement according to the letter of the law. Judex IV is on a level and can be argued with by litigants, whereas Judex III is on a pedestal and has pleas submitted to him for consideration. Egalitarians do not like it, and seek to fetter the judges' discretion in order to bring them down a peg and ensure that they are no better than themselves. It is a poor argument. It is inherent in the use of arbitration to decide disputes that the arbitrator is not *pari passu* with the disputants. Having made a man a judge over us, because we cannot otherwise resolve our disagreements, we cannot reasonably complain that he is over us and has the last word. The last word has to be his, because we cannot be relied upon to bring our argument to an end, and reach an agreed conclusion. The administration of justice is in this respect naturally inegalitarian.[1]

In other respects, however, a certain Equality before the Law is a concomitant of Justice. Justice is not served if the case of one party is incompetently presented and that of the other superbly well by the best barrister money can buy. The presentation of a case, we feel, is adventitious to its real merits, and, ideally, should be discounted. Since that cannot be altogether accomplished, we feel that counsel for two parties should be evenly matched. Here other arguments, of Freedom and of Expediency in the administration of justice, impinge. We rely heavily on our judges to discover the real merits of the case in spite of the differing abilities of counsel. But we rightly ensure by means of Legal Aid that equal access to the courts is at least not an empty Equality, and that nobody is denied a hearing through inarti-

[1] See above, § 21, pp. 91–92; § 57, p. 245.

culateness or poverty. We may call this too Equality before the Law, so long as we take care to distinguish it from Legality. The argument from Equality to Legality is weak. But the argument for a certain Equality between the parties in the procedures whereby Justice is administered, is strong. For disputes are contests. And in so far as adventitious factors can be quantified, we are right to want them equal on either side. Only so can we suppose that the best side will always win. We have Equality before the Law in order to secure a just inequality after it.

SECTION 59

EQUALITY IN THE LAW

ALL laws are inevitably equal in that they make relatively few and blunt discriminations, and treat all falling within any one category the same. They are equal in the sense of treating all (of a certain sort) alike. But the law itself may still be said to be unequal, in that the categories are wrongly specified, or the distinctions wrongly drawn, so that the law, either on the face of it, or merely in effect, discriminates between classes of people who ought not to be discriminated between. Even the most discriminatory legislation in South Africa or the South of the United States treats all black men equally, and all white men equally: but it is unequal for all that.

Equality, as applied to laws, is closely allied to Justice, and often works out the same. Nevertheless, there are differences, which are worth elucidating. Justice is concerned with relevant factors, supposed to be known, or at least capable of being adduced: Equality is concerned with factors not always known to be relevant or irrelevant, but *presumed* or *deemed* to be relevant or irrelevant.[1] Characteristically, we presume certain factors to be irrelevant, unless they can be proved to be relevant, or deem them irrelevant without possibility of rebuttal. An innkeeper must accommodate a traveller unless he is dirty, drunk, offensive, or unable to pay. There may be other features of the traveller—that he is a boy scout, that he is a Negro, that he reminds the innkeeper of a former employer, that he is a recently discharged convict—which incline the innkeeper, justifiably or unjustifiably, to refuse him: but these are irrelevant in law.

[1] See also § 62, pp. 271–2; and § 68, p. 300.

In other cases, discrimination is allowed, provided the factor on which the discrimination is grounded can be reasonably shown to be relevant. A public employer ought not to discriminate on grounds of race, religion or place of education: but he could legitimately discriminate on grounds of race if he was casting for the *rôle* of Iago; he could legitimately discriminate on grounds of religion if he was appointing to the post of British Minister to the Vatican, where religious susceptibilities could be embarrassing; and he could legitimately reject a man from one school if previous experience had shown that men from that school often failed to fulfil their promise. Here discrimination is allowed, but the onus of proof is on the discriminator.

In other cases again, discrimination is allowed, and we object to it only if the grounds for it can be shown to be irrelevant. Private employers, at least for senior posts, are assumed to be discriminating relevantly unless the contrary can be proved. If an employer says he rejected one candidate just because he was a Jew, or just because she was a woman, and agrees that these circumstances have nothing to do with the ability to perform the job, then he stands condemned. But the onus of proof is the other way. The discriminated against has to show, before he has legitimate grounds of complaint, that he was discriminated against on some clearly irrelevant factor. If an Old Etonian is not allowed to enlist as a private in the Guards, on the grounds that it might prove embarrassing for other Old Etonians who were officers, or if a works manager refuses to engage an Old Rugbeian because he remembers the film, "*I'm all right Jack*", the rejected gentlemen have no right to complain. Discretion in engaging or refusing is vested in somebody else's hands, and he is not wrong beyond all reasonable doubt in thinking that these factors may be relevant.

The extreme cases are purely personal relations. Here every factor which either party thinks is relevant, however unreasonably, is deemed relevant beyond possibility of rebuttal. If I do not like women who dye their hair blue, no blame whatever attaches to me if I refuse to consort with them. If I like Chinese, I am free to be friends with them, if I do not, I do not have to. Roman Catholics are entitled to move in Roman Catholic circles, Jews to prefer the company of Jews. It is quite wrong to criticise minorities, as some do, for being clannish, exclusive, or cliquey. It may be regrettable from the point of view of their own real interests, it may be advantageous: it is their business, and their right to decide. Sometimes, in the name of Equality, we do a lot to help minorities: we must beware we do not in the name of Equality be on occasion also intolerant.

The difficulties lie not in the paradigm cases, but in deciding where the boundaries are to be drawn between them. As we have seen, there is not a sharp separation between the public and the private sphere.[1] In the Law Courts we can deem many factors irrelevant, in the home we can deem them all relevant: but a shop is not as public as the law courts, a club not as private as a house. A large firm employing thousands of men is in a different position from two medical practitioners looking for a confidential secretary. Sometimes, as in the case of the inn, there are special arguments of utility in securing uniform treatment for everyone. In general we can say that where a relationship is with any member of an "open"[2] class there is at least a presumption of irrelevance, whereas where a relationship is with a person or persons who constitute only a "closed" class, there is a presumption of relevance. A shopkeeper deals with *any* member of the public:[3] therefore he may not pick and choose. A confidential secretary, or a personal *aide*, is admitted to all one's secrets, and has to work at close quarters: therefore he must be hand-selected. But neighbours and school-mates fall into neither of these categories very clearly. Legislation may try to prevent people picking and choosing their neighbours or their children's school-mates on racial or religious grounds: but to be effective must make formidable inroads on the principle of Freedom, and even then is likely to be circumvented. Limited Equalities, in limited respects, under limited conditions, are the most that one can be sure of achieving in a society that remains fundamentally free. For Freedom, just as it is inevitably unfair, is inherently unequal.

SECTION 60

DISTRIBUTIVE JUSTICE

EQUALITY is connected with particular Justice through Formal Equality which is another name for Equity. It is also connected with Justice considered as a property not of particular decisions but of general laws. Aristotle thought that all forms of Justice could be explicated in terms of Equality, but his account is confused and his

---

[1] § 43, p. 182.   [2] See § 29, p. 134n.   [3] § 42, pp. 179–80.

analysis awkward. With social or "distributive" justice, τὸ διανεμητικὸν δίκαιον,[1] however, some considerations of Equality are involved.

Distributive Justice is concerned with distributing the benefits or burdens accruing to a community among its members. We are concerned not with disputes which may arise between two members of the community, nor with most of the general laws which govern the life of the community, but only with those which govern certain relations between the community on the one side and each member on the other, and share out the benefits and burdens among all the members individually, assessing the share due to each individual one. Any dispute which arises is formally between the individual concerned and the community as a whole, but is felt, rightly, to be really between one individual and all the others put together. For, with a fixed benefit or burden to be distributed, the share of any one is increased or decreased only at the expense of the combined share of all the rest.

Distributive Justice in modern States is concerned with the distribution of burdens more than of benefits. Taxes and military service are what the State is most concerned to share out.[2] In the ancient world it was sometimes the other way round, and booty and the profits of public enterprise were divided among the citizens, much jealousy and dissension being thereby engendered. In the modern world the only enterprises which characteristically have cash benefits to share out are private enterprises and the concept of a "share" has been developed to provide an obvious and acceptable rule for distributing the profits of commercial associations. The one benefit which the State may have available for sharing out among its citizens is participation in the process of decision-making. This is pre-eminently, although not exclusively, constituted by the right to vote in parliamentary elections.

Distributive Justice is concerned with individuals only as members of a community. It is only in virtue of their membership of the community in question that their obligations and entitlements arise, and therefore any other features of any individual's case must be irrelevant to problems of distribution. A company should distribute its dividends among its shareholders in proportion to the number of shares held, and not according to need, or to merit, or to any utilitarian considerations. Whatever the principle of distribution is, only those features incorporated in it are relevant, and to take into consideration any other

[1] *Nicomachean Ethics*, 1131b26. See, generally, Bk. V, Ch. III, 1131a10–1131b24.
[2] Welfare payments are not share-outs. See p. 260.

factors is, when distribution is at stake, unjust. Distributive Justice demands the strong principle of universalisability, not the weak. It must be carried out in accordance with the canon of Legality, not Equity. Legality is demanded by Distributive Justice not as mere concession to human imperfection, but as representing a sort of Equality, Equality before the Law, which is logically inherent in that relationship between the community and its members with which it is concerned.

Equality before the Law, as we have already seen, does not require that all people be treated the same in all respects: nor does Distributive Justice demand that every member of a community be treated the same, but only that the principle of distribution should apply to everyone the same. What principle should be adopted is, in the modern, as well as in the ancient, world a matter for dispute. Sometimes a principle of numerical Equality is adopted, as with poll taxes and often with votes; but we should think it wrong if every shareholder had an equal dividend, irrespective of the number of shares held or the amount of money originally subscribed, and we think that taxes should sometimes be levied in accordance with the capacity to pay. Distributive Justice is, in Aristotle's terms,[1] a proportionate not a numerical Equality, though some times we may conclude that each man's share—$\dot{\alpha}\xi\acute{\iota}\alpha$—ought to be the same as everybody else's.

Equality before the Law thus characterises Distributive Justice formally, but not substantially. Substantial principles of Distributive Justice cannot be formulated in short compass. Too many other considerations are relevant. Military efficiency and economic expediency must bear upon what laws we enact for conscription or taxation. The benefits conferred by the Welfare State are to be justified on grounds of Humanity, economic expediency, or Public Interest, rather than of Distributive Justice. For although we could regard some of the non-monetary benefits as facilities analogous to the maintenance of law and order, provided by the State and available to all, yet it would be incoherent to regard moneys raised by taxation in the same light as profits or windfalls to be shared out among the members of the State. Arguments for the redistribution of monetary incomes must be arguments of Humanity, economic expediency, or something else; but not Justice. Social Justice is often taken to mean *Re*distributive Justice: but if so, it is a contradiction in terms. We should not attempt to set up an absolutely just scheme for distributing all good things.

[1] *Nicomachean Ethics*, Bk. V, Ch. IV, 1131b27–29, 1132a1–2.

The criteria of apportionment are too diverse:[1] and the compromises
required for the sake of Freedom, Humanity (in some aspects), and
other ideals preclude our ever achieving an absolute Justice in the
distribution of goods.[2] All we can say briefly is that every apportionment of benefits and burdens should be governed by the canon of
Legality, and should be carried out in strict accordance with the letter
of the law, but the content of the law itself is not determined by the
principle of Legality, and may be criticised, in another sense of
Justice or Fairness, as being just or unjust, fair or unfair.

SECTION 61

TAXATION

PROPERTY often seems less secure than life or liberty. A good government will respect the life and liberty of the subject, but even a good
government will need revenue and will levy taxes; and the subjects
may feel aggrieved and feel that they are being called up to bear
burdens unjustly; and they may then go on to claim that property
rights are absolute, and as sacred as the rights of life and liberty, and
that a citizen may lawfully be deprived of his property only if he has,
at least vicariously, consented to the tax.

Although in modern communities taxation is usually of property,
it need not always be so, nor is it only by taxation that property may
be expropriated. Conscription for service in the army or on a jury is a
tax, a tax on the time and the liberty of the subject:[3] and a compulsory purchase order for land, or the freeing of a copyright or
patent, affect the property of the subject, without in any way being
a tax. Nevertheless taxes should, so far as possible, be levied in money,
because this leaves more alternative courses of action open to the
taxpayer than a charge on his time. It is less restricting to have to pay
rates for the upkeep of roads than to have to turn out on corvée at a
stated time to put in a spell of road-mending. With military service
sometimes, and with jury service of necessity, we cannot allow the
subject to commute his obligations for a monetary payment. There

[1] Compare Aristotle, *Politics*, III, Bk. 12, 1282b30ff. The diversity of criteria
is a corollary of the infinite complexity of human beings and human situations,
asserted in § 7, p. 25.

[2] See above, § 55, pp. 242–3.

[3] So too perhaps, in Australia, the duty of voting in elections.

are still arguments, chiefly of Freedom, but also of Humanity and expediency, for alleviating the burden, partly by paying money for the time taken, more importantly by allowing those on whom it falls at a peculiarly awkward juncture to postpone their obligation until a later time—for example until the next Assizes.

It is an ancient principle in English law that there is no Equity in taxation. This is often construed that laws imposing taxes are and ought to be unfair, and that the courts are under no obligation to interpret them as justly as possible. Such an interpretation is wrong. The concepts of fairness and justice do apply to tax laws, as well as to others: but they apply in a different way. The criminal, and the ordinary civil, law differ from laws levying taxes first in being oriented towards the individual and secondly in being avoidable. A criminal court is focused on the accused, what *he* has done, and whether in consequence *he* ought to be deprived of life, liberty or property: and similarly in a civil case, attention is directed towards the two parties, and the rights and wrongs of *their* respective acts. Furthermore, it is highly praiseworthy to act so as to avoid falling foul of the criminal law or being involved in civil litigation. But taxing law is not primarily concerned with what the individual has or has not done: it is primarily concerned with general classes of persons, goods, or acts, on which are laid a duty to contribute to the Revenue, and only secondarily, in borderline cases, with the question whether a certain individual, article or act falls within the schedule laid down. One cannot rebut a tax charge by a claim of mistaken identity in quite the same way as one can rebut a criminal charge. A plea in mitigation of a penalty is always appropriate: whereas a plea in mitigation of a tax seems inappropriate, and if one were made and granted, would be unfair on all other payers of the tax. So too tax-avoidance, although regarded by the present generation of legal theorists as entirely respectable, is held in public esteem to be on a par with tax-evasion and equally discreditable.

A tax is not a penalty. It is one of the most regrettable features of modern politics that the two concepts have been confused, and it is commonplace for penal and confiscatory taxes to be imposed by the government, and met by massive tax-avoidance on the part of the governed. Penal taxation should be regarded as a contradiction in terms, and a tax should be regarded not as a penalty, to be avoided if possible, but as a contribution, to be paid with a reasonably good grace.

It is because a tax is not a penalty that it is not centrally concerned with the individual. *Nulla poena sine crimine*: it is a proper reason for not being punished that one did not *do* it; but a taxing law is not similarly concerned with what one *did*, but only with much more general classifications. Hence, except in cases of borderline ambiguity, there is no 'trial' of the taxpayer, nor onus to prove beyond reasonable doubt that he is liable; a man may not be deprived of life, liberty or property, by way of punishment, without due process of law, but he may be taxed without trial; just because, with taxes, there is no fault or crime, which they are taxes *for*, to be tried.

A tax is a *con*tribution, The taxpayer gives of his time or his money, along with many other people, in order that together they may achieve certain common purposes. The element of togetherness is reflected in the doctrine of Equality of tax-liability. Everybody ought to contribute his share; everybody ought to pull his weight; the shirker is to be despised because by evading his share of the burden he increases everybody else's. The burden is to be distributed, according to some principle or other, equally. And it is only in virtue of everybody's being, according to the relevant principle, equally liable, that anybody can reasonably be held to be liable at all. Hence it is that we require the Commissioners of Inland Revenue not to be merciful, whereas we allow the judges to temper Justice with Mercy. For the judges, so long as they ensure that the criminal law is generally respected and observed, are not being merciful at our expense.

The relative lack of concern for the individual and the emphasis on Equality which are characteristic of Distributive Justice require that taxation law should be based on the strong principle of universalisability, not the weak, on the principle of Legality rather than that of Equity. In this sense then we can accept that there is no Equity in taxation. But this is not to say that actual laws imposing taxes cannot be criticised as being inequitable, or that it does not matter if they are. Although a taxing law should be concerned to apply to classes rather than to individuals, and to maintain an equality of sacrifice, according to some principle or other, between one taxpayer and another, it is important none the less that no individual should be taxed beyond his capacity to pay, and that the principles according to which equal liability is assessed should not be outrageously irrelevant.[1] The

---

[1] The Finance Act of 1894 (57 & 58 Vict. c. 30, s. 8 (1)) granted exemption from death duties to "common seamen mariners or soldiers" dying on service. This exemption extended up to chief petty officers, sergeants, and lance-sergeants

application of taxation law should be in acccordance with Legality rather than with Equity, as we have defined these principles; but its formulation should be such as to avoid the grosser inequities, injustices, or irrationalities.

Taxes, although contributions, are not voluntary contributions. The eighteenth-century fiction that the representatives in the Legislature vicariously committed each one of their constituents to paying his taxes is difficult to elucidate; though not entirely to be dispensed with. The principle, "No taxation without representation", as it stands, cannot be sustained: even in the United States many taxes are levied on persons who are not in any way represented on the body levying the taxes;[1] and even in a modern democracy, aliens and minors would, on this principle, have to be free from conscription and monetary taxes. Nevertheless, the greater the degree of participation, the greater also, we feel, the willingness, as a matter of psychology, and the liability, as a matter of morality, to contribute time and money. And finally, as a matter of logic, there is some inconsistency in laying the burden of paying for the activities of the State on people with whom one does not share the benefit of participating in the political process. And to have a say in choosing representatives who will have a say in enacting tax laws, is to participate as much as the *average* citizen can.

SECTION 62

POLITICAL LIBERTY

FREE men are not content with Freedom under the Law and Freedom within the Law, precious though these are. Constitutional and Civil

---

[Halsbury's *Laws of England*, 3rd ed., 1956, Vol. 15, p. 54.] and although the Finance Acts of 1900 and 1924 (63 & 64 Vict. c. 7, s. 14 and 14 & 15 Geo. 5 c. 21, s. 38) made further provision for death on active service, the discrimination between commissioned officers and other ranks remained in force until 1952 (14 & 16 Geo. 6 & 1 Eliz, 2 c. 33, s. 71 (1)). Thus the eighth Duke of Northumberland who was killed at Dunkirk in 1940 made his estate liable to a higher rate of death duty, by reason of his serving his country as a lieutenant and not a private. A more canny noble would have tempered patriotism with prudence, and taken care never to accept the King's Commission with its penal consequences.

[1] Residents in Washington, D.C., are taxed by Congress, but have no representative in Congress; residents in New Jersey or Connecticut who have jobs in New York, are taxed by New York State, although they have no vote there.

Liberty are what we seek as subjects, but as citizens we seek something more, namely the opportunity of taking part in the process of government, and of having a say in the future development of the community; that is, we want Political Liberty too.

We want Political Liberty because we are conscious of ourselves not only as individuals but as members of various groups and communities, and in particular as members of nation-states. Few Britons can conceive themselves as not being British, few Americans as not being 100 per cent. American. Most men cannot conceive of themselves at all apart from possessing the nationality which they do in fact possess. Their own future is therefore bound up with their country's future, not only in the obvious external way, in which national disaster or prosperity will affect us all, but in an internal, emotional way as well. Therefore the very same reasons which lead men to want Constitutional and Civil Liberty, lead them to want Political Liberty too, in order that in that way also they may have a hand in shaping their future, and may to some extent be masters of their destiny.

Besides the emotional identifications which men often have in the present age with their nation-states, there are often good reasons for wanting Political Liberty. Some people enjoy politics. Some want to be useful, to be trusted, to be important. Some have strong views on one or two particular issues, and want to be able to secure that the community's decision is in accordance with their view of the question. Some have a lively sense that unless they are in on all the decision-taking that goes on, their own interests will suffer.

Men not only want Political Liberty but ought to have it. Two of the arguments for political obedience presuppose it.[1] Those who have participated in the making of decisions are likely to agree with the decisions made, and even when they do not agree, are likely to have felt some of the force of the arguments in favour. At the least they will be in a position not to impute bad motives to the authorities unjustifiably: some suspicions will have been dispelled.[2] Participation engenders a readiness to obey, and therefore reduces the need for coercive enforcement. And this is good. Coercion, although necessary, is a necessary evil, and coercive communities should aim to be as little coercive as may be. Furthermore, although the Rule of Law safeguards us from some sorts of unreasonable decision and the worst sorts of injustice, it cannot make, nor can we hope to have, all the decisions

[1] § 12, p. 44, IV and V.   [2] See above, § 12, p. 48.

of the authorities reasonable and just. Even though observing the procedures and principles of the Rule of Law, the authorities will often reach decisions which are wrong. It greatly softens the blow of having to abide by decisions that are wrong if the individual concerned has been involved in reaching them. Although it cannot normally be true that he has only himself to blame, the fact that he has himself among others to blame, will make him less ready to call in question the rightness of the decision. The subject can take exception to any of his ruler's decisions that are not defensible by reason alone, and can criticise freely all his faults: the citizen finds it harder to take exception to himself, and, being judge in his own cause, is likely to be more lenient to his own mistakes.

Even when a man has not actually participated in a communal decision, the fact that he could is still important. If he does not like the decision, we can reasonably ask him what different decision he would have preferred and what steps he took to obtain it. We often do fail, through idleness or indifference or the pressure of other interests, to exert ourselves over some public issue. Perhaps Political Liberty is only feasible on condition that most people are not too greatly interested in politics—indifference is, like Bagehot's stupidity, a great cement of political structures. Anyhow, men often do fail to take opportunities of opposing, and in view of their not having objected when they lawfully could have done so, are in a weaker position to obstruct or disobey after the decision has been taken. The possibility of participation transmutes apathy into acquiescence, and argues an additional obligation to conform to decisions one does not altogether like: thus Political Liberty reinforces in a further way the duty of political obedience.

Not only do we ask the grouser, rhetorically, 'Why did not you do something about it?' but, seriously, 'What alternative do you propose?' It is easy to object to decisions, easy to be unconvinced that they are necessary or right, if one is in the position of being a critic only, and not having to offer alternative solutions. Since the structure of political argument is dialectical,[1] we cannot assess the merits of a particular decision except in the context of the other decisions that could have been made in its stead. Often the chief recommendation of a course of action is the negative one that it is the lesser of two evils. It is an unwelcome truth. Men are apt to demand of the State, and of the decisions of others generally, a perfection uncontaminated by practicality,

[1] See above, § 6, pp. 22–23.

which they would not expect of themselves. By conferring on subjects the possibility of participation, we make them forfeit the status of spectators and take on the more responsible one of agents: and correspondingly change the logical level of their arguments from that of critical scepticism to that of serious consideration of practical possibilities. The sceptic always criticises, but never constructively: he always is asking questions but never feels obliged to offer any answers himself. This is his strength. His position is impregnable because he has none.[1] He maintains no position he has to defend, but merely attacks the positions maintained by others: and in politics, and indeed in all disciplines outside mathematics and formal logic, no position is so strong that it is secure from all attack and cannot ever be put in question. Thus the sceptic can always find passable reasons for objecting to communal decisions, and the subject, if arguing from the standpoint of a sceptical spectator, could maintain his grouses idly and indefinitely. By offering the opportunity of participation, we change the critic's point of view and alter his style of argument from an idle questioning to a serious assessment of the pros and cons of possible courses of action. Political Liberty makes political reasoning realistic, cogent, and likely to be effective.

A further argument for Political Liberty is sometimes given on the analogy of the *no taxation without representation* argument. For in addition to taxation, all the members of a coercive community are subject to the burden of having to obey the laws. And if they bear the burden of political obedience, they should enjoy the benefits of Political Liberty.

There is some argument here, but not a very clear one. On one side of the balance we have clear and definite burdens, on the other unclear and indefinite benefits. Many political liberties are not, and some cannot be, enjoyed by everyone. But peers, lunatics and aliens have to obey the law, just as they have to pay taxes, even though they have no vote in parliamentary elections. It is in the nature of a coercive community, as we have seen,[2] that its decisions have to be obeyed by non-participants as well as by those who have taken part. Fundamentally we are

[1] See e.g. Hume, *Two Dialogues on Natural Religion*, end of § viii, "A total suspense of judgement is here our only reasonable resource. And if every attack as is commonly observed, and no defence among theologians is successful, how complete must be *his* victory who remains always, with all mankind, on the offensive, and has himself no fixed station or abiding city which he is ever, on any occasion, obliged to defend?"

[2] § 15, p. 58.

subjects of States, not citizens, and the paramount requirement is that the State authorities themselves should be subject to the Rule of Law. If we can be citizens as well as subjects, and can participate in making decisions and not merely by having to obey them, so much the better. But it is a grace note, a way in which some States are better than others, not a requirement arising of rational necessity out of the very nature of the State.

Participation is a vague concept. We can be said to participate in any action except those which we do entirely by ourselves and those bodily movements that are induced by force. We do not speak of having a part in actions of the former class because they are wholly and entirely ours: nor of the latter class, because they are not really actions, and so not ours at all. Within these extreme limits it is difficult to draw precise distinctions. We do not know enough social psychology to be able to tell at what point a man who has had some say but not the sole say in what was done will regard the deed as his deed and not one 'forced' (in the colloquial sense, not the one defined in Section 15[1]) upon him. Sometimes it is enough simply to be in the know about what is going on, so that one is not faced with the bleak 'what' of what has been decided, but knows also the wherefore and the why. Sometimes one wants not only an ear to the ground but a voice in the process of decision-making: one wants to be able to argue and cite facts. Sometimes one wants not only a voice but a vote. Political Liberty often is equated with the right to vote. The right to vote is something definite, and clearly enables the voter to play his part in the decision procedure, and therefore seems the natural correlative of the equally clear and definite taxes that a man pays and the obligation to obey the laws. Perhaps it is. But it is far from constituting the whole of Political Liberty. The clearness and definiteness of the vote makes it also mechanical and limited. There is no argument in voting, no reaching of a common mind, no understanding of the reasons for decisions. Moreover, one's vote, although a part, is necessarily only a very small part of the decision-making process. The disadvantage of having a vote is that other people have them too, and one is always therefore in a minority of one, when one comes to think of all the things one wants. Although a voting system is often a convenient way of bringing a debate to a definite conclusion, and although the possessor of a vote is likely to be consulted with, argued with, and generally wooed, the bare possession of a vote does not confer much

[1] Pp. 56–57.

Political Liberty, or enable a man to participate in public life to any significant degree. He is given a very small say in affairs which hardly concern him, whereas what he wants is the opportunity of taking action in those matters he cares about a lot. More important, therefore, than the authority exercised in voting are the liberties of holding views about political matters and of ventilating those views in public, the right of addressing those with whom the decision rests, and the liberty of seeking and holding office. These different liberties, authorities, and rights, may all be called political liberties, but they are not all *pari passu*. The liberties of holding and ventilating views about public affairs are special cases of more general freedoms—Freedom of Thought, Freedom of Speech.[1] The right of addressing decision-makers means that corresponding duties must be imposed on the relevant authorities. The liberty of seeking and holding office is liable to many egalitarian confusions.

In no case can we lay down rigid rules, valid for all communities and in all circumstances. Just as the Rule of Law is based on the ideal of rationality, qualified by counsels of imperfection, so Political Liberty is based on the ideal of participation, qualified by the exigencies of practicality. We have a general argument in favour of participation, on which we lay great store, and against it have to set many particular arguments against the participation taking particular forms. The arguments will balance out in different ways under different conditions, and the outcome will be a series of untidy compromises. Every participant will have some cause for dissatisfaction, for he will never have participated fully—of necessity, since participation is by definition only partial. Nobody can participate enough to be completely satisfied. But on the other hand, the smallest degree to which he does participate may seem objectionable to others, either as derogating from their own power to control the course of events, or merely as being a clog on administrative efficiency. As with legal liberties, so with political liberties we strike a balance. But the principles by which the true balance is to be found are even more unclear.

The right to address decision-makers, the right to be heard, the duty on decision-makers *audi alteram partem*, is, as we have seen,[2] based on three principles. It is partly a recognition of man's humanity—since men can talk, they should be allowed to, and not just bundled about like chessmen. It is also, and importantly a canon of good administration. The good administrator, knowing that truth is many-sided,

---

[1] See below, §§ 69, 70, 72.   [2] § 28, pp. 132–3.

attempts to see every side of the case: and allowing interested parties to make representations is one way of achieving this. But it could be achieved in other ways. A member of the department might be detailed to play devil's advocate, without the devil himself being granted any right to be represented in reality. Provided all points of view are put forward somehow, and all relevant facts are elicited somehow, it does not matter how they are elicited; to give interested parties a hearing is one way, an administratively convenient way, of doing this, but nothing more. The right to be heard, however, is not just this. It reflects also our belief that each man ought himself to have some say of his own in his own future, and that each man ought to count, to count as being himself, and not merely as one instance among many of the human species. We therefore think each man ought to be able to instruct his own counsel (or appear in person) to represent his own views, not merely those views which a benevolent authority might deem him to hold. This is the argument from Political Liberty. We require that each man should be free to take some steps to shape the future of his community according to his own wishes, and there-fore he should have some say in how the political and legal decisions of his community should be made. In particular, on a matter on which he is likely to have very strong wishes, namely where a decision (judicial or administrative) is in danger of being taken adversely to his interests, he should have a chartered right of having a say, that is, the authority has a duty to hear him.

The duty of decision-makers to give a hearing to all and sundry is one which is clearly subject to heavy practical restrictions. In British constitutional theory, Peers of the Realm and the Speaker of the House of Commons have the right of access to the Monarch; though if all the Peers chose to exercise this right frequently and lengthily, constitutional chaos would ensue. Nobody, other than the Monarch and members of the two Houses, has the right to address Parliament, though parliamentary committees may invite representations from particular quarters. Americans do not have any legal right to address either the President or Congress; nor would it be wise to extend the possibilities of filibuster to the whole American people. Nevertheless, the fact that one is at liberty to express one's views to anybody, including members of the Legislature,—i.e. there is no law against it,— combined with the fact that members of Congress and of the House of Commons need their constituents' votes to obtain re-election, combine to make it possible for any citizen with a serious argument to have that argument aired. So far as the Legislature is concerned, arguments can be represented to it, though persons not. The chartered right of personal participation has to be restricted to voting at elections for reasons of practical necessity. The reasonable man with a case can in fact achieve much more; but he cannot have a legal right, which might be exercised by cranks, of wasting parliamentary time or boring M.P.s individually.

The counter arguments of practicality are less weighty in the case of administrative authorities that are reaching quasi-legislative decisions. Arguments of Political Liberty are especially relevant then because they go further than arguments of Natural Justice. Not only when the central interests of named individuals are in jeopardy, but when any clearly identifiable interests are likely to be affected, there should be a right to argue against proposals, just because this is what it is to have a say in those political decisions of the community that are of the greatest concern.[1]

The liberty of holding office is difficult to elucidate, because officials are elected, selected, or appointed usually on some grounds of merit, and people who, in the eyes of the electing, selecting, or appointing body, lack merit are effectively debarred from office. There is no legal prohibition on a Roman Catholic being Prime Minister of Britain or on a Jew or a Negro being President of the United States: but it is sometimes alleged that members of these religions or racial groups are effectively debarred from office. When the consulship in ancient Rome was opened to the plebeians, plebeian candidates were still passed over in favour of patrician candidates, and it was not until one consulship was closed against the patricians, that plebeians were able in practice to be consuls. In order to secure that members of certain groups actually do hold certain offices, it may be necessary to reserve certain offices to them. There may, on occasion, be arguments in favour of doing this but they will be based on the Political Liberty (or some other political rights) of the group as a group, not on any arguments of the Political Liberty of the individual.

A more serious difficulty is that often there are good reasons for disqualifying certain classes of people from holding certain sorts of office. Communists, fascists and fellow travellers ought not to be appointed to any position in the Civil Service where they would have access to secret documents. A Roman Catholic cannot be Lord Chancellor for fear that he would favour other Roman Catholics when

[1] See above, § 46, pp. 197–8; § 52, pp. 223–4; § 53, p. 227.

appointing judges, and thus undermine the Judiciary. In nearly all countries except Great Britain, only citizens are allowed to be legislators. It would be unreasonable for a Briton to complain that he could not sit in the French Assembly or the American Senate; and although communists do complain that they cannot get jobs in the Civil Service, their complaints do not deserve much sympathy. Political Liberty should be a secondary rather than a primary consideration in selecting for most offices. The first duty of the selecting body is to select good men, able and likely to discharge their office well. It should, however, out of consideration for Political Liberty, be wary of taking into account certain sorts of feature—a man's political affiliations, his religion, his race—unless there are strong grounds for believing them to be pertinent to the candidate's competence and reliability in the office in question. Political Liberty, that is, requires us to make certain presumptions of irrelevance when choosing officials, which we otherwise might not make.[1] This presumption, however, can be rebutted, either in individual cases—there is no general rule against nazis being appointed to teach in State schools, but an individual nazi may, rightly, be refused a job because he is a nazi, and his nazi views make him unsuitable to instruct the young—or in a whole range of cases—communists and men married to alien wives cannot hold posts in the American State Department.

In a democracy there are further arguments for being peculiarly reluctant to impose disqualifications for *elected* office. Few disqualifications except on grounds of nationality or age are imposed in most countries. But these arguments are based not so much on grounds of Political Liberty as on those of democracy. In order that the electorate may have as wide a choice as possible, as many people as possible should be eligible.

SECTION 63

INDIVIDUALISM

THE principles of legal, political, intellectual, and religious liberty gain their force from the recognition of the importance of the individual person. Sometimes this is called Individualism. But the term is unclear. It may mean that individual persons are important, which is

---

[1] Compare above, § 56, pp. 244–5; § 59, pp. 256ff.

true; or that individual persons alone are important, and that communities are unreal or unimportant, which is false. It may be understood in an evaluative sense, that individual persons are worthy of respect, or in an ontological sense, that individual persons do exist, but that communities do not. Or it may be a mixture of these.

Historically, Individualism started in religion. Corporations have no souls. The Protestants maintained that the only thing that mattered was the individual's relationship with God. Similarly in Kantian morality, only individuals can have the Good Will, and the only thing that mattered was that individuals should act autonomously. In social and political philosophy it has often been maintained that only individuals exist, and recently the programme of "Methodological Individualism" has attempted to give a reductive analysis of social and political concepts in purely individual terms. Correspondingly in the field of values it has often been thought that only individuals can have or can achieve values, and that only individual self-fulfilment is worth while. The State cannot, or at least ought not, to stand for any values on its own. Its sole function is to enable individuals to realise their purposes; its sole end to provide individuals with the means of achieving their ends: and if it presumes to aspire more highly, it oversteps the limits of Constitutionalism and is on the way to becoming a totalitarian Leviathan.

All these contentions are false. The general reason is simple: man is a social animal and an imperfect one. Although each man is himself an individual, he becomes himself, is born, brought up, finds and fulfils himself, only in social life.[1] Other people—parents, friends, fiancées, colleagues, spouse, and children—are among the most important things to a man, among the most important things about a man. What other people mean to a man, what other people think of a man, constitute a large and essential part of what it is to be that individual man. To neglect this, and to talk of individuals as though they could be considered in isolation, apart from their relations with other people, is to court confusion. Not that individuals are merely the sum of their social relations. What gives Individualism its attractiveness, and indeed makes the positive part of it true, is that man is not just simply a social animal. Each one of us is conscious of himself as an entity, as something over and above his absorbing social life and personal relationships. A man can, in his mind, detach himself from his ordinary life, and step outside himself, and commune with himself

[1] See § 13, p. 52.

in isolation. The fact that the soul can thus soliloquise is what makes us think that we are centres of consciousness, ends-in-ourselves, moral agents, supremely worth while—in short that we have souls. And we are right to think so; but wrong to conclude that these isolated meta-physical moments are typical of human life, or alone are valuable parts of it. What man does with his solitude is important. But equally, what man does in company of his fellows. And we cannot construct a political philosophy, or give a true account of human life on the assumption that we all are windowless monads, who never really interact with one another. Nor, to take another version, can we accept the argument from autonomy. Although there are often sound liberal arguments for individuals being free to make moral choices, it does not follow that the individual always knows best what he should do. Often he does not. Often, nevertheless, he should be allowed to do it, but that is a different argument. Individuals are not, as some Individualists assert, the sole arbiters of what is right or wrong, nor are values created by the individual's avowal of them. Therefore to restrict the individ-ual's freedom of choice, although often deplorable on other grounds, is not necessarily to create a state of affairs that must be less good than it otherwise might have been. Individualists have a wrong view of human nature. They fail to recognise how sociable and how fallible we are. Their view, indeed, not only is false, but if true, would make it unnecessary to have a State at all.

So much for the general thesis. In addition there are particular arguments for particular types of Individualism, and always the burden of proof lies on those who would restrict the individual and prevent him, in the name of religious conformity, corporate morality, concern for truth, or social solidarity, from doing what he wants. The particular arguments are often sound, and the burden of proof is rightly put in favour of Freedom and against those who would stop people from doing what they want to. But the arguments are not always conclusive, and the burden of proof may be discharged. On live issues, the Individualist is likely to be on the right side, but the theory of Individualism, in spite of many attractions, always proves untenable. Apart from its shaky foundations, it nearly always demands too much at the same time as defending too little on behalf of the individual. The Kantian demands an almost Existentialist autonomy in the name of freedom, but one that is apparently compatible with a passive acceptance of deeply illiberal legal systems. Mill in the name of Liberal-ism demands complete moral licence in matters which do not affect

other people, but in those that do, concedes to the community an
unfettered right to restrict individual Freedom.[1] Freedom of Speech
is often construed as an absolute privilege to say what one likes,
without any concern either to maintain standards of truth, or to protect
those who tell the truth from private sanctions.[2] Individualism with
respect to values has led to the secular State, on the grounds that
communities ought not to espouse values, but only individuals should.
But then, since it is in the nature of men to seek success, and success
presupposes some inter-personal, socially recognised value, the only
way left of being successful in an Individualist society, is to acquire
money, since money must be inter-personal, and must be socially
recognised as having value. The American liberals attempted to free
men from all the false gods of social values, in order that each might
pursue happiness his own way and serve his God authentically; but
succeeded only in installing Mammon in the place of the departed
gods. The Marxist critique of Liberalism is a fair one of Individualism
carried to its logical extremes where it denies all those shared social
values which make a society worth living in, while admitting, and
elevating to be an end, the one value, money value, which does not
make life worth living, and in as much as it is valuable, is valuable
solely as a means and not at all as an end.

We therefore treat all doctrines of Individualism with suspicion
and respect. Often they enshrine sound arguments for Freedom. But
often they overlook possible arguments on the other side, and would
lead us to deny the most obvious facts of social existence or its most
worthwhile values. We consider first the issues raised by Individualism
as regards communities and associations generally; then certain
Individualist issues in political theory; and then some of the issues
raised by the clash between individual freedom and social values and
moralities.

SECTION 64

ASSOCIATIONS

MEN are always associating with one another; sometimes casually for
fun, sometimes in marriage for life, sometimes as members of the same
regiment or same firm or same profession, or as citizens of the same

---

[1] See above, § 41, pp. 173–5; and below, § 75, pp. 343–5.   [2] § 69.

State. In many cases, for instance when I associate with my friends or professional colleagues, our association is not a community in the sense of Section 3,[1] because we have no decision procedure for reaching a common decision on disputed issues. I shall use the word 'group' for social gatherings which are less than communities in that they lack a decision procedure. This is not to say that groups cannot ever be said to have a common view on some question, but only that they cannot always. Some groups on some issues do sometimes evolve a common mind on the matter: but they do so informally. They have no formal procedure for making up their common mind, and often it will be doubtful what the common mind of a group on a particular matter is, or whether, indeed, it has one at all. The Anglican Communion is in this sense a group, in contrast to the Roman Catholic Communion which has a definite decision procedure, and is therefore a community in the sense of Section 3. On some issues the Anglican Communion does evolve a common view, but slowly and with no clear-cut criteria of exactly when it has made up its mind, or what exactly its decision is. Groups are, to a greater or lesser extent, amorphous. They lack the firm, formal structure given by a formal, generally applicable, decision procedure. Typically, they are studied by the sociologist and social psychologist rather than by the political philosopher, because, lacking a decision procedure, they do not pose peculiarly *political* problems. Nevertheless they form the background against which the decision procedures of communities do operate, and a political philosopher cannot ignore the existence and importance of informal groups.

The political philosopher must also be concerned with the formal associations defined in Section 14.[2] Associations there are defined as a subclass of communities, namely those communities whose decisions are *not* enforceable by *coercive* (in the sense of Section 15) sanctions. We further distinguish those *voluntary associations*, whose decisions are not enforceable by *any* sanctions, from other associations, whose decisions are enforceable by sanctions, which although not coercive in the sense we have given to 'coercive', are none the less effective.

The "Right of Association" is variously construed. It can be a minimal recognition of men's need to belong to social groups, which may be other than the coercive community of the State: it can be a maximal claim that the State should take no cognisance of the activities of any association except as being activities of certain individuals; and

---

[1] p. 11; or below, p. 366.   [2] p. 55, or below, p. 367.

that anything an individual may lawfully do on his own, he may lawfully do also in concert with other people, or acting as the official of some association. Or, as in the United States, it can secure to individuals the right to associate in a particular way and for particular purposes.[1]

The need to belong to social groups other than the unselective community of the State follows from the fact that men do not have all their values in common. The State, therefore, cannot endorse all the values of all its citizens, and therefore cannot provide a vehicle for the corporate expression of some values of some of its citizens. If these citizens are to fulfil themselves as men, they must be able to give expression—which often needs to be corporate expression—of values not shared by all their fellow citizens and not endorsed by the State. Therefore they need to belong to, and if necessary form, groups other than that constituted by the State.

This argument is not to be taken to mean that every value held by some citizen must be expressed: the values of the criminal classes are not thus to be cherished. But among those activities which are not demanded by the State, there is a distinction between some, which are forbidden, and many others, which are neither required nor prohibited. And it is the mark of a free society that this distinction is observed, and that corporate activities which the State does not itself engage in should not *eo ipso* be forbidden. Although the ideal of collectivism has often had its charms—men have wanted to merge their individual existences on the collective whole of one πόλις or republic or monastery—no large community, such as the modern nation-state, can achieve monolithic solidarity, except at the Procrustean price of denying spontaneity, and even humanity, to its subjects. Only all animals can be equal: it is inherent in being human to be different.

If we allow that men are not all the same, and that values must sometimes be expressed corporately if at all, we see the need for associations, in which people sharing the same values, not endorsed by the State, can give corporate expression to them. We therefore need the "Right of Association" in its minimal sense. We need not, on that account, concede the maximal claim that the State should take no account of any associations as such. Apart from the metaphysical

[1] The First Amendment to the Constitution lays down: Congress shall make no law . . . abridging . . . the right of the people peaceably to assemble, and to petition the government for a redress of grievances.

argument that communities and social groups do not really exist, there is a feeling that since by definition associations are non-coercive, they are therefore voluntary, and that every member of an association carries out the association's decisions of his own free will. And what a man does of his own free will is, provided it is lawful, his own affair and not any concern of the State's.

This argument turns upon an equivocation on the word 'voluntary'. Although a man is not subject to coercive sanctions if he fails to conform to a decision of an association, he may be subject to sanctions none the less.[1] He may lose his livelihood; he may lose the amenities and social opportunities afforded by a club; he may lose his reputation. Although his obedience, therefore, may be voluntary in the sense that it is not coerced, it is not voluntary in the sense that it is given for no other reason than the desire that the decisions of the association should be carried out. No argument from Freedom, therefore, can be adduced for complete non-concern on the part of the State in the affairs of associations. Such an argument, if it applies at all, applies only to voluntary associations strictly so called, associations whose decisions are not enforceable at all. Associations other than voluntary associations are able to exercise sanctions, although not coercive ones. A member may feel obliged to conform to some communal decision for fear of some non-coercive sanction, under heading Ia(ii) of Section 12.[2] He feels compelled rather than convinced. The threat of sanctions, although often effective, is intellectually opaque; and therefore itself needs further justification. Although associations, far more than coercive communities, are founded on the participation of their members, yet if they have effective sanctions at their disposal, they are still, though less so than the State, subject to the Rule of Law. And therefore, as with the State because it can exercise coercive sanctions, so, to a lesser extent, with associations which have any effective sanctions at their disposal, we demand that this power be controlled and responsibly used.

To some small extent, as we have seen earlier,[3] the State must concern itself with associations—if they hold property, and there is some dispute over ownership, and the law courts have to adjudicate. More generally, the State, by making its legal facilities available to associations, and allowing them to be "incorporated" and acquire some legal "personality", may reasonably require in return that the incorporated association should observe certain general rules of fair

[1] See above, § 14, pp. 54–55.   [2] p. 43.   [3] § 17, pp. 71–72.

play, even in their internal dealings with their members. Limited liability companies are subject to elaborate rules to safeguard the interests of shareholders. Even clubs may be required to observe at least the procedures of Natural Justice in deciding whether to expel a member. At the other end of the spectrum, universities, the Church, some schools, and various professional bodies, live in a complicated, almost symbiotic, relationship with the State. These communities are neither mere departments of the State nor completely independent of it. The values held in common by members of a university or members of a church are ones which are unlikely all to be shared by the members of an unselective community, although some of the values for which the Universities or the Church stand are likely to be endorsed by the State. The State is wise not to adjudicate all intellectual or religious issues itself, but wise also not to regard all questions of truth, morality or religion with indifference. Such issues are best decided by autonomous sub-communities within the State, which have the values in question as their *raison d'être*. The State, which shares some of these values, but only to a limited extent, and only in conjunction with many other, often more pressing, concerns, may provide some support, or some recognition, or some niche in the body politic, and may occasionally exercise some general oversight, without attempting to secure any detailed control.[1]

SECTION 65

COLLECTIVE ACTIONS
AND CORPORATE MORALITIES

ASSOCIATIONS act. So far as ordinary speech goes, we are quite prepared to allow collective nouns to be the subjects of verbs in the same way as personal nouns and pronouns can be, although this does not mean, as some philosophers have thought, that collective nouns are in every way the same as personal nouns. We talk of an association as though it were a person, though we do not really believe that it is either an individual person or a metaphysical super-person. An association "acts" only in and through the actions of its individual members: but not in its members acting in any way. To say that a

---

[1] For a much fuller discussion, see J. D. Mabbott, *The State and the Citizen*, Hutchinson University Library, London, 1948, Ch. XII.

rambling club went rambling in the Chilterns is not simply to say that each and every member of the rambling club went rambling in the Chilterns though it may imply that: to be a case of the club going for a ramble, it is necessary that its members did not go their independent ways which happened to coincide, but that they deliberately chose to go together, that they were conscious, to a greater or less extent, of this being a club activity, and that they had organised their individual actions to a greater or less extent, in order to bring about the result of their all acting in concert. To take another example: if I say that the family went to Brighton for the Bank Holiday, it entails that the individual members of the family did go to Brighton during the Bank Holiday: but it is not a case of the family going to Brighton for Bank Holiday, if each member of the family gets on his scooter, and without any previous consultation or planning, goes his separate way and happens to choose to go to Brighton. A mass of holiday-makers all travelling to the sea independently is a typical non-association, an unorganised crowd of separate units. The essential characteristic of an association is not simply that each member of it acts in conformity with some pattern, but that each member has not merely happened to act in such a way. It is not just a fortuitous coincidence of individual whims, but a deliberate subordination on the part of each member of his will to the common plan—not that this subordination is felt as being difficult, only that if asked why he was acting as he was, he would be able to answer with reference to what other members of the association were doing and what the general plan was.

To talk of an association's acting requires that the association is fairly highly organised, formally or informally. The larger the association is, the more formal the organisation will have to be. It does not matter whether the association is purely voluntary in the sense of Section 14,[1] or whether it has at its disposal sanctions for the indirect enforcement of any decision it makes, or whether it can enforce its decisions directly by coercion: in each case we can talk of the association acting—the family goes to the sea, the university alters its programme of studies, the State pays compensation to victims of an earthquake.

For an association to act, a fair degree of organisation is necessary. We also talk of associations feeling, thinking, holding views, adopting attitudes, upholding standards, and many other things, and, for these, much less organisation is essential. If a university is to be said to have

[1] p. 55.

altered its syllabus, then, clearly, rather carefully specified criteria must be satisfied: much less exact criteria need apply if we are to say that a university has a strong bent towards the biological sciences, or maintains a strong classical tradition, or is given to clear thinking, or is intellectually conservative. But collective sentiments, if we may so term them for convenience, are like collective actions in this, that they are constituted by the sentiments of individuals, but are not simply the sum total of the sentiments of a number of individuals. The sentiments of an association are discovered in what its individual members say and do, especially when together, or would say and would do, were they faced by certain hypothetical questions. In some associations, especially small or closely-knit ones, the body of collective sentiments form a definite *ethos*, which is sometimes so definite as to incline us to speak of a "corporate personality". But there is no need to posit special metaphysical entities over and above the ordinary persons we meet and talk with. It is simply that men think and act differently when they are together and influencing one another from when they are separate. A corporate personality manifests itself in ordinary people thinking and doing things, but in a special frame of mind, conscious of other men's thoughts and actions, and influenced by them.

Where we can talk of actions, attitudes, and thoughts, we can talk of principles of actions, moral attitudes, and evaluations. Therefore, if there can be collective actions, group attitudes and corporate personalities, there can be principles of collective action that are moral principles, group attitudes that are moral attitudes, and corporate personalities that adhere to certain moral values. It is thus intelligible to say that the State has a moral duty to provide for the victims of earthquake; or that the university ought not to give degrees in physical training; or that the rambling club ought sometimes to have rambles on week-days. Just as a collective action is not simply a number of individual actions, so a collective obligation is not simply a number of individual obligations, and a corporate morality is not simply a number of individual moralities. A collective obligation is, rather, an organised system of obligations, which are obligations upon individuals to act in various ways, not necessarily all the same way, and these obligations are imposed upon or accepted by the individuals concerned not as individuals but as members or officials of the association in question. So too a corporate morality is not a sum of individual moralities. Each individual considers himself not simply as an individual but as a member of a community or group, having certain values in common.[1] Each is concerned not only with what he himself does, but with what other members do, and each recognises that others have an interest in what he does. We are concerned about one another's doings. Parents care what their children do. Lovers care passionately about each other's actions. Similarly, at a lower temperature, we care about what our friends, our colleagues, our compatriots and our co-religionists are up to. Nor is our interest entirely unselfish: for we expand ourselves to embrace our interests. A man identifies himself with his children, his wife, his business, his club, or his country. Their successes are his successes, their failures his failures. Although he may be concerned quite disinterestedly that they should make autonomous moral judgements, he is also concerned interestedly that their actions should redound to the credit of the community of which he is a member, and should not be such as to bring dishonour to its name. He would rather that they conformed their actions to the corporate moral standard heteronomously than that they should autonomously flout them. And he in his turn will be guided in his actions not simply by his own individual views of what is right and wrong, but by a respect for the moral values shared by other members of his community. Other men's views will to a lesser or greater extent seem external to him. At one extreme, he will be anxious not to let the side down: at the other, he will sense that his own interest lies in keeping in with them and not getting into their bad books. Corporate moralities are thus not altogether autonomous. How far they involve heteronomy depends on the degree of dissociation felt by the individual between himself and the community in question. We seldom are all of one mind, and therefore seldom are at one with a community on all issues. But we often are conscious of ourselves as members of a community, and identified with it in spite of some differences of opinion. We cannot say precisely how heteronomous a corporate morality is because our own consciousness and concern knows of no precise limits. Indeed, Kant's whole distinction between autonomy and heteronomy presupposes a psychology that is not humanly possible. Although we are individuals, we are conscious of one another, and therefore can have corporate, as well as purely personal, moralities.

As with morality, so with religion: it may be wrong, but it is intelligible to talk of an association performing collectively a religious observance. Corporations may have no souls, but they quite often go to church—schools and colleges, regiments and town councils, livery

[1] See above, § 13, p. 52.

companies and friendly societies—and there is no inconsistency in the idea of corporate worship. Indeed in some Christian Churches, e.g. those of the Anglican Communion, the central act of worship can only be undertaken corporately. And here again, there is, in corporate worship, a certain loss of individual initiative and spontaneity. A man may make his private prayers at whatever time, and in whatever form, the spirit moves him; but, for the British Legion Remembrance Day service, he must go on Armistice Sunday and say and do only what is laid down. People can feel a conflict of religious duties. A man may feel impelled to testify during the singing of the anthem, or to say 'Hallelujah' in a loud voice during the sermon; but he is required to desist. Extreme Protestants sometimes have felt it their duty to protest at papistical practices in the Church of England. Roman Catholic mayors and officials have often been under the impression that they must absent themselves from all corporate religious services in which non-Roman Catholics took part. The possibilities of conflict are endless.

Where an association is purely voluntary, no political problem arises if the association has a collective morality or engages in a corporate religious observance which is contrary to the conscience of a member. The issue will be fought out *in foro conscientiae* of that member, who is free either to remain in the association and conform to its requirements, or to leave the association and act as his conscience suggests. For this reason, Individualists, and lovers of Freedom generally, have been peculiarly attracted to voluntary associations, and have felt that it was unobjectionable for voluntary associations to espouse moral or other values, whereas there was a threat to the individual's Freedom of Conscience if the State did. But, as we have seen,[1] they have often failed to see that not all associations are voluntary, and that there is not a simple dichotomy between the State, with coercive sanctions at its disposal, and all other communities with none. Many associations do have effective sanctions at their disposal, although not coercive ones, and are able to enforce, although only indirectly, a collective morality or religious observance. We cannot solve the problem of the possible tension between corporate morality and individual freedom by allowing only associations, and not the State, to espouse moral principles. Whenever an association is not purely voluntary, an individual member is not really free[2] to avoid

[1] § 64, p. 278.
[2] In the extended sense, generally excluded in § 16, pp. 56–57.

conforming to its moral requirements. It we allow any private powers,[1] as any believer in Freedom must, associations will be able to exercise powers, and will be able to use them as sanctions, and will be able sometimes to enforce its moral standards on individuals. The problem is thus inherent in the concept of Freedom itself, and cannot be solved by any individualist doctrine of a Minimum State founded on Contract alone.

SECTION 66

CONTRACT AND CONSENT

THE individualist inspiration has expressed itself in political theory in the doctrines of the Social Contract and Government by Consent. The State is seen, so far as possible, as a voluntary association of individuals, banded together for mutual protection and the maintenance of law and order, and where all questions of political obligation can be answered by the two rejoinders, 'You promised to' or 'It is what you really want'.

The attraction of such doctrines for Individualists is clear. Instead of starting, as I do in this book, with communities, decision procedures, and their enforcement, we start, as in Section 16 with conflicts and the avoidance of violence, both of which can be understood purely in terms of individuals; and contract and consent are the two ways an individual can enter into obligations which were created by him, and had no antecedent hold upon him. It seems possible in this way to explain all facets of political life in terms of individuals alone, without recourse to the concepts of *the community* or of *Natural Law* as fundamental, ineliminable ones. Moreover, in its historical setting, after the age of Feudalism, Contract theories seemed more natural than they do now. Law had largely been reconstructed on the two pillars of contract and inheritance, and it seemed plausible that a man might inherit his liberties, as he did his lands, from his ancestors, subject to whatever obligations they had originally entered into.

The demerits of such a theory are well known. We are as sure as we ever can be about questions of historical or prehistorical fact, that there never was and never has been any contract between rulers and ruled; and even if there had been, it would not, to our unfilial minds, have been binding upon subsequent generations, without successive

[1] See above, § 45, pp. 191ff.

re-endorsement by each. Historical considerations apart, it is not possible to spell out in advance all the rights and obligations either of governments or of their subjects.[1] A contract is nothing if it is not precise. And this is just what the Social Contract cannot be.

These demerits are enough to discredit the Contract theory. Before dismissing it, however, we should consider such merits as it has. They cannot be expressed in terms of contracts, but may be re-expressed in other ways. The Contract theory has the great merit of providing for some measure of consent, greater than purely coercive theories do, and on a more realistic basis than the straight theories of consent: that is, it does not have to deny the real measure of dissent that often exists, or pretend that it can be conjured away by voting procedures or talk of the general will. It admits the real disadvantages of being governed, but claims that the benefits are so great that all in all it is a good bargain. An all-in-all consent, which involves taking the rough with the smooth, is more realistic than any doctrine of piecemeal consent can ever be.

The Contract theory supports some principles of Constitutional Criticism. A contract is necessarily two-sided. There must be some *quid pro quo*. The subject takes on an obligation to obey the sovereign, and therefore the sovereign must take on *some* obligations. He is not absolutely free to do what he likes. At the least, the first thesis of Unlimited Sovereignty must be false. Not everything is lawful to the supreme authority. We can go further, and argue more specifically, that the sovereign is not entitled to make decisions arbitrarily, nor to be guided solely by considerations of self-interest. For arbitrary decisions and purely self-interested decisions do not represent any "*quid*". The sovereign is not giving up anything if he is free to act arbitrarily or solely on the basis of self-interest. For this is what his position would be if his subjects had given themselves over unconditionally into his hands. Therefore any terms on which he holds his sovereignty must give him an authority less absolute than this. His authority must stem from an accountable office, not an absolute privilege. And so we can argue for the principles of non-arbitrariness and non-egocentricity on a basis of Contract theory as well as that of the Rule of Law.[2] Many advocates of Contract theories have been concerned to make just these points against the absolutist doctrines of the age of despots. They have wanted only to deny '*quod placuit principi, legis vigorem habet*' and Machiavellian doctrines that a prince

[1] See above, §§ 7 and 10.   [2] See above, § 27, p. 123, pp. 125–9.

should consider only his own interests. And against these two tenets, the Social Contract does tell. But the bare existence of a Contract, whose terms are not known, establishes fewer principles of Constitutional Criticism than the Rule of Law. A Social Contract might not have laid down that the decisions of the authorities need be relevant, rational, or universalisable, nor that the procedures of Natural Justice need be followed. As a source of these principles of Constitutional Criticism, the Contract theory adds nothing to the Rule of Law and achieves less.

Supporters of the Contract theory have sought to extract more specific Constitutional principles. They use the "*quid pro quo*" principle to argue that the balance of advantages and disadvantages for the subject must be such that every reasonable man would want to adhere to the State, and from this to the limitations there must be upon the obligations of the subject and the authority of the government. The subject cannot be required *in general* to forgo all his natural interests: the government cannot adopt a policy of frustrating all its subjects' interests: a law that everybody should forthwith commit suicide would be ruled out by a Contract theory: so would one that set out systematically to persecute some section of society. Subjects may be required to take on contingent liabilities, and these may work out to their great disadvantage—conscript soldiers who are made to lose their lives—, but the general balance of interest is still in their favour. If one actually had to choose between taking on the obligation to obey the law, including the one that in certain contingencies one might have to sacrifice one's life, and not living under the protection of the laws, it would still be reasonable to choose to accept the responsibilities and enjoy the benefits of civil society.

The argument is attractive, particularly in giving a rationale of the rights of minorities, but is subject to the great difficulty that in the absence of an actual context of bargaining, any contract might have been offered by the government and might well have been accepted. The benefits of civil society are so great, the evils of anarchy so fearsome, that it would be reasonable to put up with even a fairly bad government rather than replace it by none. The government could drive a very hard bargain with its subjects, which would still be one they would be wise to accept.

The Contract theory is also used by Individualists not to determine what the government may or may not require of the subject, but to determine what the general purposes of government are. The nature of the State is inferred from the implied contract by which men accept its claims over them. In particular, by considering what is the least that a reasonable man could want of a government, and which therefore all reasonable men must be supposed to want, we obtain the theory of the Minimum State—an unselective, coercive community with no functions, purposes, or ideals other than the maintenance of law and order—which Locke argued for and Jefferson tried to put into practice. Instead of asking what bargain a reasonable man might, if pressed, be prepared to accept, we ask why he would enter into a bargain at all, and are told that the one reason that every man has is to establish law and order and enjoy security of life, limb and property. The real *raison d'être* of the State is therefore the maintenance of law and order, and its authority should be confined to just what is necessary for that. Everything else should be left to the individual and voluntary associations.

SECTION 67

THE MINIMUM STATE

BESIDES Contract theories of the State, three other factors have been instrumental in furthering the doctrine of the Minimum State. They have been, first, a fear of totalitarianism, either as professed in the writings of e.g. Hobbes, or as practised in, e.g. Russia or France. There has been secondly the crucial fact of religious dissension— Puritans in England, Episcopalians in Scotland, Huguenots in France, Roman Catholics in Holland. The doctrines held have often been far from liberal: but the fact that they were held, led in practice to a general acceptance of non-conformity in a sphere thought at the time to be the most important of all, and hence to a lowly and limited *rôle* for the State. Thirdly there has been an explicit doctrine of Individualism, that the individual needs liberty in which to fulfil himself, and that this is all he needs from the State.

The fear of totalitarianism has been entirely justified. Since the end of the Middle Ages it has been an ever-present threat to mankind. The doctrine of the Minimum State is an effective counter, but more than sufficient. All Minimum States are non-totalitarian, but many nonminimum ones are so too. Although in politics it has often been an advantage to have an extreme and fairly clear-cut doctrine, in political philosophy it is not. As a counter to totalitarianism we may pay our respects to the historical utility of the doctrine of the Minimum State: but should recognise that it is not the only alternative.

The fact of religious dissension provides no justification for the Minimum State. At the most, it could only be cited in support of a secular State. Since all the dissensions were dissensions within the Christian religion, the differences do not appear to us to be as great as they seemed at the time, and the measure of agreement was very much greater than that supposed by the secular State. The importance of religious dissension was not that it paved the way for the Minimum State, but that it was the one effective force working against the monolithic Maximum State in which the sovereign was in practice and in theory omnicompetent. Religion made martyrs, who could neither be coerced into conformity nor persuaded that they ought to obey in all things, although usually very willing to obey in all non-religious matters. In the end, they wore down the resistance of governments, who found that they could get everything else they wanted except religious conformity, and were usually ready to settle for less than absolute obedience—it would be a reasonable bargain from a government's point of view, if faced with highly selective but fanatically determined disobedience.

The Individualist argument has already been stated.[1] There is, or may be, an incompatibility between the ideals and moral principles of an individual and those of the State. Therefore, in order to give full reign to the individual's ideals and moral principles, we proscribe the State's having any collective ideals or corporate morality over and above the canons arising inevitably from the nature of the individual and the purposes for which individuals must be assumed to have constituted States. This is the doctrine of the Minimum State. It maintains that the State, being an unselective community, should not select any corporate ideals, but should eschew them all equally, allowing its members the Right of Association (in its wide sense)[2], so that they can form themselves into voluntary associations to pursue any corporate ideals they want, but remaining itself indifferent to all ideals and values, save only those of maintaining law and order, which are inherent in the idea of a coercive community.

It can be argued, furthermore, that the *raison d'être* of the machinery of adjudication and law enforcement is the settlement of unresolved disputes, and that this is therefore all that the State should take upon

[1] § 63.   [2] See above, § 64, pp. 276-7.

itself. And we can support this by saying secondly that whereas a reasonable man may reasonably dissent from other purposes it is proposed that the State should adopt, he cannot dissent from this one without thereby proclaiming his desire to be an outlaw. Hence the Minimum State can justify, under the sixth heading in Section 12,[1] political obedience from all its subjects, whereas any other State will be forced back through the fourth and third headings to rely upon the second and first, and ultimately on the first alone. And this, as we have seen, is rationally unsatisfactory.

We note that both these arguments rely on the persistent quarrelsomeness of men. It is because men sometimes quarrel that we need the machinery of the law; but although, in view of our inability always to agree, some method of settling disputes is essential to a community, it does not follow that it is the *raison d'être* of that community. We do not join communities in order to settle disputes, but settle disputes in order to maintain communities. The word 'State' has itself lent colour to this false emphasis. We use it sometimes in a narrow sense, where it refers to the machinery for adjudicating disputes and enforcing decisions, sometimes in a wide sense to refer to any issue of public concern or public policy. If we concentrate our attention upon the magistrates' courts and on the police force, there is some plausibility in the contention that their primary function is the maintenance of law and order: if we consider the activities of civil servants, Members of Parliament, journalists, and commentators, it is much less plausible to claim that they are primarily concerned with the maintenance of law and order, even though this is a necessary condition of their other activities. The part of the State concerned with the settlement of disputes attracts notice not only because it is essential, but because in order to be effective it has to be definite in form and prominent— we all have to be able to recognise a policeman when we see one; and therefore we are naturally led to identify this as constituting the whole of the State, and think of the State as being solely a glorified policeman. But this is wrong. As we have seen,[2] although the machinery of the State is called into being by the fact of there being unresolved disputes, it can function only on the condition of there also being a large measure of agreement. The various ways in which agreement is reached are just as essential to the maintenance of a State as the activities of magistrates and policemen: but we notice them less, because they are less formal, and because agreement generally attracts less notice than

[1] p. 44.   [2] § 5, pp. 18–19, § 8, p. 33.

disagreement, and because there is no need to publicise agreements as there is to publicise methods of settling disputes. Thus we are led unwittingly to stress the maintenance of law and order and to forget the equal importance of fellow feeling and shared ideals. But if men were always quarrelling, so that the sole communal activity was the settling of disputes, then that activity too would be impossible, and there would be no point in their living together at all.

The second argument likewise makes out the reasonable man to be much given to dissent: he is to be likely to disagree with every proposed purpose of the State, save for the bare one of maintaining law and order. But to be as disagreeable as this is to be cantankerous rather than reasonable. We need to distinguish the true proposition that a reasonable man may question any, or almost any, moral or political principle, from the false proposition that a reasonable man may question every, or almost every, moral or political principle. A man who doubts everything cannot argue rationally because there is no starting-point to argue from: and a man who disagrees with his fellow countrymen on every question cuts himself off from the possibility of rational argument with them; he declares himself a non-participant in all political processes, and cannot reasonably require that very much respect be paid to his views. The sceptic can remain unconvinced of the validity of any purpose of State other than that of maintaining law and order: but provided law and order is maintained, he is not in a very strong position to push any particular objection very far. The argument from scepticism for the Minimum State is two-edged; for although to the sceptic only the Minimum State will be justified, yet since he has contracted out of all political argument save for the pure Hobbesian one of the need for avoiding the law of the jungle, he will have to accept, if need be, a Hobbesian Leviathan which does maintain law and order, without enthusiasm, but without any rational ground for objection.[1]

The argument from the possibility of dissent cannot, if it is to be serious, be an argument from general scepticism, but must be more limited. The typical case of dissent is where only some principles are rejected, but many are held in common with the dominant party in the State, and those that are rejected are replaced by others, equally well articulated and equally firmly held. Protestants were not prepared to accept papal supremacy, to attend Mass, or to respect the monastic ideal of life: but Protestant and Roman Catholic alike professed the

[1] See above, § 66, p. 286.

same devotion to the person of our Lord, the same respect for his teaching, and acknowledged substantially the same moral law; and the distinctive Protestant doctrines, such as the supremacy of the Bible, the priesthood of all believers, and the sanctity of the secular life, were as definite and as strongly believed as those that they replaced. Neither party had any commitment to the doctrine of the Minimum State, nor was there any need for a Minimum State in order to accommodate them both. A certain measure of religious and civil liberty was required, but this is a far cry from a Minimum State.

A more serious argument arises when we consider not the classical case of one dominant and one dissenting view, but of a multitude of different dissenting views. For, although one man cannot dissent on every issue without being unreasonably idiosyncratic, different men might dissent on different issues, so that on every question of general policy some man, not evidently unreasonable, had sincere and conscientious objections. One might think that euthanasia ought to be allowed, but not abortion, and another *vice versa*: one might be for permitting homosexuality between consenting adult males but entirely against divorce, and again another the other way round. Thus in a large society it would be possible for every principle of public morality to be brought in question, so that the only safe course was to confine the purposes of the State to those of maintaining law and order, and leave everything else to voluntary associations.

The argument as now stated seems free of fallacies: it seems quite plausible that every purpose of State over and above the minimum ones of maintaining law and order might be objected to by some person, different in each case, who was sincere, and according to his lights reasonable. Certainly many public purposes of State in Great Britain and the United States are sincerely objected to by worthy and honest men. Britain is a Christian country, although many Britons are not Christians, and some are convinced opponents of the Christian religion: the United States does not officially support any religion, but does officially support education, although many Americans are highly hostile to intellectual values. Any country that has public libraries which supply "good books" more readily than "light fiction" is implementing a purpose of State which many people disagree with.[1]

---

[1] Compare the following letter to *The Times*, 1 September 1956.

Sir—Your leading article of August 28 "Why?" makes me see red. Why on earth should not public libraries provide the books their subscribers (the rate-payers) want? The fact that you may prefer a book on philosophy or ancient Rome does not mean that these particular books make you a better citizen in any

Thus unless we are prepared to confine the purposes of the State to the minimum ones of maintaining law and order, we may be, and in actual practice often are, wishing upon people purposes to which they not only do not subscribe but sometimes take strong exception.

There are nevertheless objections to the Minimum State so weighty as to outweigh the argument for it. The first objection is that it is simply not feasible to have a Minimum State which has no other purpose than the maintenance of law and order. The second objection takes up the point made about associations in Sections 45 and 64,[1] and shows that even if we confine the State to a minimum we shall not avoid people being pressed to subscribe to purposes they do not really approve. The third objection is simply that we do not find the Minimum State desirable.

A State which was really morally neutral, which was indifferent to all values, other than that of maintaining law and order, would not command enough allegiance to survive at all. A soldier may sacrifice his life for Queen and Country, but hardly for the Minimum State. A policeman, believing in Natural Law and immutable right and wrong, may tackle an armed desperado: but not if he regards himself as an employee of a Mutual Protection and Assurance Society, constructed from the cautious contracts of prudent individuals. Some ideals are necessary to inspire those without whose free co-operation the State would not survive. We may be able to secure that the State is neutral on this or that issue, but not on all. Moreover, the concept of a Minimum State, which is indifferent to all values save the one of maintaining law and order is indeterminate. There are many different systems which maintain law and order: which one are we to choose? Shall we have the institution of private property? If so, under what

---

way. If you spent your whole day fitting together horrid little parts on a conveyor belt or watching a dozen bobbins whizzing round and round, you, too, might feel in need of a nice relaxing novel at the end of the day. And a "nice romance" is just what the tired mother needs when she has at last got her family to bed— it does her far more good than an educational book and helps her to keep her reason.

Perhaps you think that everyone can afford to buy books (at 12s. 6d. a time) as you appear to think everyone can afford to go to cinemas and theatres. They cannot afford either and the public library is a godsend. What does it matter if the books may not improve our minds if they help improve our humdrum lives?

Yours truly,
Jacinth Whittaker.

3 West Road, Bury St. Edmunds.

[1] pp. 192, 278.

rules? What laws of inheritance? What laws of transfer? Merely to say that no public purpose is to be manifest in our legal system is to give us no guidance about how our system is to be framed—except that it should not be carefully and rationally thought out. In any case the goal of maintaining law and order involves the concepts of force, hurt and harm, which the maintenance of law and order is intended to avoid: and these concepts are not themselves determinate, but are determined by the values held in common by a State. In deciding what shall count as a harm, the State is taking a view of human nature, and what human beings ought to be. For this reason alone we cannot have the State merely maintain law and order, without thereby deciding which harms are to be tolerated, which prevented, which sorts of force are banned, which other sorts are to be considered as merely meta-phorical.

The second objection takes up one natural extension of the concept of force. We have in Section 14 distinguished direct from indirect enforcement of decisions, and in colloquial speech either can be described as an application of force. Let us, however, retain the distinc-tion between the use of force, properly so called, and the use of sanctions, but note that the fundamental objection (given in Section 12, pp. 45–46) to force as a method of securing political obedience applies almost as much to sanctions. And, as we saw in Section 45, once we have even a Minimum State whose decisions are directly enforceable, we shall have individuals and associations able to enforce their decisions in-directly, by the means of sanctions; and this power, although only indirectly enforceable, is sometimes as great as that of the State, and often as much open to abuse. The power of employers in the nine-teenth century under *laissez-faire* and of trade unions in many coun-tries in the twentieth century are examples. It may be true that no American capitalist wielded the absolute power of a Nero or a Ghengis Khan, and that no British trade union has behaved like the populace of Athens or of France during the Terror: but a man had a much better chance of securing justice from a mediaeval monarch than from many a modern employer, and trade union executives have shown a contempt for the rights of the individual that would have brought discredit on any ancient Legislature. The Minimum States burkes the problem of power. It is so far indifferent to values that it is indifferent to Justice. But the maintenance of law and order without regard to Justice, although possibly a good, is a minimal good, no more than that offered by Leviathan. Thus again the arguments in favour of the Minimum State turn out to give it no more support than they do to a totalitarian one.

The third objection to the Minimum State is simply that men do not want it. They conceivably might think of banding together solely for the maintenance of law and order, but in fact associate for many other reasons and want to keep it like that. Patriotism has always been a powerful emotion, and in this nationalistic age, the nation-state has appeared not simply as a coercive system but as the most real and natural social unit. A British atheist may regret the Establishment of the Church of England, but would not wish to purchase disestablishment at the cost of banning all collective action and aspiration on the part of the United Kingdom. He still will want, for example, Britain to be collectively concerned with the improvement of people's health, the encouragement of education, and the elimination of poverty. An American businessman may have a rooted suspicion of eggheads, but is none the less a devoted believer in the American Way of Life, and in the ideals set forth in the Declaration of Independence. Neither dissentient would choose to secure the abandonment of the purpose objected to by having his nation abandon all purposes whatever. The maintenance of law and order may be essential for the good life, but is not by itself enough.

Our desire for collective action on the part of the State is not simply a prejudice. Even the most hardened Individualist will concede that most people desire to engage in collective activities some times, and that in some fields the only feasible activity is collective activity. People want public recognition of those killed in war: people want roads and communications and medical research. Although with sufficient ingenuity it would often be possible to form, for the purpose of carrying on these collective activities, associations whose decisions were only indirectly enforceable, the system would be cumbrous without any corresponding advantages. A highway association might provide highways for its members, promulgate a highway code and enforce it by threat of expulsion. Fire brigades could be, as originally they were, paid for by subscribers—and available only for their use— they would go then, as they used originally to go, to the scene of each fire, and if it proved not to be the property of a subscriber, would return and leave it to burn. Nobody need be made to support medical research, the benefits of which would be reserved exclusively for those that had. Where such a system was feasible, it would not present the individual with any real freedom. He would be faced with a natural monopoly or natural oligopoly and would have no alternative but to subscribe on the terms laid down. On every occasion of life he would be having to prove himself to be a member of the relevant association. It might be feasible always to wear a bracelet entitling the wearer to medical attention in case he were found unconscious, but it would hardly be convenient. And in some cases it would be not merely awkward but impossible to engage on collective action without decisions being directly enforceable. We cannot use wirelesses unless everyone is prohibited from transmitting without a licence. We cannot have the benefits of the law of copyright unless we are prepared to use the law of the land to prohibit breaches of copyright, and enforce it, if necessary, directly. In such cases we must either forgo all possibility of collective action, with all its advantages and benefits, or we must accept the use of the law not simply to resolve ordinary disputes but to enforce some degree of uniformity. And in the other cases, although we might be able to avoid involving the law directly to enforce the uniformities required for collective action, it would be cumbersome to do so, and would require us to introduce into society a large number of additional distinctions—we should always need to know whether a particular man was a member of this or that association—, without producing any corresponding advantages. It is reasonable and natural to accept the State as an association for other purposes as well as that of maintaining law and order. This is not to say that we should accept it as the one and only association for every collective purpose—far from it: it is merely to say that we do not need to disallow all purposes of State other than that of maintaining law and order; and in particular those purposes that if they are to be undertaken at all would have to be undertaken by the State, and those purposes which if they were to be undertaken by some other association, would require, or at least suggest, that the membership of the association should be coextensive with that of the State.

SECTION 68

TOLERATION

IF WE cannot have the Minimum State, we are faced with the problem of dissent. A man, not utterly unreasonable, disagrees with some ideal acknowledged by the State. What is to be done? How is the conflict to be resolved?

There is no simple formula for toleration. All attempts to demarcate areas of tolerance fail, by excluding too much as well as claiming too much. Tolerance is a habit of mind, a style of argument, rather than a formula. It is an argument for not doing some things believed to be desirable, *in spite of* the fact that they are desirable, *because* doing them would show too little respect for another human being, wrong *though* he be. Toleration is not indifference. One can tolerate only when one cares, when one believes oneself to be right, and the other man to be wrong. Else there is no problem. One can achieve an easy acquiescence in another man's actions by not caring at all what he does: but if a man could not care less, there is no virtue in his not objecting. Toleration, therefore, is always a *counter*-argument, not the absence of a conclusion. Only when a man has an argument for doing something can counter-arguments of toleration lead him not to do it after all.

It follows that toleration is always under a strain and is never complete. If a man cares about something and thinks it desirable he will make some attempt to bring it about—else it would be hard to say that he really cared. But he will not attempt to bring it about by every means within his power, because certain means will be ruled out as showing too little respect for the personality of some one else involved. A man may support one political party and his friend another. They will argue, perhaps vehemently, each attempting to win the other round to his own allegiance. Not to argue would show a lack of interest in politics. Tolerance is shown not by not arguing but by not arguing always, and by not breaking off the association because of the other's obtuseness. Tolerance is under a strain, having to avoid at once the two extremes, of indifference—not arguing ever—and of intolerance—arguing remorselessly all the time. Exactly what is the happy mean depends on circumstances and cannot be laid down for all cases in advance.

Toleration is never complete. Although a tolerant man may take care, out of respect for another man's personality, not to press him too hard, he cannot succeed in not pressing him at all on issues that matter, except by not communicating with him at all. If they exchange views, and disagree on an important issue, then each is going to feel some pressure to reach agreement, and if one man particularly values the other's good opinion of him, he may find himself under great psychological pressure to bring his own views into line. This often happens, and is the ineliminable pressure which arises between people who differ in their views. Often there are more tangible pressures too. Dissenters were not persecuted in the eighteenth century, but were not promoted to public positions of power or profit, and therefore a Roman Catholic who wanted to get on in the world was under pressure to become an Anglican, just as an Anglican now who wishes to marry a Roman Catholic is under pressure to become one. Whether these pressures were and are proper, and what pressures in general are proper, are debatable questions. But there must be some pressures. We want people to agree with us on matters of importance. If they will not, we may be willing not to coerce them, but we will not choose them to rule over us, or to live with us, because having the opinions which they do have, we do not trust them enough or do not agree with them enough to give ourselves over unreservedly into their power or into their company.

To be tolerated is, thus, not to be free of any pressure[1] whatever, but only of pressures of certain kinds. Mill is being quite unreasonable when he protests at the "tyranny" of public opinion. For, except in matters of indifference, public opinion ought to be expressed, and will exert pressure. The unbeliever in the last century, the supporter of *Apartheid* in this, occupy unpopular positions, and cannot expect it to be otherwise except at the cost of what they stand for being reduced to insignificance. If I, an Englishman in the second half of the twentieth century, were to give vent to anti-Semite views, I should be tolerated, rightly, but ridiculed and despised, also rightly.

Toleration can be considered from the point of view of the man exercising tolerance or from that of the man being tolerated. The former is primary. The man exercising tolerance wants the other to agree with him, or at least to go along with him, but, out of respect for his personality, is not prepared to press him by all means at his command. It may operate at two levels. It operates at the high level when what is desired from the man is something which must be given whole-heartedly or not at all. Love must be unforced. So must belief. I cannot, logically cannot, pressure a woman into loving me by threatening to hold her up to ridicule and contempt, any more than by threatening to bankrupt her, or by threatening to kill her. Threats and inducements may make her amenable to my lust, but cannot win me her love. Similarly if I argue, I want to convince my opponent, not extort his affirmation by browbeating him, deceiving him, threatening him or cajoling him. Such methods may elicit verbal assent, but cannot give

[1] See § 15, pp. 56–57.
[2] J. S. Mill, *On Liberty*, Ch. I, p. 68 (Everyman edition).

me what I want. Sometimes, indeed, in order to obtain what I want—his free and considered conviction—I may go to great lengths to conceal my views for a season in order that he may be swayed only by arguments and not by any desire to stand well with me. So too with religious belief, only heartfelt convictions are any good, and therefore it is logically incoherent, if I want a man to believe, to use external pressures on him.

The high-level respect for personality is so high as to be almost outside the ambit of political thought. In personal relations, in the pursuit of truth, in the worship of God, we demand complete conviction and integrity; but political discourse is at a lower level, in which we are concerned not with whole-hearted responses and commitments, but limited acquiescences and liabilities. Respect for personality operates at the lower level too. Characteristically, we want some overt action or outward conformity, and do not mind whether it is whole-hearted or not, but do not want to secure it at the cost of showing contempt for the man as a rational agent. Pressures which lie in the logic of the situation we can properly exert: but extraneous pressures, even though legally or constitutionally available, we do not feel at liberty to use. We do not use coercion. We avoid, so far as we can, the use of what would be regarded as sanctions by any normal human being—e.g. loss of employment. We avoid, so far as we can, the use of sanctions as such; that is, although if a person persists in opinions or actions we think wrong, we may treat him less favourably than we would otherwise, we treat him less favourably not *in order to* make him change his opinions or behaviour but only *in consequence of* his not having changed them. A Roman Catholic refuses to marry someone who will not become a Roman Catholic too. This may be felt as pressure, but is not intended as a sanction: marriage is refused not in order to make the other become a Roman Catholic, but only in consequence of the other's not being one.

Toleration is a matter of degree. We show some toleration for dissentients by not coercing them, more by not debarring them from ordinary public offices, more still by not exercising extraneous financial pressures on them. What is the right degree of toleration that the reasonable man ought to exercise depends very heavily on the issue in dispute and the relationship between the parties. In personal relationships and politics we demand rather little toleration: we do not blame men for choosing wives and friends whose views and habits are entirely agreeable to them; nor am I under an obligation to vote,

out of respect for his personality, for a politician whose views I regard
as pernicious, misguided, or mistaken; for a representative has to
represent his constituents' views, and therefore his own views are
highly relevant to his constituents' choice. A motor dealer could
reasonably dismiss a salesman who expressed to customers the sincerely held view that cars ought to be abolished or that the make he
was selling was no good; whereas it would be intolerant for a Roman
Catholic car dealer to refuse to employ a salesman who was not himself a Roman Catholic. It would be reasonable for an Anglican school
to refuse to employ a Roman Catholic teacher, unreasonable to refuse
to employ a master because he did not share the political views of the
board of governors. If I have an argument with my grocer about
capital punishment, and threaten to take away my custom unless he
renounces his abolitionist views, I show intolerance; but if I have an
argument with him about sweated labour, and threaten to remove my
custom unless he abandons his opposition to a Shop Assistants'
Charter, I show no unbecoming zeal in furthering my own ideals.

The tolerant man wants to achieve a certain state of affairs but
recognises that what stands in his way is the opposition of a human
being, and will not ride rough-shod over another human being, another
partially rational agent. He will press him, but only smoothly; so far
as possible, rationally. He has respect for him, not merely as a human
being, a bare sentient consciousness, but as a partially rational one.
It is in the nature of a fallible rational agent to be sometimes wrong, but
wrong conclusions bear witness to a process of reasoning which we
still respect. 'There, but for the grace of God, go I', the rational man,
whose beliefs are right, thinks of the man whose beliefs are wrong. The
tolerant man does not think that he is, or might be, wrong on the issue
in dispute; 'Have you never considered that you might be wrong?' is
wrongly construed if it is taken that one should be doubtful of the
rightness of one's conclusions, and for that reason hesitate to press
them. Rather, it means that a reasonable man knows that however
right he is on the issue in dispute, he can be, and has been, wrong on
other issues, and this is inherent in being a rational, fallible agent. And
he does wrong to Reason if he does not allow it on occasion to be
wrong, and respect its conclusions for being reasoned even when not
for being right.

Toleration from the point of view of the tolerated wears a different
aspect. The tolerated man feels himself under pressure to conform his
opinions or behaviour to an alien standard, but cannot know what

limits there are to the pressure that may be exerted. It may be true that the tolerant man will only argue with him but will not withdraw his friendship, but the tolerated man does not know this, and therefore may feel himself under greater pressure than the tolerant man intended to exert. The interviewing panel may be sure in their own minds that they do not care what views the man interviewed expresses, and are concerned only with the skill with which he defends them, but the latter, not knowing or not believing this, is likely to feel his personal convictions and his whole personality being squeezed into an approved stereotype. If his personality is really to be respected, therefore, he must be assured of some chartered freedoms, of some guarantee that certain sorts of opinion or behaviour will not be subject to certain sorts of pressure.

We therefore need to formulate principles of toleration, even though toleration cannot really be reduced to a formula. In order to protect the tolerated from pressures he may suspect are going to be exerted, even though they are not actually going to be exerted, we may impose on those who need to be tolerant certain principles of indifference which they cannot whole-heartedly hold. Just because men's religious opinions have so often been a matter of concern, we lay it down that over a wide variety of transactions they are to be deemed to be irrelevant. I have a duty to be indifferent to men's religious opinions when selecting candidates for the Civil Service, not because I am indifferent, nor because they are irrelevant, but because otherwise the candidates may feel themselves under too much pressure to conform to what they suppose to be acceptable standards. Since governors of schools often are politicians, and might be supposed to favour candidates of their own party, they are debarred from enquiring into candidates' political affiliations, in order to preserve schoolmasters' rights to form and hold what political views they like. It is not really a matter of indifference; but it needs to be made so. So again in business transactions, there is a general argument for generally disregarding the political, religious, or intellectual views of people with whom we do business, not because we really do not care, but because it is only by seeming indifferent that we can free them from pressures that derogate from their rationality.

Principles of toleration are necessarily crude and inadequate. Certain issues, about which people are peculiarly sensitive, are to be disregarded, but others, which to a particular person may be equally important, are not similarly shielded—I may not be told to change my political allegiance on pain of dismissal, but may be told to get my hair cut if I want to keep my job. Even where convictions are protected, the protection is not complete. Although some pressures are not to be brought to bear on a dissentient, not all pressures are excluded. The dissentient may, in some cases, be secured against coercion or financial loss, but may still suffer social ostracism, and sometimes rightly. If I, an Oxford don, make vague and sweeping charges against my colleagues in the University of Oxford, I may not be liable under the law of libel, and may be safe against dismissal: but I may find that my colleagues like me less for what I have said, however sincere I was in saying it. It is inevitable, as we have seen, that however much tolerance is being exercised, some residual pressure will still be brought to bear. A tolerant man can be required to feign indifference in some respects, but not in all.

Principles of toleration are also incomplete in that even where they do operate, they operate only for some dissenting opinions, not for all. Socialist schoolmasters have a right that their political opinions be disregarded by Conservative governors: but communists, nazis and fascists are quite rightly debarred from occupying any position where they could corrupt the minds of the young. The logic of the position is not that school teachers have a natural right to their convictions which we fail to respect in the case of communists, nazis and fascists, but that school-teachers' opinions are naturally an object of concern to parents and governors—much as politicians' opinions are of concern to voters—, only, we artificially abridge this concern to some extent in order to avoid greater evils. Such a toleration, however, is limited. It allows a certain range of opinions, but not all. And one can justify tolerating some and not others.

Thus we cannot usefully formulate rules of toleration. They depend too much on particular circumstances. Fundamentally, the tolerant man will regard the person as well as his overt actions and avowed opinions, and therefore will walk delicately in attempting to secure conformity. Secondarily, in order to reassure dissentients and relieve them from imagined pressures, we adopt various *ad hoc* rules, for certain sorts of relationships and in respect of issues on which people are peculiarly sensitive. The rules lay down that these issues are to be deemed irrelevant in those relationships; such rules are difficult to enact as laws, and have to be left as vague directives. They remain crude, and, as we have seen, in two ways incomplete.

SECTION 69

FREEDOM OF SPEECH

TOLERATION is too vague to encapsulate in legal form. But if a State is to be tolerant at all, it needs to forswear the use of some pressures—at least some coercive ones—against some sorts of dissentient. These limitations must be embodied in legal form. There must be some occasions therefore on which a legal privilege is conferred on somebody, which entitles that person to act wrongly. There are in fact good reasons for conferring these privileges very widely.[1] But sometimes, even beyond a general tenor of argument in favour of Freedom, there are special arguments for conferring chartered liberties, especially on issues where otherwise, in view of certain other arguments which could plausibly be adduced, there would be a case for denying them altogether. Freedom of Speech can obviously be used to criticise and weaken the common values acknowledged by the community: Freedom of Worship can be exercised in the worship of strange and wicked deities, and in the furtherance of odious blasphemies. Freedom of moral choice can be invoked to cover gross and possibly unacceptable lapses from the common standards of the community. Nevertheless there are further arguments in favour of Freedom, not always conclusive but usually so.

In each case, although some formulation must be found, it cannot be neat. It is often thought, with these Freedoms, as with individuals' Freedoms *vis-à-vis* one another, that certain *spheres* can be demarcated, within which a man ought to be absolutely free. It has been claimed that a man ought to be privileged to say exactly what he likes, to worship whatever God in whatever way he likes, to practise whatever sexual morality he likes: but perjury, suttee, and incest have been prohibited by many States without it being evident thereby that they are intolerant. Blanket immunities cannot be conferred. The arguments for and against certain Freedoms under certain conditions need to be made explicit before we can strike a balance between them.

Some conformities are imposed not in order to prevent harm being done—as with the traffic laws—but in order to invest certain forms or patterns with conventional significance. Currency, trade-marks, official signs, and notices, all obtain their meaning from the fact that

[1] See above, § 38.

we are in general not free to use these forms just as we please. It is the prohibition which invests the form with its significance. The un-freedom creates the value. In a complicated society therefore we may enact many artificial unfreedoms as artifices for the conveyance of valuable information; nor need this be felt as restrictive, provided there are alternative forms or patterns not appropriated for symbolic use. I can reasonably be forbidden to dress myself up as a policeman or a soldier, provided there are other uniforms I can wear.[1] I can reasonably be prohibited from engraving "five-pound notes", because there are so many other designs I can engrave. Conventions are essentially generally recognised rules to do things one way rather than another when it is in itself a matter of indifference which way we do them, but we want to do them all the same way. Hence, where there is a convention, there is also an alternative, in itself no less acceptable than the form reserved for symbolic purposes. Hence conventions, and their supporting prohibitions, pose no problem for Freedom.

The pre-eminent example of behaviour subject to conventions whereby significance is obtained, is language. Communication is a social activity entirely dependent on our observing various syntactic and semantic rules. In particular, communication would be impossible unless people did in general tell the truth. The common view, that speech is inherently free, is thus exactly the reverse of the truth, if by free speech is meant that everyone is entitled to say exactly what he pleases or what suits his book, regardless of whether what he says is true or false. The offences of perjury, misrepresentation, and false pretences are indications of our not really believing that speech should in this sense be free.

The view that men ought to be free to speak as they like, is part of a wider doctrine, that men ought to be free to think as they like. It started as a religious principle. Luther argued for Freedom of Thought on religious grounds because the soul is necessarily free. He says: "We ought to remember that in every Christian there are two natures, a spiritual and a bodily. In as far as he possesses a soul, a Christian is a spiritual person, an inward, regenerate self; and in as far as he possesses flesh and blood, he is a sensual person, an outward, unregenerate self . . . When we consider the inner, spiritual man, and see what belongs to him if he is to be a free and devout Christian . . . it is evident that, whatever the name, no outward thing can make him either free or religious. For his religion and freedom, and, moreover,

[1] See above, § 4, pp. 14–16; § 42, pp. 176–7.

his sinfulness and servitude, are neither bodily nor outward. What avail is it to the soul if the body is free, active, and healthy; or eats, drinks, and lives as it likes? Again, what harm does it do to the soul if the body is imprisoned, ill and weakly; or is hungry, thirsty, and in pain, even if one does not bear it gladly. This sort of thing never touches the soul a little bit, nor makes it free or captive, religious or sinful."[1] From this Luther is led to the conclusion that "The civil authority should not prevent anyone from teaching and believing what he likes, be it Gospel or falsehood".[2] The civil authorities should not interfere, first because beliefs are harmless to them, and therefore there was no need to interfere, so far as their interests were concerned; and secondly because forced beliefs, if not a contradition in terms,[3] are without value to the man who holds them, so that there could be no justification for interfering for the sake of the individual's spiritual welfare. "Since it depends on each one's conscience to know what he must believe, and no harm is done in this to the secular authority, this authority should keep quiet, busy itself with its own affairs, and let each one believe this or that as he can and as he chooses, and not use any force with anyone on this account." And again, "In matters of faith we have to deal with a free action towards which no one can be forced. Indeed, it is a divine action in the Spirit, and it is therefore out of the question that an outside power can obtain it by force. Hence the well-known saying quoted by St. Augustine: one neither can nor should compel anyone to believe."[4]

Luther's argument falls into two parts. He is arguing first that thought is inherently free, because no one else can know what is going on in a man's mind. He is arguing secondly that thought ought to be free, because otherwise it is of no value. The first thesis, the essential privacy of thought, has come in for some philosophical criticisms, and, more seriously, is threatened by the use of "truth-drugs" and encephalograms. We need not, however, discuss it, because this argument, whatever its validity, is an argument solely for Freedom of Thought, and is necessarily irrelevant to Freedom of Speech, which, if it is to be defended at all, cannot be defended on the

---

[1] *The Freedom of a Christian*, §§ 2, 3. Translated in Bertram Lee Wolf, *Reformation Writings of Martin Luther*, Vol. I, pp. 357–8.
[2] Ermahnung zum Frieden auf die zwölf Artikel der Bauerschaft in Schwaben (1525), *Werke*, t. xviii, p. 209.
[3] See above, § 68, pp. 297–8, and below, § 71, pp. 318–19, and § 75, p. 343.
[4] Luther, Von weltlicher Obrigkeit, *Werke*, t. xi, p. 264.

grounds that speech is essentially private, so that nobody can know what another man is really saying.

Luther's second argument, that Freedom, in some sense, is a necessary condition of thought having any real value, is a cogent one, and applies not only to thought and worship, which were the chief concern of the original Protestants, but to speech, personal relations, personal morality, artistic creation, and many other activities as well. It is part of the general case for Freedom, which continues after all the particular objections have been made, and all the particular restrictions have been imposed, and requires us to ensure that at the end of it all, people are still, in one way or another, free. But it is a general argument, which applies to all sorts of activities, and not just the activity of speaking. We cannot rest a plea for a special Freedom of Speech on this argument. Instead of regarding speech as peculiarly private, we should say of it what Mill said of trade: "Trade is a social act. Whoever undertakes to sell any description of goods to the public, does what affects the interests of other people, and of society in general; and thus his conduct, in principle, comes within the jurisdiction of society."[1] And just as Mill having made this concession, goes on to maintain that there are nevertheless sound arguments for Free Trade, so we, having conceded the essentially social nature of language, need to establish on other grounds the doctrine of Freedom of Speech.

There are two decisive arguments against legislating for truthfulness: that it is not necessary; and that it is not possible. It is not necessary to legislate against lying generally, because other sanctions are adequate. Truth is objective, and is therefore inter-subjectively testable. If a man tells an untruth, he can in principle be found out; and if a man is often untruthful, he will be found out. He will then acquire a reputation for unreliability, and people will cease to accept his word, and this will be a great inconvenience to him. He will, in effect, have deprived himself of the use of speech, since sounds coming out of his mouth will no longer be taken to carry the information he wants them to bear.

The non-legal sanctions against untruthfulness are effective only under certain conditions which do not always obtain. It is clear that they cannot obtain when a vendor is describing his wares to a prospective purchaser: for the purchaser will be in a position to check the truth of the vendor's description only after he has purchased the goods, and then it will be too late. Therefore we have legal restrictions

[1] J. S. Mill, *On Liberty*, Ch. V. p. 150 (Everyman edition).

on the vendor's freedom to misrepresent his goods to prospective purchasers.

Again, the assessments society can make of a man's truthfulness are characteristically dispositional. We can discover that a man is a habitual liar or habitually inaccurate, but it is difficult for society to form a firm judgement about the truth of what a man says on a particular occasion. But sometimes we need to be assured that a man is telling the truth not as a general habit but on a particular occasion; for example, in a court of law: and then we do enact legal sanctions against dishonesty, in order that we may reasonably rely on a witness's sworn testimony, even though it may be uncorroborated, and in spite of our inability to check his general truthfulness.

The non-legal sanctions against dishonesty will be completely effective only in a small society, where everybody knows everybody else, and nobody can escape from the reputation he has earned. As society becomes larger and more mobile and more anonymous, these sanctions become less effective. It would, however, be regrettable if strangers could not trust each other, and if we were brought up, like peasants, to regard every stranger with suspicion. It is better to secure public confidence by legislating against the offence of "obtaining money by false pretences". It is a case where the argument for security outweighs the argument for Freedom—indeed, necessarily so in this case, because if there were not the security, and the corresponding restrictions on Freedom, there would be no hope of having one's words believed by strangers, even though one's words were true.

The non-legal sanctions against dishonesty work slowly, and lies, before they come home to roost, may have done much damage while in flight. The laws of libel and slander are intended to redress the balance. We may think the present law unsatisfactory. It often stifles fair comment and the disclosure of facts which ought to be made known: and often fails to give the individual enough protection against the Press. Nevertheless, the principle is acceptable enough: if one man causes another man harm by telling lies about him, he should be liable for damages.

All these, however, are exceptional cases. In general, legal sanctions are not needed, because in general we have alternative means of checking the truth of a statement that we need to be able to rely on, and these are effective, non-legal sanctions against lying. It is not necessary to have a general law against lying. Nor would it be possible. For dishonesty is not the only cause of falsehood. Men say things that are not true, far more often because they are themselves mistaken than because they are trying to mislead others. If we punished falsehood as such, and therefore error as well as deceit, we should, among fallible men, merely be putting a premium on silence. If however we seek to distinguish deceit from error, we shall find many borderline cases, and it will be difficult to draw up a legal criterion to distinguish the one clearly from the other. All we can do is to pick out certain clear cases of deceit, when a man either from the context or from what he actually says, is under a clear obligation to say, not what he thinks, but only what he knows, and yet has said something which he must have known was not true. And this is just what we do do when there is some further reason why we should. But in the absence of further reasons, we are rightly reluctant to frame a difficult law to achieve an unnecessary end.

The religious origin of the demand for Freedom of Speech is important. What men had in mind when they claimed that they should be free to speak as they thought fit, was not that they should be entitled to make false statements of fact, but that they should be entitled to *argue* freely. There is an important difference between statements and arguments. The paradigm statement is one which, although it could be checked, is intended to be accepted unchecked, on the authority of the man making the statement: the paradigm argument is one which if it is to be accepted at all must be accepted on its own authority, not that of the man who puts it forward. Statements vouch for the truth of the facts asserted: arguments merely suggest to the hearer how he should view a situation; they point out the implications of what he already knows. But it remains for the hearer to decide for himself whether the argument suggested is really sound, to see whether the implications pointed out really do hold.

Needless to say, the distinction between statements and arguments is not usually as sharp as this. Some statements cannot help being checked by the hearer: some arguments are so complicated, or so evenly balanced, that we do depend very much on the authority of the man who puts the argument forward—very commonly, for instance, in history, or in jurisprudence. We need not, however, enter into these points; it is sufficient to note that a large part of the plea for Freedom of Speech has really been a plea for Freedom of Discussion, and that this has been justified by the self-authenticating nature of argument. The ideal of what we call Areopagite society, composed of serious-minded, though fallible, rational arguers, is one which has had immense attraction for all lovers of Freedom. We shall consider first the presuppositions of Areopagite society, and secondly the conditions under which we can regard parts of our actual society as being sufficiently Areopagite to be free.

SECTION 70

AREOPAGITE SOCIETY

AREOPAGITE society is composed of finite and fallible men, like the rest of us, but of ones who are rational and responsible to a higher degree than is common among men. Because they are finite, no one of them knows everything or has considered everything: because they are fallible, any one of them, or all of them together, may be wrong. The classical arguments for Freedom of Speech have been based on man's finitude and fallibility. Free Speech, it is argued, is a corrective for both: one man's limitations in a freely speaking society will be supplemented by another man's knowledge; and one man's errors will be corrected fearlessly by others. People ought to allow a man to express an opinion, however unpalatable, because, says Mill "if the opinion is right, they are deprived of an opportunity of exchanging error for truth."[2]

Areopagites must also be rational and responsible, if Areopagite society is to elicit the truth. There would be no virtue in true opinions being aired, unless when aired they had a better chance of being believed than false ones. A sufficient number of fallible speakers would enunciate some true statements along with many false ones, upon the same principle as a sufficiency of monkeys typing out Shakespeare; but this Tower of Babel would be without merit so far as the discovery of truth was concerned. Milton and Mill both make explicit their assumption that truth will prevail and that men have a *nisus* towards the rational and away from irrationality. "For who knows not that truth is strong, next to the Almighty; she needs no policies, nor stratagems, nor licensings to make her victorious; those are the shifts and the defences that error uses against her power".[1] "Why is it, then, that there is on the whole a preponderance among mankind of rational opinions and rational conduct? If there really is this preponderance— which there must be unless human affairs are, and always have been,

---

[1] J. S. Mill, *On Liberty*, Ch. II, p. 79 (Everyman edition).
[2] John Milton, *Areopagitica*.

in an almost desperate state—it is owing to a quality of the human mind, the source of everything respectable in man either as an intellectual or as a moral being, namely that his errors are corrigible. He is capable of rectifying his mistakes, by discussion and experience."[1] Granted some assumptions of this sort, Areopagite society will elicit truth in a way that no monolithic system can.

The concepts of rationality and truth employed in Areopagite arguments are not very clear—there is some reason for supposing that they never could be made absolutely clear. There must be some common standards of value, and although an Areopagite, like anybody else, may prefer his opinion to another's, he must in general prefer that his opinions should be true rather than that they should be his own, and must feel vulnerable on the score of the truth of what he says—he must feel that he has lost caste, so to speak, if what he had maintained turns out to be false, and must be concerned that this should not happen. We note, therefore, that Areopagite nature is an intellectualised version of human nature. Areopagites interact, have some shared values, suffer from fallible judgement, from *amour propre*, and from imperfect information. The chief difference is that the Areopagite is not as vulnerable as an ordinary man, nor as selfish. It is much easier to cause a man pain than to expose his errors: it needs much less humility to achieve power than intellectual eminence.

It is not enough, however, that Areopagites should have common standards. We need to say, rather, in part, different ideas of truth, different apprehensions of rationality, but a common propensity to prefer the true to the false, the rational to the irrational, *when the issue is put to them*. We cannot simply say that man needs must love the truest when he sees it, without adding the gloss that he very often will not see the truest unless it is pointed out to him. If truth were as objective as the external world, if our standards of rationality were as uniformly shared as our rules for the application of descriptive language, there would be no Areopagite argument: we should deal with dissenters as we do with liars; moral blindness would really be *pari passu* with colour-blindness. The Areopagite arguments hold only because truth is both many-sided and share-able by all, if not by all shared; only because different people reason differently, but yet all can hope to agree on the validity of reasons adduced.

The second head we can best consider negatively: that is, we consider the conditions under which the Areopagite ideal is clearly

[1] J. S. Mill, *On Liberty*, Ch. II, p. 82 (Everyman edition).

impracticable. Even Mill concedes that "opinions lose their immunity when the circumstances in which they are expressed are such as to constitute their expression a positive instigation to some mischievous act. An opinion that corn-dealers are starvers of the poor, or that private property is robbery, ought to be unmolested when simply circulated through the Press, but may justly incur punishment when delivered orally to an excited mob assembled before the house of a corn-dealer".[1] We may call this incitement. Ideal Areopagites cannot be incited. Their opinions are the same at all times and in all circumstances—they cannot be carried away by mass hysteria, or bamboozled by demagogy. They may be wrong, but they are never unreasonable, and therefore no special precautions have to be taken to prevent their being swept away in unpropitious circumstances by their emotions.

Areopagites need no laws against obscenity for the same reason as they need none against incitement: they are no more susceptible to salacious pornography than they are to mob oratory: and for people who can err but cannot be corrupted, no protection against themselves is needed or can be devised.

Areopagites need no law of libel because other methods are effective in securing justice to defamed individuals. With Areopagites as with ordinary men defamation can occur—Areopagites can make mistakes about one another, just as much as we can. And because Areopagites are limited, like other men, an unwarranted aspersion could easily go a long way without anyone giving the lie to it, unless Areopagites had some means of enabling a defamed man to attract attention to the truth. These means are provided by social rather than legal institutions. A wronged Areopagite can write a letter to *The Times*, and vindicate himself before the court of public opinion. The sanction of public opinion is for many people, not only Areopagites, as effective as those imposed by law: the procedure will be as effective, only if there are not too many cases, so that everybody can attend with care to those that do arise; and only if editors and correspondents are as responsible and as competent as judges and barristers. These conditions granted, trial by public, learned opinion can be quite as fair and effective as trial by judge and jury. But where the public is too much occupied by other cares to follow a case in detail, and in as much as many people are not competent to disentangle all the issues involved, the non-Areopagite practice of deputing judgement to a small panel

[1] J. S. Mill, *On Liberty*, Ch. III, p. 114 (Everyman edition).

who can go into the question fully, has much to recommend it. Even in the quasi-Areopagite society of the academic world, it is often found advisable to depute the assessment of personal worth to selection committees or electoral boards.

In one final respect, even Areopagite society departs from the ideal of free speech: for although every Areopagite can say what he likes, he cannot be sure of being listened to. One can write what one likes, but may not be able to get it published, and even if published, it still may not be read. Areopagites cannot, because they are limited, give full attention to everybody: they have to select to whom they will devote time, and since some people are less worth listening to than others, there will be a tendency not to listen to them. Worse than this, since there are so many people and there is so little time, there will not be time to listen to each person even enough to discover whether he is worth listening to more. We have to dismiss most arguments unheard, pass over most books unread. Learned journals have *referees*, in order to save their readers wasting their time reading bad stuff. Because of the finiteness of Areopagite listeners and because of the fallibility of Areopagite speakers, Areopagite society has to be constructed so as to eliminate "noise" and amplify only those signals that are significant. This is possible in principle because men are rational, and prefer rational to irrational thoughts, and tend to note and retell the one and to ignore and forget the other. But if the rationality of men is to result in rational thoughts being amplified and irrational ones being damped down, it is necessary that our paths of communication should be coupled in certain systematic ways. If there is to be effective discussion, the debate must be disciplined. Nor are all opinions, e.g. those of the flat-earthist, equally good or equally entitled to respect. Therefore Areopagite society is not just a collection of rational agents, all equally rational, all talking at once: it is, if it is to be effective, highly structured, composed of many interlocking sub-societies, and with some individuals in a much more prominent position than others. The Republic of Letters is an aristocracy; not a monolithic monarchy, nor a disorderly democracy.

SECTION 71
MORALITY AND POLITICS

THE relationship between moral and political arguments is complex. Political considerations are complicated enough by themselves, and moral ones even more so. Many of the controversies over the bearing of moral considerations on politics stem from doubts about the nature of morality itself. These belong properly to moral philosophy, and cannot be adequately discussed here. I shall be dogmatic, in order to be brief.

Cynics claim that there is no relationship at all between morality on the one hand and politics and law on the other. Tough-minded lawyers like to think of law as completely independent of, and unconcerned with, morality. Law is something firm, external, definite, and decidable, and not at all concerned with questions of high-flown morality and philosophy, which are suitable subjects for sensitive souls or withdrawn academics, but which are of no interest to the man of affairs or the student of the law. Law, they say, is not concerned with what is just or equitable or good; it is not concerned with values, or rationality, or what should be the case or what ought to be the case, but only with what will be the case, what the courts will decide, what will be the respective results of undertaking this, or some alternative, proposed course of action. Law is what the bad man gets told about by his solicitor.

In the same vein politicians sometimes seek to exclude moral issues from politics. They claim to be pragmatists—concerned with what is practicable, what is prudent, what is expedient, what is feasible. These, rather than any moral principles, are the terms in which political argument ought to be carried on. The aim is achievement, not aspiration after unrealistic ideals. Politics is the art of the possible—what one can get away with; and its sole criterion success.

The arguments, such as they are, are invalid. Apart from those of moral scepticism, they are mostly a misappreciation of a perfectly valid logical distinction between the meaning of the words 'moral' on the one hand and 'legal' and 'political' on the other. Whatever the relations between morality and politics, the words do not mean the same.[1] It does not follow, as a matter of deductive logic, from an action's being morally good that it is politically good, nor does its being legally obligatory entail its being morally obligatory. It is always intelligible to say of a proposed course of action that it is legal—i.e. lawful according to the legal system in force—but morally wrong: or that it is impolitic, though morally right. This distinction keeps available for us the linguistic tools for the *moral* criticism of

---

[1] See also below § 73, pp. 323–4.

legal and political action.[1] From the fact that a particular course of action is enjoined by law, it does not follow that it is morally right, and it is important that it should be open to us to say *both* that it is legal *and* that it is morally wrong nonetheless. Similarly in politics we want to be free to assess political actions or progammes in moral, as well as purely political, terms. But from the fact that moral considerations are not necessarily the same as legal or political ones, it does not follow that they are necessarily different, and are not relevant at all. It is quite clear, as a matter of history, that moral beliefs have affected, and been affected by, legal and political doctrines, and also that the connexion has been thought to be a rational, and not a bare causal one. On many issues moral and legal or political considerations interact. We have a *prima facie* moral obligation to obey the law of the land; and *per contra*, the law will not remain effective,[2] if it loses altogether the moral respect of the people. In interpreting the law in unclear cases, the judges may be guided by considerations of Natural Law, Equity, and Justice,[3] and some laws may specifically require the judges to be so guided in deciding their application in certain respects.[4] Because of its omnicompetence,[5] the law may on occasion have to pronounce on questions of morality, as it may on any other question. The laws of libel and slander will on occasion have to consider whether a plaintiff has been defamed in regard to his moral character. Often the law may be interested in the moral character of witnesses, or in certain circumstances even of the accused, to determine how far their evidence is to be relied upon. The oaths which witnesses, jurors, and judges swear would be pointless if moral obligations meant nothing. Questions of honest intent, good faith and moral sincerity arise time and again in the course of the law of contract, of sale, of negligence, and in nearly every other branch of the law. And finally the law may be concerned to promote, to protect, or to enforce public morality, by various means and methods[6]

[1] See H. L. A. Hart, 'Positivism and the Separation of Law and Morals', *Harvard Law Review*, Vol. 71, 1958, pp. 597–9, 620–1; reprinted in Frederick A. Olafson, *Society, Law and Morality*, Prentice-Hall, 1961, pp. 442–3, 462.

[2] § 11; § 18, pp. 75–77; and § 31, p. 141.

[3] § 51, pp. 216–22.

[4] For example, The Austrian Code of 1811, quoted by P. Vinogradoff, *Common Sense in Law*, 2nd ed., O.U.P., 1946, p. 172. The Rent Act 1965 (12 & 13 Eliz. 2, c. 75) makes repeated reference to *fair* rents (e.g. in Schedule 3, paras. 10–12), and lays upon Rent Officers and Rent Assessment Committees the duty of determining fair rents.

[5] § 17, pp. 68–72.   [6] See below, § 75.

Tough-minded lawyers take too limited a view of the law. What the solicitor tells the bad man is of interest to the bad man and to budding solicitors, who may be called upon one day to give similar advice to a similar client. But to us, who are neither solicitors nor altogether bad, this particular type of legal advice is not of absorbing nor of exclusive interest. Granted, the State, being an unselective community, contains bad men; and even bad men have rights; and we allow the law to be abused by subjects for the sake of Constitutional Freedom[1] and in order that it may not be abused by the authorities.[2] But the latitude given to bad men, and to all of us in our bad moments, is only feasible and, more, only intelligible, against the background assumption that we are not all of us altogether bad all the time. No community can exist unless there are some values held in common by its members— at least by almost all of them;[3] and it is only because human beings, although selfish, are not totally selfish, that human society in general is viable, and the institutions of Freedom, in particular, workable.[4] We can, and do, accommodate in our theory and practice of the State, that there are some utterly unscrupulous people, completely devoid of any sense of obligation, who are, so far as their emotions and wills go, outlaws, and will not accept decisions as binding unless they can be forced to comply with them. That was why we needed coercive machinery for the State. But outlaws are necessarily only a minority: else there would be no law. For law to exist, it is essential, as we have seen,[5] that it be accorded varying degrees of acquiescence, acceptance, consent, respect, and co-operation by various sections of the community. Some of these need quite explicitly to be moral. The law would wear a very different aspect if juries were composed of Twelve Bad Men and False. The very advice which the bad man and his legal admirers value, would be different if the solicitor were not acting entirely disinterestedly in accordance with his professional obligation to give the best advice he could. If the bad man went to a bad solicitor whose object in advising his clients was to obtain the maximum amount of advantage and remuneration for himself, the law would be represented in a different light.

The advice given to a bad man by a good solicitor is thus a useful conceptual tool for determining certain limits, but does not constitute

---

[1] See above, §§ 34, 35.   [2] See above, § 30, p. 137; § 31, p. 138, n1.
[3] See above, § 1, p. 1; § 8, p. 33.
[4] See above, § 21, esp. pp. 91–93; and § 22, esp. pp. 95, 99–102.
[5] § 18, pp. 75–77.

the whole of the law. The law is not an isolated phenomenon, something apart from the rest of society, which could be studied "autonomously" in isolation from all other social considerations, convenient though this might be for professional academics: the law is part of the fabric of the community, interwoven with multitudinous other strands of social intercourse. It cannot be taken out of its context, and considered as though it were something that existed on its own. To understand it, we have to view it in connexion with many other disciplines, and the complex interplay between legal and sociological, economic, political—and moral—considerations.

The cynics' claim that politics and law are totally divorced from morality is often a protest against the *simpliste* view that they are identical, and that, as many good men aver, there is no distinction between political and moral arguments. They mean it well. They believe that if a course of action is morally right then it is politically right, and if it is morally wrong then it is politically wrong, without any further argument. But all too often having espoused a political cause they make the converse inference that since some course of action is politically expedient therefore it is morally right, or that since some opposition is politically awkward therefore it is morally wrong. By assimilating the vocabulary of moral assessment to that of political argument they deprive themselves of the ability to make purely moral, as opposed to partly moral partly political, assessments, and therefore weaken rather than enhance the effectiveness of purely moral considerations, unalloyed by any considerations of expediency.

Nevertheless it may seem harsh to say that one could do other than have a moral duty to act morally even in politics. Yet this is so. For it is inherent in any political enterprise that it is a joint one. In politics we are not arguing about what I should do, but what we should do. And although we have many values in common, we do not all have all values in common. And therefore if we are to reach agreement on what is to be done on some occasion, it may be that the agreed course of action will be different from what one person would have done if he alone had had the say. It is incoherent to engage in political argument without conceding the possibility that one may not get things all one's own way. If two people argue each on the basis that it is for the other to agree with him, their argument is doomed to sterility from the outset. It is a prerequisite of reasonable argument generally, and not only of political argument, that each person would rather modify his position for the sake of truth than maintain it by means of turning a deaf ear to all argument for the sake of *amour propre*. Only if each recognises himself, and believes the other, to be subject to the common tribunal of reason, in the sense that each would rather reach the right solution than merely have his own way, is it worth arguing at all. But whereas academic arguments may fail to end in an agreed conclusion, and we may in the end have to agree to differ, the whole object of political argument is not to have to agree to differ, but to reach some workable agreement which shall be the basis of action, action we can co-operate in taking together. It is incoherent to seek, or even envisage, *co*-operation entirely on one's *own* terms. But one's conscience is entirely one's own. To insist that political action shall be judged purely in moral terms is to insist, thanks to the principle of autonomy, that it shall be judged entirely in accordance with one's own morality; with which other people may, in part, disagree. So, if the object of the argument is to reach agreement here and now on a plan of joint action, it cannot be always a purely moral argument. If we are talking politics, although we shall be concerned with moral issues, we shall not be concerned with them as moralists. It is inherent in the idea of political discussion that principles should be compromised, and that we should be willing to forsake the planning of the New Jerusalem in order that the earthly polities which actually do exist should not fall apart around us. Political discussion is not immoral, but does require a resolute acceptance of the second-best. Unlike moral argument, it is not concerned solely with the question 'what is the (morally) right course?' but chiefly with the very different question 'how can people who deeply disagree nevertheless live peaceably together?' and though moral issues are often, and quite properly, raised, the whole tone of the debate is suffused with the note of its being better to suffer sweet violence to one's own conscience than do rough violence to other men's bodies. We have therefore a moral duty *not* to insist on what we would consider, in the absence of other people's opposition, to be the morally right action. The word 'moral', as we shall shortly see, has many senses. Here we need to distinguish what I, after argument and deliberation, honestly believe to be the morally right course, from what, in view of the, often unreasonable, obstruction of other people, I finally decide to go along with. Both are moral decisions. The error lies in confusing them, and arguing that since I must make a final decision, and am morally responsible for whatever decision I make, therefore I should always stick to my own opinion, and that to act against one's better judgement is always morally wrong, and that the good man will never compromise his principles or allow his ultimate decision to be influenced by any "political" considerations of what other people are willing to agree to.[1]

Morality is not all of one piece. We need to distinguish, as here, different stages at which different considerations come into play,[2] and also different strands or styles of moral argument. Besides the highly personal, individualist mode in which each man autonomously affirms his own moral judgements for himself entirely on his own responsibility, we have, as we have seen,[3] corporate moralities. We may distinguish, thirdly, rational morality, the morality thought to be incumbent on all men in virtue of their being rational agents.

These moralities differ in emphasis and application rather than in kind. Personal morality stresses the autonomy of the agent: it is what I really and truly in my heart of hearts believe to be right. Corporate and rational moralities stress autonomy less than does personal morality, in order to emphasise other aspects more. Corporate morality emphasises the social side of moral behaviour; it plays down the first person singular, in order to concern itself more with the first person plural. Rational morality pays less attention to existential commitment and conviction and concentrates on the rationality and universality of moral beliefs.

Although they emphasise different aspects of morality, none of them denies the other aspects. Personal morality is not subjective nor does it abandon its claim to universal and objective validity. The whole point of the argument about fornication is that it is *not* a question of pre-marital intercourse being wrong *for me* but not *for you*; it is whether it is wrong *tout court*. Similarly with euthanasia, people may differ, but they cannot, logically, agree to differ. These moral views are thus not subjective. But they are autonomous. We always keep open the logical possibility of idiosyncratic personal moral views. Although we cannot agree to differ, we do reserve the right not to be convinced. It is always intelligible (though not always reasonable) to say at the end of an argument about personal morality, 'but I still think it is right' or 'I still think it is wrong'. Corporate and rational moralities although less autonomous, are not completely external. Hence the rub. A member of a group or community is under pressure not merely to conform to its corporate morality but to believe in it, and in so far as he does not

[1] See further, § 72, pp. 319ff.
[2] See also below, § 72, § 73, pp. 330–1.
[3] § 65, pp. 281–4.

accept it wholeheartedly, he is not at one with his fellows. A man ought, *qua* rational agent, to endorse rational morality, and if he does not, we think him unreasonable, and will argue with him in an effort to show him the error of his ways. We can *understand* what he is saying if he says that is it morally right to murder, to steal, to lie, or to cheat; but we have no hesitation in dismissing his views as wrong, and as ones he ought not to be holding, without more ado. What he says is intelligible, but not reasonable. We understand the views that Nietzsche held; but do not think them tenable for that. In one sense, we do *not* think Nietzsche was free to hold the views that he did—he was not rationally free to hold his views, because they were not rational views; and we want him not only to see the rationality of rational morality, but to make it his own, and be autonomously a rational moral agent.

Rational morality combines with the corporate morality of a State to form its public morality. The public morality of a State consists partly of those central tenets of morality which no reasonable man, we think, can reasonably dissent from; and partly of those collective aspirations and ideals which the community, either implicitly in the course of its history, or explicitly by deliberate avowal, has collectively adopted or affirmed. It is contrary to public morality to murder, to steal, to lie, to cheat. Cruelty to animals is also contrary to public morality in England. It cannot be maintained that this prohibition either is essential to the maintenance of communal existence or is universally observed in all countries. Nevertheless we affirm it here. Although men could associate together in the British Isles without having the avoidance of cruelty to animals as one of their shared values, in fact we do have this as one of our values, not perhaps a central one but nevertheless one we cherish. Nor is there any reason why we should not. We associate together not merely for the maintenance of law and order but, at least in part, for the good life. We want to realise collective aspirations together: and even though we could manage without some one of them, this in itself is no reason why we should.

These different forms of morality interact with law in different ways. A man may find some part of the law incompatible with his personal morality, and be faced with a personal problem of whether and to what extent he ought to obey or co-operate with the law. Similarly the law may be incompatible with the corporate morality of some association or group—the Mormons in nineteenth-century America, the Doukhobors in Canada, the communists in many contemporary States. On the other hand, it is logically incoherent for a State or an association

to attempt to enforce a purely personal morality, which must be autonomous if it is to be anything.

The relationship between the law and public morality is much more
complex. The law in part embodies public morality, in part is guided by
it. It may seek to promote or encourage public morality, and may
enforce certain standards of behaviour on grounds of public morality
alone. In the other direction, the law may be at variance with public
morality, and may, in extreme cases, raise problems not only of
personal morality but of constitutional principle, whether we ought to
observe our moral obligations or whether we should fulfil our obligation, also grounded in public morality, to obey the law of the land.

SECTION 72

FREEDOM AND DISSENT

A MAN may be under a legal duty to do what his personal morality
forbids, or may be legally prohibited from doing what his morality
enjoins. The problem is primarily one of moral philosophy, but there
is a political problem too, that of preventing the moral problem from
actually arising. The moral problem is not simply an issue of morality
versus expediency, but of one moral obligation against another. It is
not, as simple-minded moralists make out,[1] that we ought simply to do
what our morality requires and incur whatever penalties the law lays
down; that although men may not in practice be brave enough or
strong enough to do what they ought to do and face the consequences,
yet in principle the path of duty is quite clear. Rather, there is a conflict
of duty itself, and the bare fact that we are under a legal duty or a legal
prohibition creates some moral obligation on us to do, or abstain from
doing, as the law directs.

Even with personal morality there is some obligation to submit one's
judgement to the ruling of the law. For even an autonomous agent is
not autarkic. Men are not simply isolated individuals, each pursuing
moral self-fulfilment, authentically and autonomously, but acting
independently of other people. At the very least, men live among other
men. If a man is to treat other men as ends-in-themselves, and not
merely as means to his own moral self-fulfilment, a man must recognise them as independent agents by being prepared on occasion to do

[1] See above, § 71, pp. 315–17.

what they want and what they deem best, and not be entirely a moral law unto himself. I do not really recognise you as another initiator of action unless I sometimes say 'Not as I will, but as thou wilt'. Loyalty and friendship, at least among finite, fallible, imperfect beings, are necessarily heteronomous virtues. If I am to be human, I cannot be completely captain of my soul, but must submit myself in part to the judgement of others.

The existentialist position of extreme autonomy is absurd. It is moral solipsism, and, like all forms of solipsism, incoherent. It cannot be intelligibly maintained that I ought always to do that which is right in my own eyes, because it is part of the meaning of the word 'right' that it is intersubjective and independent of the will. Autonomy in this sense (not in the different sense that I am always answerable for the actions I undertake) cannot be absolute. Although I alone must make the final decision and am finally responsible for what I do, I must be prepared sometimes to act against my better judgement, or else I shall be laying claim to an infallibility that no mortal can possess or should pretend to. Therefore it is in principle possible for there to be a moral obligation to act against what, other considerations apart, one would take to be one's moral duty. In the case of political and social obliga-tions, the argument goes further. For man not only lives among other men, but acts with them. And as we have seen,[1] if a man is to find fulfilment in acting together with other men, he cannot hope always to achieve it autonomously. There is necessarily the possibility of acting heteronomously in acting socially; and therefore in being a member of any group or community, a man is renouncing the absolute right of private judgement. To be a member of a community is to be not always on one's own: and although on any particular issue a man may find himself impelled, after due discussion with others and careful con-sideration by himself, to be out on a limb, this cannot be rightly a normal position for any one.

A man *may* be under a moral obligation to subordinate his own moral scruples to the requirements of the law: not necessarily, not always; but may be. Often, especially in a free society, it is possible to resolve the conflict of obligation without having to override either, for the law often provides opportunities for alternative courses of action involving other legal obligations than those that run counter to morality as he understands it. A barrister who believes capital punishment is wrong does not have to accept briefs for the prosecution

[1] § 12, pp. 48–49; § 13, pp. 52–53; §63, pp. 273–4; § 67, pp. 281–3.

in murder cases, nor need a Roman Catholic become a judge in the divorce courts, where he will have to grant decrees of divorce. This is not to say that he should not, but only shows how if he comes to the conclusion that, all the arguments to the contrary notwithstanding,[1] he ought not to play any part in any legal proceedings for judicial execution or dissolution of marriage, then he can follow his conscience without breaking the law: and, *per contra*, if he decides not to opt out of some office which may impose unpalatable obligations, then he must carry out the obligations of his office, his own conscientious objections notwithstanding. It is possible to arrange that most of the more exacting obligations attach to offices which are avoidable rather than to bare membership of a non-selective community, which is not. Apart from military service and the payment of taxes, the laws impose mostly negative obligations which leave many reasonable alternatives open to a man with scruples of conscience. Only extremely uncompromising moralists—Jehovah's Witnesses, Nietzscheans or communists—are likely to be locked in unavoidable conflict with the law. Otherwise, a man with a tender conscience can preserve it from bruising, if he will tread delicately, and accept the concomitant inconveniences and loss of opportunities.

Freedom of conscience is secured at the price of non-participation. The morally onerous, but morally rewarding, obligations attach to offices one can opt out of, rather than to membership of the community by itself, and therefore there can easily be a division into activists and passivists, the leaders, the moral Mamelukes[2] who are involved and play a full part in the life of the community, and the led, for whom Political Liberty is an unrealised option, and for whom the State takes on an external and negative aspect. This is regrettable but inevitable. Perfect democracy must be totalitarian democracy, because if everyone is to participate fully in the political process, everyone must be of one mind, and nobody may dissent from the prevailing opinion. If people are to be free to be out of sympathy with public opinion, they must be able to opt out of the higher levels of involvement, and settle for a low minimum of external conformity. And if any can, then many will, apathy and indifference being common human characteristics. A large majority may be acquiescent rather than active, with the government of the country being run by an aristocracy–"the Establishment" or "the Party"—, an *élite*, a selected minority of activists, who enthusiastically endorse the established *ethos* of the State, largely self-

[1] See above, § 22, pp. 99–102.   [2] See above, § 18, pp. 75–76.

selected by virtue of their voluntary and active avowal of the shared values of the community. Freedom, here as often, is two-faced. Political Freedom argues for democracy; moral and religious Freedom for the possibility of aristocracy, in which it is open to dissenters to opt out of the obligations of office.

The problem can be eased but not resolved. A free society cannot function unless men—many men—will volunteer for public office; for only thus can coercion be controlled. But those who do volunteer will encounter the same conflicts of conscience that non-participation enables others to avoid. Involvement does not betoken less sensitivity than withdrawal. Often there will be a conflict between what a man seriously and sincerely believes to be right and what he must, in his official capacity, perhaps as the result of the ignorance or imperceptiveness of others, set himself to do. It is a personal moral problem. We cannot say where the balance of obligation will lie, in advance of actual cases. All we can do is first to provide an honourable entry for argument—one can, and sometimes must, be under a moral obligation to subordinate one's personal moral scruples to the public obligations of one's office—, and secondly, in case the burden becomes too heavy for conscience to bear, to secure an honourable exit.

But equally for the dissenter, who spiritually secedes from the rough-and-tumble of public life in order to preserve his soul untarnished by the world, the solution is not altogether satisfactory. Not only does he cut himself off from political activity, but he feels out of sympathy with some collective aspirations of his age and society. The conscientious bear-baiter and the enthusiastic bull-fighter would feel out of tune with the values of contemporary England. The Anglican in Afganistan, the Roman Catholic in America, the Protestant in Italy, all feel out on a limb. They are not persecuted: but they are not altogether at one with the values accepted by their countries. This gives them just cause for repine, but not for complaint. For it is incoherent to be a member of a community and to demand that all its actions and aspirations should be just those that one would choose oneself. Neither dissenter nor supporter of the Establishment can expect to be entirely at home in any earthly city. Some degree of alienation is the price we have to pay for being individuals who yet seek their identity in being members of a community or group.

SECTION 73

THE RIGHT OF REBELLION AND THE DUTY OF DISOBEDIENCE

THE law of the land may come into conflict with rational or public morality, as well as with personal morality. There is then not only a personal problem, but a political one as well. There is, as in the case of the conflict with personal morality, the final decision to be taken by each man separately, of how he shall act; and in view of the likely consequences of disobedience, it may be an extremely hard decision to take. But with laws which run counter to public morality, there is an additional question that does not arise with those that are in conflict only with one's personal morality. For if a law is contrary to one's personal morality, there is no doubt that there is still some *prima facie* obligation to obey it. Hence the moral problem: we are torn between conflicting moral obligations, and whichever way we decide, some *prima facie* obligation is going to be overridden. But if a law is contrary to public morality, there is some doubt whether it is really a law at all, and hence whether there is any *prima facie* obligation to obey it. There may still be compelling other reasons for obedience— fear of sanctions—, but there may be no obligation to obey. Normally, if I break the law, I have acted wrongly (morally wrongly), even if I am not found out and do not suffer for it: but the Resistance fighters who contravened nazi ordinances were not law-breakers, but, on the contrary, heroes.

The issues are clouded by a terminological wrangle. People ask whether wicked laws really are laws at all, and are told by upholders of Natural Law that bad laws, if sufficiently bad, are not laws, and are void and totally invalid. Against this, Legal Positivists from Austin onwards have protested that the assessment of a law's moral virtue and of its legal validity are two totally different things, not to be confused with each other. The existence of law is one thing, says Austin; its merit or demerit is another.[1] We have seen[2] that as a logical doctrine about the meanings of words, the Positivists' protests are incontestable. It is one thing to say of a law that it is a bad law, and quite another

---

[1] J. Austin, *The Province of Jurisprudence Determined*, p. 184 (Library of Ideas, ed. 1954).

[2] § 71, pp. 312–13.

22—P.P.

thing to say of a putative law that it is invalid and no law at all. But, equally clearly, to point out this difference of meaning is not to show that there can be no connexion. It is at least intelligible to say that a putative law is invalid *because* very bad. It cannot follow simply from these being different concepts that there can never be an argument linking them. What makes it appear so, is a further belief that the criteria of validity for laws must always be formal criteria. And for this belief there is some justification, in that laws along with the rest of the decision procedure would fail in their function of settling disputes unless everybody could be sure what was the decision procedure and what was the law, even though they did not all agree with the actual decisions yielded by the decision procedure and the actual content of the laws.[1]

There is thus some reason for adopting a formal definition of the decision procedure, and therefore of the laws, because we can agree on formal criteria whereas we can never hope all to be agreed on all matters of substance. We know who the Queen is. We know who are members of the House of Lords and the House of Commons. We can count votes, and be certain whether a Bill has been passed by a majority vote three times in each House, and whether the Queen has said '*La reine le veult.*' If these conditions are fulfilled, the Bill is an Act of Parliament and has the force of law, and there can be no disputing it. There is thus a natural tendency to make the criteria of validity—the Rule of Recognition as some legal philosophers put it[2]— purely formal, and to disallow any question of the merits or demerits of a law from entering into questions of its validity, and to deny that outrageous wickedness should be capable of impugning the validity of a law.

Nevertheless the pure doctrine of legal formalism is wrong for the same reason that the first thesis of Unlimited Sovereignty is wrong.[3] Formal criteria are not the only ones we can agree on, although they are the easiest to handle. We agree not only about the number of people present at a given time, their personal identities, and the way they vote, but also about questions of value; and we should not be able to live together at all unless we did. It is against this general background of agreement that our decision procedures are to be understood. We may use only formal criteria to define a decision procedure, because

---

[1] § 4, pp. 13–14.
[2] H. L. A. Hart, *The Concept of Law*, Ch. VI, § 1, pp. 92–93.
[3] See above, § 8, esp. pp. 33–34; § 9, pp. 36–37.

formal criteria are most apt for the purpose: but we adopt, and continue to accept, the decision procedure that we do, because it yields results which are, by and large, in accordance with our common, agreed values. The definition is a formal one, true: but what is defined is of useful application because of its substantial virtues in practice, not simply because it has been defined; and if it did not possess these substantial virtues, we should never have bothered to define it. Formalism fails because it extrapolates too rigidly from normal to abnormal conditions. In normal conditions, formalism may give an adequate account of the law, and one which enables us to distinguish legal from moral and other non-legal considerations. But in extreme circumstances, and in particular when the moral assumptions which form part of the shared values of a community are outrageously flouted, the tacit conditions which are taken for granted by our normal criteria for legal validity, are called in question, and may have to be made explicit.

Even Legal Positivists concede that whatever its formal merits, a legal system is not valid unless it is effective.[1] The legitimate heir of the Romanovs may issue a *ukase*, and it may satisfy all the formal criteria for validity in the Tsarist legal system: but it will be of none effect, and therefore not valid. Effectiveness is a necessary pre-condition for formal validity: but effectiveness is neither a formal nor a tidy notion. We can recognise central cases and say, when presented with standard examples of legal systems, whether they are effective or not. But we cannot neatly distinguish all hypothetical cases into the two categories 'effective' and 'ineffective'. We cannot say what would happen were Parliament to prohibit marriage or the Supreme Court to rule Queen Elizabeth II perpetual President of the United States. Since these are unreal possibilities we do not need to anticipate them and either agree that such decisions would be valid law or write into the criteria of validity the additional, non-formal, stipulation that decisions to these effects shall not be valid. Nor need we anticipate other, less absurd, cases. It is enough that our decision procedure can settle disputes that actually arise.[2] But in so far as we do not anticipate hypothetical cases, our criteria of validity are not being fully formulated. Criteria of validity tell us under what conditions a law, or decision, *would, if* it satisfied them, be valid. And therefore we do not know fully what the criteria of validity are, because we cannot say which way many hypothetical cases would be settled. We can, with great confidence, extrapolate

[1] See above, § 11.   [2] § 8, pp. 31-32.

a little in the law: we can be sure what the legal effect of a will would be if the testator left his watch to his eldest son instead of to a godson, and we can be sure what would be the legal effect of an Act of Parliament lowering the age at which people can marry from sixteen to fifteen. But we cannot with equal confidence extrapolate to abnormal cases, for then the question of whether a particular law is valid is not purely and simply a factual question. It is necessary first to *extract* and formulate the rule, and "enter into the spirit of the constitution" rather than merely apply some formal test. Often there will be a divergence of views on how the rule is to be formulated, and often formulations will be, partly, in terms of Equity, Justice, or Natural Law. Nor does a divergence of views about the Rule of Recognition matter, so long as there are no actual cases where its application is in doubt—so long, that is, as there are no putative laws passed that are palpably inequitable, unjust or wicked. Although the jurisconsult will naturally yearn for a tidy Rule of Recognition giving formal criteria of validity, his yearning need not be gratified. Throughout most of its existence, English law has had no tightly formulated, universally accepted, formal criterion of validity.[1] It is only for the last two hundred years that the enactments of the King-in-Parliament have been accepted without qualification or reserve. Before that, as throughout mediaeval Europe, there was no single rule, and validity was assessed as much by reference to considerations of morality and Natural Justice as by any formal criterion. Rules of Recognition, in fact, have often not been rules.

Thus even effectiveness is not a purely factual matter. And effectiveness is not the only pre-condition of validity, unless we redefine validity so that is shall be. And even if we do, we shall not thereby secure that questions of validity are purely questions of fact and never matters of evaluative assessment. There is therefore nothing to be gained by extrapolating from normal to abnormal conditions, and attempting to formulate formal criteria of validity which shall hold irrespective of background conditions. If, nevertheless, we were to do this, we should be sacrificing the conceptual point made in the last section that there is at least a *prima facie* obligation to obey the law. There is not even a *prima facie* obligation to obey the laws of the Tsars, of pre-revolutionary France, or of ancient Rome. They are formal systems, worthy of study in jurisprudence, but totally lacking in

[1] See J. W. Gough, *Fundamental Law in English Constitutional History*, Oxford, 1955.

authority, as well as power, over us. If a legal philosopher wishes to, he may treat his subject formally, thus preserving it from the corrupting contact of other disciplines. But in treating law in isolation from other considerations, he is divorcing it from the realities which make law an important phenomenon in the eyes of the ordinary man. For the ordinary man, the law is something which he ought, at least in the absence of overriding arguments to the contrary, to obey, as well as something which will, by and large, be enforced on the recalcitrant. I shall therefore continue to use the terminology of Natural Law rather than that of the Legal Positivists, and allow the locution in which a putative law may be said to be invalid and no law at all, in spite of satisfying all formal criteria of validity.

Systems of law operating under abnormal conditions I call *pathological*. A legal system can be pathological in many different ways. It may be partly or completely ineffective. It may indulge so much in retrospective legislation, that subjects never know where they stand with the law, and cannot take steps to obey some ordinance that later may be deemed to have been in force. Or the laws may never be published, so that again subjects cannot, even if willing, take steps to act in accordance with the law. Or there may be no access to the courts, so that the legal system does not in fact provide a procedure for deciding disputes.[1] Or the adjudications of the courts may be arbitrary and absurd: as when men are "punished" for crimes they are not even alleged to have committed, or are held responsible for the actions of others over whom they have no control. Or the government may have usurped power by insurrection or *coup d'état*, or may be a foreign occupying power having successfully invaded the territory in question. Or the legally constituted authorities, although legitimate according to the constitutional law of the land, may set about enacting outrageously wicked and evil edicts, after the manner of the nazis.

In each of these pathological cases, formal criteria of validity, even if they exist, are insufficient to enable us to answer all the questions we naturally ask about a law. Formal criteria of validity, as we have seen, can be significant only if certain substantial conditions are, at least tacitly, presupposed. "Matters of State and Government . . . are to be interpreted according to the Tacite Conditions and foundations of Government, of which *The preservation of the community* is the

---

[1] See above, § 18, p. 76.

chiefest."[1] *Salus populi suprema lex esto*,[2] not in the modern tyrannical, Jacobin sense, but as giving part of the background against which it makes sense to have any formal criterion of legal validity. Effectiveness is one such condition, in the absence of which we are under no obligation to obey laws, however formally valid they may be within their ineffective system. Laws not enforced are not in force, true. Austin is right. But so also is Augustine: States without justice are but robber bands enlarged.[3] There are other conditions besides effectiveness, in the absence of which we are under no obligation to obey putative laws whatever their formal credentials to validity. If the Queen-in-Parliament, or any Hobbesian sovereign, were to enact that every subject was to take his own life, it would fail to be a valid law to the same extent, although for a different reason, as a duly promulgated *ukase* of the legitimate heir to the Tsars of Russia. Hart gives a full account[4] of the pathology of legal systems when the condition of effectiveness is not fully satisfied, but fails to allow that systems can be pathological by reason of other defects too. The nazi system was pathological, not because its penalties were not enforced, but because it was evil and insane. We may on occasion be obliged to obey in the sense that if we do not we shall be shot: but we are under no *moral* obligation to obey, as we are with the laws of a legitimate government, and in this important sense the "laws" of tyrants are not laws.

Under pathological systems the arguments[5] for political obligation fall apart. With a totally ineffective system I cannot be moved to obey by fear of sanctions if I did not, nor by any *quid pro quo* argument that I ought to give obedience in return for protection, nor by the argument of communal unity. I cannot be obliged to obey a usurping or occupying power because I promised to, nor because I can be said to want to really, nor because I was consulted, nor because it is the communal decision of my community. And with an entirely wicked government I can have none of these reasons for obeying their edicts, nor any reason based on Natural Law; no reason whatever, in fact, save fear of the penalties for disobedience. And this is not enough to make a law a law. Although it gives part of our sense of what it is to be obliged to obey the law, it gives only part. At least for the officials, the Mamelukes, and in fact not only for them, the obligation to obey the law

---

[1] A. Ascham. *A Discourse*, London, 1648, p. 66.
[2] Cicero, *De Legibus*, III, iii, 8.
[3] *City of God*, IV, iv, *remota justitia, quid sunt regna nisi magna latrocinia?*
[4] *Concept of Law*, pp. 114–20.   [5] § 12, pp. 43–45.

must be construed as an internal, partly rational, ground for obedience, not a purely external, opaque, fear of sanctions for disobedience. And therefore, to be a law, a rule cannot be obeyed by everyone for fear alone. Some people may never obey the law for any other motive than fear of sanctions: everyone may on occasion obey partly from this motive. But a law characteristically makes a greater claim on our obedience than merely that secured by threats, and in order to remain effective a legal system must at least on some occasions win some respect on the part of some. Some people must sometimes feel there is some moral obligation to keep the law. This is both part of the meaning of the concept, and a necessary condition of effectiveness.

Under some pathological *régimes* there may still be some obligation to obey the law in some cases. One may have a duty to co-operate even with a usurping or occupying power for the suppression of gross crimes. A man in occupied Europe would still be under a duty not to murder, and would be right to reveal the whereabouts of a murderer to the Germans, even though he would not be under an obligation to desist from listening to the B.B.C., or to co-operate with the Germans in their war economy drives. A citizen of France under Louis Napoleon or of South Africa after the elimination of the entrenched clauses from the Constitution would likewise be faced with a *de facto* government with no, or only a dubious, *de jure* title. The formally valid enactments of the Third Empire or the Union of South Africa, lose, for at least some time after the unconstitutional action, at least some of the claim to obedience possessed by the laws of Great Britain and the United States. What measure of resistance is justified and called for, is difficult to determine. Not all laws are equally infected. A man would not be justified in breaking a new traffic act of the South African government, although he might in failing to comply with some racial requirement. Chiefly, however, an unconstitutional government forfeits the "benefit of the doubt" to which constitutional governments are entitled. A constitutional government may often reach decisions some of its subjects disagree with, often pass laws they think are wrong, sometimes even wicked. But it is entitled to a presumption of having acted in good faith, just because it does observe the letter and the spirit of the constitution. It thereby shows willing. Even if it is wrong on a particular issue it is as it were by mistake, not by evil intent. There is therefore a strong obligation on the subject to bear with it, even in its errors, rather than set himself up as a judge above the law. Not so with an unconstitutional government. It has to prove its good faith in each of its ordinances, rather than have it taken for granted. Until it has earned a patent of respectability by good behaviour over a period of years, its title to obedience is open to question in each particular case, and although the subject does not have a complete licence to disobey an established unconstitutional government, the onus of argument is shifted.

Unconstitutional *régimes*, which are *de facto* only and not *de jure* governments, although pathological, are likely to be cured by the passage of time. Almost every *régime* finds its origin in unconstitutional action. William I was a conqueror and William III a usurper according to the letter of the law, and the Founding Fathers were rebel colonists before they bound themselves by the Constitution. So, too, ineffectiveness either is cured or else kills. But other pathological *régimes* can continue for long periods without amendment or supersession. Although the pressures towards good behaviour on the part of the government are great,[1] they are resistable. The nazis were perhaps optimistic in thinking their New Order would last a thousand years, but it might well have survived and continued in its odious ways for several generations if the Allies had not liberated Europe by force of arms. The subject of such a tyranny is under no obligation to obey its wicked and iniquitous "laws". If he can contravene them with impunity, he is morally free to do so. Sometimes he may have a moral duty to, sometimes even at the price of incurring all the penalities they may choose to inflict.

Many writers have argued for the right of rebellion, but have failed to distinguish the case where a particular law conflicts with a person's private morality from that where a whole system of laws runs counter to public morality. The former poses agonizing personal problems, but so far as politics is concerned, the individual's view must ultimately give way to that of the State: the latter case is, fortunately, rare, but where it does arise, it raises fundamental questions in political philosophy of the government's right to govern. If we fail to draw the distinction, the right of rebellion becomes a crude and untenable doctrine of Private Judgement. If we do draw the distinction we see that there are two stages at which the normal argument for political obligation may fail. It may fail at the end, when a private individual, having acknowledged that the law in question is a valid law, and that he has a *prima facie* obligation to obey it, goes on to enter a final 'but',

---

[1] See above, § 18, pp. 75–78.

and says 'but that does not conclude the matter;[1] there are still moral arguments on the other side, and these overweigh the argument for obeying the law'. But the argument may also fail at the beginning. It may never get off the ground, because it is denied that this is the law,[2] or that anyone has any obligation at all to obey it. We have shown that the latter is a possible argument, but only under abnormal conditions where the system is pathological. Normally we have no right of rebellion. Therefore the doctrine is tenable. But under extreme conditions we may. And this is enough to make the doctrine important.

The right of rebellion is a moral right. It is taken for granted that it could not be a legal right, or we should be legalising anarchy. In large part this is so, but it is one of the unrecognised advantages of Constitutional Monarchy, that it does institutionalise the right of rebellion in legal form. The Queen may—legally may—refuse her assent to a wicked or unconstitutional law: and if she does, every subject may— legally may—refuse his assent too. The *veto* of the Crown differs from that of the House of Lords. The House of Lords can, and sometimes does, throw out a Bill. Its *veto* is meant to be used, although not too often and not too obstinately, to make the House of Commons have second thoughts. The *veto* of the Crown is meant not to be used. The Royal Assent always could, but never should, be withheld. It represents not the second thoughts which we need to provide for in view of the dialectical nature of political reasoning,[3] but the final legislative 'but'. Only if a Bill is vitiated by utter unconstitutionality or wickedness should a Constitutional Monarch interpose to prevent its achieving formal legal validity. Provided a Bill is at all within the bounds of reason and morality, the Queen should approve it, even though it is far from what she thinks is best, wise, prudent, expedient or right. If she approves a Bill, it will have the force of law, and we shall have a legal, and well-founded *prima facie* moral, obligation also to approve, to the extent of obeying it. But if she were to refuse her assent, it would not have the force of law, and we should be under no obligation to obey it. If she had refused her assent wrongly, she would

---

[1] Compare H. L. A. Hart, 'Positivism and the Separation of Law and Morals', *Harvard Law Review*, Vol. 71, 1958, p. 618; reprinted in Frederick A. Olafson, *Society, Law and Morality*, Prentice-Hall, 1961, p. 460.

[2] I am using the terminology of Natural Law: a Legal Positivist would say that although it was a valid law of a certain system, the system was one such that, contrary to the usual rule, there was no *prima facie* obligation to obey any rule of that system.

[3] See above, § 53, p. 230.

very soon have to give in, and might well lose her throne. But if she were right, the government would have to go, and the unconstitutional or wicked law would never have been in force. There would have been a rebellion without the loss of a single life.

The final *veto*, like the ultimate deterrent, is never to be used, although always capable of being called upon. The Constitutional Monarch embodies the Reasonable Man. On all questions of Public Interest, many of Justice, many of other political goods, reasonable men may reasonably disagree: and to decide such questions we have recourse to the ordinary decision procedures of the State. Only in extreme circumstances, where every reasonable man would criticise and condemn a proposed measure as utterly unconstitutional, should a Constitutional Monarch convert a valid Constitutional Criticism into a legal Constitutional Limitation; only under a pathological *régime* should a Constitutional Monarch play an active *rôle* and re-interpret "the Tacite Conditions and foundations of Government". It was right in Rhodesia in 1965–6. It would have been right to refuse the Royal Assent in October 1964 to a Bill prolonging the life of the Parliament then assembled.[1] For any man in Rhodesia after the Unilateral Declaration of Independence was morally entitled to dis-obey the enactments of the illegal *régime*, as any man in Britain would have been, had Parliament not been dissolved in October 1964. We cannot allow any man the legal right of disobeying a formally valid law, nor can we arrange to consult all men together on questions of Constitutionality. The Constitutional Monarch is a particular person, who therefore can be consulted, but a representative particular person, who is the mouthpiece for all his subjects, and stands for them, in respect of their recourse to the ultimate remedy of rebellion. The modern Monarch is no longer sovereign; but in ceasing to be sover-eign, has become the supreme personification of the subject.

SECTION 74

NATURAL LAW

MANY of the problems concerning the relationship of law and public morality have traditionally been discussed under the heading of Natural Law. Unfortunately the term has been used in different, though

[1] See above, § 9, pp. 34–35.

connected, senses, not clearly distinguished from one another. In consequence all the doctrines and arguments put forward under the title of Natural Law have fallen into a disrepute not always deserved. I shall first distinguish three senses of the term, and criticise some of its tenets, in order then to restate those of its contentions that are valid.

Natural Law was sometimes equated with the *Jus Gentium*,[1] the common core of rules which all communities observe, and, it would seem, must observe if they are to survive. All communities forbid murder among their members, some bodily assaults, theft and treason. Even a gang of brigands cannot be, as Plato put it,[2] παμπόνηροι: they can only be ἡμιμόχθηροι if they are to live together at all. There must be some honour among thieves, some consideration for one another, some mutual forbearance, for "without such a content, laws and morals could not forward the minimum purpose of survival which men have in associating with each other".[3]

Natural Law was also sometimes contrasted with the *Jus Gentium* as well as with the Positive law of particular polities (the *Jus Civile*).[4] Here it seems to be "not a complete and ready-made system of rules, but a means of interpretation".[5] It is not a part of a system of law, co-ordinate with Positive law, but is, so to speak, *meta*-law, in terms of which we may assess, criticize and understand actual legal systems. The student of Natural Law is not concerned simply with the municipal law of his own community, in the sense that a practising lawyer, solicitor, or attorney is. He is not concerned merely to draw up valid wills, or advise clients on their legal obligations under some given contract. Rather, he is concerned to understand the phenomenon of law, of wills and contracts, courts and cases, generally; and in the light of his general understanding of law, to assess the value of particular legal rules or legal institutions. It is legal[6] philosophy, partly descriptive in the contemporary fashion—the modern discipline of jurisprudence; partly prescriptive—the principle of Constitutional Criticism as I have called it.[7]

In its third sense Natural Law is almost identified with rational

---

[1] e.g. by Gaius, see Justinian's *Digest* I, i, 9.
[2] *Republic*, I, 352c. So too Augustine, *City of God*, IV, iv.
[3] H. L. A. Hart, *The Concept of Law*, p. 189.
[4] By Ulpian, see *Digest*, I, i, 1; and Paulus, see *Digest*, I, i, 11.
[5] A. P. d'Entrèves: *Natural Law*, London, 1951, pp. 29–30.
[6] In a wide sense of the word 'legal' equivalent to that of the word 'political' in this book. See p. 20, n 1, or p. 336.
[7] § 9.

morality, but with the added claim that it has the full force of law without further formality. It is of this that Cicero writes[1] that it is a sin to try to alter it, "nor is it allowable to attempt to repeal any part of it, and it is impossible to abolish it entirely. We cannot be freed from its obligations by Senate or People, and we need not look outside ourselves for an expounder or interpreter of it."

Cicero's words, although eloquent, are equivocal. They could be taken as simply charting the logical geography of rational morality, and calling it a sort of law—much as we today talk of the Moral law: the Moral law differs from ordinary law—Positive law—in that the concept of legislation does not apply to the Moral law,[2] neither, correspondingly, is there any need for it to be promulgated and published. Moreover, in cases where the Moral law comes into conflict with the Positive law, there remains a moral obligation to obey the Moral law, all positive enactments to the contrary notwithstanding.

This interpretation, however, although acceptable on its own, as an account of rational morality, is not what Cicero meant. Natural Law for him is not mere morality; it is a form of law, a *para*-law, so to speak, different from Positive law, but comparable with it and overriding it. Legislators ought to legislate in accordance with Natural Law, at least in the negative sense of not enacting laws that are immoral and wicked. Not only can no positive enactment abrogate the Natural Law, but any putative positive enactment to the contrary is *eo ipso* void, and we are under no obligation to obey it, however well it may satisfy formal criteria of validity. Finally, we know what Natural Law is without its needing to be promulgated, and are obliged to obey it irrespective of whether it has been incorporated by enactment in Positive law or not.

The unifying thread in all these different accounts of Natural Law is a negative one. The word 'natural', like many other words, obtains its sense from what it is being contrasted with. Here the contrast is always with Positive law, the particular detailed legal system of a particular community, whether based on custom or self-consciously promulgated by a legislative authority. Positive law, depending on the arbitrary *fiats* of individual men or communities, is variable and irrational: Natural Law is unchanging and intelligible and rationally

---

[1] *De Republica*, III, xxii, 33. *Huic legi nec obrogari fas est, neque derogari aliquid ex hac licet, neque tota abrogari potest, nec vero aut per senatum aut per populum solvi hac lege possumus, neque est quaerendus explanator aut interpres.*

[2] See further H. L. A. Hart, *The Concept of Law*, Ch. VIII, pp. 171–3.

justifiable, everything that Positive law is not. So Grotius,[1] "Those who have consecrated themselves to true justice should undertake to treat the parts of the natural unchangeable philosophy of law, after having removed all that has its origin in the will of men." But that is impossible. We cannot purge law of everything arbitrary, nor can we give any account of law, having removed all that has its origin in the will of men, because it is only in the context of the wills of men, imperfectly informed, incompletely unselfish and fallible men, that we need to have laws at all. Natural Law, negatively defined as law with all Positive law left out, is no law at all, but a vacuous nothing.

The mistake lies in erecting a perfectly proper protest into a rigid rule. It is right to protest against the first thesis of Unlimited Sovereignty.[2] Sovereigns neither should, nor can, issue arbitrary *fiats*: *quod placuit principi* does not have the force of law unless it satisfies many other conditions. Although the sovereign has the last word in one sense, yet the fact that the sovereign has spoken does not mean there must be an end to argument, and even the edicts of the sovereign may have their legal validity impugned, if the "Tacite Conditions of Government"[3] are not satisfied. But the advocates of Natural Law go much further than this. They elevate the arguments of Constitutional Criticism into definite laws of Constitutional Limitation,[4] and maintain not merely that law does not totally depend upon the arbitrary will of sovereigns, but that it does not depend at all on the wills of human beings. Indeed, on Cicero's account, we should not need any Positive law at all. There is a Stoic assumption of perfect information, which would make unnecessary arbitrary assignments by *fiat*.[5] But not in fact possessing perfect information, we need at least conventions to guide us in matters of indifference, and these must have their origin in the will of men.

Natural Law cannot be conceived of as the negation of Positive law. Nor can it be thought of, as by some mediaeval thinkers, as simply adjoined to Positive law. We cannot assign to Positive law the function of making conventions in matters that are in themselves indifferent— e.g. whether we should drive on the right-hand side of the road or the left—, and reserve for Natural Law the *rôle* of laying down the law in

[1] *De Iure Belli ac Pacis*, Prol., Section 31. *Quod si qui verae iustitiae sacerdotes naturalis et perpetuae iurisprudentiae partes tractandas susciperent, semotis iis quae ex voluntate libera ortum habent*, . . . quoted by A. P. d'Entrèves, *Natural Law*, London, 1951, p. 78.
[2] § 7, pp. 26–29; § 8, pp. 33–34.   [3] See above, § 73, p. 327.
[4] See above, § 9, pp. 34–37   [5] See above, § 2, pp. 6–7.

morally important matters. For Positive law, although partly conventional, is not wholly so. Whether we drive on the right-hand side of the road or the left may be a matter of indifference, but whether we give right of way to cars on the main road, as in Britain, or cars entering from the side, as on the Continent, is not a matter of indifference but one where there are arguments for and against each course. And this is typical of Positive law. It is not simply a matter of convention, but is also subject to rational criticism and appraisal, sometimes even to moral criticism and appraisal. Positive law does not simply conflict or fail to conflict with Natural Law, as it would if Natural Law was a co-ordinate type of law, comparable with Positive law, adjoined to it. Rather, Positive law is, typically, appraised by Natural Law as being better or worse, and only in extreme cases do we talk of incompatibility or conflict.

The reason for this is that men are not only imperfectly informed but fallible in their judgement. Contrary to what Cicero suggests, we do not always know of ourselves what rational morality requires of us. Our judgement is fallible, our light uncertain.[1] We ought always to know what Natural Law lays down, perhaps: but in fact we sometimes do not, even though we think we do. Nor have we any method of demonstrating beyond doubt the cogency of valid moral arguments or the invalidity of others.[2] Natural Law lacks the definiteness ascribed to it by Cicero. It is for this reason that we need to have Positive law in order to embody it in definite legal form, and furnish us with an effective decision procedure, which otherwise we should not have; and it is for this reason also that Natural Law and Positive law are not *pari passu*, and are not to be regarded as adjoined to each other, and do not normally either conflict or fail to conflict with each other.

Natural Law, therefore, is not to be thought of either as the negation of Positive law or as a complementary system of law adjoined to it. But this is not to say that we can make no sense of Natural Law. We can understand the three traditional doctrines[3] of Natural Law if we take them as principles of Constitutional Criticism, based on some of the moral values cherished by the community. They provide a set

---

[1] So Locke: "For though the laws of nature be plain and intelligible to all rational creatures, yet men, being biassed by their interest, as well as ignorant for want of study of it, are not apt to allow of it as a law binding to them in the application of it to their particular case." *Second Treatise on Civil Government*, Ch. IX, § 123.

[2] See above, § 6, pp. 20–23.

[3] See above, p. 333, ll. 6–15; p. 333, ll. 16–32; pp. 333–4.

of vague, but not vacuous, moral qualifications to the two theses of Unlimited Sovereignty and the elevation of Legality into an absolute principle. Not all things are possible to the supreme power—witness the fact that although different legal systems differ in many respects, they do not differ in all, and there is a common core of rules which all systems incorporate, and which none could disregard if it was to remain effective. Nor are all things lawful to the supreme authority. However supreme the supreme authority is, it is not above criticism. Its enactments may be valid Positive law, but still we can question their virtue, and not from the private standpoint of a personal morality only, but from that of public morality built into the very system from which the supreme authority obtains its credentials. Nor does Legality exhaust all the content of the Rule of Law, nor is it our sole criterion. And, contrary to the teaching of Bentham, Austin, and Hart,[1] the fact that a rule violated standards of morality could, in extreme circumstances, vitiate its validity as a legal rule, and conversely, the fact that a rule was morally desirable could be a reason for regarding it as a valid legal rule.

Natural Law arguments stem from the shared values of the community. We share values. If we did not, we should not be able to have any community with one another at all. Our shared values are vague, true; and therefore we need to establish a decision procedure so that we can settle those disputes we cannot resolve by argument or good nature alone. But our disagreements are few in comparison with our agreements, and although our agreement does not reach the very high standard of unanimity in all serious cases, which would enable us to dispense with having a decision procedure, yet it is sufficient on many matters of substance to form the background against which alone it makes sense to have a decision procedure.

It is thus that Natural Law offers an account of why we should obey the law and of what things may lawfully be ordained. The reason why we should obey the law is because what it lays down is something which we ought to do anyhow, something we have always agreed to in substance. The short answer the upholder of Natural Law gives to the question, 'Why should I obey this law?' is the second one listed in Section 12, 'Because you ought'. God according to Cicero,[2] is "the

---

[1] H. L. A. Hart, 'Positivism and the Separation of Law and Morals,' *Harvard Law Review*, Vol. 71, 1958, p. 599; reprinted in Frederick A. Olafson: *Society, Law and Morality*, Prentice-Hall, 1961, p. 444.

[2] *De Republica*, III, § xxii, ⟨*deus*⟩ *legis huius inventor, disceptator, lator; cui qui non parebit, ipse se fugiet, ac naturam hominis aspernatus hoc ipso luet maximas poenas, etiamsi cetera supplicia quae putantur effugerit.*

author of Natural Law, its promulgator, and its enforcing judge, and whoever is disobedient is fleeing from himself and denying his human nature, and by reason of this fact will suffer the worst penalties, even if he escapes what is commonly considered punishment." Our obligation to obey Natural Law depends on its content, not its form; on what is ordained, not by whom, nor by what procedure, it was enacted. Natural Law is independent of the decision procedure,[1] because it enshrines the shared values on which the very existence of the community depends. So, too, it guides and limits legislators in the laws they may enact. They ought to enact laws which express, and are conducive to the realisation of, moral values, and in any case must not enact laws which run counter to them.

Natural Law, on this interpretation, represents the principle of Constitutionalism in its moral aspect. It provides us with a ground for Constitutional Criticism, and affords us, correspondingly, with a reason for political obedience. Its fundamental importance for political theory lies in the fact that Natural Law arguments, like some Rule of Law arguments,[2] are independent of the decision procedure adopted; they concern not the form of the law, but its substance—a rare virtue. For we do often agree in matters of substance. Although we do not all agree all the time in all cases, there is a large measure of agreement between most of us most of the time about many things. And therefore often, though not always, we can agree about the rights and wrongs of a case independently of the verdict of the formal decision procedure that has been set up. And therefore we have available an independent standard of assessment of the decisions yielded by the decision procedure, and can criticise the decision procedure if it consistently yields the wrong decisions. The point about a decision procedure is not that it is the only method of settling disputes, but that it is the only method of being able *always* to settle disputes. This is reason enough for having a decision procedure: but is also reason why the decision procedure is not our sole standard, nor the Positive law our only guide to what is right and wrong. We do not need a formal decision of the procedure set up for resolving disputes to validate a value about which there is no dispute. We have a general exception to, or extension of, the two principles of Legality, *Nulla poena sine lege, Nullum crimen sine lege,*—

---

[1] See quotation on p. 334, n 1, *ad fin., neque est quaerendus explanator aut interpres.* "We need not look outside ourselves for an expounder or interpreter of it."

[2] See above, § 13, pp. 50–51; § 24, pp. 107–8.

exception if we take '*lex*' to mean Positive law, extension if we are hereby allowing Natural Law to count.

We need to tread warily. The counter-arguments for Legality, based on imperfection and Freedom, remain cogent. The argument from Natural Law does not invalidate the arguments for Legality; rather, it shows the need for them, that there is an argument which they are needed to override. If it were not for the Natural Law argument, it would be obvious that in the absence of a specific Positive law there could be no crime and should be no punishment. But if, as we have argued, the function of Positive law is often to demarcate, rather than always to constitute, what is lawful and what unlawful, then where it fails to demarcate properly, we can invoke general moral principles, which only have not been already made explicit because they have never before been brought in question. We can. Nevertheless there are arguments why we should not. We are dealing with imperfect men, who even in fairly clear cases, are capable of great self-deception about where their duty lies. We value Freedom, and therefore want to make law external, like the Positive law admittedly is, rather than internal, as Natural Law must seek to be. For these reasons we normally resist the argument from Natural Law. Normally. Normally we are dealing with mature legal systems that have embodied their values in an explicit set of statutes and precedents, which give unambiguous rulings on most questions. In such cases the arguments for Legality are applicable and conclusive. But, as we have seen,[1] they are not always applicable. Even in a mature legal system there are some unclear cases, where Legality gives no guidance, and in them Natural Law offers canons for Judicial Interpretation. Moreover, mature legal systems were not always mature, but have developed from primitive ones in which many values had not been embodied in explicit statutes and precedents. A primitive legal system often cannot be guided much by the canon of Legality. It is still in process of formulating its laws and often the only guidance available to the judges is that of the shared values of the community together with other vague legal "policies". It is only by Judicial Innovation[2] that a primitive legal system can develop into a mature one, and a mature one continue to develop.

The third, and most important, case where the arguments for Legality do not apply is when the legal system is pathological,[3] when some of the conditions normally obtaining, and presupposed by any

[1] §§ 31, 34, 35, 73.　　[2] § 47, p. 204; § 51, pp. 219–21.
[3] See above, § 73, p. 327, or below, p. 370.

legal system, do not in fact obtain; in an absolute monarchy, if the Monarch has gone off his head; in an age and area where no one legal system is completely effective, but different jurisdictions appear to be in force on different occasions; where a legal system is so wicked as to have forfeited all claim for obedience; or where those in authority have abused their position and conferred upon themselves a licence to commit the most heinous crimes with impunity. In such cases, where the Positive law is defective or in abeyance we may adduce Natural Law arguments that are not overridden by considerations of Legality. In the Nürnberg trials the fact that the accused had acted in accordance with the Positive law of the nazi State was no defence, because the nazi legal system was pathological; and, in particular, it had been manipulated by the accused to provide a legal cover for their misdeeds. If we accept the principle of Constitutionalism at all, and deny that *all things are lawful to the supreme authority*, then we are thereby denying the absolute sway of the principle of Legality: for the supreme authority is by definition able to invest all its doings with the cloak of Legality, and therefore if none the less not all things are lawful to it, Legality cannot be an absolute guarantee of lawfulness. Therefore, at least as regards the supreme authorities and their associates, we cannot accept without qualification the principle *Nullum crimen sine lege* in the narrow sense of '*lex*', or we shall be conferring on them an absolute unlimited sovereignty. Nor, by the same tokens, can we affirm *Nulla poena sine lege* unqualifiedly without thereby granting them immunity for any misdeeds they care to commit under pretence of law. We must either make exceptions to these principles, or, better, extend the meaning of the word '*lex*' to cover not only Positive law but Natural Law as well.

This course is preferable to that of allowing retrospective legislation,[1] because Natural Law is unlegislatable, whereas retrospective legislation, with whatever safeguards, is not. The principles behind Legality which we wish to preserve are first that men, being imperfectly moral,[2] should not be expected to be perfectly moral all the time, and secondly that men being imperfectly wise[3] cannot know where they stand or all that is required of them unless it is codified

---

[1] See above, § 53, pp. 228–9. See also H. L. A. Hart, 'Positivism and the Separation of Law and Morals', *Harvard Law Review*, Vol. 71, 1958, pp. 619–20; reprinted in Frederick A. Olafson, *Society, Law and Morality*, Prentice-Hall, 1961, pp. 460–2.

[2] i.e. imperfectly unselfish and imperfectly rational, B(i) and B(ii) in § 1, p. 2.

[3] i.e. imperfectly rational and imperfectly informed, B(ii) and B(iii).

and reduced to a limited number of definite demands. But we can allow men not to be saints without condoning their being fiends: and although often we can deceive ourselves into not recognising that what we are doing is wrong, it is in the nature of our knowledge of right and wrong that we do sometimes know that we are doing wrong, and if ever anyone knew he was doing wrong, the nazi leaders must have known.

In extreme cases, therefore, where what he did was wicked, and where he must have known at the time that he should avoid doing it, a man cannot plead arguments either of imperfection or of Freedom. But only in extreme cases, only where the ordinary conditions for Legality do not obtain. Where we can, we should confine '*lex*' to Positive law, and not try people according to Natural Law, for Natural Law is in most cases too doubtful and indefinite to be a safe guide when men who are fallible are being judged by other men who are fallible too.

Our shared values are too vague to constitute a sort of law by themselves, but not so vague as to be vacuous. For the sake of invariable decidability they need to be embodied in Positive laws, but Positive laws can be assessed as better or worse by reference to them, and could, in extreme cases, be condemned as being clean contrary to them. It was consideration of this possibility that led philosophers to construe Natural Law as *para*-law rather than *meta*-law. But in actual fact it is normally a case of a Positive law being a better or worse one, rather than of its conflicting and being incompatible with our moral values. Some of our laws can be criticised from a moral point of view; but very few, if any, are so bad that there is nothing to be said for them, and that they are completely incompatible with the moral values we cherish. Our history has been a happy one. We have been able to hold Leviathan by the ears.

SECTION 75

FREEDOM AND MORALITY

THE Wolfenden Report[1] focused attention of the plight of male

---

[1] Report of the Committee on *Homosexual Offences and Prostitution*, 1957, Cmd. 247. See also Patrick Devlin, The Enforcement of Morals, *Proceedings of the British Academy*, O.U.P., 1963; and H. L. A. Hart, *The Morality of the Criminal Law*, O.U.P., 1965. See further, Patrick Devlin, *The Enforcement of Morals*, O.U.P., 1965, esp. pp. xiii-xiv for a full bibliography.

homosexuals, and recommended, among other things, that homosexual conduct between consenting adults should not be prohibited by the criminal law. Its conclusions were admirable, although its arguments were inadequate. Public discussion has suffered since from oversimplification. It has suffered also from concentrating on a few Wolfenden-type topics, where many other arguments sway our sympathies, and from not considering the much wider range of the law's concern for morals.

The Wolfenden solution is in terms of delimitation. It distinguishes public from private morality, and will allow the one to be enforced by law, and claims unassailable immunity against the law for the other. "There must remain a realm of private morality and immorality", said the Wolfenden Report,[1] "which is, in brief and crude terms, not the law's business." The absolute privilege which the early Protestants claimed for a man's spiritual relationship with God, the modern liberals claim for a man's sexual relationship with his fellow men and women. A man's soul was once his impregnable fortress: and now at least an Englishman's bed is his castle.

The delimitation of spheres of influence for public and private morality will not work. The real distinction between them is one of arguments, not actions.[2] It is not that there are certain deeds which are necessarily outside the law's cognisance, but that there are certain spontaneities which cannot be compelled. Moreover the "realm of private morality and immorality" is at once too narrow and too wide. It is too narrow, because a man needs Freedom in far more than some private sphere of influence if he is to lead a full and effective life. He needs to be able to initiate and carry out plans in public as well as in private. He needs to be free from excessive pressure from the law in all his normal transactions with other people, not only those done in secret. At the same time the sphere of private morality is made too wide. Sexual emotions are powerful, and sexual acts committed in private can have important repercussions outside. The law must in general be prepared to take cognisance of activities on which family life and blood relationships are based, and which characteristically can result in the arrival of a new member of society. The original sphere claimed for religious freedom failed in the same way. In giving a man freedom to worship God in the privacy of his own soul it did not give enough, because men need also freedom to worship God

[1] § 61.   [2] See above, § 71, pp. 317–18.

together in public, and to work out this worship in their everyday, and even on occasion in their political, life. It also conceded too much. A man's innermost convictions, just because they are likely to flower into action, may be of public, and not merely private, concern. Communist beliefs, however sincerely held, are a disqualification for certain important offices, just as, in an earlier age, Roman Catholic ones were. We screen civil servants by reference to their beliefs, not merely their actions; and quite rightly.

Instead of delimitations, we need to consider arguments. Arguments for and against enforcement, arguments for and against protection. The position is essentially a dialectical one, with sound arguments on either side, which do not admit of a neat resolution by delimiting separate realms or spheres, but which work out in a number of untidy compromises. The point at issue then becomes whether the protection or enforcement of morals is by itself ever an argument which should weigh with us.

It would be logically incoherent for a State, or indeed any association, to attempt to enforce a purely personal morality, which must be autonomous if it is to be anything. Its definition is a matter of motives, not actions. It is like personal religion. It depends essentially upon inward frames of mind and not exclusively on outward behaviour; and hence purely external conformity is not worth securing. He who receives the Holy Sacrament in order to qualify for an office of State is not being a Christian but is eating the body and blood of Christ to his own damnation. No amount of conformity to the monastic rule or practice of monkish exercises was enough to save Luther's soul, only the inward conviction that Christ had died for him in order that he might be saved: and this inward conviction could not be coerced. Therefore, whatever other reasons for insisting upon conformity there may be, there cannot be the simple one that people ought, as a personal religious or moral obligation, to conform to the practice in question. For, by enforcing conformity, we deprive it of all religious and moral merit as the action of the person concerned.

With corporate and rational morality, however, it is not logically absurd to enforce moral behaviour by threat of sanctions.[1] Much of public morality is embodied in the law—murder, theft, perjury, incest, cruelty to animals are prohibited by law as well as being contrary to public morality: but often it is the safety of potential victims rather than the salvation of potential criminals that we have

[1] See above, § 65, pp. 281–2.

primarily in mind. We forbid murder not so much because it is wrong for the killer to kill as because it is bad for the killed to be dead. We may forbid cruelty to animals because we think it disgusting and degrading, and want our community to have no lot or part in it: but we may be extending to animals the concern we normally have for human beings: with most people both arguments operate, but some philosophers have maintained that the former consideration is never by itself adequate, and that we ought never to enforce or forbid anything on grounds of public morality alone. So Mill: "The sole end for which mankind are warranted, individually or collectively, in interfering with the liberty of action of any of their number, is self-protection . . the only purpose for which power can be rightfully exercised over any member of a civilised community, against his will is to prevent harm to others. His own good, either physical or moral, is not a sufficient warrant. He cannot rightfully be compelled to do or forbear because it will make him happier, because, in the opinion of others, to do so would be wise, or even right. These are good reasons for remonstrating with him, or reasoning with him, or persuading him, or entreating him, but not for compelling him, or visiting him with any evil in case he do otherwise."[1] Mill wants people to make their moral choices without being subject to any pressure whatever, not even "the moral coercion of public opinion",[2] because his view of man is an extremely individualistic one. Men are, fundamentally, isolated, separate units, who act on one another, but never with one another. They can hurt one another, and need to be prevented from doing so, but apart from that, each is the master of his own fate, the captain of his own soul. "The only part of the conduct of any one, for which he is amenable[3] to society, is that which concerns others. In the part which merely concerns himself, his independence is, of right, absolute. Over himself, over his own body and mind, the individual is sovereign".[4] Mill is part Protestant, part sceptic. He is sceptical of the religious and metaphysical bases of morality, and, like Kant, thinks that only freely affirmed moral values are valid: and these are just what cannot be encouraged by any legal or social penalty or pressure. The State is, regrettably, necessary, because people are liable to hurt and harm one another, unless prevented: but the sole purpose of the State is to prevent people hurting one another, and it ought not

[1] J. S. Mill, *On Liberty*, Ch. I, pp. 72–73 (Everyman edition).
[2] Op. cit., p. 72.   [3] i.e. accountable.   [4] Op. cit., p. 73.

to have any other purpose, or allow its coercive machinery to be used for any other purpose, than that of leaving people free to lead their own lives according to their own lights.

Hart[1] softens the uncompromising rigour of Mill's individualism, by admitting the paternalistic argument, that the law may properly be employed to prevent an individual from harming himself, and by stretching the concept of public decency to justify our laws against bigamy. His argument is attractive, but still, I think, wrong. It rests upon the concept of harm, which although an essential concept, is, as we have seen,[2] too elastic a one to support a sole and sufficient criterion. In its narrowest sense, although fairly definite, harm is far too narrow. Even Mill has to construe it more widely to save himself from absurdity.[3] But if once we start enlarging it, there is no limit to its expansion. By invoking moral or spiritual harm the Inquisition could justify their activities within the framework of Hart's paternalism. Nor need this be special pleading. What is regarded as harmful depends upon the common values of a community and the ideal patterns of life cherished by it. It does not provide a separate system of values, but rather is a specification of some of the values we already have. It is a negative value which can, in the particular case, be assigned to some individual, and is of a generic type to be valued negatively by nearly all.

Emphasis on harm manifests an underlying individualism, which, as we have already seen,[4] cannot be sustained. We cannot have a value-free Minimum State. There are different ways in which law and order may be maintained, exemplifying different communal values, and we have to adopt some and not others.[5] Nor do we want a morally neutral Minimum State. We want to be able to identify ourselves as members of the State, and therefore we want it to mean more than a public utility company for the provision of police and sewers. However sceptical we may be of religion and metaphysics, it remains a fact that men do have values in common and want to realise them in common. And we may therefore put pressure on members of a community to conform to some standard which we want the community as a whole to observe. If we have in common an ideal of human dignity which drunkenness derogates from, we may prefer having England sober by

[1] H. L. A. Hart, *Law, Liberty and Morality*, O.U.P., 1963.
[2] § 41, pp. 173-4.
[3] J. S. Mill, *Essay on Liberty*, p. 73 (Everyman edition); see above, § 41, p. 173.
[4] § 67, pp. 292-5.   [5] § 39, pp. 167ff; § 67, pp. 292-3.

Act of Parliament to having it freely drunk. Prohibition, licensing laws, and taxes on spirits may be more or less open to objection on other grounds, but not on that of its being wrong for the community to exercise any pressure on any member to conform to any moral ideal.

The argument between Freedom and Morality is thus a complicated one. The State is not morally neutral. It may, and sometimes must, take sides. That an action contravenes public morality, or runs counter to any of the shared values of a community, is *a* reason, although not necessarily a sufficient or conclusive reason, for discriminating against it in the working of the community's decision procedure. We may restrict Freedom for the sake of Morality, in the same way as we do for the sake of Justice, Equality, or economic expediency. We may protect public morals and public worship in the same spirit as we protect public truthfulness,[1] public conventions of meaning and public symbols of authority:[2] but there are arguments on the other side. There is a tension between the demands of Morality and those of Freedom. To leave people entirely free to do as they please is to suggest that morality does not matter,[3] and might prove ultimately subversive of the fabric of the State and the continued maintenance of law and order: but to enforce morality is to deny moral Freedom. Although the argument from public morality is an argument, it is an argument to be advanced with extreme caution, and even when advanced, will be met by counter-arguments from Freedom which cannot be lightly brushed aside.

We have two reasons for caution in urging the argument from public morality. They stem from the two characteristic features of the State, that it is unselective in its membership and has at its disposal coercive power[4]. Other communities, though often not voluntary associations,[5] do leave open some option of contracting out,[6] and therefore can make more stringent demands on those who choose to remain members than should the State. Because it lacks a safety-valve, it should be chary of putting pressure on its members to accept stringent obligations or conform to very high standards. It should be peculiarly tolerant towards dissenters, just because dissenters cannot normally help having the nationality that they have. Similarly, the

---

[1] § 69, pp. 305–6.   [2] § 43, pp. 175–7; § 4, pp. 14–16.
[3] See above, § 13, p. 53, and § 32, p. 145,   [4] See above, § 15, pp. 57–58.
[5] See above, § 14, p. 55, or below, p. 367.
[6] But see above, § 64, p. 278; § 65, pp. 283–4.

State should be reluctant to use coercive sanctions just because they are sure-fire sanctions. The decisions of the courts are enforced on subjects willy-nilly. But effectiveness is purchased at the cost of sensitivity, and we do not want to wear jackboots when treading in a region where toes often stick a long way out.

Even if we do advance the argument from public morality, there are weighty arguments on the other side. Where enforcement by direct prohibition is proposed, there is a strong presumption in favour of Freedom, as well as many practical arguments against putting penal laws on the Statute Book if we can possibly avoid it. Lying is contrary to public morality, but except in court on oath and under other special conditions, is not prohibited by law. We have seen why.[1] Similar reasons often hold for not making a law against something, even though it is wrong and people ought not to do it. It is bad to have laws which are difficult to enforce, and are likely to be broken by a number of people:[2] for not only the particular laws, but the whole legal system, is thereby brought into disrepute. It is for the same reason bad to pass laws which do not command a considerable measure of respect from the majority of law-abiding people. It is bad to have laws which give opportunities for blackmail. It is an argument against a law that it will both fail in its object and cause a large amount of suffering in the process.

In the detailed argument between Freedom and Morality the principle of alternatives[3] is of decisive importance. If the State does not adopt one rule, what other rules can it adopt, and with what effects? If a man cannot pursue one course of action, what other courses are open to him, and how satisfactory are they? Where the State is balancing one man's liberty against another man's rights,[4] the arguments will be fairly evenly balanced whatever rule it adopts, and therefore the argument from morality can easily be decisive. To enforce a contract is to give one party the Hohfeldian right that the other should not leave his side of the bargain unfulfilled, and thus is to deny to that other party the Hohfeldian liberty of not doing it. We may reasonably strike the balance in favour of enforceability in most cases, but allow the argument from morality to tip the balance the other way, in favour of leaving a person who has entered into a contract for "immoral purposes" at liberty to choose whether she will fulfil it or

---

[1] § 69, pp. 306–7.   [2] Compare § 11, p. 42.
[3] See above, § 44, pp. 180–82.   [4] See above, § 36, pp. 156–7.

not.[1] More generally, a liberty needs to be supplemented by ancillary rights,[2] and by increasing or decreasing these, the State can make the liberty more easy or more difficult to exercise, without needing to curtail the liberty itself. It is easy for an Englishman to travel in England; for not only is there no law prohibiting it, but there are many laws prohibiting people from preventing him: it is difficult for an Englishman to acquire a *harem* in England; for while there is no law against having *harems*, there are no rights which facilitate the acquisition of one; the would-be possessor may not advertise vacancies, nor may he invite individual members of the public to occupy one, nor may he offer financial inducements to any third person to secure candidates, nor will the courts enforce any contract he may enter into with any woman who accepts such employment. In these ways, without forbidding concubinage, the law discourages it. Similarly, in striking a balance between one man's liberty and another's security, the law shows its disapproval of gambling, dissipation, and para-military training; and its approval of marriage, of work, and of religious, educational, and other charitable institutions. But it does not demand, on pain of penalties, that we, in the one case desist from, or in the other engage in, any of these activities.

The law's concern for morality is chiefly shown in these many unspectacular ways where it strikes one balance between liberties and rights rather than another. Sometimes, however, the direct enforcement of some moral standard is in question. It may be that there is no alternative way of securing compliance—in a free society it is designedly easy to get round the law.[3] It may be felt that only if the State enforces a certain principle, does it really take it seriously—a principle not enforced is merely a pious exhortation which it does not expect people to live up to.[4] These claims cannot be ruled out of court. But the argument from alternatives also applies on the other side.

Our attitude to homosexuality has been decisively altered by our

---

[1] The application of the principle in English law is wide. The courts refuse to enforce contracts not only to leave people free not to be immoral in spite of their undertakings, but to deny them the facility of entering into binding contracts (compare § 42, pp. 177–8); see, for example, *Uphill* v. *Wright* (1911), 1 K.B. 506.

[2] See above, § 36, p. 157–8; § 39, p. 168.

[3] See above, §§ 34, 35.

[4] See also J. F. Stephen, *A History of the Criminal Law in England*, London, 1883, II, pp. 81–82, and the Report of the Royal Commission on *Capital Punishment*, 1953, Cmd. 8932, § 53, both discussed by H. L. A. Hart, *Law, Liberty and Morality*, O.U.P., 1963, pp. 60–69.

changed view of the facts. We now believe that homosexuals for the most part cannot help having the feelings they do have, and that it is not to any large extent "catching". The second fact, if true, bears on the issue in an obvious way by countering the otherwise cogent argument that we need to suppress all manifestations of homosexuality in order to protect innocent people from corruption in much the same way as we "suppress" smallpox sufferers in isolation hospitals in order to protect other people from the infection. The first fact operates in a more fundamental way. It shows that homosexuality is much less an optional form of perversity than has been hitherto supposed. Not only does this lead us to assimilate homosexuality to kleptomania, but it shows that the homosexual has no alternative form of sexuality open to him. If we forbid drunken driving, a man is still free to go on driving while he is not drunk, and to go on drinking when he is not going to drive. But homosexuals, we believe, cannot obtain comparable satisfactions in other, normal ways. And while it is far from being the case that every one has or ought to have some form of sexual life, it is true that most people either have it or can hope to have it one day, and that it can, for some, be a great hardship to be totally deprived of all prospect of it.

The question of prohibiting homosexuality should be contrasted with that of prohibiting the profanation of the sacred mysteries. In many parts of Christendom the celebration of the Black Mass has been forbidden by law, even by consenting adults in private. No objection can be sustained on the score of Freedom. For to celebrate the Black Mass *is* perverse. The rite obtains its significance only in the context of belief in the God it seeks to blaspheme. Prohibition denies no natural urge its only outlet. The blasphemer, like the forger, is debarred from complaining. What is forbidden is forbidden in virtue of certain conventions, conventions of speech and action in the one case, of design in the other. But where significance is secured by convention, no natural difference inheres apart from convention, and therefore the man who wishes to abuse the convention has no just complaint, since there remain open to him alternative courses of action which should be, from his external point of view, equally acceptable.[1] It is clearly reasonable for a Christian community to set great store by its behaviour towards God, and to seek to ensure that none of its members should deliberately desecrate a divine institution. And the atheist, who claims

[1] See above, § 69, pp. 302-3.

it does not matter, cannot for that very reason complain much at not being allowed to do it.

Corporate moralities may be encouraged and promoted, and, subject to heavy qualifications, even enforced. Our common ideal is not and cannot be simply and solely that individuals shall have opportunities of manifesting a Kantian goodwill, and making moral choices entirely authentically and autonomously, so that we ought not ever to exercise any pressure whatever on anyone at all. To be a member of a community is to be subject to pressure.[1] Communities do have values in common which they are anxious to promote, and may want to enforce. An Englishman may regard it as a stain upon the honour of England that any Englishman should commit sodomy or perform experiments upon alive (though anaesthetized) animals or eat meat; and may therefore conclude that there ought to be a law against these things.

It is a possible, but remains always a dangerous, conclusion. The argument, if carried to extremes, would make all the doings of a member of a State subject to direction by the law of the land. Many States have taken upon themselves the task of directing and supervising their subjects very closely. In the circumstances of the modern nation-state, which is large and very far from being a voluntary society, the ideal, articulated by Hegel and partly put into practice in the totalitarian states of Germany, Italy, and Russia in our own age, is neither fully feasible nor innocuous.

The totalitarian morality is not fully feasible because it is concerned only with what members of the State should do *qua* members of the State; and this one characterisation of individuals is very far from exhausting the complexity either of individuals themselves or the situations in which they find themselves. A totalitarian morality is, like a legal code, a blunt instrument. A legal code lays down certain rights and duties of citizens, but can only consider a limited number of circumstances, and must deem irrelevant many circumstances which most men would reckon to be morally relevant. Similarly the totalitarian moralities seem to be wooden. They lack the sensibilities of the individual consciences of the West. Nor is this surprising: if the State decides everything, the individual will never learn how to make decisions for himself: and if the emphasis is to be on monolithic solidarity, we should expect judgements to be crude and undiscriminating. Thus totalitarian moralities, quite apart from other failings, are inadequate. Much of our life is concerned with people not

[1] See above, e.g., § 12, p. 49; § 64, p. 278.

as Russians or Englishmen, nor as barristers or doctors, but as individual persons: and we need a more subtle and finely drawn morality
than any promulgated and imposed by the State. The State simply
cannot cope with the whole of morality: even if it wishes to be a
totalitarian State it must in practice allow its public morality to be
supplemented by personal morality. The totalitarian, or Maximum,
State is as impossible as the Minimum State.

Moreover a public morality can be enforced only at some cost to
personal morality, and the more that this is done, the more morality
will be an external legalistic code of conventional behaviour, and the
less it will be the sincere authentic choice of a rational agent. Morality,
unless it is being constantly renewed by people free to make their own
appraisals and their own decisions, becomes ossified and moribund.
A public morality enforced by law is peculiarly susceptible to this
sort of senescence and decay: for if it is enforced by law it must be
fairly static, whereas to be living and vigorous a morality must be
dynamic, often questioned and rediscovered and re-endorsed by free
agents who are acting without constraint.

Thus although we cannot say for certain that all legal enforcement
of public morality as such is wrong, we can usually achieve the end of
protecting, promoting or encouraging morality without invoking
actual legal enforcement; and wherever a principle of public morality
is enforced which a man might reasonably or naturally be averse to
observing, something is lost. And if it happens often, much will be
lost. Totalitarianism is a greater evil than non-enforcement of public
morality: for if too little public morality is enforced by law, it still
can be inculcated by other means; but if too much is enforced by
law, then no room is left for the exercise of individual moral choice.

SECTION 76

FREEDOM AND REASON

A FREE Society is one in which 'I chose to', 'I decided to' or 'I
wanted to' is often a sufficient answer to the question, 'Why did
you?'[1] This means that there may be no further rationale of actions,
and hence of arrangements, than the brute, rationally opaque, fact
that somebody wanted it so. It does not mean that there can be no

[1] See above, § 38, p. 167.

rationale of actions—men, even when possessed of absolute discretion may still act rationally; in particular, although legally they may
not be accountable for their actions at all, they remain morally responsible; they may be ready to furnish an account to all-knowing and
all-understanding God, which is not therefore limited by the finitude
of human powers of communication; they may be feeling their way
to some ideal of self-fulfilment, intelligible in retrospect but imperfectly comprehended at the time even by themselves. All these may
be the case; for men are partly rational, partly disinterested: but they
may not; for men are not wholly rational, not wholly disinterested.
And therefore the price of Freedom is some measure of rational
opacity. People will act in ways which cannot be justified rationally;
and if they are free, exercising a legal privilege according to their
absolute discretion, there is no way of bringing them to book. A man
may, from purely selfish motives, back out of a moral commitment:
a girl may throw up her job in a fit of temperament; an old lady may
leave her money to found a cat's home; a young man may spend all
his time with the worthless and spiteful Sue, while the amiable,
attractive, loyal, and sensible Pru is eating out her heart for him; the
investor, trying hard to invest wisely and sensibly, miscalculates the
future market, and loses his life's savings. All this, and much more. And
these errors accumulate. One man's unreasonable action creates the
situation in which another has to act: which in turn is one of the
circumstances with which subsequent agents have to deal. The fabric
of history and the development of institutions is constituted by the
concomitance, often fortuitous, of individual actions, often irrational.
Gibbon overstated it when he said that history was nothing but the
record of the crimes, the follies, and the misfortunes of mankind;
but men often do act wrongly, often do act stupidly, and often their
actions have unfortunate consequences, and although the historian
may be able to understand how it is that things came to happen
as they did, he cannot give a rational justification of the result. The
outcome is the result of people often acting as they wanted to act, and
quite often wanting to act unreasonably. And this result stands. It will
happen anyway, human nature being what it is, but the believer in
Freedom goes further and accepts that it will happen, as the price, well
worth paying, of having people free.

The believer in Freedom, therefore, will make heavy qualifications
on Hegel's dictum "in a political constitution nothing should be
recognised as valid unless its recognition accord[s] with the right of

reason".[1] For although it is right and proper to make a rational critique of the institutions of any community, there are rational grounds for often accepting the absence of a rational justification. If we allow Freedom we accept some measure of rational opacity: and it is rational to allow Freedom. This is not to say that we must never criticise institutions, nor that we must always accept what is the case as being right, nor that we ought to allow people to do exactly as they like on all occasions in all circumstances. Every system of law is in contradiction with the principle of absolute licence: for very good reasons the most important rights and authorities are conferred in the form of accountable offices, not legal privileges with absolute discretion. And the principle of Constitutional Criticism entitles us to criticise decisions —and procedures and institutions—even when there is no legal remedy available for setting them to rights. We may criticise: we may hold people accountable for their actions: we may transform legal privileges into accountable offices: we may restrict some sorts of Freedom. But always we must remember that the burden of proof is a heavy one. Existing institutions may not be the most rational ones, but the fact that they have arisen out of the free actions of many people means that they are not lightly to be overthrown; it is not enough that they are less than perfect—they must be less than tolerable before we are justified in undoing the deeds of other men whose Freedom we profess to cherish. Existing distributions of property cannot be justified on pure grounds of rationality alone, but only if we give great weight to the free dispositions of the dead as well as of the living. The radical rationalist may well be impatient of the dead hand of the past— but before he dismisses it, and sets about a root and branch reform, he must himself face the problem of Freedom. Either he must abolish it, as the communists have attempted to do; or if he allows men to be free, they will make mistakes and act arbitrarily and abuse it as well as use it, and then, however clean he wipes the slate at the outset of his reforms, new encrustations of error will begin to accumulate, and the last state will be no better than the first, though undoubtedly different. Even in purely intellectual matters, the lover of Freedom must not take too cavalier a stand. Other people's opinions may only be prejudices, but still, their opinions are their own, and even if wrong are

---

[1] Proceedings of the Estates Assembly in Wurtenburg: in *Schriften zur Politik und Rechtsphilosophie*, hrsg. von George Lasson, 2nd ed. Leipzig, 1923, p. 197. English translation in *Hegel's Political Writings*, by T. M. Knox and Z. A. Pelczynski (Oxford, 1964), p. 281.

worthy of some respect, not because of what they are but because of those who hold them. We may reason with people, sometimes perhaps satirise, sometimes perhaps ridicule them: we may even have to override them, particularly if they are very wrong-headed. But *if* we have to—and we should take care not to constitute ourselves the sole judges of this question—we should do so with reluctance. What is wrong with the rationalist and the radical is not that they want to be given reasons nor that they want to reform and remedy the many wrongs they find, but that they are impatient, unwilling to accept that the consequences of other men's Freedom constitute any sort of reason which they ought to respect, and unready to recognise other men's errors as worthy of regard. The rationalist and the radical suffer from the vice of *egotheism*, believing oneself to be God, omnipotent, omniscient, infallible, utterly unselfish. It is easy to think out plans for the world, irritating to find that other people will not fall in with them. Since sometimes the error, or unwillingness to co-operate, is clearly on the part of other people, it is tempting to assume that it always is; and since one is trying to be unselfish onself, it is tempting to assume that one has succeeded in being completely disinterested. Hence one comes to imagine how much better, fairer, and more reasonable the world would be if only everyone would do as he was supposed to—supposed to by oneself. The incomplete control and imperfect intelligibility, which are the inevitable corollaries of Freedom, are seen as blemishes, that prevent one from achieving the complete control and perfect intelligibility in the event, which one has already achieved in one's thoughts. But to have the same mastery over the world as one has over one's thoughts is to be God. And we may doubt whether any radical, however full of righteous indignation, or any rationalist, however reasonable, is really up to being God. But if one is not prepared to be God, one must accept the limitations of humanity: among them that one cannot hope to have everything justified to one's own satisfaction.

The extreme demands of reason cannot be met. Quite apart from any question of Freedom, it is unreasonable for a finite being to think that everything should be rationally transparent to him: and if he further considers that he is only one among many, and that he ought to make the same allowances to others for their finitude, fallibility, and imperfection, that he would expect to be made to himself, it becomes clear that no one is entitled to be too demanding. But this does not mean, as many conservative thinkers have concluded, that we should not ask for reasons, nor that we should not attempt reforms. It is only that having asked for reasons, we should not prove too difficult to satisfy: and that in recommending reforms we should not be too ready to regard everybody else as wrong. Contrary to what the conservatives feel, we ought to seek a rational critique of our institutions, and ought not to think that whatever is, is right, nor to contemplate the continuance of existing abuses with an air of bland acceptance. We should ask 'why?' but recognise that the reason will often be simply the contingent fact that other people happened to want it so; and we should accept this as being often, although not always, an adequate answer. We should seek to remedy wrongs, but in doing so should make sure that we shall not be thereby bringing about greater. Above all we should avoid the frightening *schadenfreude* of some reformers, who seem to be motivated by the belief that the real reason for making omelettes is that it provides an excuse for breaking eggs.

SECTION 77

RADICALISM AND REFORM

THE love of Freedom greatly blunts the argument for radical reform. Even if he makes a clean sweep of the past, the lover of Freedom knows that he is committed to the errors and follies of the future. And this thought will give pause to many who feel the urge to make a break with the old ways, and to start afresh. But nevertheless it could be that the past and present were so bad that they were worse than the future was ever likely to become if once there could be a lightening of the burden and a new start made. Easy radicalism will not go with a love of Freedom, but, in straitened times, a heroic radicalism might. Even so, there are objections.

The first is the seemingly trivial one that a policy of change will not universalise. If I were to propose sweeping reforms as a universal maxim, I should commit myself to the conclusion that whatever reforms I myself instituted ought in turn to be swept away in the name of change. Reform itself must be reformed, and there is no state of affairs with which the thorough-going reformer can rest content, so that he cannot even describe what it is that he is trying to achieve. A policy of complete change, as such and for its own sake, is inconsistent and incoherent. A policy of rigid conservatism—no change at all—is intelligible, if not always sensible; and a policy of piecemeal reform—

change only where necessary—is universalisable, intelligible, and, although not very informative, unobjectionable. Radicalism, easy or heroic, is not, as such, a tenable principle of action.

Radical measures may be called for by the occasion, rather than as part of a way of thought. Although Radicalism is in fact often a temper of mind—against which the argument from non-universalisability tells heavily—it usually goes under the pretext of being a once-for-all emergency programme intended to deal, once and for all time, with the complete mess that former generations have landed us in: and sometimes, though not as often as radicals make out, this is the real radical position. Plato was not an advocate of change for change's sake: he believed that if once he could make a fresh start, with a generation uncorrupted by the errors of their elders, he could thereafter maintain a policy of rigid conservativism.[1] Such a radicalism can be formulated so as to avoid the objection of non-universalisability. To do so, the radical must specify, in reasonable detail, the goal he is trying to achieve, not merely the actuality he wishes to avoid. It is easy to agree that the present is awful and that the future must be different—but this will not universalise: it is difficult to propose a plan for the future, involving great dislocation but perhaps offering great benefits; if one does do so, it will not lead to any inconsistency when universalised —but it may be difficult to secure agreement on it, and will necessarily, if the dislocation is to be great, be impracticable.

A community is not something static, but a complicated pattern of interlocking lives. We cannot, as when making a blue-print, rub the slate clean, and start again; life must go on. People cannot be put into a state of suspended animation, while the planners rearrange everything, and organise new patterns of life. People have to continue to live, even in a time of rapid change, and can only adjust and readjust themselves relatively slowly, and will carry with them into the future memories and habits formed in the past.

If human affairs were relatively simple, instead of infinitely complex, it would have been possible for Plato and his companions to devise the ideal constitution, and then take in a draft of ten-year-olds, tell them what to do, and start them in their new life. But people cannot simply be told. Each man needs to acquire many habits and many skills, as well as a store of factual information, in order to be able to live in the situation in which he grows up. He cannot simply be told how to live, but has to learn, and this takes time. Plato could not just

[1] *Republic*, VII, 540d–541b.

read the *Republic* aloud to his ten-year-olds, but would have to bring them up, feed them, rear them, and educate them for many years; and it would be more than Plato and his friends could manage un-aided. They would need nurses, servants, gym-instructors, cooks, perhaps even a few extra teachers of geometry—and from all of these the old corruption would continue to come into the minds of the young.

Even on the score of factual information—the one thing which does not take long to assimilate—human affairs are too complex for us to be able to start everything afresh. We can make changes: but only against a background of un-change. In the course of years we may make many further changes, changing what had at other times been part of the stable background. But there is still only a rapid develop-ment, not a clean break. We cannot think up or carry through a root-and-branch reform, which shall really make all things new. We cannot think it up, because we can only plan a finite, small, number of details, so that our plan is always only an outline plan, leaving people to carry on the rest of their affairs in unaltered ways: and we cannot carry such a reform through, because people are not malleable enough, but are often old and unable or unwilling to learn new tricks, and often have memories which from the reformer's point of view are in-conveniently long.

SECTION 78

RATIONALISM AND EMPIRICISM

THE conclusions of the previous two sections are those of Burke. Although we may need to carry out reforms, we should do so with some reluctance and great caution, always showing reverence towards the institutions of our fathers, and respect, and even tenderness, towards the vested interests of our brothers. Burke also advocates the use of experience rather than reason as a guide to political action. We may sympathise with him here too, but it is difficult to say exactly what is meant by the words 'experience' and 'reason', both of which have a multitude of meanings, often heavily charged with emotional significance.

The word 'experience' is often used in its original sense of the process whereby a man becomes expert. We demand of a ship's captain that he should have had a lot of experience of the sea. He should have spent much time sailing, sometimes under adverse conditions; he should have often had to take decisions, and have tried one course and another, and have learnt from his mistakes and successes. A man gains experience in this sense partly by the passage of time, partly by having acquired an *expertise* by a process of trial and error. We sometimes even use the word 'experienced' simply as a euphemism for 'old', but more properly require there to have been some element of having *tried*. The Greek word for experience '*ἐμπειρία*' is derived from the verb '*πείρω*' 'I try'.

The second sense of the word 'experience' derives from the former sense of 'experienced'. Not only the man who tries, but the woman who merely feels, gains experience in this sense. Hope, jealousy, love, fear, are experiences. Anything which could enter into a detailed autobiography can be called an experience, and especially what could enter only into an autobiographical account, and could not be reported on by any external observer. My experience on first reading Homer, on first being able to swim, on failing an important examination, are typical experiences, because these are characteristically known only through my telling other people about them.

The shift from the "trial" to the "autobiographical" sense of 'experience' is a reasonable one. For what is of interest about the well-tried mariner is not simply that he has knocked about a lot, but that he has often had to take decisions in difficult circumstances, and knows what it is like to be in a tricky situation, and will not lose his head. The taking of decisions is something peculiarly lonely and private. Other people can observe my decisions as they are carried out, but they cannot take my decisions themselves, and therefore cannot stand in my place when I am taking a decision. Therefore decision-taking needs to be viewed autobiographically. And therefore the "trial" sense of 'experience' leads naturally to the autobiographical.

The third sense of the word 'experience' is that of 'sense-experience'. It is the experience a man has on account of, or by use of, or through, his senses—the experiences of taste, feeling, smell, sight, and sound. A proposition is based on experience, in this sense, if it is based on what can be seen or heard, and not, for instance, on pure argument, or intuition, or speculation. Locke wanted to point out that our knowledge of the world of nature is not a matter of pure thought alone, but depends on our using our eyes and ears, fingers and noses to discover what the world is like. It has proved an unfortunate use of the word 'experience' but is connected with both the other two. It is connected with the second in that it is something given. I cannot help seeing the sights or hearing the sounds I see or hear in much the same way as the woman cannot help experiencing anguish or elation at the sight of her beloved. Sense-experience, together with emotional experience, is what one's life is made up of. One has these experiences, and they are the *data* from which all our ideas are derived. The concept of sense-experience is also connected with the idea of trying, through that of experiment. If one wants to know about nature, it is not enough simply to sit in a study and theorise. One must put one's theories to the test, one must try and see; try out the theories, and see, in a literal sense, whether predictions derived from the theories come out true or not. The experimental method is both a putting of theories to the test, trying them out in practice, and a use of sense-experience to determine whether they are in fact correct.

The three uses of the word 'experience' are thus linked. Nevertheless it has been unfortunate that one word has been used in these three senses; and much bad philosophy has been done in consequence. For political thinking we need only the original sense of 'trying'. 'Experience has shown that . . .' in a political context means that we have tried an institution, a principle, or a method, and have found that it does work in practice;[1] or that we tried alternatives and have found that they do not work. 'The empirical approach' means that we proceed by trial and error; we try out a plan, and find out whether it does work or not.

The word 'reason' is used in a variety of senses too. We have used it in its widest sense; but have had to distinguish a separate and narrower sense when used in the plural; reasons, we said,[2] are stateable reasons. A person, we allowed, might be acting with reason, although unable to say what his reasons were. Other uses of 'reason' are more restricted still. Some philosophers—Plato and Hume—have thought that the only real reasons properly so called are deductive arguments. Many others have allowed inductive arguments to be reasons, but nothing further. Others again have put forward certain principles, e.g. that all men are free, or that all men are equal, as self-evident truths of reason, and have proceeded to argue briskly and brusquely from them.

We cannot formulate neat definitions of 'experience' and 'reason' in which Burke's contention comes out as true. The words are not

[1] See, for example, footnote 1, on p. 80.
[2] § 38, pp. 164–5.

natural opposites. In several important senses of 'experience' we should want to deny that experience was particularly important in politics, and in our sense of reason we want to insist that reason should be a guide. Nevertheless, Burke is making three important points.

The first stems from the impossibility of generalising about human affairs with complete precision.[1] If we speak in few words, we do not speak precisely: if we would speak precisely, we should have to use many, many words. We may have, as an idea of reason, the idea of a political maxim analogous to that of a physical law, which is perfectly precise, and will apply to a given set of initial conditions, automatically and with complete rigour. If we have such an idea, we have to recognise that the political maxim, unlike the physical law, is infinitely complex, and cannot be formulated *in toto*. We can only hope to formulate that part of a political maxim which is applicable to the actually existing conditions. The rationalist who produces a blue-print is therefore to be distrusted. We have already, in the previous section, seen the impossibility of making an entirely fresh start. A politician must start with the situation as it actually is, and go on from there. We now see, further, that the relevant part of an ideal political maxim will depend on the situation it is to be applied to, and that what is to be prescribed will vary—and vary very much—in accordance with the situation. An Englishman may believe in trial by jury: but if he applies it in India, where jurors are subject to many inducements and intimidations, and where the ideal of a true verdict is not widely valued, he will merely multiply injustice. An American may believe in free enterprise: but if he attempts to apply it in Africa, where the ideal of the industrious acquisition of wealth lacks wide appeal, he will merely produce chaos. It is necessary first to have experience of the actual situation, to know what the relevant conditions are, before formulating the relevant part of a political maxim.

Burke's second point is that we are not very good at formulating parts of political maxims or at foreseeing what the consequences of their application will be. Even if we have studied the actual situation, and are attempting to formulate a principle which is relevant to that, we may get it wrong; and even when we are right in principle, there may be snags in practice which we had not reckoned with. There is therefore a considerable balance of advantage in existing procedures and institutions, which have already been tried and have stood the test of time. They may not be perfect, but we know where we are with

[1] See above, § 7, pp. 25–26; § 30, pp. 137–8.

them, and at least they work moderately well. We need to be very cautious before scrapping them in favour of some new-fangled scheme, however excellent in theory. And, if we must innovate, it is well to do it first on a small scale. A pilot scheme will show up the snags and suggest ways of avoiding them. And so we can avoid disastrous or costly mistakes later on. This is not a protest against reason as such, but against the easy assumption of rational transparency in human affairs which rationalists are often tempted to make. We have seen already how it is that, on grounds of Freedom, we ought to abjure the search for rational transparency: but considerations of Freedom apart, it would be wildly unwise for anyone to expect it in the affairs of imperfect and fallible men. The wise rationalist knows that he may make mistakes in formulating his maxims, that other men may fail to fall in with his plans for them, and that he does not know all the relevant factors; and therefore he will be modest in laying down the law. Like his brother, the natural scientist, who is dealing with things which although less complicated are even more opaque than men, the rationalist should always be ready to "try and see", to put his theories to the test, to learn not only from theory but from actual experiment. In this, original, sense of 'empiricist' we all ought to be empiricists, we all ought to adopt an empirical approach, we all ought to be guided by experience. For in so far as we are dealing with what is rationally opaque, it is the only other guide left to us: and fallible, selfish and finite men are, at least in part, rationally opaque to other fallible, selfish, and finite men. So that only God could be a perfect rationalist, and not even He, if He allows men to be free and respects their private judgement. Men cannot be perfect rationalists. Whatever schemes they think up, there is a possibility that they will not work out as intended; and a failure to work in practice is a valid criticism of any scheme.

Burke's third point is about the method rather than the tone of political thinking. It is tentative and dialectic, not deductive and absolute. As against Locke and the Americans,[1] he does not think that political arguments can be put into deductions from simple self-evident principles. The simple apothegms that wise men have coined, although often true, are not automatic in their application. We may say 'suum cuique', and yet hold it right to deprive a homicidal maniac of his gun.

Burke's three contentions are interconnected, and all tell against the

[1] See above, § 6, pp. 20–22.

deductive absolutism of the extreme rationalist. Any principles that could serve as premisses would, according to the first contention, be too complicated ever to formulate. Such principles as have been formulated are, according to the third contention, not premisses for deductive arguments, but guides to reason, which still leave room for a 'but'. And the great virtue of the empirical test of time is that it produces 'buts' which according to the second contention, the political thinker cannot always anticipate.

As counters to extreme rationalism, all three contentions are valid; but as a positive doctrine, empiricism fails. The great defect of experience is that it is not, or at least not fully, communicable; the great virtue of reasons is that they are. If a politician formulates his principles, they can be discussed, criticised, and shared: if he merely lays claim to an empirical approach, and says that we must be guided by experience, we do not really know what he stands for. He is asking to be trusted, without in return entrusting his views to the public. But the community depends on there being values held in common, and in so far as it is not a static community, there needs to be a process of public discussion and criticism, whereby the community can come to share new values. The practice of political empiricism tends to run counter to this principle. On many minor issues it does not greatly matter,— not every minor issue can be discussed by everyone anyhow—but the habit of not discussing political principles, if it becomes pervasive, is bad. It is bad for any community, but especially bad for one that cherishes Constitutional Freedom. For one of the safeguards of Constitutional Freedom is that many subjects should participate in the various aspects of government, voluntarily and freely. And this is possible only if there is a wide measure of understanding and agreement between them. The political empiricist is apt to make too much of *expertise*, and to make it too difficult for outsiders who have not been initiated into the art of government to join in, or understand what is going on. Highly attractive though this may be to rulers, it runs contrary to any hope of Constitutional Freedom that there should be a curtain between ruler and ruled.

Constitutionalism requires that Rex, like Judex, should think aloud in public. Judex III was a good Judge, because he laid himself open to the charge of inconsistency if he was inconsistent; because he made it possible for critics to point out errors in his reasoning; and because he made it possible for lawyers to anticipate his future decisions. For similar, though not exactly the same, reasons Rex should open his thoughts to public inspection. He must let the Laity in, and formulate his principles of action. In Britain, this is largely achieved by parliamentary debate. But *Hansard* is long, and few people can read it all. Further compression and simplification is needed if people are to be able to enter into political discussion. As with all simplifications, there is a danger of over-simplification. The political empiricist's slightly aristocratic disdain for government by slogan is highly understandable. But if government is not to be government by closed shop, there must be some attempt to open the thought-processes of government to public inspection, criticism and appraisal, and this requires that there should be a corresponding attempt to formulate the relevant principles of political action. Such formulations are always incomplete: and the shorter and sharper they are, the more incomplete they are. But even catch-phrases are effective in securing the co-operation of the people at large. The watchwords of the French Revolution, muddled and misguided though they were, set the peoples of the world on the march: the parliamentary speeches of Burke, statesmanlike and sensible, merely emptied the House.

The statesman needs to communicate his thoughts in order that other people may think as he does, so that government may be as much as possible government by consent, and as little as need be government by force. The means he should adopt vary with the occasion: most people are not passionately interested in politics, and many are inclined to be apathetic. We must not expect too much. Political action should be rational: but, knowing that our capacities are limited and our information imperfect, we are rational to prefer, where possible, institutions and procedures which have been tried and found to work, rather than other schemes which may fail on any one of innumerable circumstances. Where we have to innovate, we are wise to prepare for the worst rather than to count on the best; and to make our plans run the gauntlet of criticism, and, where possible, small-scale experiment, before being implemented fully. There are good reasons why the principles of political action should be formulated, so far as is reasonably feasible, both before and after the event: but such formulations are never complete or precise, and should be treated as guides only to political reasoning, not as premises for deductive arguments. It is impossible to formulate completely and precisely maxims which will cover every situation, and politicians should not attempt to formulate detailed theories for all eventualities, but make detailed proposals only for actual situations, or contingencies which are reasonably like to arise; and then, even when they have been made, allow that they could be wrong, could be open to objection, could benefit by criticism.

English public life is based on Burke. The Englishman distrusts abstract speculation, high-flown principle and radical remedies. Politics, he reckons, requires practical know-how much more than theoretical principles, an ability to anticipate snags and circumvent difficulties, rather than an assumption that because one's arguments are deductively rigorous, nothing can conceivably go wrong. The Englishman defers to the man with long experience and sound judgement, believes in the empirical approach, dislikes appeal to principle, and prides himself on his lack of logic. In much of this he is wise. Nevertheless he needs to think. He may eschew doctrinaire solutions supported by specious reasoning, but he has to use reason none the less in order to extract the relevant lessons from his experience. Experience has to be interpreted. Feeling one's way is a rational activity. The political empiricist may pitch his thoughts in a different, and often lower, key than the extreme rationalist; he may be averse to grandiloquent formulae: he may be unready, too unready, to formulate his thoughts: but he thinks, and thinks rationally. Else no amount of experience would stand him in any stead. Moreover, he ought to formulate his thoughts. He ought, diffidently, but nevertheless definitely, to extract the principles of his *expertise*, and hold them up for examination, both by others and by himself. After all, he may be wrong. Experience is no guarantee against error. Only by saying what he thinks, does he expose his errors to correction. To say nothing for fear of saying something wrong can be as much a refuge of cowardice or pride as a mark of becoming modesty. Also, others may be wrong. In spite of their expertise, experts often differ. Only by rational discussion and debate can experience be shared, differences resolved, and a common mind achieved. Even where the professionals are agreed and are right, they should still reason together and articulate their arguments, to enable outsiders to listen in, and thereby be included in, the processes of government. And finally, even from his own point of view, the professional politician needs to think things out and come to know what his principles are. It is the *sine qua non* of success, the condition of real achievement. It is not enough to have held high office. Office offers opportunities, but only a good use of them constitutes an achievement to be proud of. And to decide wisely needs rational thought. Without it, empiricism and professionalism degenerate into flabbiness. It is easy to excuse oneself, on the grounds that one ought not to be doctrinaire and inflexible, from all serious thought whatever; and from not having thought out one's principles in advance, one becomes incapable of reasoning sensibly in the event, or of giving one's reasons afterwards. In avoiding the danger of inflexibility, one courts the equal danger of opportunism. The important principle of realism, that "politics is the art of the possible" degenerates into a weak-kneed readiness always to take the line of least resistance. Political power is not worth holding on those terms: for they constitute the abdication of power. Political power is only worth having if one can use it to achieve something worth while: and this means that one must have some idea of what things are worth while—some principles—and must be ready to overcome difficulties and opposition in order to achieve them. Not to have any principle, save that of staying in power, and being always willing to take the easiest way out, is to achieve nothing, and to hand over power to those who can make things easy or difficult for one. The final fate of the extreme political empiricist is to be always grasping at the semblance of power while yielding the reality, and to have opportunities of action which he fails, through opportunism, ever to take. Only the man who stands for something can be a statesman. Only the man who knows what is worth doing can hope to achieve anything worthwhile.

DEFINITIONS

Some verbal changes have been made from
the forms of words used in the text

1   The word 'political' is to be taken throughout the book, except where the context implies the contrary, in its wide, original sense, in which it applies not only to politics in the modern, narrow sense, but to social and legal affairs, and all that pertains to men's public life. §6 p. 20n

2   A *community* is a body of individuals who have in common a method of deciding disputes. §3 pp. 10–11

3   A *group* is a social gathering which lacks a decision procedure. §64 p. 276

4   A *dispute* is a question that arises among or between members of a community about what shall be done by, or in the name of, their community. It cannot be resolved by argument alone. §3 p. 11

5   A *conflict* arises when two agents capable of interacting with each other are taking steps to bring about incompatible states of affairs. §16 p. 63

6 A *violent conflict* is one in which at least one of the parties to the conflict uses every means within his power that he thinks will be effective for getting his own way. §16 p. 63

7   A *decision procedure* is the method of deciding disputes that is common to members of a community. §3 pp. 10–11
In mathematical logic, the phrase 'decision procedure' is used in a technical sense, different from that in this book. §4 p. 13n

8   A man, or body of men, has *authority* if it follows from his saying, 'Let X happen', that X ought to happen. An authority is a man or body having authority. §4 p. 16

9   A man, or body of men, has *power* if it results from his saying, 'Let X happen', that X does happen. A power is a man or body having power. §4 p. 16

10 A man, or body of men, has *influence* if the result of his saying, 'Let *X* happen', is that other people will say (perhaps only to themselves), 'Let *X* happen'. § 4 p. 16

11 A decision is *directly enforceable* against a party when it can be carried out against his wishes and in spite of any obstruction he may offer. § 14 p. 54

12 A decision is *indirectly enforceable* if it can be arranged that if he does not co-operate in carrying it out or acquiescing in its being carried out, then he shall either have carried out against him further measures which he would like to, but is unable to, resist, or be prevented from doing some range of things he would like to do. § 14 p. 54

13 Decisions which are enforceable but not directly enforceable are enforced by means of *sanctions*; a *sanction* is an alteration in a person's position carried out against his will and itself enforceable directly or indirectly. § 14 p. 54

14 *States* are those communities whose decision procedures are made effective by coercion. § 14 p. 55; § 15 p. 57

15 *Associations* are those communities which do not have coercive sanctions at their disposal. § 14 p. 55

16 *Voluntary associations* are those communities which have no serious sanctions at their disposal. § 14 p. 55

17 A man is being *coerced* when either force is being used against him or his behaviour is being determined by the threat of force. § 15 p. 57

18 *Force* is being used against a man, if in his private experience or in his environment either something is being done which he does not want done but which he is unable to prevent in spite of all his efforts, or he is being prevented, in spite of all his efforts, from doing something which he wants to do, and which he otherwise could have done by himself alone. § 14 p. 57 (see also § 36 pp. 158–9); § 16 pp. 63–64

19 A person is *using force*, or has *resorted to force*, or has *resorted to violence*, if he uses every means within his power that he thinks will be effective for getting his own way in a conflict. § 16 p. 63

20 *Judex I* decides individual cases, but does not record decisions or give reasons.

Judex II decides individual cases, treating like cases alike, and records his decisions, but does not give reasons.

Judex III decides individual cases, treating like cases alike, records his decisions, and gives his reasons.

Judex IV subsumes individual cases under general, antecedently promulgated, laws, but, ideally, has not authority to interpret the law or make any innovation in it. § 30

21 A man is *free to* perform a particular action if he is not forbidden by an identifiable rule or person that is authoritative. § 32 p. 145

22 A man is *free from* some real or apprehended evil, if the evil neither does happen, nor would happen, nor would be likely to happen, were he not to take avoiding action which, apart from the need to avoid the evil, he would not have wanted to take.

§ 32 p. 145

23 *Liberty* is freedom to do something; it is being able to do whatever it is that we want to do, without there being any authoritative rule or person to tell us not to.

§ 33 p. 147 (see also § 32 pp. 145–6)

24 *Security* or *Immunity* is freedom from some real or apprehended evil. § 33 p. 147

25 *Hohfeldian Liberty*, *duty*, *right* and *no-right*.

§ 36 p. 156; See table p. 157

26 A *legal privilege* is a Hohfeldian legal liberty to act, combined with a further Hohfeldian legal liberty not to give or have any good reasons for one's act. § 37 pp. 160–61

27 *Private property* is a legal privilege of using and disposing of some good, together with a security (a Hohfeldian right) against other people using or disposing of it. § 45 p. 183

28 An *official* is a person or a body entrusted with some duty or task or commission, granted some authority to carry it out, and responsible for the exercise of that authority. § 26 p. 117

29 An *office* is a combination of duty, discretion, authority, and responsibility. § 26 p. 118

30   To be *responsible* is to be able or obliged to give one's reasons for one's actions or inactions in answer to the questions, 'Why did you do it?' or 'Why did you fail to do it?'   § 26 p. 118

31   To be *responsible to* a person or body is to be obliged to give one's reasons for one's actions or inactions if asked for them by that person or that body.   § 26 p. 121

32   The ideal of *Equity* corresponds to the weak principle of universalisability. The ideally Equitable decision is purely rational, taking into account all the relevant factors of the case. § 29 p. 133
(see further § 55 p. 235)

33   The ideal of *Legality* corresponds to the strong principle of universalisability. The decision altogether in accord with Legality is purely deductive, basing itself only on the finite number of features antecedently specified as relevant by the statute.
§ 29 pp. 133–4

34   A *free* community is one in which 'I want to' is always a good, although not a conclusive, reason for allowing a man to act in the way which he desires.   § 38 p. 167

35   *Justice* is a rational regard for the individual, taking into account all and only all the circumstances of the individual case, and not merely some of them, and not any other extraneous, and properly irrelevant ones.   § 55 p. 235

36   *Formal Equality* is the same as Equity.   § 56 p. 246

37   *Equality before the Law* is the same as Legality.   § 56 p. 246
(but see further § 58 pp. 255–256)

38   *Equality of Respect* is the same as Humanity.   § 56 p. 246

39   Arguments of *Humanity* are arguments based on the fact that men are human, and ought to be treated in certain ways (or better, ought not to be treated in certain other ways) in virtue of the fact that they are human.   § 57 p. 250

40   *Equality in the Law* is concerned with factors not always known to be relevant or irrelevant, but *presumed* or *deemed* to be relevant or irrelevant.   § 59 p. 256

41   A *Minimum State* is an unselective, coercive community with no functions, purposes, or ideals, other than the maintenance of law and order.   § 66 p. 287

42   A *pathological* system of law is one operating under any of the following abnormal conditions: it is ineffective; its legislation is characteristically retrospective; the laws are not published; there is no access to the courts; the adjudications of the courts are arbitrary and absurd; the government lacks legitimacy; or the laws are quite outrageously wicked.   § 74 p. 327

TABLE OF HUMAN NATURE AND
IDEAL COMMUNITIES[1]

We make five assumptions about human nature:

A(i)   Some Interaction
A(ii)   Some Shared Values

B(i)   Incomplete Unselfishness
B(ii)   Fallible Judgement
B(iii) Imperfect Information

These can be denied in two ways, pessimistically, in the E form, and optimistically, in the A form.

A(i)E	No Interaction	A(i)A	Total Interaction (i.e. No Privacy)
A(ii)E	No Shared Values	A(ii)A	Total Concord (i.e. No Divergence of Values)
B(i)E	No Unselfishness (i.e. Total Selfishness)	B(i)A	Complete Unselfishness
B(ii)E	No Judgement (i.e. Total Unreasonableness)	B(ii)A	Infallible Judgement (i.e. Total Reasonableness)
B(iii)E	No Information	B(iii)A	Perfect Information

We do not consider either of the denials of A(i) or A(ii) further; nor the assumption B(iii)E.

If we have assumptions

A(i), A(ii), **B(i)E** B(ii), B(iii) we have	Hobbes' philosophy
A(i), A(ii), B(i), **B(ii)E**, B(iii)	Modern political philosophy
A(i), A(ii), B(i), B(ii) B(iii)	Actual Human Society
A(i), A(ii), **B(i)A**, B(ii), B(iii)	Areopagite Society
A(i), A(ii), B(i), **B(ii)A**, B(iii)	MRA[2] Society
A(i), A(ii), B(i), B(ii), **B(iii)A**	Stoic Society
A(i), A(ii), B(i), **B(ii)A, B(iii)A**	Kantian[3] Society
A(i), A(ii), **B(i)A** B(ii), **B(iii)A**	Civil Service Society
A(i), A(ii), **B(i)A B(ii)A,** B(iii)	Church Society
A(i), A(ii), **B(i)A B(ii)A, B(iii)A**	Heaven

---

[1] See § 2, pp. 5–10.   [2] or Eisenhower.   [3] or Hare-ian.

INDEX

Accountable, Accountability, 117–123, 160–2
  useful criterion of, 161, 164, 194, 285
  See also Responsible, Answerability
Adjudication
  defined, 134; discussed, 133–5; 197ff.
Administration, Administrative, 193–202
  Compared with Executive, 114f.
  The Administration always has a majority, 210
Advowson, 162, 183
Ahab, 188, 190, 196
Alternatives, 181ff, 187, 195, 200, 261
America, American, Americans, U.S.A., 11f., 22f., 30f., 34, 38, 79, 80, 91, 116, 184, 217, 223, 239, 265, 270, 275, 293, 294, 360, 361
  American Constitution, the, 38ff., 79, 83, 114, 213, 277
  U.S.A., 38ff., 30ff., 71, 80, 83, 114, 199, 213, 217, 264, 291, 329
  President of U.S.A., 80, 106, 213, 270, 271, 325, 35
  Congress, 39, 71, 106, 213, 229ff., 270, 35
  Senate, 79, 213, 218, 272
  Supreme Court, 39–41, 114, 217f., 223, 325
Anglican, 100, 297, 299, 322
  Anglican Communion, 276, 283
  See also Church of England
Answerability for Actions, 83, 80, 90, 109f.
  See also Responsibility
Aquinas, 235
Arbitrary, Arbitrariness, 7, 19, 23ff., 123, 124, 147, 171, 215, 216, 242
  Non-arbitrariness, 19, 126, 285

Arbitration, Arbitrators, 16ff., 108ff., 123ff., 198
  Inegalitarian implications of, 255
Areopagite, 308–11, 7, 91, 307f.
Argue, Argument, 20ff., 36, 48, 111, 174, 203, 213, 230, 250, 266, 270f., 290, 296, 298, 307, 312, 315ff., 343
Aristotle, 26, 242, 244,, 258f., 260, 261
Ascham, 138, 328
Assignment of Responsibilities. *See under* Responsible
Associations, 47, 54, 61, 294f.
  defined, 55 (*also* 367)
  discussed, 275–84
  not all associations voluntary, 283
  See also Voluntary Associations
Athens, Athenians, 37, 91, 100, 293
Attainder, 36f., 84, 113, 115f., 225f.
  defined, 226
audi alteram partem, 132f., 269ff.
Augustine, 305, 338, 333
Austin, 148, 159, 323, 328, 337
Authority
  defined, 16f.
  follows power, 69, 147
  of officials, 117f., 208ff.
  lacked by ineffective systems, 41, 325ff., 148
Autonomy, 6, 101, 273f., 282, 316f., 319f., 343, 350
Bad Man, The, 154, 198, 254, 312, 314
Bagehot, 266
Bentham, 337
Bill, Private. *See* Private Bill
Black Mass, 349f.
Blimp, Col., 103
Bloody-minded, 54ff., 58, 1, 11, 20, 94, 108

373